EVERTON F.C.

THE
MEN FROM THE HILL COUNTRY

The development of Everton Football Club
During the reign of Queen Victoria

by

Tony Onslow

First published 2002 by Countyvise Limited,
14 Appin Road, Birkenhead, Merseyside, CH41 9HH

Copyright © 2002 Tony Onslow

The right of Tony Onslow to be identified as the author of this work has
been asserted by him in accordance with the Copyright, Design and
Patents Act 1988.

British Library Cataloguing in Publication Data.
A Catalogue record for this book is available from the British Library.

ISBN 1 901231 29 1

Printed and Typeset by Birkenhead Press Limited,
14 Appin Road, Birkenhead, Merseyside, CH41 9HH

Acknowledgements

Alex Onslow

Joan Onslow

The Local Studies Department of the following Libraries.
Accrington, Belfast, Birkenhead, Blackburn, Bolton, Blackpool,
Burnley, Darwen, Derby, Glasgow, Nottingham, Oswestry,
Sefton, Sheffield, St. Helens, Wallasey, Wrexham,

The Lancashire Football Association, Leyland.

Kevin La Vall.

David Barber, Librarian at The Football Association, London.

The Staff of Penketh Library, Warrington.

Above all, The staff of Liverpool Record Office & Local Studies,
William Brown Street.

Contents

Introduction   Page vi

Stanley Park   Page 1

    The 1880/81 Season
    The 1881/82 Season
    The 1882/83 Season
    The 1883/84 Season

Anfield   Page 34

    The 1884/85 Season
    The 1885/86 Season
    The 1886/87 Season
    The 1887/88 Season

The FA Cup: The Early Years   Page 59

    Merseyside Enters The Competition
    Everton's Early Years
    Everton at Goodison Park

The Football League: The Anfield Years   Page 84

    Champions
    Goodison Park

Bibliography

Thomas Keats. History of the Everton Football club 1878 - 1928.
David Pickering. The Cassell Soccer Companion.
F N S Creek. History of the Corinthian Football Club.
Bryon Butler. The Official History of The Football Association.
Bryon Butler. The Official Illustrated History of the FA Cup.
Gareth M Davies, Ian Garland.
Who's who of Welsh International Soccer Players.
T Walvin. The Peoples Game.
Stephen. The History of Liverpool Ramblers AFC 1882 - 1951.
Peter Swain. The Birth of Modern Football in Bolton and District.
Ian Ross, Gordon Smailes. Everton the complete record.

Introduction

This book is an attempt to highlight the difficulties encountered by the early pioneers of Association Football on Merseyside, centred in and around Everton Football Club. It goes on to record the club's first visits to many present day venues.

Referring to Everton's geographical location the title, The Men From The Hill Country, was first used by a reporter calling himself "The Grumbler", who covered the game in Liverpool for the Bolton based sports paper, The Football Field. First published on the 20th September 1884, this newspaper was the first to cover all the teams in the North West and Midlands. It was sold every Saturday evening at The Tarleton Hotel in Church Street and was very popular with the early followers of the game in Liverpool.

I have confined my research to the period spent by Everton Football Club under the reign of Queen Victoria.

This book is dedicated to all the away followers of Everton Football Club, whose friendship and loyalty I have been fortunate enough to share.

Stanley Park

It's a well known fact that when Prince Rupert came to besiege Liverpool during the English civil war, he pitched his camp near Everton village, the year being 1644. The village in those days standing between Eastbourne Street and Breck Road. He placed his gun batteries on the hill overlooking the town which he boasted was "A mere crows nest", but it took the Prince eighteen days to take the town, losing one thousand, five hundred men in the process. Many streets around the village later bore his name in acknowledgement of his visit.

In the Seventeenth century a local merchant named George Campbell traded rum and sugar from the West Indies, one of the islands being Santa Domingo, where he captured a French prize ship and with the proceeds he built a fine house near Mere Lane which he called St. Domingo House. Soon the whole area became known as St. Domingo.

In the year 1736 Mary (Molly) Johnson was born in the village. At the age of twenty three a local doctor, who was attending Molly during a pulmonary illness, was struck with her industry and her way of making slender means go a long way and suggested to her that she should make and sell toffee. The kindly doctor gave Molly a good recipe that he recommended to his patients for colds and sore throats. On an open air oven behind her little cottage where she lived alone Molly secretly perfected the now famous Everton toffee. The local population soon found the toffee to be very tasty for those even in the best of health, so to cope with the demand Molly opened the first toffee shop, at her cottage in Village Street. Molly got married in 1761 to a man named Bushell, at St. Thomas' Church in Park Lane. When, in

1810, her first cottage was demolished she moved her business to 21 Village Street where she was assisted by her niece Mrs Cooper. Molly died in 1818 and was buried in Walton Churchyard. The Cooper family continued to make the toffee until the shop was demolished in 1884.

On a triangle of land opposite Molly's last shop stood a fenced off enclosure, which was used for keeping strayed and distrained cattle. In the centre stood a round building with a

Everton Village 1856 showing Prince Ruperts Castle (right) with Everton toffee shop opposite

conical roof, which was the old village bridewell. In those days it was called 'The barn of the hill', but in later years to the children of the area it was known as 'Prince Rupert's Castle'.

Stanley Park, which is situated to the north east of the village, was opened to the general public in 1870 at a time when Rugby dominated the winter sporting activities of Merseyside. In

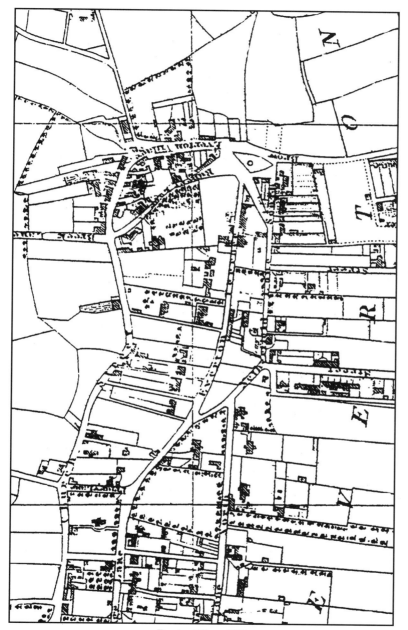

Everton Village 1820

the same year a Methodist Chapel was opened on Breckfield Road at a cost of two thousand, two hundred pounds. A church hall was later added and a manse purchased at 128 Queens Road for a further fifty pounds. To this church, in 1877, Benjamin Swift Chambers was appointed minister. Reverend Chambers was born near Huddersfield on the 30th August 1845 where he served his apprenticeship as a high class engraver, in which work he soon distinguished himself. In 1867 he entered the Methodist College from where two years later he took his first chapel at Ashton, before moving to St. Domingo. Later in 1890 he moved back to his native Yorkshire to take up a ministry in Leeds, where

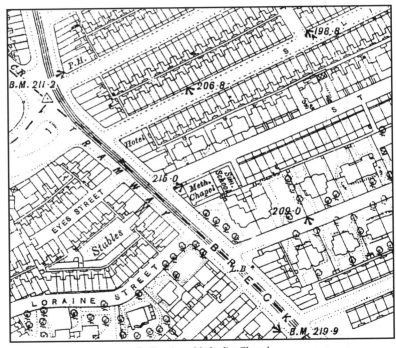

St. Domingo Methodist Chapel

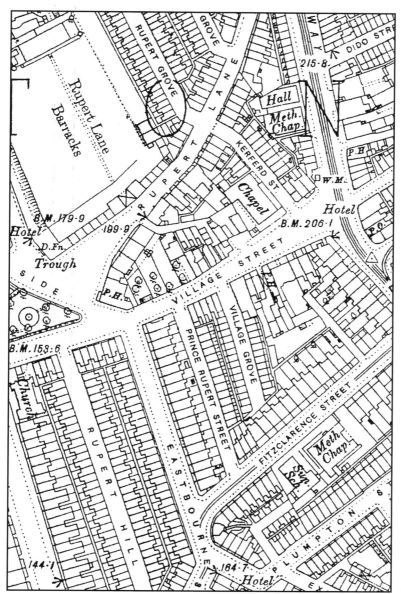

Everton Village 1890. The toffee shop has been demolished.
The Queens Head is shown on the corner of Village Street.

he remained until his death on the 28th November 1901 and was interred at Shepley.

At the time of Reverend Chambers appointment to St. Domingo, Queen Victoria had just assumed the title 'Empress of India' and sat at the head of the world's first industrialised nation, with massive overseas investments. Benjamin Disraeli was Prime Minister and war was narrowly averted in the Balkans by the treaty of Berlin and the expanding seaport of Liverpool was slowly swallowing up the little hill top village of Everton.

It had been nearly fifty years since the opening of the world's first major railway line between Liverpool and Manchester and now a great railway network linked all the major manufacturing towns with the two great seaports of London and Liverpool. Steam had replaced sail on the high seas and in Liverpool the electric tramcars were fast replacing the horse drawn trams. New routes were stretching out like tentacles to the outskirts of the town. For the first time people could catch a tram at the corner of their street to one of Liverpool's three main terminal stations and take a train to the destination of their choice. The apparatus was now in place for the development of the new game of Association Football.

The main reason why Liverpool was not involved in the early development of the game was the late arrival on Merseyside of the Saturday afternoon off. While the steelworkers of Sheffield and the cotton workers of Lancashire, bound together by a single industry, had received this concession some ten years earlier.

When St. Domingo's first formed a football section in 1878 they rented a pitch in the South Eastern corner of Stanley

Park, where they quickly became the best side in the area, drawing in the top players from neighbouring teams. Eventually at a meeting held at the Queens Head, a public house in Village Street, it was decided to adopt the local name of Everton. The Landlord, Mr J W Clarke, being a keen follower of the new sport, allowed the Queens Head to become the new club's first head quarters. The local school master, Frank Brettell, who lived in

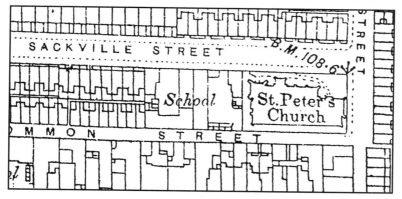

Location of Everton's first opponent's St. Peter's Sackville Street Everton.

nearby Gregson Street, was later appointed club secretary. The central feature of the village, Prince Rupert's Castle, became the club insignia, with Molly's famous product supplying the nickname 'The Toffee's'.

The new club's first game was played on the 23rd December 1879 and their opponents were local neighbours St. Peters. The church, which at the time stood in Sackville Street, is today sadly no more as it was destroyed in the bombings during World War Two.

1880/81 Season

Before the start of the season the club engaged the services of Ayrshire born Jack McGill, formerly of Glasgow Rangers, who quickly took over the position of player coach. The Association game was already well established north of the border, thanks mainly to the Queens Park club from Glasgow, who were the unofficial custodians of the Association rules in Scotland. Founded in 1867 they enjoyed a run of seven seasons without defeat, five without conceding a goal.

During the summer break Everton along with their would be first opponent's of the new season, Liverpool Association, had joined the Lancashire Football Association and together had entered the Lancashire Cup. Liverpool Association club had been formed by a local solicitor, Edwin Berry, who in later years was to sign for Everton. The Liverpool Association team were made up of well appointed players, who included former Edinburgh University captain, J Harvey. They acquired possibly the first private football ground in Liverpool, near Sandown Lane in Wavertree, where on the 9th October 1880 they lost 3-1 to Everton. Liverpool Association then became the first Merseyside team to play in Manchester, where they were beaten 3-1 by Manchester Wanderers at Brookes Bar.

In September of the same year the draw for the first round of the Lancashire Cup was made in Blackburn. Liverpool Association received a home tie with Great Harwood but Everton, however, were less fortunate in drawing Great Lever, a well established team from Bolton.

Leaving from Liverpool Exchange Station the team made what was the first railway excursion in the club's history to the match which took place at the Woodside Ground on Manchester Road. Everton returned home with a creditable 1-1 draw. They lost the replay 8-1 at Stanley Park, the contest being ruined by the referee who was also a member of the Great Lever committee. Everton protested to the Lancashire FA who, at a meeting on the 13th of November, ruled in favour of the Merseyside club and it was decided to replay the game at Great Lever with Mr Yeats, a prominent member of the Lancashire FA committee, being appointed as referee.

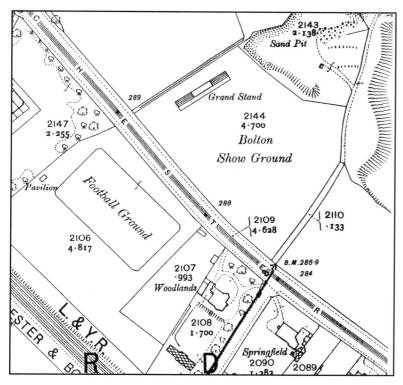

The Woodside home of Great Lever F.C. venue of Everton Lancashire Cup Games 1880

The two teams met for the third time at Woodside in November 1880, the match leaving Everton with many unpleasant memories of their return visit to the area. They arrived at the ground to find the field of play surrounded by a large partisan crowd. To say the welcome was hostile is putting a mild interpretation upon the behaviour of the home supporters. Great Lever won a close game 1-0, but even this did not reconcile the indigenous population, whose actions caused even Mr Yeats to sense its intimidating presence. As the Everton players left the ground, they were surrounded and taunted with such remarks as, "Tha'll get no cheese an bacon ta neet Everton", followed by other abusive local expressions.

Early in the new year Everton again travelled from Exchange Station for a match with Burscough. This rural community had formed a football team which in those early days played their home matches on various fields around the village. Everton won this first encounter 5-1.

During the month of February Everton played two matches on consecutive Saturdays against coal mining teams from South East Lancashire on the same ground. The players and club officials travelled to the ground first by train and then by tram, which passed the ground on Park Road Blackbrook, about one mile from St. Helens town centre and continued to Haydock from where their first opponents were situated. Everton won a hard physical game 3-2. The opposition for the second visit was provided by Garswood Park, a team formed by the workers at a colliery of that name situated on Liverpool Road, half way between Haydock and Ashton-in-Makerfield. Everton dominated the first half but failed to score. After the break the visitors continued to press forward and, after fine work by McGill, Aston scored for Everton. The goal was hotly disputed by the home side on a plea of off side. After a long discussion the game continued with the goal being held in dispute. From this set back Garswood Park adopted a more defensive approach, stationing three or four men permanently on the goal line, the result being Everton attacking for the rest of the game that ended 1-0.

In 1876 a certain Robert E Lythgoe had been appointed agent for The Shropshire Union Canal Company at their offices

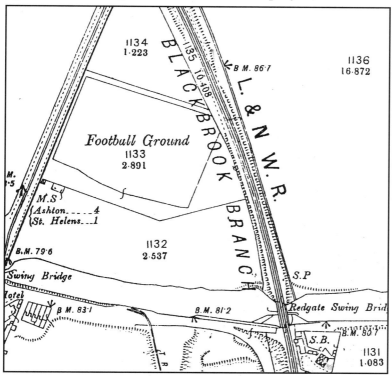

Blackbrook, St. Helens venue of Everton v Haydock and Garswood Park Matches 1881

in New Ferry. Mr Lythgoe was a keen follower of the Association game having previously played for The Druids, who where based at Ruabon in North Wales. A tireless and perspicacious man, he settled at 2 Irwell Street, Liverpool before joining the newly formed Bootle FC. Later at a meeting in the Cocoa rooms at 107 Chester Street he also helped form Birkenhead FC, the new club's first ground being Mr Heathcock's Field, which was located between Chester Street and Church Street and was the venue for their first meeting with Everton. Everton, being the more experienced of the two teams, won the match comfortably 7-0. The Chester Street ground was later enclosed and used by the club until it was taken over by The 1st (Cheshire) Engineers and used as a parade ground.

Everton made their last excursion of the season to Earlestown, situated at the spot where the West Coast main railway line crosses the Liverpool to Manchester line. The

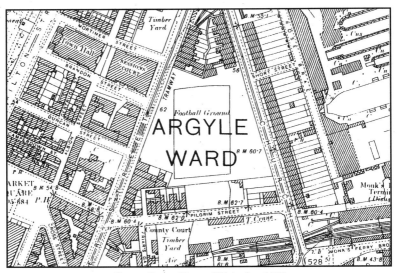

Chester Street, Home of Birkenhead F.C.
Everton first played here March 12th 1881

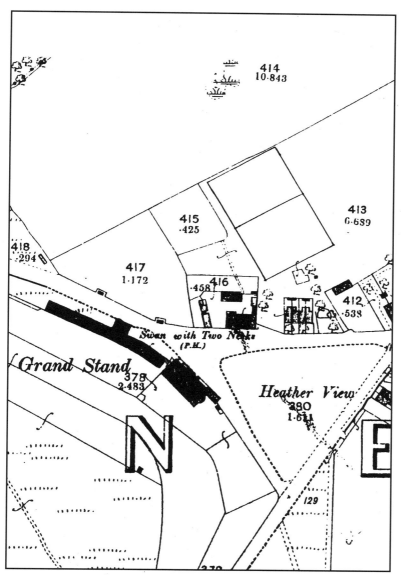

Earlestown ground behind the Swan with two nicks,
large grandstand shown is Newton-Le- Willows racecourse

enterprising Earle Family from Allerton, had constructed their Wagon Works near to the junction, thus giving their name to the town. Like many of the early football grounds, the local club had placed their pitch near to a hotel, whose facilities could be utilized on the day of the match. The present case being The Swan with Two Nicks, which in those days faced the grandstand of Newton-le-Willows racecourse. Everton won a close game 1-0 and the two sides became great friends and rivals in the coming years.

1881/82 Season

The season began with a trip to Northwich Victoria, one of four fixtures arranged by the club secretary that year, with teams belonging to the Cheshire Association. For years the main industry of the area was mining salt. When Ludwig Mond and J T Brunner placed their alkali works nearby, the town began to grow. Northwich Victoria were a well established club who were formed in 1874. They were one of the strongest teams in the County, playing their home game's opposite the Drill Hall on the old parade ground of the local militia, which was on the banks of the River Dane. After arriving by train Everton walked the short journey to the ground and left with a 2-0 victory.

On the 5th of November Everton paid their second visit to Cheshire to play Chester Rovers, a team who were playing their home fixtures on the Roodee Racecourse. Owing to a mix up on the trains Everton arrived at Chester Station with only seven of their first team players. The facilities of the racecourse grandstand were probably used for the match. Everton it is reported, took to the field with local substitutes who in the course of the game proved to be of little use. Owing to this handicap Everton were forced to play a defensive game, but still managed to achieve a 1-1 draw.

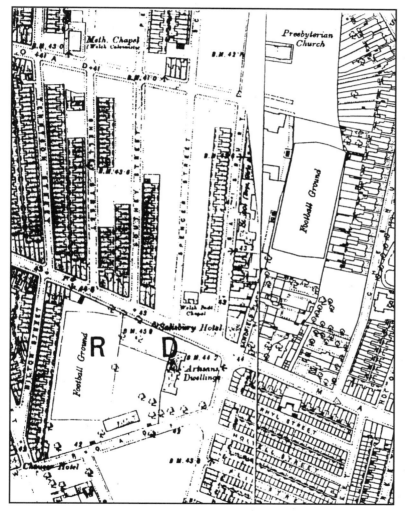

(Lower Left) Marsh Lane Home of Bootle F.C (Higher Right) home of Bottle Wanderers

Early in the new year Everton paid their first visit to the Bootle ground on Marsh Lane. Considerable interest was shown in the area and some five hundred people assembled around the tight little ground. After going a goal down, Everton slowly began to take control with Jack McGill having an outstanding game, scoring all the goals in a 4-1 victory. The Rev. A W Keely refereed the game and Bob Lythgoe was an umpire. After the match the players and officials sat down to tea together at the Derby Arms.

Everton next met their third Cheshire Association club, in the form of Over Wanderers. To fulfil the fixture the team took a train from Lime Street Station and alighted at Winsford, a town comprising of the three local townships of Over, Swanlow and Wharton. The surrounding countryside was given over to the production of salt and chemicals, which was evident in its appearance.

The Everton party, which consisted of only eight players, walked eastwards from the station along Wharton Road to find a large playing area surrounded by a cinder running track. Owing to the late arrival of the train it was decided that the match would be of one hour's duration, with Everton once again taking to the field after securing the services of three locally recruited substitutes. At the start of the game a strong wind acted in favour of the home side, but at half time the score line was blank. After the interval, with the wind in their favour, the Merseysider's superiority began to show with Jack McGill being head and shoulders above the rest. He had an outstanding game repeating his performance at Marsh Lane by scoring all the goals in a 4-0 victory. Over Wanderers are today known as Winsford United.

Everton's next visit was to the North Shropshire Town of Oswestry. This rural market town grew in size owing to the building of the headquarters of the Cambrian Railway Company. The match against the local White Star club took place at the Cricket Ground on Victoria Road with play commencing at 3:35pm, twenty minutes after the advertised time. Everton lost 1-0 in a game that was reported to have been played in a "most friendly spirit", which considerably enhanced the pleasure of the moderate attendance of spectators. Afterwards the teams had tea together at the Queens Arms. Everton revisited the town the following year and after the match signed George Farmer who, along with George Dobson, became the Merseysider's first professional players.

George Farmer was born in Oswestry in 1863 and had recently been capped twice for Wales while playing for the local White Star club. He was employed as a skinner and lived with his parents in Oswestry at Vine Cottage, Rope Walk. He quickly established himself in the Everton team scoring a hat-trick in a 8-2 victory at Haydock. He went on to score seventy goals during his time at Everton and was noted for his neat passing and was equally at home in attack or defence. In 1890 he left the club to join the newly formed Liverpool South End. He also played for Liverpool Caledonians and Rock Ferry before he retired from the game. He later settled in West Derby where he lived until his death in 1906.

With regards to George Dobson there is no account in the club records of him ever playing for Bolton Wanderers, so it's possible he was signed from Great Lever or Halliwell. He was well known in the area, for upon signing for Everton he was appointed agent for R Mercer of 35 Market Street, Bolton, who were at the time famous for the manufacture of football goods. He lived at Blessington Road, Anfield and played only one league season at Anfield before leaving the club during the summer of 1890.

For the final club fixture of the season Everton travelled to Bolton for a game with Halliwell, a team formed at the local Jubilee club, which was situated about two miles from the town centre. After alighting from the tram on Halliwell Road the Everton players walked down a footpath to find a large semi-circular field on Bennetts Lane where they enjoyed a 6-1 victory.

Earlier in the season, despite their unpleasant past experiences in this competition, Everton, along with Bootle, Liverpool Association and local neighbours St Peters, had once again entered the Lancashire Cup, where they received a home tie with Middleton whom they beat 5-0.

In the second round Everton were drawn away at Turton, the oldest club in Lancashire. The club was formed in 1871 by the Kaye Family who, with the help of 'The Flying Shuttle,' had acquired great wealth from the cotton industry and purchased the nearby Turton Tower estate. One of their son's, John, attended Harrow Public School where he came under the influence of C J Alcock, who was destined to become the secretary of the Football Association. During his time at school, John developed a love for the game of football. He played under the Harrow rules and when he returned to Turton, with the help of village school master W T Dixon, he quickly formed Turton Football Club. Through the old boy network a match was arranged with Brookhouse Ramblers, a team formed by an Old Harrovian, son of the Hornby family at Blackburn. Turton established a headquarters at The Chetham

Arms and found a ground at nearby Tower Street. The club was also a founder members of the Lancashire FA.

Arriving at the local railway station, the Everton party walked the short distance to the local hamlet of Chapel town to find the Chetham Arms, which was in the High Street, near to where the ground was located. The game kicked off at 3:20pm with the home team scoring within five minutes and adding two more goals before the break. Everton played a much better game in the second half, but lost the match 3-1. The Lancashire FA took three shillings and nine pence (thirty four and half new pence) as their quarter share of the gate money. This being possibly the first official receipt for a game involving Everton. The largest share of the round being two pounds and two shillings from Blackburn Olympic making it clear to all concerned that, at this stage of its development, association football in the cotton towns of Lancashire was more advanced than the game on Merseyside.

1882/83 Season

The season began for Everton with a trip over the Mersey to play a team of former public schoolboys playing under the name of The Wirral Association. The team had played one or two games the previous year as the Wirral Old Public School Men. Their fixture list for the coming season was quite impressive. At a time when most players met their own travelling expenses, they were travelling far afield in order to fulfil their fixtures. The club secretary was A W Tetley who arranged the match with Everton that took place at Shrewsbury Park, Oxon, with the visitors winning 5-0.

The ground, which was located in an affluent area, was a fairly simple affair and some teams appeared to have had difficulty in finding it's location. The Daily Post dated the 21st October 1882 stated, "When the Whitchurch Club visited earlier in the season, it was getting close to half past four by the time they reached the ground, but I can understand as Shrewsbury Park is not a place readily reached".

The following Saturday Bob Lythgoe, who appeared to be known to the Wirral players, acted as their umpire for the visit of the famous 'Sheffield Club'.

Everton had arranged a fixture with Bolton based club Eagley on the same day, but Jack McGill kindly consented to turn out for the Wirral Club in an attempt to strengthen the side in the face of such strong opposition. Despite playing well and scoring, Jack could not prevent the Yorkshire men from running out 5-2 winners. Also in the Wirral team that day was Mr W H Bailey who played at full back. The Wirral Association were also one of the founder members of the Liverpool FA, but sadly they played only one season under that name and then disappeared forever.

In November Everton made their first visit to North Wales at the invitation of Wrexham. The game at that time being well established in the principality largely due to men like Chirk schoolmaster J T Thomas who taught the skills of the game at school and in his leisure time. Many a good player passed through his hands, the most famous being a local miner from Black Park Colliery, called Billy Meredith who went on to win major honours with both Manchester United and Manchester City. Wrexham were formed in 1873, at the Turf Hotel by the members of the local cricket club. They began playing on the

Racecourse, but an increase in rent forced them to move to the Rhosddu Recreation Ground to where Everton made the short walk from the local railway station. After winning the toss, Everton kicked off against the breeze. Despite being the better team for most of the game they faded towards the end and two late goals by R Davies sealed a 5-3 win for the Welshmen.

On the 9th of December Everton travelled to the railway town of Crewe to meet Crewe Alexandra. They arrived with a well below strength team and made the short walk to the Alexandra ground, which was situated next to the railway station on Nantwich Road. Their opponents, formed by the local railway workers, were an extension of Alexandra Cricket Club and became the strongest of the four clubs founded in the town. Everton lost the match 2-1 with their reserve forward, Westland, being the goal scorer.

In the meantime the draw had been made for the first round of that year's Lancashire Cup. Out of the five clubs from Merseyside who entered that year's competition, Everton received the worse possible fixture, an away trip to face firm favourites for the trophy, Blackburn Rovers, at the Leamington Ground.

The Leamington Ground had been Blackburn's home since the 15th October 1881. When they took the lease the first thing they did was to build a grandstand costing five hundred pounds which could seat seven hundred people. The ground contained a pavilion with dressing rooms and a large refreshment area. During Blackburn's nine years at the Leamington Ground they had one of their most successful periods in the club's history. They won the FA cup three times in successive years and also

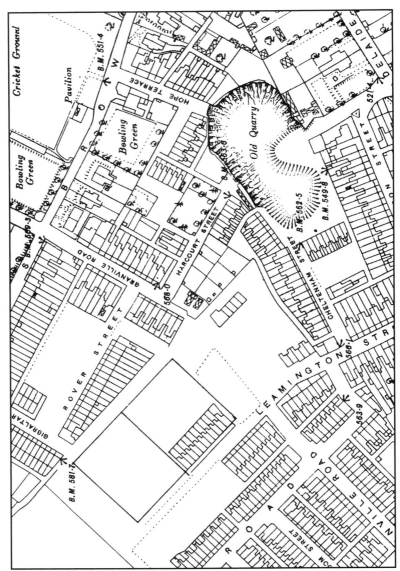

The Leamington Ground shortly after Blackburn Rovers move to Ewood park.
Rovers had previously played on Alexandra Meadows (Top Left)

entered the Football League. The ground received recognition from the FA by being selected as the venue for three England international matches. Prior to the 1890-91 season the club officials were unwilling to succumb to new rent demands and gambled on finding a new home. As a result of their decision Rovers opened that season at Ewood Park. The Leamington Ground was quickly covered with terraced housing.

There were seven hundred spectators present at the ground for the Everton visit and, not surprisingly, the gulf between the two sides was enormous the visitors losing 8-0. The Preston Herald covered the game and remarked, "Although the visitors were exceedingly fine players, they were a little too impetuous and very careless with regard to observing their respective positions. For sometime, getting the ball appeared to be the entire object of their endeavours and it was generally a race to be first to touch the ball".

After the match, Jack McGill was persuaded to sign for Accrington. Everton missed Jack and struggled in his absence, but he was back for the start of the next season.

The newly formed Liverpool Ramblers had also entered the Lancashire Cup competition, but were unable to play their tie at Blackpool based Great Marton. Ramblers secretary, Percy Bateson, wrote to the Great Marton club to say "I exceedingly regret, that this morning I was obliged to send you a telegram, saying that we could not get a team to go so far away and therefore must scratch in your favour. Most of our players being in offices here, are unable to get away at such a time as 12:25pm and there was no later train that would suit. I am very sorry if you have gone to any great expense, but to recompense that you have won (practically speaking) your first tie. Of course you will inform the association that we have scratched to you".

Back in Liverpool in October time of 1882, steps were being taken to form a Liverpool Football Association. The main driving force behind the idea was Bob Lythgoe. Publishing a letter in the local press he went on to say, "Having observed in some of your recent issues, correspondence advocating the advisability of forming an Association in this district and being also of the opinion that the time has now arrived for the formation of such an organisation here (similar to those of Birmingham and Sheffield) which will not only enable us to put a thoroughly representative team - playing under the Association rules - in the field but will also in a large measure benefit the local charities as in the towns already named. It has occurred to me that the time for action has already arrived and there is nothing to prevent our forming an association at once and selecting our committee, so that we may have our first draw for the charity cup competition at the end of this season and play all the ties in the month of March and April, similar to the arrangement of the Yorkshire Rules. Towards the end of this season we should be well organised and in a position to place a good representative team in the field, which should be able to play a well contested game with some of the best clubs in the country, one or two of which we then could have here to meet our association the proceeds of course, to go to the charity fund, also the proceeds of the final tie. It is obvious that the first thing wanted is a charity cup and I think it only remains for the association, when formed to appeal to a few of the more wealthy and charitable gentlemen to obtain the desired object. To accomplish all this it is therefore evident our first step is to have a meeting on an early date and I now ask all association clubs in the district to meet at the Tarleton Hotel on Thursday at 8 o'clock".

One week later at a crowded and enthusiastic meeting, it was decided to form a confederation of clubs in the district. The twelve clubs represented were as follows: Liverpool Association, Bootle, Everton, Wirral Association, Birkenhead, Liverpool Stanley, St. Peters, Liverpool Rovers, Anfield, St. Mary's, St. Benedict's and St. Georges. Mr R M Sloan of Bootle presided and briefly explained that the objects of the meeting were as follows:- That an association of clubs playing within a radius of six miles be formed under the title of Liverpool and District Football Association. After a short discussion the resolution was carried unanimously. Mr Edwin Berry (Liverpool Association) then moved that each club represented at the meeting, be entitled to nominate two members as a temporary committee, which was carried without dissent. On the motion of Mr T Evans (Everton), Mr R E Lythgoe was elected Hon Sec (pro tem). The question of a trophy was mooted, the prevailing opinion being in favour of a shield. At the meeting the following week the draw for the first round of the challenge cup took place with the following teams being drawn against each other; Bootle v St. Mary's (Kirkdale), Liverpool Stanley v St. Peters, Liverpool Rovers v Wirral Association, St. Benedicts v Anfield, Liverpool Association v Everton, Toxteth Wanderers v Liverpool Ramblers and Birkenhead v Bootle Wanderers. All the ties were to be played on or before the 24th January 1883. In response to an unanimous wish Lord Claude John Hamilton MP, accepted the office of President of the Association.

The meeting was also informed "That as a result of local negotiation, with the object of aiding the efforts now being made in the district, it has been decided to play the England v Ireland international match at Liverpool. The fixture being arranged for the 17th February 1883". The game actually took place on the

24th February 1883 at the new Liverpool Cricket Ground at Aigburth which had just been completed that summer. The ground contained a handsome pavilion designed by Mr Harrison and built by Cubbits. It was amongst the finest of it's kind in the country and this fine building still stands today as a monument to local Victorian self confidence. This was the second occasion the Irish Association had met it's older and more experienced rivals and were anxious to improve on the13-0 defeat they had suffered the season before.

The day of the match was cold with brilliant sunshine which favoured the fashionable attendance of two thousand, five hundred spectators who turned up to view the proceedings. The pitch was in magnificent condition, in all probability the best in Liverpool at the time and favoured the passing game. England scored three times in a six minute spell to give them a 3-0 lead at half time. They scored another four goals in the second half to finish 7-0 winners.

The England team that day was, Harry Albermarle Swepstone (Pilgrams London), Percy John de Paravicini (Cambridge Uni), Henry Thomas Moore (Notts. County), John Hudson (Sheffield Wednesday), Oliver Wheatley (Aston Villa), Stuart Macrae (Notts County), Francis William Pawson (Cambridge Uni), Arthur Tempest Blakiston Dunn (Cambridge Uni), Harry Chester Goodhart (Old Etonians, London), Henry Alfred Cursham (Notts. County), William Neville Cobbold (Cambridge Uni). After the contest the teams dined together at the Bear's Paw Restaurant in Liverpool.

Everton meanwhile, had reached the semi final of the Liverpool Cup, where a game with Bootle awaited them. The venue was to be the Liverpool College Ground, Fairfield, which attracted a large crowd. Public interest also centred on the fact that the proceeds arising from the match were to be handed over to the Hospital Saturday Fund. Bootle dominated the first half and led 3-0 at the break, giving Everton club secretary and goalkeeper Frank Brettell a torrid time in the process. Immediately after the change of end, Cartwright scored a lucky goal for Everton, the ball striking a Bootle defender and glancing through the posts. Everton pressed strongly but could not break down a resolute Bootle defence who deservedly took the game 3-1.

The following Saturday Liverpool Ramblers beat Birkenhead 6-0 at the same venue. They then met Bootle in the final which also took place on the College Ground. Bootle carried off the trophy with a 3-1 victory. The proceeds of all the three games went to the hospital fund.

1883/84 Season

Everton were by now emerging as one of the strongest teams in the city and by far the most popular. Fixtures with such clubs as Bolton Wanderers had already attracted large crowds to Stanley Park which were becoming difficult to control and, more importantly, the fans were viewing the proceeding free of charge. The answer was to have an enclosed ground.

Overlooking the park on Priory Road, a wealthy cattle importer Mr William Cruitt had recently purchased a fine house named Coney Green, with a large adjacent field. Mr Cruitt agreed to rent the field to Everton Football Club and during the summer months club members and players worked to enclose the area,

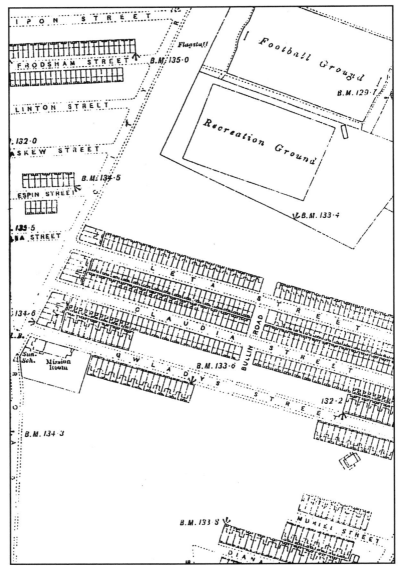

(Top of Picture) Walton Stiles Ground used by Everton for a home match v Southport, Sepember 1883. It was also the venue for the Liverpool Cup Final Everton v Bootle April 1886

building dressing rooms and erecting a small stand. But it soon became clear to all concerned that the ground would not be ready in time to host the opening fixture that the club secretary had arranged with Southport on the 15th September 1883.

A solution was quite literally close at hand. The Liverpool Association, who had folded during the closed season, had moved to a new ground at Walton Stiles the previous season. The pitch was still in good playing order so Everton made their first move, albeit for one game, to a ground not one hundred yards from what was to later become the famous Goodison Park. Everton won this one off encounter quite comfortably 3-0.

While awaiting the completion of their new enclosed ground Everton had to content themselves with a series of away matches. The first being a trip to Bolton for a fixture with Eagley, a well established team, sharing a ground with the local cricket club. The venue was located near the Dunscar Bridge tram terminus, about two miles north of the town centre. The Everton party arrived late and the match kicked off at 4:02pm. It proved to be a tough game for the visitors, who after trailing 3-2, finished strongly and registered a 4-3 victory.

By the end of October the new ground was ready. The opening fixture, arranged by Bob Lythgoe, was to be a representative match between Liverpool and District and Walsall and District. Despite special omnibuses being laid on from Exchange Station the attendance was disappointing. The game ended 3-3.

The honour of being the first club side to visit the new ground fell to the little Northwich based team Hartford St. Johns, who gave a good account of themselves before going down 3-1. Jack McGill scoring the first goal on the Priory Road ground.

Two weeks later the powerful North Midlands outfit Burslam Port Vale were the visitors. The fifty mile journey made by the club was the longest made by any team to fulfil a fixture with Everton at that time. A large muster of spectators witnessed a tight match, but it was the visitors who returned to the Potteries with a 1-0 victory .

The previous Saturday Everton had defeated St. Peters 10-0 in the first round of that year's Liverpool Cup and next faced Liverpool Ramblers. The Ramblers club had been formed in 1882 at the offices of local solicitor James Bateson, which were situated at 14, Castle Street, Liverpool. The prevailing uncertainty as to the location resulted in the crowd not being as large as expected with the match eventually taking place at the College Ground at Fairfield. Owing to the late fixture of the goal posts, the game eventually kicked off at 3:30pm. The first half was an even contest with Pilkington being outstanding for Ramblers, but in the second period Everton played a much better game and won the contest 4-1. The Ramblers goalkeeper Percy Eccles was unfortunate to not see the final goal in what was by then near darkness.

In December Everton made their longest journey to date for a return fixture with Burslam Port Vale. After arriving by train at Stoke they took the recently opened Tunstall branch line to the Brownhills area of the Five Towns. The ground was located near the Brownhills railway station on a field adjoining the local cricket ground, whose pavilion was perhaps used for the players to change, as the map of the time shows no changing facilities were available at the football ground. After an entertaining game Everton were no worse for their long excursion and returned home with a 2-2 draw.

Back home in the Liverpool Cup, Everton's next opponents were Bootle Wanderers, a team who at the time were playing their home games at Seaview Place, off Marsh Lane. Despite gaining a home draw, Wanderers elected to play the tie at Priory Road where they lost 5-2.

As there were now only three teams left in the competition Everton received a bye into the final with Earlestown who beat Liverpool Stanley 2-1 for the right to play them. Bootle had by now left their cramped little ground on Marsh Lane and amalgamated with the local Cricket Club at Hawthorne Road where the final was to be played. Amongst the two thousand, five hundred present, were Mr W E Earle, Mr E Stewart-Brown and Mr R Lythgoe. The Earlestown men put in a prompt appearance and when Everton entered the arena they were most cordially received. The game commenced at 3:30pm and by half time the score was still 0-0. Twenty minutes into the second half Edwin Berry broke down the left wing, crossed the ball and after a confused struggle in the Earlestown goalmouth, Parry rushed in to score what turned out to be the winning goal to the great delight of the Everton followers. Amidst tremendous cheering Everton kept up the pressure and at the final whistle there was great rejoicing. The winning team were driven triumphantly through the streets back to the 'Hill Country' by horse and carriage, so ending what was to date the club's most successful season, a new ground and their first trophy.

Alas, all was not well in the leafy suburbs of North Liverpool. The euphoria surrounding the club's win, was brought to an abrupt end by landlord Mr Cruitt's refusal to allow the club to use Priory Road for the following season. The reason presumably being the large number of followers the team had accumulated and the noise they generated disturbed the tranquillity of the surrounding area, so once again Everton were on the move.

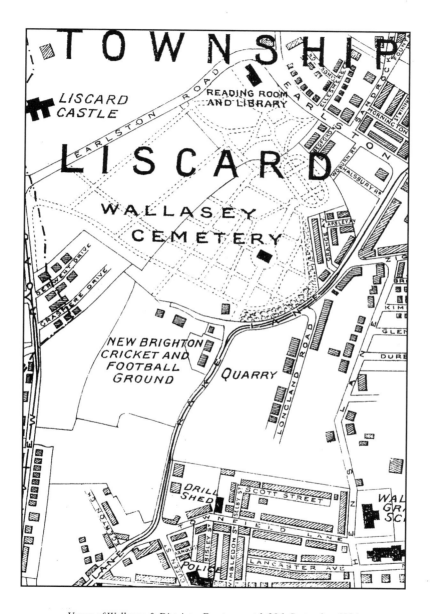

Venue of Wallasey & District v Everton match 20th September 1884

Anfield

The committee quickly secured a new ground at the former home of Everton Cricket Club in Walton Breck Road, on land belonging to local brewers, John and Joseph Orrell. The now well known terms were:- "That we, the Everton Football Club, keep the existing walls in good repair, pay the taxes, do not cause ourselves to be a nuisance to Mr Orrell and other tenants adjoining, and also to pay a small sum as rent, or subscribe a donation each year to the Stanley Hospital in the name of Mr Orrell".

The club members and players were by now more experienced and galvanised by a common cause. They quickly set about their task with great enthusiasm. During the summer months the site was a scene of constant activity, as all concerned quickly turned the field into an enclosed ground, with a fence around the pitch and an open grandstand on the Northern side. It was also decided to use the Sandon Hotel, owned by the newly elected president Mr John Holding, as the club's headquarters and changing rooms. Everything was once again in place ready for the coming season.

During the pre-season meeting of the Liverpool and District Association it was announced that the number of members had now increased to thirty six teams. The new clubs being:- Argyl, Burscough, Crescent (Southport), Christ Church (Southport), Christ Church (Bootle), Earlestown Wanderers, Golbourne, Gymnasium, Haydock, St. James (Haydock), Temperance, High Park, Liverpool Cambrian, Liverpool Linden, Liver, Newsham, Ormskirk, Oakfield Rovers, Southport, Southport Wanderers, Skelmersdale, Tranmere, Warrington, and Wallasey and District.

1884/85 Season

Everton began the season by accepting a kind invitation from their old friends and rivals Burslam Port Vale, to provide the opposition for a match to celebrate the opening of their new ground in the Potteries. The enclosure which was reported to be well appointed stood on Waterloo Road, close to Corbridge Railway Station, with a tramline passing the main entrance. The pitch was surrounded by a cinder running track, which was a quarter of a mile in circumference, a grandstand which could provide accommodation for one thousand six hundred spectators and a large pavilion. Given the primitive state of the visitor's Walton Breck Road ground, it is fair to say that this development was at the time far superior. The local press described the encounter as being played before two thousand spectators. The home team had the best of the first half and lead 1-0 at the break. In the second half of the contest the home team again had matters pretty much their own way adding six more goals to their total. The poor weather conditions told severely on the under strength Everton side.

Everton next crossed the Mersey for an encounter with the newly formed Wallasey and District Football Association. The match was played on the ground of New Brighton Rugby Club. Unlike Shrewsbury Park, the ground, situated on Seaview Road, Liscard was easily reached by the tram from New Brighton Railway Station. Mr C T Bowering and Mr G W Turner were the only two players in the home side who had turned out for the Wirral Association team against Everton the previous season. The weather on the day, we are told, was beautiful. Everton won the toss and attacked the lower goal. The Liverpool team once again proved too strong for the team from over the water and won 5-1.

Saturday the 27th September 1884 marked the opening of Everton's new ground on Walton Breck Road. The beaten finalists in last years Liverpool Cup, Earlestown, kindly accepted the invitation to provide the opposition. The two teams changed at the Sandon Hotel before making the short walk to the new enclosure. At 3:50pm the visitors kicked off towards the Anfield Road end, with the slope in their favour. The large crowd that had gathered for the grand opening were soon cheering the first goal for Everton, as Higgins went into the history books by being the first player to score a goal on the new ground. The rest of the match was very much in Everton's favour with further goals from Whittle scoring two, Gibson and Richards scoring one a piece, adding to the total as Everton ran out 5-0 winners.

Everton next began their defence of the Liverpool Cup with a 7-0 victory over Sefton Park based, Toxteth Wanderers, before setting off on their next new adventure to the Cheshire village of Davenham. How such a small rural community could provide such a strong team is a mystery, but they were well respected members of the Cheshire FA, who had already knocked Crewe Alexandra out of the FA Cup. In what manner Everton travelled the two miles from Northwich Station is not clear, as the map shows no tramline, but arrive they did, and after changing in the Odd Fellows Arms, they made their way to the National School Field on Northwich Road.

The pitch was on a incline where the home team captain won the toss and elected to kick downhill. A close game followed and in the closing stages, with the score standing at 1-1, a shot from Gibson was fisted out by the home goalkeeper Shaw and the ball fell conveniently for Jack McGill, who scored the winning goal.

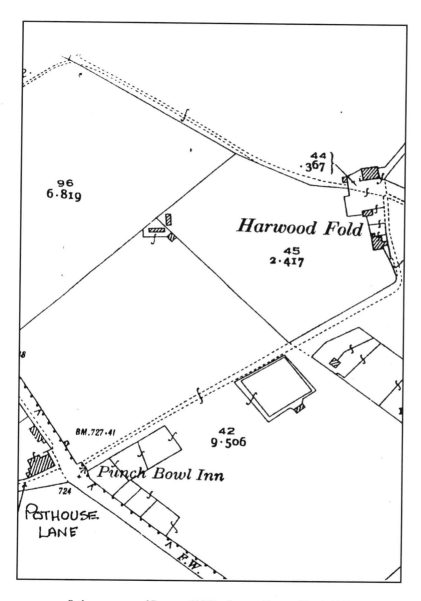

Pothouse, venue of Darwen Old Wanderers v Everton March 1885

Everton next returned to the Walton stiles enclosure as the visiting team to inflict a 2-1 defeat on the new tenants of the ground, Liverpool Stanley.

By February 1885 Everton had once again fought their way through to the final of the Liverpool Cup when, after disposing of Southport, Bootle and Golbourne, respectively, they once again faced their old rivals Earlestown. The match took place at Hawthorn Road, Bootle, where around five thousand people packed the ground, which included two thousand who had made the journey from Earlestown and were conspicuous by the blue cards stuck in their hats on which was inscribed, "Play up Earlestown". The game was well contested although occasionally a little rough. The Everton captain was absent through injury, but they still dominated the game. Everton were thwarted by the aptly named Earlestown goalkeeper Champion, who held the Everton forwards at bay with a brilliant all round performance. Earlestown eventually took the trophy back to the Junction Town with a 1-0 victory.

Before the season ended, Everton still had new paths to travel and made their first visit to the football mad town of Darwen. The team they had to face consisted of local coal miners calling themselves 'Darwen Old Wanderers'. Everton, who did not send their strongest team, arrived at the local Railway Station and travelled to Pothouse on the outskirts of the town, where they found the playing area to be only one hundred yards by fifty yards with a deeply pitted surface. They did, however, have a small pavilion. Everton lost the match 7-0. After the game hospitality, one imagines, was dispensed at the nearby Punch Bowl Inn.

Darwen was to be the last new venue of the season, Everton did however send a strong team to Haydock for a charity match in aid of the new Cottage Hospital which was to be built on Clipsey Lane. During the Whitsun weekend, Everton played two charity matches in aid of Stanley Hospital with club president John Holding being well to the fore in arranging the event. His guests included his Worship The Mayor, Alderman Ratcliffe, and Major Lester, the Chairman of the hospital. On the Whit Saturday, the 23rd May 1885, they beat a Liverpool Select 5-2 with the help of Fergus Suter of Blackburn Rovers, possibly the world's first professional footballer. Bolton Wanderers provided the opposition on the Whit Monday and after the match John Holding entertained his guests at his house overlooking Stanley Park.

1885/86 Season

Burnley paid their first visit to Liverpool for the opening game of the season, which was followed by a procession of home matches against clubs from East Lancashire in which Everton failed to register a single victory. The Lancashire Association found the club to be of not proven ability and relegated them to the newly formed Junior Cup Competition. This was clearly disheartening for Everton who, never-the-less, beat Adlington 8-1 in the first round. They were then drawn away to Peel Park, who were based in Accrington, for the second round of the contest. Everton sent a weak team who arrived late at the ground, which turned out to be a large recreational area complete with bowling greens and a large Hotel that was used on match days. The match eventually kicked off at 3:55pm consequently darkness was setting in before the match finished. Despite taking an early lead, Everton lost their way in the gloom going down 5-1.

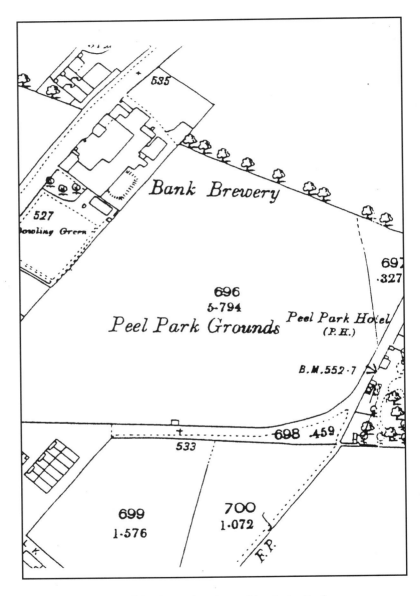

Peel Park Accrington, later home of Accrington Stanley

The following weekend, with all but two of their first team players, Everton travelled to North Wales to encounter the Druids, a team that contained mostly coal miners, who had captured the public's imagination in 1883 by dismissing Bolton Wanderers from the FA Cup; before losing to the eventual winners Blackburn Olympic. After leaving the train at Ruabon Station the Everton team would have enjoyed a pleasant stroll through the Wynnstay Estate before arriving at the playing field. The Driuds team, which contained many Welsh internationals, proved too strong for Everton who went down 4-0.

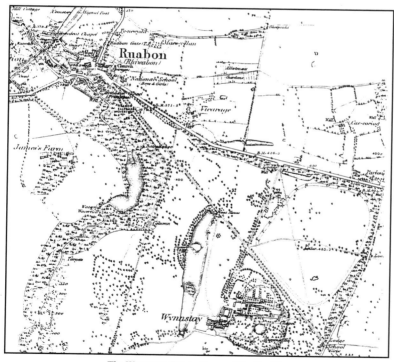

The Wynnstay Estate Home of the Druids.
The pitch was located inside the training ground to the right

On New Years Day 1886 Partick Thistle became the first Scottish club to visit Anfield winning a sporting game 3-0. The following day Irish club Limavady became the first overseas team to play against Everton at Anfield, beating the home team 1-0. Towards the end of the month, Everton again visited the town of Blackburn to play a locally based team called Witton taking a strong side with them. The ground which was situated on Preston Old Road, on the outskirts of the town, contained a small Grandstand, but no local transport link. This resulted in the visitors arriving late, so play was limited to forty minutes each way. After drawing 1-1 at the break Everton faded badly and went down 4-2.

On Saturday the 23rd January 1886, Everton met Bootle for the first time at Hawthorne Road where an immense crowd assembled for the match. Mr Ormerod, a Lancashire FA committee member, arrived from Accrington to take charge in the middle. Everton took an early lead through Wilding, then the defence took command, well marshalled by George Dobson. Bootle could do nothing to budge them, with Mr Ormerod's presence preventing the game from boiling over. Everton won the match 1-0.

Liverpool Ramblers were now using the Liverpool Cricket ground at Aigburth as their headquarters during the winter months and Everton played a fixture there in February winning 5-0. The Daily Post reporter referring to them as "A well oiled machine". By the end of the same month, after beating Southport Wanderers and New Ferry, Everton had progressed to the third round of the Liverpool Cup where their next opposition was High Park, a junior club based in Southport. Eight hundred spectators gathered on Devonshire Road for a match that aroused great interest in the town. Everton led 2-0 at half-time. High Park pulled a goal back just after the break, but Everton hung on to the end for a 2-1 win, with George Dobson once again being their outstanding player.

The following weekend Everton had arranged a fixture with their neighbour Stanley, but a heavy fall of snow put the game in doubt. The club posted notices in the area asking for one hundred men to clear the ground of snow on the morning of the match for a small reward. Such an advertisement today would perhaps receive a warm response, but in times of great hardship things were different. The first one hundred to arrive were quickly put to work, but from all directions people continued to engulf the ground. The club directors began to lose control of the situation and, when a gang of local tough guys known as the 'High Rip Gang' appeared on the scene, matters threatened to get out of hand. The local constabulary were quickly sent for and, through a combination of free tickets and good police work, order was soon restored. The pitch was cleared of snow and the match went ahead as planned.

The draw for the semi final of The Liverpool Cup paired Everton with Liverpool Stanley. The match took place at a neutral venue, Hawthorn Road, Bootle. Five thousand people paid gate receipts of eighty pounds, the bulk of them coming from the Hill Country. This was evident by the great cheer which greeted the Everton team on their arrival on the pitch. The first half was evenly contested, but in the second period Everton pressed forward strongly and a sense of impending defeat seemed to take possession of the Stanley players. Stanley's outstanding player, Sandy Dick, was forced into an error from which Everton took the lead. A second goal quickly followed and Stanley eventually lost 3-0. Bootle won the other semi final and the stage was set for these two deadly rivals to meet in the final.

The venue chosen for the final was the Liverpool Stanley ground at Walton Stiles, which by this time had developed into a simple enclosure. Eight thousand people are reported to have somehow crammed into the ground to watch the match. The press reporters of the day complained of having to do their work without any seating or cover. Mr Ormerod returned to Liverpool to take charge in the middle, bringing with him Mr J Lewis from Blackburn Rovers to act as umpire, with Mr C J Hughes, the secretary of The Cheshire Association, travelling from Northwich to act as the other official. Amid great excitement Bootle kicked off with the sun in their eyes. The early exchanges were evenly balanced until mid way into the first half, Gibson, with a brilliant drive, scored to give Everton the lead which they held until the break. Upon resumption the striped shirts bore down on the Everton goal, with the Bootle captain, Eyton Jones, having a fine game on the left wing. George Dobson and his men were in no mood to lose the trophy two years running and defended stoically. For the last few minutes Everton applied strong pressure on the Bootle goal and when time was called, Everton were the victors of a fine game winning 1-0. The men from the Hill Country then celebrated in great style, escorting the trophy back to the Sandon amid great cheers. After the match the Liverpool and District committee decided to donate one hundred and thirty pounds to local charities, a princely sum in those days.

The season however was to have a sting in the tail. Liverpool Athletic Club had recently moved from their former headquarters on Low Hill to a fine new ground on Prescot Road in Fairfield. The committee decided, as a means of drawing public attention to this new venture, to invite local football clubs to compete in a tournament on the ground at Whitsuntide, with a silver shield being offered as the prize for the winners. Eight

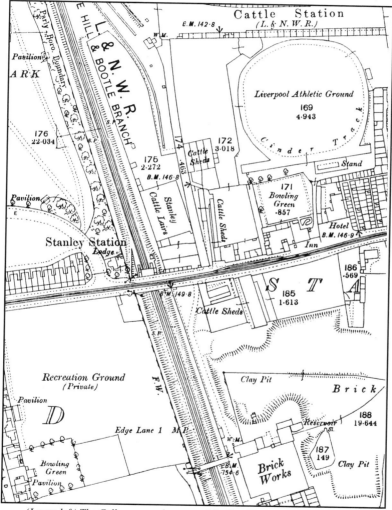

(Lower left) The College grounds venue of the first Liverpool Cup Final 1883.
(Upper right) Liverpool Athletic Ground venue of the Bootle v Everton Athletic Shield Final May 1886

clubs took part and true to form, the final saw Everton pitted against old rivals Bootle. Eight thousand people assembled on the Monday evening for a game which for excitement had never been surpassed in Liverpool. The Liverpool Ramblers player, Mr W H Bailey, kindly consented to act as referee and by the end of the night must have wished he was somewhere else. The game was intensely exciting from the start, Bootle determined to avenge their cup defeat, took an early lead through Hutton, which they held until the break. Early in the second half a shot from George Farmer was fisted out by Bootle goalkeeper Galbraith. Everton claimed the ball had crossed the line and Mr Bailey ruled in their favour.

The decision was hotly disputed by the Bootle umpire and play was held up for a while amid great confusion. The incident clearly upset the striped shirted players, who upon the resumption, attacked their opponents goal with renewed vigour. Following confusion in the Everton goalmouth, Bootle forward Routhledge forced the ball over the line. Their jubilation was short lived, when Mr Bailey disallowed the goal for off side. The Bootle side were clearly miffed by the decision and lost their composure for a while, but were soon back on the attack claiming a goal which was once again denied. At full time the score was level, so a period of extra time was played. With a few minutes remaining, Wilding grabbed what turned out to be the winning goal for Everton. The Bootle players and officials were still upset, claiming all the referee's decisions had gone in their opponents favour and refused to concede defeat. The Athletic Company retained the trophy and the matter was put for decision before the Liverpool and District committee, who decided to award the shield to Everton.

During the summer months Everton signed Jimmy Costley from Blackburn Olympic. He was born in Liverpool on the 18th January 1862 and brought up in Rathbone Street, Toxteth. He moved with the rest of his family to Blackburn, where after leaving school he gained employment as a Cotton Spinner in the Brookhouse Mill. While playing for Brookhouse Ramblers, Jimmy was induced to turn professional with Olympic. In March 1883 he was selected to play in the FA Cup semi final against the much fancied Old Carthusians. He scored one of the goals in a 4-0 victory. Costley was then selected to play in the final, which took place at The Oval Cricket ground in London, where their opponents were to be the Old Etonians. They were holders of the trophy and were captained by the great Lord Kinnaird. At full time the score was 1-1 and the contest went into extra time. With only a few minutes remaining, Costley cut in from the left and scored the winning goal that broke the hold of the Southern Amateurs on the FA Cup forever. When his career ended he returned to Blackburn and settled in his old trade at Brookhouse Mill, where he eventually died in 1930 and became the first Liverpool born football hero.

1886/87 Season

The season began true to form with a string of nine home matches. Why Everton began in this manner is not clear, but they had to wait until October before the club fulfilled an away fixture. This was to be at Ashton - Under - Lyne, to encounter a team by the name of Hurst. The match, which was played at Surrey Street, ended 2-2. The home team are today known as Ashton United.

Everton next encountered The Lancashire Cup, being once again invited to compete in the Junior competition. After disposing of Fleetwood Zingari 9-0, they were drawn against Bells Temperance, an Accrington based side from the Woodnock area of the town. Known locally as the Watermen, they arrived at Anfield to find a weak Everton side awaiting them with only three first team players present. The day was bitterly cold with the ground being almost devoid of grass. The Lancashire FA sent their Hon-Sec Mr R P Gregson to referee the match in which Everton went down 3-2 before a crowd of one thousand five hundred spectators.

The draw for the first round of The Liverpool Cup was made in November pairing Everton with Bootle. The town experienced what was to be its first taste of Cup Fever.

It was perhaps a little sad that the two leading clubs in the area had to fight it out in the first round of the contest. On the day of the match, trains between Liverpool Exchange and Kirkdale were full to capacity. An estimated crowd of ten thousand people, the largest to date to watch a match on Merseyside, descended on Bootle Cricket Ground. Many of the crowd climbed the hoardings when unable to gain admission at the legitimate entrance. All the leading figures from the Liverpool Association were present in the pavilion, including Bob Lythgoe, no doubt pleased to see the success of the competition.

The Bootle team were first to take to the field and, from the roar that greeted them, it sounded like the whole of Marsh Lane was present. When a few minutes later Everton left the pavilion it was clear by their reception that many of their followers from the Hill Country were also at the ground. The referee, Mr Bentley, called the captains to the middle. The crowd, who pressed hard on the ropes, presented an imposing sight and a protest was lodged by both captains. After due consideration, the home team kicked off with the wind in their favour. The first half was, to say the least, a 'full-blooded affair' with both sets of players accepting the barging and hacking as an occupational hazard. The excitement generated by the rough play frequently caused a hold up by bringing the crowd on to the field of play. Bootle had the best of the first period, but failed to turn their advantage in to goals and at half time the score line was blank.

When the second half resumed the home team kept up the pressure and soon claimed the first goal, but the Bootle umpire showed great integrity when he informed the referee that the ball had passed the wrong side of the upright. With twenty

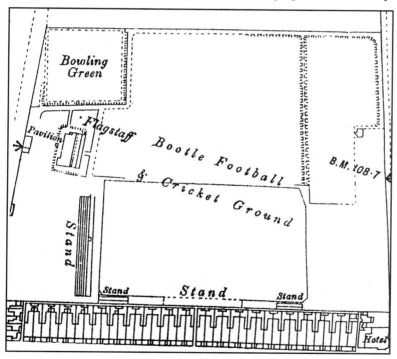

Bootle Cricket and Football Ground 1892

A sketch of the Bootle Football ground around 1890.
The pavilion can be clearly seen in the corner of the ground as the home team attacks
towards Stanley Road

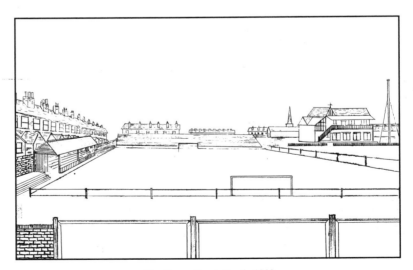

Hawthorne Road, Bootle 1892

minutes gone in the second period the Bootle goalkeeper, clearly unnerved by the noise generated by the schoolboys standing on his goal line, dropped a centre from the left and Briscoe nipped in to give Everton the lead. The Bootle captain urged his men forward and only a goal line clearance by George Dobson prevented them from equalizing. Once again the crowd encroached upon the pitch and play was held up until the ground was cleared by the club stewards. Shortly after the play restarted a melee occurred in the home team's goalmouth, amid great confusion the ball was forced over the line for a second Everton goal.

With one and a half minutes left to play, the ball cannoned off the crowd causing Mr Bentley to blow his whistle for a throw in. Thinking the game was over, the crowd quickly engulfed the playing area. The Bootle captain appealed to the referee to play the full ninety minutes, but Mr Bentley insisted on having the pitch cleared. As this seemed impossible the Everton fans chaired their players back to the pavilion where the argument continued. George Dobson eventually led his players back on to the pitch, their opponents, who had began to get changed, declined the invitation to follow, leaving Everton to collect the trophy and return it to the Sandon.

Looking at the map of the period, it is clear to see that the energetic committee of Bootle were in the process of developing the enclosure for football. A large terrace, along with three small stands are clearly visible to the right of the pavilion. This area of the ground is today partly covered by Wadham Road. The original Pavilion, though still standing today, is shortly to be replaced by a new head quarters for Bootle Cricket Club.

In December Everton again visited Bolton to play Astley Bridge, a small club situated at the southern end of the town, but who, never-the-less, had their own enclosed ground. Everton won a close game 2-1.

During the festive season Anfield was honoured by the first ever visit of the crack amateur outfit The Corinthians, the first London based team to visit Liverpool. The club, which was formed in 1882, was the brainchild of N L Jackson who hoped to establish a team to rival Queens Park, who at the time were supplying most of the Scottish International team. Their superior team work was reflected in the results of the early encounters between the two countries. The England team at the time consisted mostly of ex public school boys and university players, from an assortment of clubs. The team needed to practice together if they were to match the team work so readily displayed by the Scots.

Mr Jackson collected the most gifted of these players and quickly developed a superior pattern of play, while entertaining the top clubs of the day at such London venues as Queens Club Kensington and the Oval Cricket Ground. Twice during this period the England national team was made up entirely of Corinthian players.

A fall of snow greeted them on their arrival in Liverpool, but this did not stop a crowd of over three thousand people flocking to the ground to see players drawn from the elite of Victorian Society. A reporter, who accompanied the visiting team, gave a visual description of the ground at the time, describing it as having, "No shelter from the icy blast as we sit huddled up on the open grandstand, snow for a cushion, ditto for a foot stool, ditto everywhere".

The famous Queens Park centre forward, Dr J Smith, made a guest appearance in the Corinthian colours. He broke a bone in his hand after a tussle with Everton defender Sandy Dick, who had recently been signed from Liverpool Stanley. Despite this, the Southern Amateurs went on to win 4-2. What a dash they must have cut, when leaving the Sandon that evening, sporting top hats and canes.

During the 1920's, Liverpool born Benjamin Howard-Baker was the Corinthian star goalkeeper and also an Olympic High Jumper, Hurdler and Discus Thrower. He once teamed up with Dixie Dean, to keep goal for Everton in a match against Leicester City. During the summer months he regularly turned out for Liverpool Cricket Club, at Aigburth, near where he lived in Grassendale. He died in 1987, age 95, the last of the old Corinthians.

Early in the new year, Everton made the first of what was to turn out to be many visits to Burnley. The local Gazzette describing them as, "The crack Liverpool Club". They arrived in the town considerably later than expected and reached their destination to find the home team waiting on the pitch. The match took place on the area of Turf Moor opposite the Wellington Hotel which still stands today on the corner of Brunshaw Road and Melveders Road. Burnley Cricket and Football Club had recently taken over an extra seven acres on Turf Moor, giving them 13 acres in all. The ground on the day was reported to be in splendid order and, owing probably in great measure to the summer-like weather, a large crowd was reported to have gathered around the pitch.

Everton struggled from the start to contain the lively home forwards. Names like McNee, McRae and McFetterridge, suggested one or two Scottish players were present in the Burnley team. Despite having the incline in their favour for the second half, the visitors could not withstand the late flourish inflicted upon them and went down 5-0.

The Easter Holiday period saw Everton make their first ever overseas trip to Belfast to play an Ulster Select. The game was scheduled for Saturday, but had to be postponed until Easter Monday on account of the non-arrival of the visitors whose ship was fog bound on the River Mersey. The match took place at The Ballynafiegh Cricket Ground, on Ormeau Road, where a large crowd saw Everton win 2-1. The goals were scored by Gibson and Dobson.

Returning home, Everton next sent a modest side to Accrington to compete in a fixture arranged with Church, a team who at the time were using a ground located in Pickup Street behind the Pickup Arms. This ground was shared with the local cricket club. The pitch that day was covered with three inches of snow and the sun shone brightly. The effect was very dazzling and Everton were beaten 5-3. Church returned the visit to Anfield the following Saturday, where a full strength home side avenged the defeat with a 4-1 victory.

By April Everton had once again reached the final of the Liverpool Cup without a great deal of effort disposing ofHaydock 5-0, Linacre 13-0 and Tranmere Rovers 9-1 respectively and now faced Oakfield Rovers, a team consisting mainly of former pupils of Anfield Road Sunday School. Oakfield Rovers played their home matches on Breck Park and were captained by Billy Hughes, a Caernarfon born player, who had earlier moved to Liverpool. Hughes later signed for Bootle and was ever present during their one and only season in the football league. After the early elimination of Bootle, interest in the competition had dwindled and the crowd of under three thousand that had assembled at Hawthorne Road witnessed an easy victory for Everton who, despite losing Briscoe in the first minute, cruised to a 5-0 victory. The Mayor of Bootle presented the trophy to the Everton President, Mr John Holding. The prize was then conveyed by horse and carriage back to the Sandon and if enthusiasm had been lacking at Bootle it was certainly unbounded in the Everton headquarters where the team and their supporters passed a pleasant and convivial evening.

Later in the month, Everton enjoyed a visit to the locally termed, peaceful valley of Rossendale, in Lancashire, accompanied by a number of supporters. They arrived late at Newchurch station and made all haste to the ground. But this was no easy matter as an ascent of probably half a mile by a pathway which was almost perpendicular had to be climbed to reach a table of land on the side of the hill where the match was to be played.

The Rossendale club had recently taken over the Dark Lane ground from the local Rugby Club as the Association game began to take over in the valley. Everton were no worse for their ordeal and won a sporting game 3-0.

On the Whitsuntide weekend, Everton made their final new excursion of the season when they journeyed to the seaside town of Blackpool to play South Shore. The match was played at Cow Gap Lane, which today is an extension of Waterloo Road. This little club had the previous season caused a sensation when they knocked Notts. County out of the FA Cup. South Shore were separate from Blackpool FC, who were formed later in 1887 from the nucleus of St. John's FC who played their home matches at Raikes Hall Gardens. The two teams amalgamated in 1889 before moving to Bloomfield Road. The side Everton elected to send were well below full strength and were well beaten 7-2.

The same afternoon, Anfield was chosen to host The Lancashire Junior Cup Final, in which Bells Temperance defeated Lower Hurst 1-0, before a crowd of five thousand.

1887/88 Season

Of the thirty five matches that were arranged by club secretary Alexander Nesbit for the season, only four were to take Everton to play at new venues. The first being the opening day of the season when they made a trip to Cheshire, for a match against Chester St. Oswalds on their ground at Exton Park. Many Everton supporters were present in a crowd that numbered over two thousand, despite the inclement weather. The visitors won the toss and elected to play downhill, forcing the pace and leading 2-1 at the break. With the slope now in their favour, Saints quickly evened matters, then took a 3-2 lead. Everton equalised with ten minutes to go, only for the home side to grab a dramatic winner in the closing stages.

Everton next revisited Church, where a local newspaper reporter gave this account of his meeting with the early away followers of the club. "Meeting one or two of the Everton supporters at Bethels prior to the match, I was a little surprised at the airs, which they gave themselves. The Toffy Lads (the reporter's spelling), in their opinion, evidently being a tip top organisation. 'Can you win today?' was a question which appeared a little absurd to them, and I was informed that the Everton team considered themselves quite able to tackle any club bar North End". "What do you think of us here ?" the Everton fans asked, "Well we look upon you as a pretty smart team, but scarcely up to the mark of such clubs as North End, Blackburn Rovers, Accrington, Bolton Wanderers and others". Discussing interest in football in the Everton district my friend informed me that, "A gate of six thousand was not unusual, but the average was about three thousand".

When the match eventually started the crowd numbered around one thousand. The home team were nicknamed 'The Turkey Reds', from the colour of their shorts, treated at the local Steiners Dye Works. They quickly found themselves trailing 2-0, but hit back strongly to level the contest 2-2. On the whole, the visitors had the better of the play and Church had their defence to thank for preventing a defeat.

Church Football Club had to move in 1889 when the land was needed to build a factory. They sold their grandstand and found a new ground at Foxhill Bank, but seemed to disappear shortly after.

In October, Everton broke new ground by accepting an invitation by Nottingham County to play a match during the city's annual 'Goose Fair' celebrations. On their arrival at Liverpool Central Station, the players and officials were delighted to find that, for this special occasion, the Cheshire Lines Committee had placed a palatial new saloon coach at their disposal. Following a pleasant journey through the Derbyshire countryside the party arrived at Nottingham Midland Station and quickly settled down for lunch at The Wellington Hotel. Later they took the short tram ride along London Road, alighted at the terminus and walked across Trent Bridge to the cricket ground. They were greeted at the large pavilion by the officials of Notts. County Football Club. The over night rain. had made the ground slippery, but despite this handicap, the two teams played out an entertaining game which ended 1-1.

Following the game the Everton party were treated to a substantial tea in the pavilion and later took the tram back to the market square, where they mingled with the vast crowd at the fair, before taking the train for the return journey back to Liverpool.

Early in the new year Everton paid another visit to the Lancashire Mill Town of Darwen to play the town's top team, Darwen. The famous cup side shared their ground with the local Cricket club at Barley Bank. Darwen celebrated the Everton visit by fielding their strongest eleven and routed the visitors 5-2.

Over the Easter Holiday Everton again embarked for a second trip to Belfast to play two matches. Firstly taking on an Ulster Select at Ballynafiegh on the Saturday where, after enduring a very rough sea crossing, they looked very much out of sorts and went down 3-2. The following day they crossed the city to play Cliftonville. The match took place on the Cricket Ground which is situated across the road from the present day Solitude Ground. Everton proved too strong for the Irish Club side, winning 10-1, with Briscoe scoring six of the Everton goals. The Belfast Newsletter reported that both games were well attended. Everton clearly helping to popularise the game in the Province.

Everton did not travel again that season, but on the 21st of May, Wolverhampton Wanderers paid their first visit to the city. This was the shape of things to come. During the summer months both clubs were to become founder members of 'The Football League'.

Ireland and the West of Scotland, which resulted in Everton being paired with Scottish giants Glasgow Rangers for their first game. The rules at the time stated that professional players had to have been with the club for a given period of time to be able to play in the competition, which left several of Everton's best players ineligible for the tournament. In the face of such strong opposition the Everton executives decided to withdraw from the competition and the game was declared a friendly.

A crowd of six thousand watched as the Clydesiders made the brighter start, taking the lead through Heggie after fifteen minutes. For the rest of the half the visitors kept up the severe pressure on the home defence but failed to add to their tally. In the second half Everton gradually began to take command, with Jimmy Costley striking the foot of the post. The latter half of the game was very much in Everton's favour, but sheer hard luck prevented them from equalising. A sporting and well fought game ended in a 1-0 win for Rangers.

The 1887-88 FA Cup Competition was to prove the most controversial. Two Scottish players, Izatt and Weir, although selected, failed to turn out for Bootle in their FA cup tie at home to Workington. Later it transpired that both players had been persuaded to join Everton. Izatt turning out on the right wing against Bolton Wanderers in a cup tie at Pikes Lane which was played on the same day.

On the 15th October 1887, in glorious weather, a large crowd gathered to witness the tie. The five hundred Everton supporters who had travelled to Bolton for the match, were reported to be "making a bigger rumpus than all the remaining units that went to constitute the five thousand present put together". Bolton Wanderers had no less than three practice matches in the week beside their ordinary training, whilst Everton did next to nothing. One of Everton's players, who had been out of town, travelled all night to play in the match. With Mr Ormerod of Accrington acting as referee, Everton kicked off at the advertised time. The early stages of game were fast and sometimes rough as the play was switched from end to end. With half time rapidly approaching, both sides were struggling for the initial advantage Steel, the Bolton half back, hit the bar with a fierce drive, the ball rebounded to the same player who forced the ball over the line. Everybody in the ground thought he scored except apparently Mr Ormerod who disallowed the goal for offside. At half time the match was goal less.

On restarting, the game again burst into life and progressed as fast as ever, as the excitement generated by the crowd spread to the players. Following a high ball from the left, Roberts waited his opportunity and cleverly lifted the ball over a crowd of players to give Bolton the lead. With time running out the Everton followers strongly urged their team on with shouts of the day such as 'do a rush'. Try as the Everton forwards did they could not make any headway against the solid Bolton defence. The final whistle went leaving a score of 1-0 in favour of the home team.

Everton secretary Alexander Nesbit, after their defeat at Bolton, questioned the late registration of the Bolton player, Struthers, which upon examination proved to be three days late. The Football Association ordered the match to be replayed at Anfield which also ended all square. Everton eventually went through at the fourth attempt which landed them an away tie with Preston North End.

The tie, which had to be postponed to await the outcome of the FA's inquiry, was finally played at Deepdale in front of a crowd of seven thousand people. Everton made three changes to the team that played at Bolton, Smalley replacing Joliffe in goal, Wier replacing Murrey at half back and Cassidy taking over from Richards on the wing. The pitch on the day was reported to be in excellent condition, the only draw back being the strong wind which blew right down the field. The powerful Preston side, which had been assembled by manager Major William Sudell, had beaten Hyde United in the previous round 26-0. This is a record for the competition which still stands to the present day. Everton won the toss and the home team kicked off up the incline against the wind. Led by England centre forward John Goodall, Preston took the lead after four minutes through Drummond, Gordon made it 2-0 after thirty six minutes to give the home side the lead at the interval. With the slope and the strong wind in the home team's favour, the second period of the game was almost entirely confined to the Everton half of the field. With shots and corners coming too frequent to mention, Everton went down 6-0. Darkness came on and, towards the end of the game, it was almost impossible to see all the field of play.

In the meantime the FA had found Bolton Wanderers' sins small compared to those of Everton's, finding the club guilty of, 'persuading players to join them by financial inducement'. They closed the Anfield ground for one month. Upon hearing the news Bob Lythgoe arrived at the Sandon in a hansom cab and to the displeasure of all present took away the Liverpool Cup which Everton held at the time. This lead to Everton's temporarily resigning from the Liverpool and District Football Association as a means of protest.

Bootle, on the other hand, undaunted by past events, had gallantly battled their way through to the last eight of the contest and were rewarded with a visit to the Oval Cricket Ground. In doing so they became the first team from Merseyside to play a cup game in the Capital. Their opponents were the popular Old Carthusians, winners of the trophy in 1881. Bootle entered the famous enclosure amid hearty cheers from the fashionable crowd of around three thousand people, with Andrew Wilson their full back being singled out for special cheers when recognised by the Surrey supporters as a once famed Corinthian. The match referee was no other than Major Marindin of The Royal Engineers and President of The Football Association. Having won the toss, Bootle chose to attack the Harleyford Road goal. After three minutes of play had elapsed the home side took the lead, through their English International W N Cobbold, which, despite heavy pressure from Bootle, they held at the interval. When ends were changed, the future Everton captain John Holt was repeatedly jeered by the home fans for his rough treatment of local favourite W N Cobbold. The Old Boys added a second goal to win the match 2-0.

The Football Association selected Anfield as a neutral venue for this season's FA Cup semi final between Preston North End and Crewe Alexandra. This was the first time Liverpool had hosted the penultimate round of the contest. On the 18th February 1888, hundreds of fans from the Ribbleside cotton town began pouring through Exchange Railway Station, while supporters from the Cheshire railway town arrived at Lime Street. The Preston team arrived at 1:30pm and took lunch at the Neptune Hotel in Clayton Square before making their way to the ground. Considerable interest was shown in the match by the local followers who swelled the crowd to around ten thousand. There had been a light overnight fall of snow which still lay on the surface of the pitch. This was soon melted by the bright warm sun which had been shining all morning. The ground looked in poor condition and Crewe handed in a protest. Preston won the toss and elected to kick down the slope with the sun on their backs. Crewe, who were much smaller in stature than the Preston side, were soon under pressure and after a one sided first half trailed 5-0 at half time. In the second half Crewe could make no impression on the solid Preston defence on a pitch that was by now ankle deep in mud and water. Preston did not add to their score and the 5-0 result was allowed to stand by the FA committee, thus over ruling Crewe's protest.

Along with the birth of 'The Football League', the 1888/89 season saw the FA introduce the qualifying rounds. Everton were drawn away to Ulster, but declined to travel because of the costs it would incur and were scratched from the contest. It was left to Liverpool Stanley to represent the city who, after beating Workington and Astley Bridge at Walton Stiles, also declined to travel to Ulster when drawn against Cliftonville.

The 1889/90 campaign saw Everton receive a home draw with Derby County for their first match. This tie was one of the few in the first round of the competition in which two league clubs faced each other. The Derby County executive having spared no pains in their endeavours to make a good show, sent their players to the Davis Hydropatic establishment at Matlock Bath in Derbyshire. Here they were put through a carefully chosen course of training. The contest drew a crowd of ten thousand to Anfield. The pitch on the day of the match was in a dreadful state, heavy and almost devoid of grass. The first half was a fairly even affair with Derby taking a 2-1 lead, before

Everton hit back to lead 3-2 at the break. After the change of ends, Everton attacked down the slope and quickly added two more goals. The Derby players were unable to make any headway whatever in the heavy ground and play was now entirely confined to the lower half of the ground. The visitors were now hopelessly beaten, the home team adding another six goals to their tally, giving Everton a club record score of 11-2. To the general surprise of their supporters no protest was made against the state of the pitch by the Derby executive who accepted their defeat with dignity.

Everton next faced Stoke City who the previous season had become the first league club to be knocked out of the cup by a non-league team when fielding their reserve side for a tie with Warwick County. The Everton team arrived in the Potteries on the evening of Friday the 2nd February 1890 and made their head quarters at The Copeland Arms Hotel. Local interest in the game was great and an hour before the kick off people began to fill the Victoria Ground. Before a crowd of seven thousand Stoke kicked off with Everton defending the Town End. Trailing 1-0 at the break, the visitors were always chasing the game and after a poor performance went down 4-2.

Bootle had also entered the contest and received a home draw against Sunderland Albion. Despite losing 3-1 at Hawthorne Road they proceeded to the next round when the Wearsider's were disqualified from the competition for fielding an illegal player. Derby Midland next visited Bootle and were beaten 2-1, which opened the way for possibly the biggest game in the history of the North Merseyside club; a home tie with firm FA Cup favourites, the great Blackburn Rovers. In drizzling rain a crowd of six thousand gathered at the Bootle Cricket Ground to watch the match. Rovers kicked off towards the Hawthorne Road end and in the first minute, future Everton player Jack Southworth gave them the lead. Bootle seemed overawed by the occasion and lost a one sided match 7-0. The quality of this Blackburn Rovers side may be measured by the fact that they went on to win the trophy, beating Sheffield Wednesday 6-1 in the final.

By general consent the most important tie in the first round of the 1890/91 contest was that between Sunderland and Everton which was to be played at the Wearsider's home, at the time Newcastle Road. A heavy fall of snow during the night caused some fear least the game should be postponed. The Sunderland officials quickly hired a gang of workmen armed with shovels and accompanied by twenty horse drawn carts in which to carry away the snow. In the course of a few hours it was announced that the stands were cleared and that the ground was in splendid condition. With an estimated twenty thousand present, the game began at 2:25pm. The home team mounted early pressure and took the lead after fifteen minutes. Everton fought back strongly, but good defensive work by the home team won the day 1-0. The gate receipts were one hundred and twenty pounds, at the time a record for a match in the North East of England.

The 1891/92 season saw Everton receive a home tie with Burnley for their first game on the 16th January 1892, in what was to be their last season playing at Anfield. Liverpool and the surrounding areas were covered in snow on the day of the match. The Anfield pitch was cleared, but small patches of frozen ice still remained. Twenty loads of sand were quickly carted from Seaforth Sands and distributed over the playing surface. The ground however was still frozen solid as the cold weather continued. Before the game began both sides entered a protest against the match being considered an FA Cup tie and played the match instead as a friendly.

The Burnley players all wore mourning for the death of Queen Victoria's grandson, Prince Albert Victor, The Duke of Clarence. The flag of the home club was flying at half mast as the Prince was a patron of both clubs.

Fred Geary was missing from the home side line up as Alex Latta kicked off before a crowd of around seven thousand. The visitors quickly raced into a two goal lead which they held until half time. Edgar Chadwick pulled a goal back for Everton just after the break, only for McLardie to restore Burnley's two goal advantage. The home fans tried to stimulate their players by playing instrumental music, but the visitors went on to win the match 4-2. The gate receipts were two hundred and fifty pounds, the visitors share, after paying expenses amounting to one hundred pounds.

At the following meeting of the Football Association committee, it was decided to replay the tie, the two teams meeting again at Anfield the following Saturday. Owing to the recent thaw in the weather the pitch was in much better condition than the previous occasion. Fred Geary was back in the Everton line up which increased the gate to ten thousand. The visitors again proved too strong for the home team winning a rough game 3-1.

A good many of the home spectators did not take kindly to the defeat and as the two sets of players walked back to the Sandon they became aggressive towards the visitors. Two of the

Burnley players, Nicol and Bowes, became detached from the rest of the team and were forced to take refuge in a bus which was followed by the crowd for some distance. The incident was noted by officials of both clubs, who quickly hired a horse drawn cab to go in pursuit with the men's clothes. The two players were found in an hotel some time later and happily for all concerned they

Anfield looking towards the Walton Breck Road end.
The two players on the right are Edgar Chadwick and Alf Milward

Everton 1 Burnley 3
FA Cup replay January 1892, showing Anfield Road end

escaped unhurt. This incident made the Everton directors think about providing dressing rooms inside the perimeter of the ground, so as not to expose the players of visiting teams to attacks of this nature.

Everton at Goodison Park

Everton drew cup holders West Bromwich Albion for their first ever cup tie at their new home of Goodison Park on the 21st January 1893, where a large crowd saw them win convincingly 4-1. Following home wins over Nottingham Forest and Sheffield Wednesday, Everton now found themselves through to their first ever FA Cup semi final, where a match with the invincible Preston North End awaited them. North End were many people's favourite to lift the trophy, having scored twenty

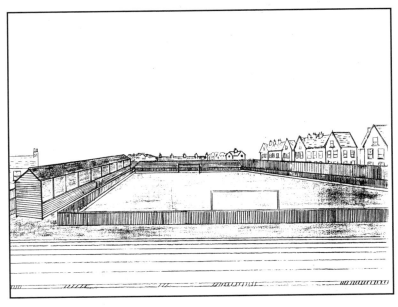

Goodison Park 1892

goals in their three cup games in that season's contest. The match, which took place at Bramall Lane, Sheffield, saw Everton rise to the occasion and held the favourites to a 2-2 draw. The replay, also at Bramall Lane, ended goalless, so the teams met for a third time at Ewood Park, Blackburn, on the Monday before the date set for that year's final.

The new ground of Blackburn Rovers was taxed to its uppermost capacity, with one of the biggest crowds ever gathered for a match in the North of England. The road from the ground to the town centre, stretching for a mile, was completely congested with vehicles and people. The gates were soon closed, but thousands of people climbed the hill behind the grandstand and had a good view of the match which must have been watched by approximately forty thousand people. Before the game commenced the crowd was so dense that hundreds of small boys were passed over the heads of the spectators to sit on the cycle track surrounding the playing area. (The scene suggested most strongly the need for the FA to make adequate provision for crowd control at the final tie the following Saturday).

The teams entered the arena to a great reception and the game kicked off on time. Everton started the brighter and took the lead through Maxwell just before the break. On resuming Preston began to gain the initiative which seemed to take a good deal out of the Everton defenders and when a cross from the left was turned in at the far post by Preston winger J Gordon to equalize, it seemed likely that North End would carry the day. With a quarter of an hour left to go, Preston laid siege to their opponents goal, but the young Everton goal keeper Williams, recently signed from Brombrough Pool, was equal to anything they could offer. With only three minutes remaining, Latta broke from defence and won a corner. The well placed centre found P Gordon unmarked who headed Everton to victory amid scenes of great jubilation. They were now to play Wolverhampton Wanderers in the final.

The gate receipts amounted to the enormous sum of seven hundred and ninety pounds, beating all previous records for a football match in Lancashire. Half the net proceeds, after paying the third class railway fares of the competing clubs, were divided as follows:- two thirds were divided between the four clubs competing in the semi-final ties, and the remaining third between the clubs competing in the final. The remaining half was taken by the Football Association.

Quite a remarkable reception awaited the Everton team upon their arrival at Exchange Station that evening. The concourse was crowded with hundreds of happy people from the hill country and every member of the team received special recognition. Williams, whose brilliant goalkeeping contributed so largely to the victory, was carried shoulder high from the station to a conveyance. The team then went off to spend the rest of the week at the Derbyshire Spa Town of Buxton.

With teams from the North West and the Midlands now dominating the competition, the committee of Surrey County Cricket Club declined to host the 1892/93 FA Cup Final at the Oval Cricket Ground. They chose instead to stage the London Senior Cup final between Old Westminsters and The Casuals.

The Football Association were forced to seek pastures new, many enclosures were suggested with the final selection being that of Manchester Athletic Club, located in the Fallowfield district of the town. The ground had been successfully tested earlier, on the occasion of the annual rugby match between Lancashire and Yorkshire, and the committee set to work straight away to perfect arrangements.

The arrangements that the committee had prepared at first seemed adequate, but the crowd, however, proved too large to control as the match aroused an exceptional amount of interest. From as early as 11:00am there were several thousand in the ground. A schoolboy match between Manchester and Sheffield preceded the main event and during the game the crowd increased enormously. It was estimated that over forty thousand people were present. Nearly an hour before the kick-off the field of play was encroached upon. So great was the pressure that the barrier near to the pavilion gave way and the crowd rushed the enclosure set up for the press and officials. Mounted police were sent for as the stewards struggled to keep control, but the crowd were good natured and everything was cheered.

Winning goal for Wolverhampton Wanderers
FA Cup Final 1893, Fallowfield Manchester

Wolverhampton entered the enclosure first from the large stand, followed four minutes later by Everton. Play began at 3:35pm with Everton kicking off with the sun in their faces and enjoyed most of the early play, but at half time the score sheet was blank. The encroachment of the crowd delayed the restart while the field was cleared. Ten minutes into the second half a long high ball from Allen deceived the young goalkeeper Williams and sailed into the net thus giving the Wanderers the only goal of the game. Wolverhampton gained a popular victory in the press, by the fact that the team was made up entirely of English players.

The 1893/94 FA Cup season saw Everton make an early exit, losing 1-0 at Stoke City in the first round. Goodison Park, however, had been chosen to host that season's FA Cup Final which was held between Bolton Wanderers and Notts. County. The selection of Goodison by the FA was a tribute to the efforts made by the Everton directors in the development of the ground. In the weeks leading up to the game two open stands had been erected on the Goodison Road side to give extra seating for six thousand people, bringing the capacity up to around fifty thousand. The two participating teams arrived on Merseyside a few days before the game. Bolton set up camp at Eastham, Notts. County chose to stay at the West Kirby Hotel. Notts. County won the game 4-1 to become the first team from the second division to lift the trophy. The attendance for the game was given as thirty seven thousand.

The 1896/7 season saw Everton again battle their way through to the final. They began with a first round victory over Burton Wanderers, winning 5-2. (Burton Wanderers made their first and only appearance in the Football League that season). Following victories over Bury and Blackburn, Everton faced Derby County in the semi final at the Victoria Ground, Stoke. A new one thousand six hundred seater grandstand had recently been opened and the ground greatly improved for the occasion. Everton spent the week before the game at Lytham St Annes for a week's training. On the day of the match they were able to field their full strength team. The first half, which was a dull affair, ended goalless. The second half, however, was played at a more frantic pace which saw Everton take the honours with a 3-2 victory. Their reward was a trip to London to face Aston Villa in the final at the Crystal Palace.

The Crystal Palace had been designed by Joseph Paxton and originally constructed in Hyde Park by Fox and Henderson in time for the Great Exhibition of 1851. Three years later the structure was dismantled and moved to a new permanent site at Sydenham, South London. A large ornamental garden and park

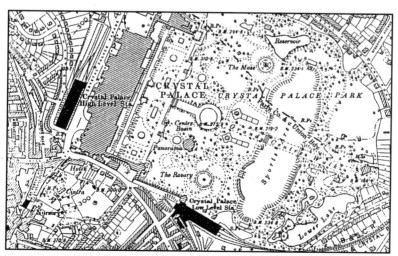

The Cystal Palace grounds, Sydenham South London.
The football field is situated on the South side of the Grand Centre Walk

were then laid out on the eastern side and a railway station on the west side. Two observation towers were placed either side of the transept and an amusement park was added. In 1870 a lake was filled in and a sports arena was laid down. A large seated pavilion was constructed, to which was added an angled grandstand on either side, giving seating accommodation for nine thousand people. A large grass covered bank stood opposite, topped in later years by an open stand.

Six special trains full of supporters left Liverpool Lime Street Station on Friday evening of the 9th April 1897. From early Saturday morning London took on a carnival atmosphere with the supporters of both club's mixing together while sight seeing. Around midday the fans crammed into Ludgate Station for the seven mile journey to Sydenham. The carriages were small and tightly packed as the engine snorted and hissed its way along the dark tunnels. With most of the trip being underground, all concerned were happy when the train suddenly burst into the green fields of South London and arrived at Crystal Palace High Level Station. The fans quickly made their way through gardens to the sports field, positioning themselves on the grass banking around the pitch. The arena at the time was overlooked by a switch back railway, on which many of the crowd were perched.

The Everton party travelled to the capital on the Friday and made their headquarters at the Tavistock Hotel in central London. Ten minutes before kick off time they appeared out of the pavilion, led by their captain Stewart, wearing light blue shirts and white shorts. The Aston Villa team they faced that day were firm favourites to lift the trophy having already secured the league title for the second year running. The match that followed has many times been described as the finest ever witnessed at the

Crystal Palace ground. All the goals came in a twenty five minute spell just before half time. The lead changing hands three times before Villa went on to do the double with a 3-2 victory.

The attendance was sixty five thousand, eight hundred and ninety one, the largest crowd to date to watch a football match in England. The Crystal Palace authorities had guaranteed the FA one thousand two hundred pounds, plus sixpence a head for every person over thirty thousand and one shilling a head over forty thousand. The company took the revenue from the reserved seats, but the main beneficiaries were the two clubs who took the remaining net profit.

The present day Crystal Palace FC were later formed in 1905 and adopted the Crystal Palace ground as their home. The FA Cup Final was played at Crystal Palace until the First World War, when the military took over the ground. On the early evening of the 30th November 1936, a small fire which began in one of the staff rooms developed into a blaze which sadly destroyed much of the building.

The following season in 1897/98, Everton, after victories over Blackburn, Stoke and Burnley, again faced Derby County in the semi final. The match took place at the Molineux Grounds, Wolverhampton, which at the time was part of the town's large recreational area, complete with gardens and skating rink. The weather on the day of the match was inclement to say the least. Water appeared in large pools on the pitch making the setting look anything but cheerful. The spectators from Liverpool were much later in arriving than those from Derby and consequently were less favoured in the matter of accommodation, the best positions naturally being taken by those first in attendance in preparation for the game.

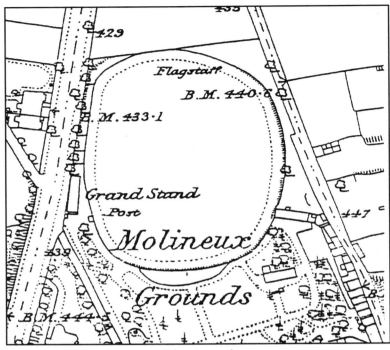

Molineux grounds,
around the time of the Derby County v Everton Cup Semi Final 1898

Everton spent some time prior to the match training at their old quarters at Lytham St. Annes under the watchful eye of their trainer Mr Lewis. Leaving Blackpool by train the Everton party lunched at Crewe before arriving at Wolverhampton at 2:00pm. By the time the teams appeared at 3:20pm the crowd had reached thirty thousand. Everton lost the toss and defended the Hotel End of the ground. They were quickly down to ten men when Stewart was carried off injured. Steve Bloomer gave Derby the lead after 25 minutes and former Preston favourite John Goodall increased the lead early in the second half. Edgar Chadwick quickly pulled one back for Everton, only to see Steve Bloomer add a third for Derby, who won the match 3-1.

This was to be Everton's last cup run of the nineteenth century and their supporters had to wait until 1906 before they eventually won the trophy, beating Newcastle United 1-0 at Crystal Palace.

The Football League: The Anfield Years

The main driving force behind the formation of the Football League was William McGregor, a Perthshire born Scot, who moved to Birmingham where he bought a drapers shop in the district of Witton. A keen follower of the Association game, he was quick to notice that football clubs had no come back if the opponents failed to appear therefore leading to a loss of revenue for the home club. Mr McGregor sent a letter to some of the most prominent football clubs of the North West and Midland areas of England, inviting them to attend a meeting at the Anderton's Hotel in London. This in turn was followed by a second meeting in Manchester which led to the formation of the Football League. Of the teams who played in the inaugural season, six were from Lancashire and six from the Midlands. The three clubs that were left out were Nottingham Forest, Sheffield Wednesday and Halliwell of Bolton.

Around this time the legendary 'Spring Heeled Jack' paid a visit to the streets of Everton. First reported in London, the leaping terror was seen one evening in Shaw Street wearing a tight fitting hood, a long black cloak and what looked like springs compressed on the soles of his boots. The large crowd that quickly gathered stood by in amazement as Jack leaped from the street to the roof top of the houses ending up eventually on the roof of St. Francis Xaviers church in Langsdale Street, but before Everton FC could offer him a contract he jumped over the roof tops of Haigh Street and disappeared into local folklore. For many years late Everton mothers would warn their children to beware of 'Spring Heeled Jack'.

Liverpool, in those early days, was well detached from the football hot-bed of East Lancashire, but was the largest town, in terms of population, in the Northern group. Why Mr McGregor invited Everton and not Bootle is now lost in the mists of time. The most likely explanation being, is that the Anfield ground was reserved for the sole purpose of Association Football. Bootle, like many other teams at the time shared their ground with the local Cricket Club.

For the forthcoming new league season, Everton strengthened their team with several new signings. During the summer, a whisper went around the hill country that the new players, along with the rest of the squad, were to take part in a practice match in a field on Belmont Road. As the players arrived for this match a crowd of three thousand were waiting to greet them.

The first league match at Anfield was favoured by beautiful weather with the contest bringing eight thousand people to the ground. The visitors, Accrington, arrived twenty minutes late so at 4:25pm on the 8th September 1888 the first football league match to take place on Merseyside kicked off. The first half was played at an even pace and with neither side gaining the advantage, the first period ended goalless. The honour of scoring the first league goal for Everton fell to Fleming, who headed them in to the lead early in the second half. The same player added a second goal as Everton went on to win the match 2-1.

For their first away match of the new campaign, Everton travelled to Birmingham to meet the great Aston Villa, one of the most progressive clubs in the land. Aston Villa were formed as early as 1874, allegedly at a meeting which took place under a gas lamp at the corner of a street. The match took place behind the tram shed in the Parr Barr area of the town, close to the local railway station. A crowd of four thousand saw the home team dominate much of the match and lead comfortably by two goals to nil for most of the match, but with five minutes to go, after a melee in the Villa goalmouth, the ball was forced over the goal line by Watson for the visiting side, therefore registering the first away goal scored by Everton in the Football league. The visitors continued to mount pressure in an attempt to draw level, but the Villa defence held out to take both points. Everton's first away match sadly ending in defeat.

Everton next visited Pikes Lane, Bolton, where they were beaten 6-2 by Bolton Wanderers in what turned out to be their heaviest defeat of the season. They next visited Trent Bridge to face a Notts. County team, that at the time contained at full back, H A Cursham, a player who had represented England in the international played against Ireland at Liverpool Cricket Ground. Also in the starting line up was H B Daft, a Corinthian, who was to win five caps for England. The same player was also to turn out for Notts. County in the 1894 FA Cup Final at Goodison Park. A crowd of four thousand watched Everton kick off towards the Gamston Lane end, against a fairly strong breeze. After three minutes, a long shot from the left deceived Smalley to give County the lead. The home team then kept up the pressure throughout the first period to lead 3-0 at the interval. During the break, Everton changed the arrangement of their side and played a much better game, with Nick Ross pulling a goal back. Towards the end of the game, the play became rough and unpleasant; the final score was a 3-1 win for County. As the players walked back to the pavilion the visitors were surrounded by a mob of angry home supporters with Sandy Dick being singled out for some rough treatment. The little Scot received a severe wound to the head when struck by a heavy stick. The County players quickly came to his aid and helped him to the pavilion where he received treatment to his injury.

The following Saturday, Everton, minus Sandy Dick, made the first ever trip to the Midland Railway town of Derby. Once again, a new saloon coach was supplied by the railway company, one of the first signs in the area that the local football club was beginning to acquire the symbol of 'Special Status'. The fixture was played on Derby Cricket Ground where the home team had been founded to provide a winter activity for the club members. The venue, which was located on Nottingham Road, one mile from the town centre, catered for all the sporting requirements of the local population. A fine cricket pavilion stood in the middle of a circular horse racing track, which in turn was overlooked by a large grandstand. The flat playing surface was well suited for football and a sporting crowd of three thousand people witnessed the first ever away win for Everton. Jimmy Costley scoring two of the goals in a 4-2 victory.

Derby later moved to the Baseball Ground in 1895. Everton played their first league game there on the 7th April 1896.

In December Everton returned to The Potteries for their first ever match with Stoke City. A team which was formed in 1868 by local railway workers and was the second oldest team in the league. The venue for the match, the Victoria Ground, took it's name from the hotel near by. The pitch was surrounded by a circular cinder running track. The only covered accommodation was the grandstand which stood on the Boothen Road side of the ground with the River Trent clearly visible on the other. The match took place on the 15th December 1888 and was watched by a crowd of one thousand, five hundred. The game ended in a 0-0 draw as the referee called time a quarter of an hour early due to heavy fog.

Later in the month, Everton returned to the Midlands to play their first ever match against West Bromwich Albion, who had been founded in the town by the workers of Slaters Spring Works. They were at the time playing their home matches at Stoney Lane in the Cronehills district of the town. The Everton team on the day were well below full strength, trailing 3-1 at the break. They ended the match with nine men, losing 4-1 in the process. The return game with Accrington took place at the end of December, at the Thornyholme Cricket ground on the outskirts of the town. The Everton party arrived to find a large square field with an excellent playing surface. The visitors kicked off towards the pavilion end. George Farmer was absent for the only time that season, his place being taken by a local born player, Parkinson, who scored Everton's only goal of the game as they went down by 3-1.

On Boxing Day morning, a touring team from Ulster were welcomed to Anfield for a friendly game. Despite the wet weather, a moderate crowd turned out to watch Everton score a 3-0 win. Lunch was then taken at The Sandon. Following a short break, they then played Blackburn Park Road in the afternoon of the same day. Everton won this Lancashire Cup Tie 4-0, which was witnessed by a separate crowd of over four thousand. The seasonal festivities no doubt rendering one or two changes of players that occurred in the home team!

The last new venue Everton visited of the first league season, came as early as January, when they travelled to the South Staffordshire, home of Wolverhampton Wanderers. Founded in 1879 in similar circumstances to Everton, the club were at the time playing their home matches on Dudley Road and using the nearby Kings Arms as their headquarters. The visitors lost the toss and kicked off uphill, facing the wind. The home team mounted continual pressure throughout the half and at the break led 4-0. After the restart, Everton's play improved a little, but the home side had the better of the contest winning 5-0. Wanderers moved to Molineux the following year.

On the 3rd March 1889, Anfield hosted it's first ever international fixture, when selected as the venue for England v Ireland match. The Irish team arrived in Liverpool on Friday morning, aboard the steam ship Dynamic, and stayed overnight at the Shaftsbury Temperance Hotel on Mount Pleasant. A reporter from the Belfast Telegraph, who accompanied the Irish party, described the Anfield ground as being "Of a most complete character. The unreserved or sixpenny portion is immediately behind both goals, where the spectators stand upon tier after tier and all have an equally good view. Two reserved stands run parallel down the field, the largest one being covered over and extending the full length of the ground, while the smaller one is "specially reserved". He also mentioned, that "The teams dressed in the Everton committee rooms, adjacent, coming on the field by an entry which prevents them from being seen until they appear in the centre of the field". This being a correct observation, the players after leaving the Sandon entered the ground by a door in the back of the Kemlyn Road Stand. As expected the Irish team, which consisted of all local players, were no match for England and were beaten 6-1. The small crowd of six thousand reflected the disappointment shown by the local fans at the omission of Everton player Johney Holt from the England side.

The season ended for Everton with a home fixture against their old rivals Bootle, in a match that was billed 'The Local Championship'. So great was the interest in the match that the committee increased the entrance charge, but this, despite many complaints, did not deter a near capacity crowd from assembling on the day of the match. Shortly after 4:00pm, the referee, Mr Fitzroy-Norris called the teams together to caution the players against rough play.

Both sides heeded the officials warning and after an even first period, the score stood at 1-1. The man who caught the eye was the new Bootle goalkeeper, Jardine. After the break, as he made his way towards the Walton Breck Road goal end, he was greeted with warm applause. With the slope now in their favour, Bootle began the second period strongly, and midway through the half took the lead following a corner. After more pressure from Bootle, the Everton captain, Nick Ross, saved a certain goal by sending the ball through a bedroom window. Minutes later the game ended with a 2-1 victory for the visitors.

Everton finished · their first league season in a disappointing eighth place with an average home gate of seven thousand, two hundred and sixty. They had acquired twenty points out of a possible forty four. The main problem had been the lack of goals. Only bottom club Stoke City registered less. To remedy the situation, Fred Geary was brought in from Notts. County, along with Alex Latta from Dunbarton, both players becoming an instant success.

On transferring to Everton, Alex Latta became known locally as 'the finest player never to have played for Dunbarton'. The reason being, during the summer months, Dunbarton had merged with neighbours Dunbarton Athletic, of whom Alex Latta was the star player. The fans at Dunbarton's Boghead Park ground, looked forward with great anticipation to his appearance. However as Dunbarton were strictly amateur, he moved south and signed for Everton as a professional football player.

Also signed that year from Chester St. Oswalds, was a young Welshman named Charlie Parry. Born in Llansilin in 1871, he made his debut for Wales against England at Wrexham in 1892, going on to win thirteen caps in all. He played five seasons at Everton, quickly becoming popular with the home crowd for his 'bone crunching tackles'. After leaving Everton, he played for Newtown, before ending his playing days at Aberystwyth. He later settled at Oswestry, where in 1921, it came to the notice of the Everton directors that their former player had 'fallen on evil days' and his health was not very good.

The club quickly despatched a strong team to North Shropshire to play a selected Oswestry and District side for his benefit. The match taking place at the local Cricket Club. An estimated crowd of around three thousand watched the match, despite blinding snow and hail storms that swept the open field during the match. The game ending in a 1-0 victory for the home side. Charlie sadly died the following year, leaving a wife and six children.

The three signings had greatly improved things at Anfield, as Everton finished their second season as runners up to the great Preston North End, Geary scoring twenty five goals.

In keeping with the times, the club secretary arranged for a pre season picnic and sports day with tickets being made available to players, club officials and fans. It is easy to envisage the kind of chaos such an event would cause today, but in those early days of the game Everton's entourage was of a small number. On Thursday the 10th August 1891 a caravan of wagonettes left Anfield conveying about one hundred people, their destination being Mr Henry Horwards field, Paradise Lane, Formby. About half of the first team players attended the function, the others filling previously arranged cricket engagements. The most noted absentee was Mr John Holding, who was at Llandudno and sent his apologies. Never the less present were, Bob Lythgoe, Alex Nesbit and former Ramblers goalkeeper W H Bailey.

Among the winners of the competitions that followed were, Fred Geary who won the 120 yards handicap and throwing the cricket ball, Alf Millward who was victorious in the long jump, with Edgar Chadwick winning the dribbling contest. The tug of war by far generated the most amusement. Afternoon tea was later taken at the nearby Grapes Hotel, where Mr Jackson, a senior member of the club, awarded the prizes before the party left for home at around at 9:00pm.

Champions

The 1890-91 Football League season was to become one of the most momentous to date in the short history of Everton Football Club. Penalty kicks were introduced for the first time as Everton began the campaign by winning their first four league matches in some style. Fred Geary scoring seven of the sixteen goals registered by the club in those first four games.

During the month of October, Everton embarked on their first ever visit north of the Border. The Scottish players in the team left Exchange Station on Monday morning to visit their respective families, while the remainder of the team left on the Wednesday, all concerned meeting up that afternoon in Edinburgh. The club secretary had arranged for the players to visit a local exhibition grandly titled 'The Edinburgh Exposition of Electrical Engineering, General Invention and Industries', situated in Colindale Road, before settling down for the night at the Albert Hotel. The next morning the party left Waverley Station on the 9:00am train to play a game that had been arranged with Third Lanark in Glasgow. The game was scheduled to kick off at 12:30pm, so as not to clash with the Celtic and Sunderland match timed for 4:00pm, thus giving the local fans time to attend both fixtures.

Everton arrived in the city in good time and took a tram ride out to Cathkin Park, which was situated in the Mount Florida area of Glasgow, close to the famous Hampden Park. The eight thousand crowd that greeted Everton as they ran out on to the pitch were treated to fine game of football. Geary gave Everton an early lead but the 'Hi Hi's' hit back in the second half to force a 1-1 draw.

In November Everton played their first game at the new home of Blackburn Rovers, Ewood Park, which at the time was located on the edge of the town. At the beginning of the season many of the local people predicted that the distance from the town centre would deter many of the supporters from attending the games, but this did not prove to be the case with attendances being up on those at the old Leamington ground.

Everton arrived to find the building work still in progress, but the large grandstand on the riverside of the ground was ready for occupation. Despite the unsuitable state of the weather over twelve thousand people were present. The large Everton following amongst them witnessed a poor performance from the visitors who slipped to their third defeat in a row.

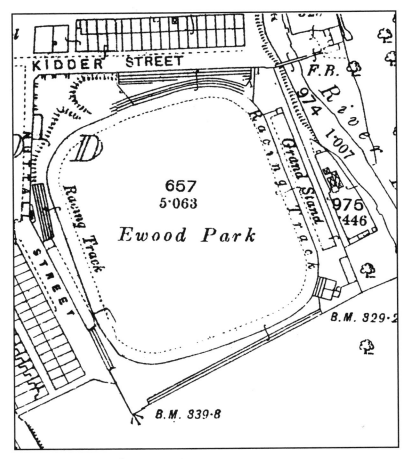

Ewood Park, Blackburn, around the time of Everton's first match

Everton attacking Darwen end goal during the 1890 game. Ewood Park is still under development in the background.
The two Everton player's are Geary and Latta

Just before Christmas Everton played their first ever league match in the North East of England against Sunderland. Sunderland were formed in 1879 by a group of local school teachers led by James Allen, who was a graduate of Glasgow University. They eventually settled at a ground on Newcastle Road and were elected to the Football League in 1890. The first encounter between these two famous clubs was a close affair with the home team winning 1-0. With the backing of wealthy local business men Sunderland moved to Roker Park in 1898. Everton played their first game there on the 12th November that year.

Early in the new year a new invention was unveiled by the Football Association, 'Goal nets'. Their designer, John Alexander Brodie was born in Liverpool in 1854 where he began his career in 1875 in the Engineering Department of the Mersey Docks Estate. Although being a keen Rugby follower, it was while watching Everton in their first league season that his attention was drawn to the difficulties encountered by referees in awarding legitimate goals when having to depend on the verdict of umpires who were appointed by the participating clubs. Mr Brodie who was at the time residing in Kelvin Grove, Toxteth, patented his design at the offices of Sloan and Lloyd Barnes in Castle Street.

They were first used on the Liverpool Ramblers ground some time later. Mr Brodie offered them for sale at sixpence (two and a half pence) with Bolton Wanderers becoming the first league club to purchase and try out the prototype. The first official use of goal nets by the Football Association was during the North v South representative match played at Nottingham in January 1891. In 1898 Mr Brodie was appointed Chief Engineer to the City of Liverpool, executing an annual expenditure of half a million pounds. He died in 1934.

With two games left to play Everton led the table with twenty nine points, closely followed by Preston North End on twenty five points. The two teams met at Anfield for the penultimate game of the season. A crowd of around fifteen thousand saw the reigning champions refuse to relinquish their title easily as they completed the double over the home side with a 1-0 victory, thus leaving Everton needing to win the one remaining match, an away game at Burnley, to be absolutely certain of the title.

During the month long break between the two fixtures, Everton embarked on the club's first visit to the capital for a tour which included three matches, the first taking place at the Oval Cricket Ground on Saturday the 24th January 1891 against The Corinthians. The visit generated a lot of interest in London on account of the visitors possible forthcoming League Championship. Everton were minus three first team players, the most noticeable absentee being Fred Geary, who was unable to travel following a recent bereavement in the family. The heavy rain on the day kept the crowd down to around two thousand, who paid one shilling each entrance fee. The Corinthians fielded a strong side which included seven internationals. There was nothing to chose between the teams during first period and at the interval the score was 1-1. Robertson gave Everton the lead with Sandilands replying for the Amateurs. After the interval the visitors began to get on top and Alf Millward, who played a splendid game throughout, gave them the lead. He then scored his second goal in the last minute, to make the final score 3-1.

On Sunday morning, the weather having changed for the better, the players and committee went on a sight seeing tour in the morning and after lunch they visited Hampton Court. Monday morning the party left Charing Cross Station to be met at Woolwich Station by the directors of Woolwich Arsenal, who had arranged for them to visit the ordnance works. The party were then taken on a two hour tour of the factory which at the time employed about eight thousand people. After lunch a match had been arranged with the works team who at the time were using the name 'Royal Arsenal'. The match took place on the club's recently acquired Invicta Ground, on Plumstead High Street. Everton making three changes from the team that played on the Saturday. The eight thousand crowd were treated to a fine exhibition of professional football from the Merseysiders who won the game 5-0.

The following day the weather again turned nasty, but this did not stop Everton from completing the last match of their scheduled tour. This was to be against Kent based amateur side Chatham, winners of the local Championship. The Everton party arrived from Charing Cross Station, to find a large square shaped cricket ground located on Park Road on the edge of a flat uninhabited piece of land known as the Great Lines. The ground contained a pavilion which was situated in the South East corner, but with little else in the way of accommodation for the spectators. The visit of the would be league champions aroused a great deal of interest in the area, bringing the largest crowd ever to the ground who clearly could not have viewed the proceedings in much comfort. Despite reports of the Chatham defence playing a magnificent game, Everton led 4-0 at the break. In the second half Chatham not only prevented Everton from adding to their tally, but from a centre by the club secretary Harry Hobert, Colvin scored for the amateurs. The Chatham News reported "His single goal was as valuable as fifty against minor teams". Chatham, home town of 1875 cup winners Royal Engineers, were later to become one of the founder members of the Southern League in 1893.

Two weeks later came the biggest game to date in Everton's short history. By way of an incentive, the committee offered each player a bonus of five pounds, plus a gold medal on securing the title. The few among the eight hundred supporters who left Exchange Station at 1:15pm by special excursion train to Burnley who had visited the town five years earlier could not help but be impressed by the ground improvements made by the followers of the association game in this East Lancashire community. The Turf Moor area had changed beyond recognition. The Cricket Club still occupied the area of the only previous encounter between the two teams, the football section having developed the eastern corner of the moor into their present day location. The Burnley committee, in anticipation of a large crowd, had recently erected a new grandstand which they had purchased from the locally defunct Union Star club. This added to the structure already in place on Brunshaw Road.

Snow and sleet fell continuously on the day leaving the pitch soft and slippery, but this did prevent a constant procession of people on to the ground causing the kick off to be delayed until 4:00pm. When the teams eventually took to the field the crowd had swelled to an estimated ten thousand; the local press reporting two thousand visiting fans were present. Mr C J Hughes of Northwich set the game in motion. Everton, having lost the toss, kicked off towards the end overlooked by The Bee Hole Colliery. Spurred on by their large following, the Merseysiders mounted most of the early pressure and were unfortunate not to take the lead, the ball twice rebounding off the crossbar. Near to the interval Everton mounted several corners, but at half time the score line was 0-0. On resuming play the visitors again made all the running, but five minutes into the half, against the run of play, Haresnape gave Burnley the lead. The goal stunned the visitors, but within two minutes they were level, Geary scoring with a low shot which was accompanied by loud cheers from their supporters. Everton kept up the pressure and fifteen minutes into the second half they took the lead following a great mix up in the Burnley goalmouth McFetteridge turned the ball into his own goal to the delight of the Everton followers. With the title in their grasp, anxiety began to creep into the visitors play and with five minutes remaining Bowes headed Burnley level. Before the cheering had died down Stewart gave the home team the lead with a thunderbolt that cannoned in off the underside of the crossbar. Everton just had enough time to mount another attack, but the ball stuck in the mud in the Burnley goalmouth. Just when it seemed they would equalize, the ball was cleared to the touchline. Almost immediately the final whistle went leaving the home team 3-2 winners.

The disappointment of the Merseyside fans was short lived for the news reached them later that evening that North End had lost 3-0 at Sunderland, making Everton League Champions. In doing so they became the first team in history to achieve a five figure attendance when their eleven home games at Anfield were watched by an average crowd of eleven thousand, eight hundred and seventy five.

The winning goal. Burnley 1 Everton 0, February 1892.
The goal is scored at the Bee hole End, the Everton goalkeeper is Jardine, the Burnley goalscorer is Hill.

During the summer months the now famous row developed between landlord and tenant concerning the rent for Anfield which resulted in the majority of the club members deciding to cross Stanley Park and set up camp on Goodison Road. The Liverpool Echo dated the 16th April 1892 reported that "Mr Holding had applied for an interim injunction against George Mahon, Dr Baxter, John Atkinson and William R Clayton to prevent them from removing any of the fixtures and fittings already in place at Anfield. The court was told that the ground contained four large stands for spectators, one on each of the said piece of land. The stand on the north side measures about 50 yards in length, the stand on the east side measures 65 yards in length, the stand on the south side (Kemlyn Road) measures about 125 yards in length and the stand on the west side about 60 yards in length. All the said stands are built practically on the same lines-viz, columns of brickwork were built into the ground, such columns rising from the height of a few bricks at the point nearest to the centre of the ground in steps till they reach the outside edge of my land at which point they are of a considerable height. On each of the steps there are beams of timber extending under the next step and firmly built into the brickwork with mortar. The cross-planking in which the people stand and sit, is nailed down and securely fastened to the said beams of timber and further secured to uprights which are let into the ground. Eight wooden buildings or sheds containing iron turnstiles surrounded by a hoarding fixed into the soil to a considerable depth".

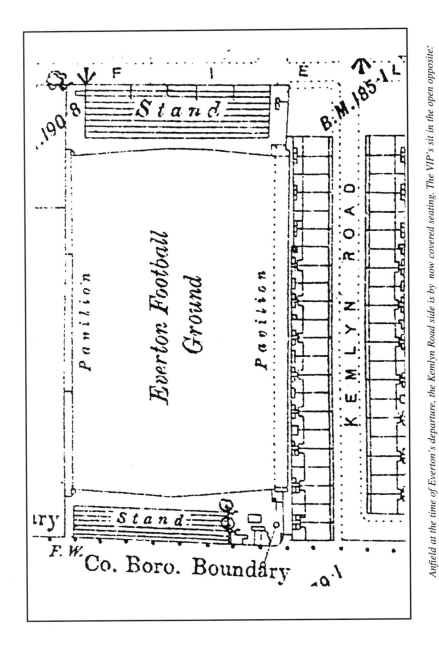

Anfield at the time of Everton's departure, the Kemlyn Road side is by now covered seating. The VIP's sit in the open opposite.'

Goodison Park

The Everton directors gave local building contractors Kelly Bros the task of having the ground ready for the forthcoming season. Taking in to consideration that no such undertaking had been attempted before, these gentlemen achieved what could only be described as a miracle. Beginning work on the 7th June 1892, they completed the job in time for the coming season. The main feature of the new ground was a large grandstand which ran almost the full length of the Mere Lane (now Bullens Road) side situated to give protection against the east winds that effected the area during the winter months. On Thursday the 27th August the president of the FA, Lord Kinnaird, arrived in a landau carriage and declared the new ground open. This in turn was followed by sporting events; a firework display and a concert by the band of The Prince of Wales Own Regiment.

The first match on the new ground took place on Friday the 2nd September 1892, Everton winning a friendly against Bolton Wanderers 4-2. The next day one of the new additions to the first division, Nottingham Forest, provided the opposition. The distinction of scoring the first goal at Goodison fell to Horace Pike, who gave Forest an early lead. Fred Geary scored the first goal for Everton in a 2-2 draw. The return match took place on the town ground Nottingham on the 12th January 1893.

Forest moved to their present day City ground in 1898 where Everton played their first match on the 1st October that year.

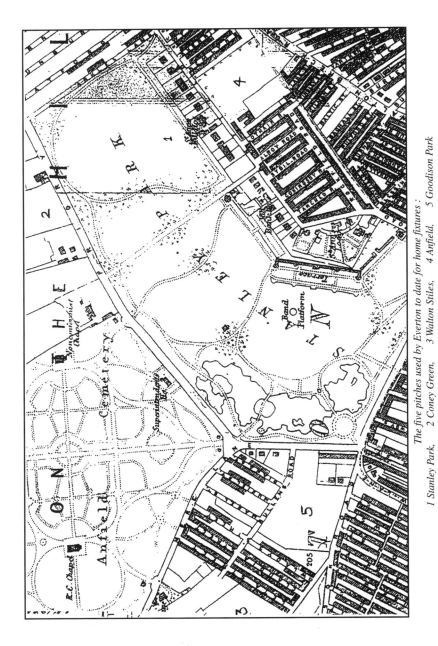

The five pitches used by Everton to date for home fixtures :

1 Stanley Park,   2 Coney Green,   3 Walton Stiles,   4 Anfield,   5 Goodison Park

Everton began the 1892/93 season's new away fixtures with their first ever trip to Manchester to play Newton Heath, a team formed by workers of The Lancashire and Yorkshire Railway Company. The match took place on North Road, in the Monsall district of the town, on ground between the companies large railway carriage and wagon works and Moston Brook. The Newton Heath club at the time were using the nearby Shears Hotel as their headquarters where the players changed before making the short walk to the ground. Newton Heath had used the North Road ground since their formation in 1878 which was described as being a 'mud heap' at one end and 'hard as flint' at the other. Just a rope barrier surrounded the pitch which also contained a small stand.

The weather on the day was reported to be rather bleak and a crowd of about four thousand being present to witness an exciting match. After leading 3-2 at half time Everton were forced to endure a lot of pressure before Farman equalised for the home team, but back came the visitors to score a late winner. All four Everton goals were scored by Alex Latta.

The venue changed next season, on the 2nd December 1893, Everton again defeated Newton Heath, 3-0, at the Old Beswick Cricket Ground which was situated in the Bradford area of Manchester.

Everton next set out on their first visit to the White Rose County, to play a league match with Sheffield Wednesday on the 13th February 1893. From as early as 1825, The Wednesday Cricket Club had been in existence in the town and in 1867 a football section was added. The association game proved very popular with the local population, for as early as 1878 there were as many as twenty six clubs playing in the town. The Wednesday were at the time occupying a ground called the Olive Grove, which was situated near Queens Road and approached by a small tunnel under the railway line that ran down one side of the pitch. An impressive grandstand stood on the other side of the enclosure which was surrounded by an iron railing and a cinder path. Everton won the match 2-0 to avenge a 5-3 defeat at Goodison the previous November.

On the 13th November 1897 Everton played their first league game at Aston lower grounds, Birmingham, the new home of Aston Villa. The playing area was part of a large Victorian leisure complex complete with dance hall, skating rink and open air gardens. The grounds were eventually transformed into the present day Villa Park.

Everton returned to the steel town next season to encounter Wednesday's newly promoted neighbours Sheffield United, formed like many other teams as a winter pastime for members of the local cricket club of the same name. Their ground at Bramall Lane was perhaps the last venue to stage both county cricket games and top flight football league matches on a regular basis. At the time of Sheffield United's first season in the top flight, their Bramall Lane ground was a large open affair boasting a fine pavilion but little else in the way of cover. The energetic committee quickly added a new stand on the John Street side, to accommodate two thousand spectators in comfort. Everton won their first game on the ground, 3-0.

The 1894-95 football season was looked forward to in Liverpool as never before, for the first time ever, the City was to be represented in the top flight by two teams and there was controversy even before the campaign began. During the summer months it came to the attention of the Everton directors that the

Liverpool president, Mr John Holding had engaged the services of their club's leading goal scorer Fred Geary to manage one of his public houses, which was situated in Thirlmere Road. Mr Holding speaking through his general manager, Mr Ramsey, informed the local press that Mr Geary had been granted a free hand to pursue his football. Everton, on the other hand, stated that they were in possession of a document signed by Mr Geary, which stated that he must give his sole time to the club. The incident increased the gulf already existing between the two clubs. Fred Geary signed for Liverpool the following season.

On the 29th August 1894, in preparation for the coming season, the Everton Directors treated the players to an eighteen mile horse and carriage ride, taking in the villages of Knowsley, Kirkby, Prescot and Huyton, before stopping for a knife and fork tea at the Childwall Abbey Hotel.

The first football league derby game between Everton and Liverpool took place at Goodison Park on the 13th October 1894. For this auspicious occasion the club invited a party of local dignitaries which included the Mayor of Liverpool, Mr W B Bowering. The home team had made a great start to the season winning all seven previous games and topping the table in the process. In preparation for the game, Liverpool had spent time training at Hightown, Everton electing to train at home.

On the day of the match the crowd began to arrive early to watch the added attraction of a schoolboy match between Liverpool and Nottingham before the main event of the day that kicked off at 3:30pm. Amidst great excitement the home team quickly got into their stride and soon took the lead. The distinction of scoring the first goal in a Merseyside Derby fell to

Scotsman, J McInnes, a recent signing from Third Lanark. Bell and Latta added further goals as Everton went on to win the match quite comfortably 3-0. The crowd was estimated at forty thousand, who paid receipts of over a thousand pounds. There were no reports of the ground being taxed to capacity.

The first new venue visited that season was Birmingham for a fixture with newly promoted Small Heath, a club that later became Birmingham City. The club were at the time playing their home fixtures on a sloping pitch at Muntz Street, in the Small Heath area of the city, which had a capacity of around thirty thousand. Although the ground contained a well equipped wooden grandstand, the most interesting feature was the ornate covering behind one of the goals, which had been purchased from local rivals Aston Villa, when they vacated their ground at Parry Barr. The first match between Everton and Small Heath ended in a 4-4 draw with Alex Latta scoring a hat-trick.

The 17th November 1894 was the date set down for Everton's first return to their old ground of Anfield. How John Holding had managed to assemble a rival top flight team in only three years clearly speaks volumes for the energy of the man. Everton stalwarts Millward and Chadwick, with clear memories of the old ground, could not fail to be impressed by the sight that greeted them. The main feature of the ground consisted of a impressive new grandstand covering the north side of the ground, which included seating for three thousand, five hundred spectators. The two teams then played out a 2-2 draw, Scotsman Bob Kelso scoring Everton's first goal as the away team on their former ground.

In the new year Everton again visited London for a two match tour. The first being a return trip to Woolwich Arsenal where they recorded a 2-0 victory. They continued with a visit to the Essex County Cricket Ground at Leyton for a match against London Casuals, a team that included seven internationals from the Corinthians as guest players. The famous amateurs began strongly and took the lead after five minutes. Everton weathered the early storm and slowly began to take control of the game. Just before the interval John Bell equalised with a fierce shot into the top of the net. The second half was a fairly equal affair with the visitors taking the honours with a late goal from Reay.

For the first away game of the 1895/96 season Everton made their first trip to Burnden Park, the new home of Bolton Wanderers. They arrived to find a pre-match cycle race in progress. Everton lost the match 3-1 before a crowd of fifteen thousand.

John Holdings new Liverpool side found life hard during their first term in the top flight and were relegated at the end of the season. The Lancashire cotton town team of Bury, was one of the clubs promoted to take their place. Bury Football Club had been founded at the Old White Horse Hotel in 1885 as a result of an amalgamation of two local church teams. From the time of their foundation they were based at Gigg Lane which is considered to be one of the finest playing surfaces in the land as a result of it once being part of the nearby Bankfield Farm. It was easily reached from the town centre by tram along Manchester Road. This ground formerly belonged to Lord Derby, as did Everton's first ground at Stanley Park.

Before the 1889 Lancashire Cup Final against Everton, the Bury chairman J T Ingham stated, "We'll give 'em a shaking.

In fact, we are the Shakers". Which remains the club's nickname to the present day. The first encounter between the two clubs ended in a 1-1 draw on the 11th January 1896.

On the 6th April 1897, Goodison Park was chosen to host an international match between England and Scotland. The England party stayed at the Alexandra Hotel in Dale Street. The Scots made their head quarters in the Crompton Hotel in Church Street. From the early hours of Saturday morning the Scottish fans began arriving in Liverpool on five special trains from Glasgow. The heavy rain that fell on the day of the match caused a postponement of the Liverpool Cup Final which was to be played on the ground before the main event. The game itself was a disappointment for the Scottish fans as England won the match 3-0. The arrangements made by the Everton committee proved excellent as the forty thousand crowd were accommodated without any reports of congestion.

In January 1899 Everton played their first ever fixture at St. James Park against Newcastle United. The Everton party arrived on Tyneside on a Friday evening and by noon the next day a thick mist accompanied by an incessant drizzle hung over the area placing the game in doubt. Shortly before 1:00pm the gloom lifted slightly, but the pitch was heavy after so much rain. Fifteen thousand people saw the visitors kick off up the slope and quickly get into their stride taking a two goal lead which they held until the break. The home team rallied strongly in the last half hour of the match which ended in a 2-2 draw.

Two more new venues were to be encounted before the end of the century, the first coming in the form of their second trip to Cottonopalis, (the city of Manchester's nick name in Victorian days), to play Manchester City. The team had originated at St. Marks Parish Church in West Gorton, later changing its name to Ardwick which lasted until 1894 when the club adopted its present day name. Everton arrived at the club headquarters, the Hyde Road Hotel in Ardwick, where they changed for the match. On leaving the hotel they passed through a set of gates located on left of the building along a short footpath that passed under a large railway viaduct to find a large irregular shaped enclosure formerly known as the 'Croft'. The match was played before a crowd of fifteen thousand who saw Everton win the match 2-1 with goals from Gray and Settle, local favourite Billy Meredith replying for Manchester City.

Later in the season Everton made a trip to the small Derbyshire town of Glossop for a match that is to date the only football league encounter between the two clubs. The fixture was played on North Road Cricket Ground with the local press referring to Everton as "One of the most costly football organisations in the country". A crowd of six thousand saw the visitors kick off towards the town end where an entertaining game ended in a 1-1 draw. Glossop is to date the smallest town, in terms of population, to be represented by a team in the top flight. This was due mainly to the help of the local business community.

By the time of the death of Queen Victoria in 1901, the association game was vastly different from the one that began in 1863. The North and Midlands now dominated the proceedings and it was to be another four years before the first professional team from the South, Woolwich Arsenal, were to reach the top flight. It had been a long journey for Everton to reach this stage of their development. Beginning from a team of local church lads, who were watched by a few friends and relatives in the

South East corner of Stanley Park, to one of the leading clubs in the land, with a ground and support that were second to none. If the beautiful game goes on for another thousand years and world wide historians of the future investigate it's origins, one of the most re-occurring names will be that of the descendants of the original men from the hill country, Everton Football Club.

for club and country

the hunt for european and world cup glory

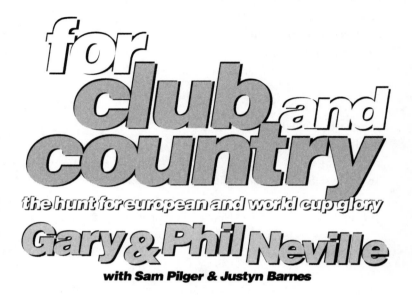

for club and country

the hunt for european and world cup glory

Gary & Phil Neville

with Sam Pilger & Justyn Barnes

First published in Great Britain in 1998
This edition published in 1999
by **Manchester United Books**
an **imprint of VCl plc**
76 Dean Street, London W1V 5HA
(www.vci.co.uk)
in association with
Manchester United Football Club plc
Old Trafford, Manchester M16 ORA

CIP data for this title is available from the British Library

ISBN   0 233 99498 X

10 9 8 7 6 5 4 3 2 1

 A Zone production

Design by **Tim Barnes** ◉
Photos by **Action Images, Allsport, Mark Leech, Empics, John Peters,
Sporting Pictures, PA News, Mike King**

Printed by CPD, Wales

Contents

Prologue   1

1   Getting started   5

2   The Italian job   29

3   Goal glut   45

4   The best team in Europe?   73

5   Sublime to the ridiculous   89

6   Munich remembered   103

7   A little miracle   129

8   Monte Carlo and bust   133

9   Slipping away   147

10   The worst day of our lives   185

11   To win or Toulouse?   207

12   Paying the penalty   227

13   Back home   243

14   The Cole and Yorke show   257

15   Farewell Kiddo   277

Epilogue   287

List of Illustrations

between pages 84 and 85
1   Eric Cantona
2   Family and friends' support
3   Early promise
4   Captaining United's Youth team
5   10 September 1997,
    England v Moldova
6   Nicky and Becks listen to some
    good advice
7   Henning Berg signs
8   13 September 1997 v West Ham (h)
9   Ken Bates
10 1 October 1997 v Juventus (h):
    Giggsy flies
11 1 October 1997 v Juventus (h):
    We were all delighted
12 11 October 1997, Italy v England (a)
13 20 October 1997 v Derby (a)
14 England coach John Gorman and
    the United lads
15 25 October 1997 v Barnsley (h):
    Andy Cole
16 28 October 1997: Roy Keane
17 5 November 1997 v Feyenoord (a)
18 9 November 1997 v Arsenal (a)

between pages 148 and 149
19 15 November 1997, England v
    Cameroon (h)
20 4 January 1998 v Chelsea (a)
21 6 February 1998, Munich Memorial
    Service at Manchester Cathedral
22 7 February 1998 v Bolton
    Wanderers (h)
23 20 February 1998:
    "Three Barnsley MPs... "
24 Alex Ferguson
25 18 February 1998 v Aston Villa (a)
26 28 February 1998 v Chelsea (a)
27 3 March 1998: Taking a break
    in Monaco

28 14 March 1998 v Arsenal (h):
    Screaming and shouting
29 14 March 1998 v Arsenal (h):
    Peter Schmeichel injured
30 18 March 1998 v Monaco (h)
31 28 March 1998 v Wimbledon (h):
    Ketsbaia-style!
32 28 March 1998 v Wimbledon (h):
    Ben Thornley
33 6 April 1998 v Blackburn Rovers (a)
34 10 April 1998 v Liverpool (h)
35 18 April 1998 v Newcastle
    United (h)
36 3 May 1998: Arsenal are
    Champions

between pages 212 and 213
37 23 May 1998, England v Saudi
    Arabia (h)
38 Glenn Hoddle
39 29 May 1998, England v
    Belgium (a)
40 Tony Adams
41 31 May 1998: Phil is left out of
    England's 22 for France '98
42 Paul Gascoigne
43 Ian Wright
44 15 June 1998, England v Tunisia:
    Paul Scholes
45 16 June 1998: Becks, Alan and me
    at Brazil v Morocco
46 22 June 1998, England v Romania
47 26 June 1998, England v Colombia:
    Becks' free-kick
48 26 june 1998, England v Colombia:
    Becks celebrates
48 30 June 1998, England v Argentina:
    Becks sent off
49 30 June 1998, England v Argentina:
    Sick and numb
50 Phil in training

Acknowledgements

Maurice Watkins

Marian Lynch

Tracey Mirkin

Howard McAlpine

Faith Mowbray

Liz Harris

Nicky Paris

Paul Steggle

James Freedman

Tim Forrester

Adam Shaw

Esther McAuliffe

Matthew Parker

James Taylor

Matt Turner

Stephanie Jones

Lou Pepper

Derek Balment

To our family, friends,
United and England team mates,
and especially the fans

Prologue

GARY: On Sunday 18 May 1997, Eric Cantona announced his retirement. It came as a big shock.

The players never had any clue that he was going to retire. In the morning, I'd seen on Teletext that there was going to be a press conference, but I thought we must be signing someone. I had played with Eric on the previous Friday evening in a testimonial match for Coventry's David Busst. There were no handshakes or mention of retirement, nothing in the dressing room after the game. Getting off the coach in Manchester that night, Eric said, "All the best for summer, lads. I'll see you later." That was the last time I saw him.

PHIL: When I heard on local radio news that Eric had retired, I was absolutely gutted. Now, I think I know why he kept it quiet – he just wanted to get away and hide and if he had told one of the lads it would have been hard for us to keep it in.

GARY: Looking back, I am not disappointed about the way Eric left. I just remember the great things he did for the club. United hadn't won the Championship for twenty-six years before he arrived and it's no coincidence that we finally won it in his first season here.

By 1993, Bryan Robson was coming to the end of his playing career and Eric became the top man on the training pitch and in matches. Just to be in the same dressing room as him was a dream. He was one of the best players I've ever seen, a genius. And when you see a naturally gifted player work so hard in training, you understand what it takes to be great.

Eric was often portrayed as an aloof, arrogant man, but he was friendly with all the lads, especially the older players. Personally, I wouldn't go up to Eric and ask what he did last night or anything like that. Like Bryan Robson before him, I respected Eric as an elder, and he had that same aura when he walked into a room.

PHIL: As captain, Eric never gave motivational speeches in the way Tony Adams does with England. He was a different kind of leader. The opposition were just frightened to death of him. They put two or three men on him and that gave the rest of us more room to play.

Eric won us many games on his own a couple of seasons ago, but since then players like Beckham, Giggs, Scholes and Cole have also emerged as match-winners. We no longer need someone to look up to. We are more of a team now.

GARY: Eric has no need to explain to us why he retired. He was immense for United and if he wants to live a life away from football, then he should be able to do what he thinks best.

The strange thing is that since we reported back for pre-season training, Eric's name has not been mentioned once among the players. Never. He's gone and the club's moved on. The confidence within the squad here is so high, we don't think the loss of one person is going to affect twenty players.

After five great years with Eric as our leader, we will have to do it all without him this season.

PHIL: 1997/98 promises to be the biggest season of our lives. Our ultimate dream is to win the European Cup with United and the World Cup with England. Four years ago, Gary and I were wondering if we would even earn a regular first-team place at United.

Gary and I were brought up in a close-knit sporting family and we've supported Manchester United all our lives. Our dad Neville and mum Jill both work at Bury Football Club – my dad is the Commercial Director and Mum is Club Secretary. Dad was a good local league cricketer, Mum used to play as a winger for her school's girls' football team and my twin sister Tracey is an England netball international. Gary and I both have steady girlfriends. My girlfiriend's name is Julie Killelea, who is a company secretary at a large construction firm. Gary goes out with Hannah Thornley, who is the sister of Ben Thornley, another player who came up through the United Youth team. She's a student at Salford University.

GARY: Phil and I wouldn't be professional footballers if it hadn't been for the support of our parents. They'd take me out of school if there was a football match – and Phil hardly went to school at all! He captained England schoolboys at cricket in the summer and then played international football in the winter. My dad always said to us, "Give this your best shot, you can do your A levels at seventy five if you want."

Between the ages of sixteen and eighteen, I gave everything to Manchester United. My attitude was that if it worked out, then good; if it didn't, I'd have no regrets. I know two lads who got offered apprenticeships at Man United but did A-levels instead because they felt it was too big a risk. I couldn't live with that decision for the rest of my life and that's why I took a chance. Now, every time I play for Man United, I get the rewards.

When I was fourteen, Phil was playing for England schoolboys and I couldn't even get into the county team, but my parents always had belief in me.

Other players came to Manchester United with a much better reputation than me – Nicky Butt, Ryan Giggs, Ben Thornley and John O'Kane had all played for England schools; Robert Savage and Keith Gillespie had played for Wales and Ireland respectively. Then there were three or four, including Paul Scholes and I, who hadn't played international football. Thankfully, everyone is given a chance at United. With hindsight, I'm glad I wasn't picked for the county side because it made me think, "I'll show them". I've enjoyed proving a lot of people wrong.

Getting started

Friday 1 August

GARY: The first League game of the 1997/98 season is eight days off. The Brazilian defender Celio Silva had his work permit rejected today. We don't seem to have much luck with the Department of Employment; we lost Jovan Kirovski this time last year, after their refusal to give us a permit. I know Jovan would have been a great player for us, as he's proving now at Borussia Dortmund. He's similar to Eric Cantona in physique and in the position he played.

Saturday 2 August

GARY: The headlines in the papers are all about David Beckham and I being rested for the Charity Shield match and the first two league matches of the season. The press seem to think the manager is giving us a slap down to stop us getting big-headed.

The fact is, Alex Ferguson told David and me before the Far East tour (which we didn't go on) that he was going to rest us at the beginning of the season. After Le Tournoi this summer, he allowed David and I to return to pre-season training a week later than everyone else.

The Gaffer is worried that I'm playing too much. Since I got into the first team, I haven't had a summer off: I played in the 1995 Umbro Cup, the 1996 European Championships and then Le Tournoi this year.

Most managers weren't too keen on their players going to Le Tournoi, but both players and managers realised a the chance to play Brazil, Italy and France couldn't be missed. The fact that we beat Italy and France and won the competition was a massive confidence boost in World Cup year, and the experience the young players from United gained there can only help club and country.

PHIL: Jordi Cruyff has decided to change the name on his shirt. He always had Jordi on his back at Barcelona, but when he arrived at United they put Cruyff on the shirt without asking him. With Cruyff on his back, he says there is more pressure on him, what with his famous dad.

Sunday 3 August   Manchester United 1 Chelsea 1
                                   United win 4–2 on penalties

PHIL: The Charity Sheild against Chelsea was quite a niggly, scrappy game. Butty and Dennis Wise had a little battle. They're both fiery characters who like to put their foot in. Dennis is always talking to you on the pitch, which we all try to ignore – sometimes unsuccessfully.

GARY: We were desperate to win today, and Chelsea chairman Ken Bates' comments in this morning's papers only increased our desire. He said he always stood up when he heard the chant, "Stand Up If You Hate Man U." He should know that if you are going to slag us off in public, you are only going to get beat.

It happened last season with Liverpool. Stan Collymore said on *The Girlie Show* that there were a few United players he could nominate for "Wanker Of The Week". After that, the lads in the United dressing room were really fired up. We should thank Stan for those comments really, but his Liverpool team-mates probably didn't.

I would be surprised if a Man United player ever came out with statements like that. I dread to think what Alex Ferguson would do.

GARY: Teddy Sheringham enjoyed picking up his first winners' medal with us. Peter Schmeichel was laughing at how excited he got.

Teddy occasionally asked us questions about life at United during England training camps, so he was obviously always interested in moving here. I said in an interview with *Manchester United* magazine last year that Teddy was one of the toughest players I'd ever played against. After losing Cantona, he's an outstanding signing for us. He already knows a lot of the players, so he's fitted in straight away.

The lads like him.

PHIL: When England played South Africa in May, the United lads were saying to Teddy, "Come and join United." The Boss had mentioned to Nicky Butt that he wanted Teddy, but Spurs wanted too much money. Originally, they were asking £6 million – the £3.5 million we paid was a good deal.

Once Eric left, we needed someone who can play in a similar role. The team had been built in recent years around Eric, who liked to drop into deeper positions than an out-an-out striker. Teddy fits that bill perfectly and he brings other qualities too, including his exceptional heading ability. People talk about his lack of pace, but there will be plenty of quick players around him at United.

GARY: I always like it when we sign British players because you know what you're getting – though we've been lucky with the foreigners who have joined United. Their attitude is superb and we've learnt from the way that they look after their bodies and the way they train.

But if you perform at United, you'll get in the side whatever your nationality, whether you cost nothing or £6 million. In the summer of 1996, after we'd won the Double, David Beckham and I were in Malta. The Gaffer had already signed five players, including one defender (Ronny Johnsen) and one right-sided midfielder (Karel Poborsky). David and I were discussing the fact that despite winning the Double, it was going to be even harder for us to get in the team next season. That's the challenge of playing for a club like United.

If United signed Roberto Carlos and he was playing better than me, or if Phil or Denis Irwin were playing better than me, I wouldn't complain about not making the team. I've supported Manchester United all my life and they should always have the best players available. If that means me, good; but if it doesn't, hard luck.

Charity Shield / Wembley Stadium / Att: 73,636

Chelsea 1
De Goey, Leboeuf, Sinclair, Clarke, Poyet, Morris (Petrescu), Wise, Di Matteo, Granville, Hughes (Vialli), Zola /
Scorer: Hughes
Manchester United 1
Schmeichel, Irwin, Johnsen, Pallister, P Neville, Keane, Butt, Scholes, Giggs (Beckham), Cole, Sheringham (Cruyff)
Scorer: Johnsen
United win 4–2 on penalties
(Scholes, Zola, Irwin, Keane, Leboeuf, Butt)

for club and country

Monday 4 August

GARY: This morning's *Sun* says that Alex Ferguson was offered the England manager's job before Glenn Hoddle. I hadn't heard that before. I'm not surprised that the FA asked him; he's got the best record of any manager in the game.

At the time, I was gutted when Terry Venables left because I could see the team was progressing. Fortunately, Glenn Hoddle has carried it on. The results, performances and team spirit just get better.

Tuesday 5 August Manchester United 2 Slavia Prague 2

PHIL: Stan Collymore is having a go at his old Liverpool team-mates, calling them 'Spice Boys'. I was surprised because when he's with the England squad he hangs around with them. I know Robbie Fowler and Steve McManaman quite well from England and you won't find two nicer lads. They're not 'Spice Boys', they take their football very seriously.

GARY: Tonight's game was a friendly match arranged as part of the deal which brought Karel Poborsky to United, so Karel wore the captain's armband. I was absolutely knackered afterwards. These Eastern Europeans are all like Olympic sprinters – strong and quick.

The Chilean central defender Dante Poli was given a run out tonight as part of his United trial. Dante did well, but we've not heard yet if he has signed. I don't think he is better than Pallister, Johnsen or May. If he joined, it would just be another person blocking the progress of homegrown players.

The lads have been giving Giggsy some stick this week as Dante looks like his long lost brother. Ryan wasn't pleased!

Friendly / Old Trafford / Att: 22,075

Manchester United 2
Van Der Gouw, G Neville, P Neville (Curtis), Poli, McClair, Pallister (Johnsen), Beckham (Mulryne), Poborsky, Cole (Cooke), Cruyff, Giggs (Thornley)
Scorers: Poborsky, Cooke
Slavia Prague 2
Sterjskal, Lerch (Labant), Kozel, Asanin, Rehak (Hysky), Vicek, Ulrich, Lasota (Vavra), Vacha, Horvath (Joarolim), Vagner (Kuchar)
Scorers: Horvath, Asanin

Wednesday 6 August

GARY: Recently, my dad, Phil and I have been talking about whether we should ask for our contracts to be upgraded. We've decided to leave it until Christmas time before we have a word with the Gaffer. We always consult him. If he says there's no point we'll drop it.

The club has always been really honest with us and upgraded our contracts to bring us in line with our team-mates when necessary. I've signed a four-year contract, a five-year contract and another five-year contract so far. That's fourteen years worth of contracts since I was eighteen, and I'm only twenty two.

United don't generally pay the ridiculous wages that you hear of other players getting in Europe. The club has a strict pay structure. I accept that some of the players in the team should be on more than me. I'm a realist. But over the past couple of years, wages in football have exploded and I feel I need to be brought into line.

Some people are jealous of the wages top players earn, and I realise how lucky I am to be doing what I'm doing. But there are hundreds of pro footballers and maybe only three percent never have to work again when they retire.

When you choose a career in football at sixteen, you are taking a massive risk. I look at Bury, where the players may not have the ability of the lads from Manchester United but work just as hard. When they retire from football, they have no academic qualifications and they still need to work for another forty years.

Alex Ferguson always said to us when we were teenagers, "If you make it at this club, fame and fortune will follow, and that's why it's worth the sacrifice." You can't be going to night clubs every night and turning up late for training.

I knew that if my football dream was realised, wealth would follow. You get used to the way of life and that drives you on. We were brought up in a two-up, two-down terraced house on the main road and we didn't have that much money in the family. My Mum and Dad gave us everything that they could, but now we're living in four-bedroom detached backing on to a golf course and we all enjoy it. Hopefully, Phil and I will keep them in a nice house for the rest of their lives. That's the way we want it to be for all they've done for us.

PHIL: The way I look at United's riches is that we get the best of everything. It's the little things: there are clean bibs for training; our boots get cleaned and taken to the game for us; our cars are parked for us on match day.

Opposing teams probably think that because somebody parks our cars we are big time charlies, but we are not. We still work harder than every other team in training. Our work-rate surprises a lot of our opponents.

Thursday 7 August

GARY: I read in the papers that Gianluca Vialli has given up smoking. A few players in English football smoke, but tend to keep it quiet. On the Continent they are more open. I remember going to a youth tournament in Sunderland when I was eighteen and the Portuguese team fumigated the corridors with smoke from their hotel rooms. I don't know any United players who smoke.

I was relieved at the news that Grobbelaar, Fashanu and Segers were aquitted of match-fixing. I don't see how a footballer can throw a football match. I've looked at the Liverpool game against Newcastle that Grobelaar was accused of throwing and I don't think he could have got anywhere near any of the three goals.

I have never caught a whiff of anything like that in the game. It's unthinkable.

Sunday 10 August   Tottenham Hotspur 0 Manchester United 2

GARY: The opening day of the season is always special, so I was gutted not to be involved today.

After Nicky Butt had given us the lead, the Gaffer told me to get stripped off because he wanted me to go on and seal it up at the back.

I said, "I'm just going to the toilet."

When I got back we had scored again and the Gaffer turned to me and said, "Get your top back on!" The other lads on the bench burst out laughing.

Teddy Sheringham got some terrible abuse from the Spurs fans, but their players gave him a warm welcome off the pitch. They take the sensible view; if they had the chance to come to United they would probably take it as well.

Premiership / White Hart Lane / Att: 26,359

Tottenham Hotspur 0
Walker, Edinburgh, Vega, Campbell, Howells, Neilsen, Carr, Ginola, Clemence (Sinton), Iversen, Ferdinand
Manchester United 2
Schmeichel, Irwin, P Neville, Johnsen, Pallister, Butt, Keane, Scholes (Beckham), Giggs, Sheringham, Cruyff
Scorer: Butt, Vega (own goal)

Monday 11 August

PHIL: I went to Old Trafford this morning and bumped into Henning Berg in the toilet.

"All right there! ave you signed for us or something?"

"Yes, I've just done it! Its all been hush-hush."

I'm really pleased. He's a great player. Like Denis Irwin, Henning's a quiet type who always does a brilliant job.

Tuesday 12 August

GARY: Henning came into the training ground this morning and shook everybody's hand in the dressing room. He immediately went to chat with Ronny and Ole, who he knows from the Norwegian team.

I've always been a big admirer of Henning. I've selected him for my PFA Team Of The Year two years running.

We do most of our training at The Cliff training ground in Salford, although we also use pitches at Littleton Road which back onto The Cliff. Strangely, you can't go directly across from The Cliff to Littleton

Road playing fields. Instead, it's a ten-minute drive to the entrance! The club is currently seeking planning permission to build a brand-new £10 million training facility in Carrington, South West Manchester.

Wednesday 13 August   **Manchester United 1 Southampton 0**

GARY: Southampton just came to defend. They put everyone behind the ball and we couldn't break them down. I was on the bench with Becks and when the manager sent him on late in the game, he got us the winner.

Premiership / Old Traffford / Att: 55,008

Manchester United 1
Schmeichel, Irwin, Johnsen (Berg), Pallister, P Neville, Keane, Butt, Scholes (Beckham), Giggs, Cruyff, Sheringham /
Scorer: Beckham
Southampton 0
Jones, Van Gobbel (Williams), Monkou, Benali, Todd, Oakley, Magilton, Maddison, Slater (Robinson), Johansen (Evans),
Ostenstad

Thursday 14 August

GARY: David Beckham and I played in a reserve game against Leeds at Halifax tonight. We got beat 3-0. As we were leaving a bloke came up to Becks' car, banged his fist on his window and ordered him to sign something. Becks said something and the bloke started abusing him. Unbelievable. People should not take take liberties like that.

Friday 15 August

GARY: The bloke from yesterday has obviously gone to the papers. The *Daily Star*'s front-page headline alleges that Becks swore at two young autograph hunters. Utter rubbish. There were no kids about.

It is a disgrace that such garbage can be published without any checks. People in the public eye have no protection from these idiots. Whether an allegation is true or not, stories like this can damage a reputation. Becks signs more autographs than anyone at the club.

When he leaves The Cliff he sometimes has to stay for ages making sure that everyone gets one. Becks and Giggsy get sackfuls of letters every week and they both reply to every request.

Sunday 17 August

GARY: This afternoon I went for my regular check-up on my barn. I bought it in May 1997 and I'm converting it. I plan to move in next summer and give my parents my current house.

I bought my first house in Bury two years ago and the whole family lives there now. Tracey is often away – she's doing a teacher training course at Bristol University. Phil just prefers to live with us and let me pay his phone bills, even though he's got a house of his own!

I've had a few teething problems with the barn. The lad who sold it to me was going to sell the surrounding land to the Forestry Commission. But I only bought the barn on the condition that I could have that land too, because they were planning public picnic areas practically on my doorstep. I don't think I'm the most popular person in Bury at the moment, but I'm not going to harm the land. It's still going to be grazing land, with cows and sheep on it.

Wednesday 20 August

PHIL: Becks told us he has become the Brylcreem Boy. A lot of the players use gel, and we all reckon he can sort us out with a big pot for the dressing room.

Friday 22 August

PHIL: Training was just a light forty-five minute session as we have a match tomorrow. We played a Youngs v Olds practice game. We scored first, but eventually lost 5-1. The Olds had Rai Van der Gouw on their side who just blocked everything, whereas we had Becks in goal who isn't the greatest!

It was only Henning Berg's second day in training and I'm really impressed. I gather Henning is a big United fan as well, which doesn't surprise me as United are very popular in Norway. A few times a year, I meet groups of Norwegian fans when they come over to Manchester.

The journey to Leicester took two-and-a-half hours. There is a speed limit on coaches of sixty two miles an hour, so all the lads moan about having to travel on a milk float. The coach has two levels: me, Nicky, Giggsy were down the front and David Beckham, Gary, Jimmy Curran our masseur, and Albert the kit man were on the other floor. The manager, Pally, Keano and Denis Irwin play cards at the back.

Our coach is easy to spot because there is a massive Red Devil crest on the side. Some cars pass three or four times, because people like to wave to us.

Saturday 23 August   Leicester City 0 Manchester United 0

PHIL: Gary got up at seven, and woke me with his rustling of the papers. When I started reading them, he told me to stop because he wanted to go back to sleep and I was disturbing him!

We had a match tactics meeting at 12.45. The Gaffer didn't announce the team, but he pulled me and Scholesy aside and told us we would be on the bench. Gary needs a game and I'm the unlucky one. I was a bit disappointed as I've played all the games up until now, but, to be honest, I expected it. He wasn't going to leave out Denis Irwin.

During the warm ups, Becks accidentally hit a young Leicester fan in the face with a shot. He went straight up to him and apologised and told him to come and see him later. After the game, Becks gave him his boots.

We knew it was going to be a difficult game as Leicester had just beaten Liverpool at Anfield, so we were reasonably pleased with a point. But to hit the post three times and not score was incredible.

Back on the coach, I found out the cricket score from the sixth Test at the Oval between England and Australia. The Aussies were one hundred for nine – when I'd last heard, England were still batting! I was just in time to see Tufnell take the last wicket.

During the series, Australian captain Mark Taylor's family has been staying at my house (the one I don't live in!) My family have been friends with him since he was the professional for Greenmount CC, my local team. Mark wanted to give his family a base so his kids didn't have to drag around from hotel to hotel.

Premiership / Filbert Street / Att: 21,221

Leicester City 0
Keller, Prior, Walsh, Elliott, Kaamark, Izzet, Lennon, Campbell (Savage), Guppy, Marshall (Claridge), Heskey
Manchester United 0
Schmeichel, Iriwn, GNeville, Berg, Pallister, Butt, Keane, Beckham, Giggs, Sheringham, Cruyff (Scholes)

Sunday 24 August

PHIL: No training today. I read the news of England's thrilling Test win. Sometimes I wonder what might have been if I had chosen cricket as my career. I think my Dad's dream was for Gary to play for Manchester United and me to play for Lancashire at Old Trafford cricket ground. I was a left-handed batsman and in my time at Lancashire I broke the records set by some famous names. In the Under-13s, I broke Mike Atherton's record of runs in a season and in the Under-15s I beat John Crawley's record too.

My best innings was probably my last for Lancashire Under-15s, against Yorkshire. People knew it was my last game of cricket before I joined Manchester United and there was a big crowd. I was facing bowling from the likes of Liam Botham, but I scored a hundred and twenty five runs without giving a catching chance until I was run out.

Gary was a good player too. He played for North of England Under-15s but missed out on England trials because of a broken finger. I've been told that current England coach David Lloyd remembers us at fourteen as the best players in our age groups. We even got a mention in Ian Botham's recent book on the state of English cricket, *The Botham Report*, as two promising cricketers who got away.

I finally chose football in a week when I got picked for England

Under-15s at both cricket and football. I played football in front of 60,000 in Berlin's Olympic Stadium and then flew home to play cricket for England, but there were no spectators except for the players' families. There just wasn't the same buzz.

My Dad used to ask Brian Kidd if it would be all right for me to go on cricket courses and play matches when the football and cricket seasons overlapped. I didn't want him to think I didn't care about football, but Kiddo just said, "Go and enjoy yourself." United didn't put any pressure on me.

Monday 25 August

PHIL: No Bank Holiday for me. I got into training about ten o'clock. There was a feeling of disappointment around because of Saturday; all the lads felt we should have won.

The lads gave Teddy a bit of stick for hitting the post from two yards on Saturday, but nothing serious. He's under enough pressure as it is.

There was an emphasis on shooting this morning. The manager wants us to sharpen up and get more shots in on goal. I never score, I just get in the way and get hit a lot!

I haven't scored for the first team yet, but I did hit the post on my debut against Wrexham over two years ago. Gary scored his first one last year against Middlesbrough and likes to have a pop at me about not managing it yet. On Saturday, he was laughing because his odds on scoring were a lot shorter than mine – Gary was 40-1 and I was 60-1! My Dad always has a fiver on me scoring and it's getting expensive.

Jordi Cruyff was really disappointed about being injured on Saturday. He told me he blamed himself because it was his poor touch that allowed the ball to run away and then he got injured trying to retrieve it.

I'm quite close to Jordi. Last season, when he was really down, I would encourage him and tell him to give it all a chance. He has done well in pre-season and in the games so far.

Before I left The Cliff, I must have signed a hundred autographs. There seem to be more people there every day.

Tuesday 26 August

PHIL: The manager announced the team for the game against Everton tomorrow. I'm a sub again. Bad news for me, with the England squad still to be announced on Friday.

We launched into a practice game with tomorrow's team playing against the other lads, who pretended to be Everton. For twenty minutes, I was Andy Hinchcliffe.

After training, we had a photo session for the new Champions' League kit, which has a brighter red shirt than the home kit and the white socks which we prefer. I had lunch with Jordi and we discussed tomorrow's game and the Champions' League. Jordi hopes we get drawn with his former club Barcelona as he would love to go back there.

In the evening, I went to see Bury play Crewe in the Coca-Cola Cup with my Dad. As both my parents work there, Bury has always been my second team and I try to see as many of their home games as possible. We don't get treated like superstars; we have been going there for years. Tonight they drew 2-2.

Wednesday 27 August   Everton 0 Manchester United 2

GARY: I met up with the other lads at Old Trafford where we got the coach to Liverpool. We had some lunch and then all went to our rooms. Phil and I slept for about three and half hours until 4.30 pm. I always sleep in the afternoons before a game – it refreshes me.

Before leaving the hotel, we had a snack and then the manager went over our match tactics again. Ronny Johnsen was in the team announced yesterday, but he pulled out injured so Henning is in. Giggsy's new role in the side was discussed – he's going to play centre forward, with Teddy and Scholesy behind him.

We set off from the hotel at about 6.15 pm with a police escort. Sometimes we'll leave an away ground and stop at traffic lights by a pub with opposition supporters standing outside and they'll gesture and throw things. It happened at Tottenham for the opening game of the season, but fortunately we have shatter-proof glass fitted on our coaches! Foreign coaches don't though, so last year in Turkey we got showered in glass when someone threw a stone.

PHIL: David Beckham has been voted the best-looking man in the world by readers of the *Sun*. Some players gave him stick, saying that he had gone out and bought every copy in England, but he protested that he hadn't even seen the article. We had a laugh at Giggsy who was way down in thirty-fourth place.

Becks is getting more and more attention, and I think he is handling it really well. He is working even harder at his football. He is so much under the microscope that he has to play well in every game.

GARY: Tonight was one of the finest away performances I can remember. Giggsy was world class in the striker's role. In the second half, the way he gave Slaven Bilic a two-yard start and beat him in a straight sprint for the ball was frightening. We only scored two, but it could have been five. We were all pleased for Teddy, who got his first goal. His son Charlie was up to see the game as well.

That is four games played and four clean sheets. At this stage last year, we had already let in five. Before this season started, the manager told us that the number of League goals we let in last season (forty four) was unacceptable. He said we must improve and I think we have.

Premiership / Goodison Park / Att: 40,029

Everton 0
Southall, Watson (Thomas), Bilic, Short (Branch), Barrett, Stuart, Williamson, Speed, Phelan, Barmby (Oster), Ferguson
Manchester United 2
Schmeichel, Irwin, G Neville, Berg, Pallister, Butt, Keane, Beckham, Giggs, Sheringham, Scholes (Cole)
Scorers: Beckham, Sheringham

Thursday 28 August

PHIL: Ronny Johnsen had to pull out of training today. He won't be fit for Saturday's game. I sat next to Jordi and Ole Gunnar at lunch. Ole's injury isn't progressing as quickly as he hoped, but he should be back before the first European game.

I haven't seen Dennis Bergkamp's hat-trick against Leicester yet, but

Jordi and Ole were raving about it. Jordi is good friends with Dennis and was really pleased for him.

Friday 29 August

PHIL: There were loads of photographers and cameramen at The Cliff today because it's the European draw today, so the lads had to watch their language a bit. Before the Youngs v Olds game, the oldies were saying that it wasn't worth playing because they always beat us. We beat them 4–3! Giggsy is the oldest of the youngsters. He has pledged never to play for the Olds, even when he's drawing his pension. On the other hand, Rai Van Der Gouw went in goal for us. He is actually older than Peter but Schmikes says he would never go in goal for us!

Afterwards I posed for a few photos for *Glory Glory Man United* magazine. I am the new editor of the letters page.

Later, Gary rang me on the mobile to tell me who we had drawn in our Champions' League group. We've got Juventus (again!), Feyenoord and Kosice. I think Gaz is more interested in what the food will be like after some bad food experiences in Volgograd with United and in Poland with England ... Otherwise, we were all quite happy with the draw. Hopefully our experience of playing Juventus last year will help. I don't know much about Feyenoord, but our senior players have fond memories of winning the 1991 Cup Winners' Cup in Rotterdam.

GARY: In the afternoon, Phil and I had a question and answer session with the Larne supporters' association, of which I am president, who were over from Northern Ireland. My Dad was at the back of the audience. During the session, he found out we'd been selected for the England squad to play Moldova. A thumbs up let us know we were both in.

Saturday 30 August   **Manchester United 3 Coventry City 0**

PHIL: I arrived at Old Trafford at midday, had a light pre-match meal and then went to relax in the players' lounge. No friends or family are allowed in before the game, only the players. We have a players rota for doing presentations up in the VIP suites and it was my turn. Everyone has to do three or four each season.

At about 1.30 pm, we all filed into the dressing room where the Gaffer announced the team. He had told me earlier in the week that I would be playing, but it was nice to get confirmation.

After going through the match tactics, the Gaffer disappeared until ten to three as usual. We passed the time by watching *Grandstand* and old United videos. Peter likes to go in the warm-up room, but I had a kick about and did some stretches. The goalkeepers always go out on the pitch before us and the rest of us join them for the warm-ups about half an hour before kick-off when the ground is still quite empty. At about ten to three, Kiddo walks to the tunnel and that is the signal to follow him back in. Today, Becks stayed out for a couple of Player of the Year presentations.

Then comes the moment when everyone shakes hands and wishes each other all the best. I'm usually third in the line and our captain Roy Keane leads us out.

We scored really early against Coventry last year, so it was *déjà vu* when Coley scored after only a minute. I had to mark Darren Huckerby who is very fast, but I thought I did well against him. I was taken off in the second half after my head accidentally clashed with Paul Telfer's elbow.

The final score flattered us. Afterwards in the dressing room, the manager told us he was pleased with the win, but not with the performance. He said we shouldn't be complacent against teams like Coventry.

GARY: The atmosphere at Old Trafford was very flat today. Our fans at away games are brilliant, but 55,000 people at home should really make more noise. During today's game there were a few bad passes and the crowd started moaning. I remember Michael Appleton's debut at Old Trafford last season, against Swindon in the League Cup. His first two or three passes were bad and the crowd started giving him a hard time. He came through it well, but at the time I thought, "Give him a break, he's a young lad and it's his first game."

I sometimes think the best way to improve the atmosphere is to start losing! Last season when we played Arsenal at home after losing to

Fenerbahçe, Southampton and Newcastle, the "Stand Up for the Champions" chant started. It generated the best atmosphere at a League game since I started in the first team.

Other than that game and our game against Juventus, I can't remember a match with an outstanding atmosphere, and that's very sad. When I used to go and watch, the fans would lift the roof off every match – and there were more poor performances back then.

Premiership / Old Trafford / Att: 55,074

Manchester United 2
Schmeichel, P Neville (Irwin), G Neville, Berg, Pallister, Butt, Keane, Beckham, Giggs, Sheringham, Cole (Poborksy)
Scorers: Cole, Keane
Coventry City 0
Ogrizovic, Shaw, Burrows, Williams, Huckerby, Dublin, Salako, Telfer, Richardson, Hall, Nilsson

Sunday 31 August

GARY: At 1.30 this morning, I woke to the terrible news that Diana Princess of Wales had been badly injured in a car crash. Later the news came through that she was dead.

I had never met her, but whenever anyone asked me who I thought was the best-looking woman in the world, I would say Diana. Becks used to laugh at me about that. He and I were having a silly argument about it on the coach one day, until Giggsy turned round and told us that he had met her and she was absolutely unbelievable.

Today's game between Newcastle and Liverpool was called off, which I think was the right decision. I would have found it difficult to play – I was numb. Our family just sat in front of the television all day.

Wednesday 3 September

GARY: I thought England's World Cup tie against Moldova might be postponed as well, but it was on so we went down to Burnham Beeches.

Rio Ferdinand was dropped from the squad yesterday after being found guilty of drink-driving at the weekend. He's staying with the squad but won't be selected for the team. I think he's been unlucky. He went out celebrating his call-up to the England squad, had a few drinks with his mates and was caught when he drove the following morning.

At United, we are encouraged to keep our drinking to an absolute minimum. You've got to remember that you are always representing Manchester United and maintain a certain standard of behaviour. I'm not that big a drinker anyway. Footballers have a lot of spare time, but you must be professional. Alex Ferguson will not tolerate people going so far that they are doing a disservice to their body and letting down their team-mates. He takes responsibility for your behaviour. You don't want to do anything wrong because his trust for you will diminish.

Thursday 4 September

PHIL: Teddy has gone back to Manchester because he cracked some ribs. He played through the injury for a few weeks and now he's been told to take four weeks rest. At the start of his United career, the last thing he wants is to be injured.

Friday 5 September

PHIL: None of the players have mentioned Diana's death. Possibly we're still in a state of shock. I suppose if we talked about it too much we would get depressed before the game. Only Glenn Hoddle raised the subject. He said, "You'll be under pressure because of what has happened this week. Let's just be dignified and put on a good performance."

Saturday 6 September

GARY: The FA allowed us to go home to watch Diana's funeral. It was one of the most moving things I have ever seen. I thought Earl Spencer's speech said it all.

Monday 8 September

PHIL: Rio Ferdinand has been quiet. Glenn Hoddle made him report to see what he was missing out on. I haven't spoken to Rio about it; it's difficult when you don't know somebody well and I didn't want to be nosey. He knows what he has done wrong.

Wednesday 10 September   England 4   Moldova 0

PHIL: Standing in the tunnel listening to Elton John's "Candle in the Wind", I felt overwhelmed by it all – I was shivering. Ian Wright said later it was the most significant match of his life.

Before kick-off we discovered that Italy only got a 0-0 draw in Georgia. Added to the emotion of the occasion, we were all up for the game. We played on instinct and everything came naturally. Ian Wright scored twice, and Glenn Hoddle said afterwards, "I'm going to the bookies tomorrow to put my mortgage on Wrighty breaking the record on Saturday." He's close to Cliff Bastin's all-time scoring record for Arsenal.

Everyone was so happy after the game. My mum and dad gave me a big hug in the players' lounge afterwards. We had only beaten Moldova, but there was such a special edge to the whole night.

Now we only need to get one point in Rome to qualify.

World Cup qualifier / Wembley Stadium

England 4
Seaman, G Neville, P Neville, Batty, Campbell, Southgate, Beckham (Ripley; Butt), Gascoigne, Ferdinand (Collymore), Wright, Scholes
Scorers: Scholes, Wright 2, Gascoigne
Moldova 0
Romanenko, Fistican, Siroanko, Testimitanu, Spinu, Rebeja, Shishkine (Popovici), Curtlanu, Culbaba (Suharev), Miterev, Rogaciou (Shibolar)

Thursday 11 September

PHIL: Paul Gascoigne was brilliant last night. Glenn Hoddle has been saying that Gazza has got to be careful about his drinking and his diet. I think Glenn is trying to keep him focused for the World Cup if we get there. It's obvious he's placing a lot of importance on him.

Gazza is one of the nicest, funniest blokes I have ever met. I hope that if we get to France, he's with us. When you are in a hotel for a month you need people like him.

Friday 12 September

GARY: We heard that the club had got a letter from Eric Cantona, saying that he would not be coming to the club's Championship celebration banquet. It would have been nice for the fans to see him one last time. They would want to pay him a special tribute. I hope they get a chance eventually.

Saturday 13 September   Manchester United 2 West Ham United 1

GARY: David Beckham was on the end of some disgusting chants from the West Ham fans about his girlfriend. We went a goal down, but after Keaney equalised Becks, Roy and I ran over to them as if to say, "Have some of that!"

I don't know how Becks copes with the abuse. Sadly, I think it's just going to get worse. Becks knew he was going to get the press attention going out with Victoria, but why should he be slaughtered like this?

Premiership / Old Trafford / 55,068

Manchester United 2
Schmeichel, G Neville, P Neville, Pallister, Berg, Keane, Butt, Beckham, Giggs (Poborsky), Scholes, Cole (McClair)
Scorers: Keane, Scholes
West Ham United 1
Miklosko, Potts, Ferdinand, Unsworth, Breacker, Berkovic, Moncur (Lampard), Lomas, Hughes, Hartson, Kitson
Scorer: Hartson

PHIL: Sure enough, Ian Wright broke the Arsenal goalscoring record today with a hat-trick against Bolton. Glenn Hoddle must be counting his winnings.

Wednesday 17 September   Manchester United 3 Kosice 0

GARY: We were all a bit apprehensive about the trip to Slovakia, but it turned out fine. Travelling to Eastern Europe hasn't always been good. Two years ago we went to Volgograd and it was an absolute hell hole. The hotel was infested with cockroaches – a couple of the lads were bitten and others woke up covered in spots. There were no towels and no hot water!

This game turned out to be a stroll in the park. With a crowd of just 8,000 fans, it seemed like a practice match. Kosice seemed to be in awe of us, in the same way that we were in awe of Juventus last season.

Champions' League / Lokomotiva / Att: 9,950

FC Kosice 0
Molnar, Spilar, Telek, Kozak, Janocko, Ljubarskij (Rusnak), Koslej (Faktor), Semenik, Zvara, Sovic, Kral
Manchester United 3
Schmeichel, G Neville, Irwin, Pallister, Berg, Keane, Butt, Beckham (McClair), Poborksy, Scholes, Cole
Scorers: Irwin, Berg, Cole

Thursday 18 September

PHIL: We started off our Champions' League campaign with a solid 3-0 away win, but the papers have decided to concentrate on a couple of misses by Andy Cole. Can you believe it? In a game where he set up our first goal and then scored the third himself!

The treatment Andy gets is a disgrace. He's the £7 million man, so he's expected to score forty goals a season just as he did at Newcastle. But no player has ever done that at Manchester United. Andy is now involved in the build-up, whereas at Newcastle he was a pure goal poacher. At United you can't afford to have someone who just hangs around the box.

Coley has won two Championships and an FA Cup winner's medal at United. Nobody can argue with that.

GARY: The manager took me aside this morning to let me know personally that I wasn't in the Dream Team he has selected from the best players from his eleven years at Old Trafford for a video launched next Monday.

Here's the Gaffer's first eleven:

Peter Schmeichel

Philip Neville	Steve Bruce	Gary Pallister	Denis Irwin
David Beckham	Roy Keane	Bryan Robson	Ryan Giggs
	Eric Cantona	Mark Hughes	

He told me that when he made his selection he didn't know which was my best position, centre half or right back. At least I'm a sub! The likes of Paul Ince and Andrei Kanchelskis didn't make it into the side either, so I'm in good company.

PHIL: I was absolutely amazed and honoured to be selected. Being so young, I didn't expect it at all.

Saturday 20 September   **Bolton 0   Manchester United 0**

GARY: Bolton are one of my least favourite teams. People from Bolton have a very aggressive streak!

Bolton fans are the worst for singing songs about Munich. Today, people in the crowd were doing aeroplane impressions and singing, "Who's that lying on the runway?" Sick, absolutely sick.

While I was warming up, a Bolton fan shouted, "We know where you live, Neville!" Charming! I also saw four lads in the crowd who I used to play cricket with in Bolton, and they gave Philip some terrible abuse during the game. Bolton's players had obviously been sent out to rile us. I think they are still hurting from when we beat them 6-0 last year. Nathan Blake's tackle on Pally was an absolute disgrace. He ran his studs down the back of Pally's calf and could have caused serious ligament damage. Pally didn't even react that badly when Blake took a swing at him. I couldn't believe the referee sent Pally off as well.

Premiership / Reebok Stadium / Att: 25,000

Bolton Wanderers 0
Brannagan, Frandsen, Taggart, Pollock, Sellars (Beardsley), Blake, McGinlay, Thompson, Bergsson, Fish, Whitlow
Manchester United 0
Schmeichel, G Neville, Irwin, Pallister, Berg, Poborsky (P Neville), Beckham, Keane, Butt, Scholes (Solskjaer), Cole

Wednesday 24 September   **Manchester United 2 Chelsea 2**

GARY: Tonight we had our usual battle with Chelsea. There always seem to be incidents during games between us and players get into trouble.

At half-time, I was walking up the tunnel alongside Roy Keane when we heard a commotion at the entrance. I turned around to see a melée of players. There was a lot of pushing and shoving, but the security lads soon sorted it out. The last I saw, a Chelsea player launched headfirst into the scramble. That was the signal for most of us to head for the dressing room!

In the second half, all the trouble seemed to be forgotten.

It was disappointing not to win, as Chelsea could be our fiercest rivals this season. Their Chairman, Ken Bates, has also been quoted as saying that we are just a club from the slum side of Manchester. To me, Chelsea could move their stadium to the middle of Harrods and win fifteen championships on the trot, and even if you moved Old Trafford to downtown Beirut they still wouldn't be as big as us. At the moment, they haven't got the tradition or history of United, Liverpool or Arsenal.

PHIL: Watching from the stands, I was really impressed with Chelsea. They were the best team to play at Old Trafford for a while and I thought we were lucky to get a draw with a brilliant late equaliser from Ole, who is back after being injured for so long.

Ole wore a huge smile in the dressing room afterwards, but no one else did. The manager was not happy at all!

Premiership / Old Trafford / Att: 55,163

Manchester United 2
Schmeichel, G Neville (Giggs), Irwin, Berg, Pallister, Butt, Keane, Scholes (Sheringham), Beckham, Poborsky (Solskjaer), Cole
Scorers: Scholes, Solskjaer
Chelsea 2
De Goey, Hughes, Leboeuf, Myers, Le Saux, Poyet, Wise, Lambourde, Zola (Flo), Petrescu, Hughes
Scorers: Berg (own goal), Hughes

Saturday 27 September   **Leeds United 1 Manchester United 0**

GARY: After Bolton, we had the hospitable atmosphere of Leeds.

It was the worst I've ever known at Elland Road today. When our coach pulled up, hundreds of Leeds fans were waiting for us. There were men with their kids on their shoulders making obscene gestures at us. You could see the hatred in their eyes. We were spat at and had coins thrown at us. Elland Road is the only away game my Dad won't go to.

The manager said, "The last time they beat us here, they were selling videos at nine o'clock the next morning. Don't let them make another video." Unfortunately, we didn't produce the goods and Leeds played like the away team, putting eleven men behind the ball.

More worrying than the defeat was our captain Roy Keane being stretchered off with a knee injury.

Premiership / Elland Road / Att: 39,952

Leeds United 1
Martyn, Gunnar, Wetherall, Radebe, Robertson, Kelly, Hopkin (Molenaar), Ribeiro, Haaland, Kewell, Wallace /
Scorer: Wetherall
Manchester United 0
Schmeichel, G Neville (P Neville), Irwin, Pallister, Berg, Beckham, Keane, Poborsky (Thornley), Scholes (Johnsen),
Sheringham, Solskjaer

2

The Italian job

Monday 29 September

GARY: We trained in the afternoon, which is unusual for us, in preparation for the visit of Juventus on Wednesday. The manager had us watching videos all morning: our first half performance against Juventus at home last season, followed by their last game against Sampdoria.

Ron Atkinson said on the commentary to the first half of the Juve game how nervous we looked, and the Gaffer agreed: "He's right, you were." He wants us to relax and believe in ourselves this time.

It's difficult to see what's happening on a video. The best I've seen are the ones that Glenn Hoddle shows us with England. He gets a cameraman to film the game from up in the gantry and they're brilliant – you can see the runs players make and the team formation.

During the meeting, the Gaffer named the team for Juventus. Then he told us that Roy was having a scan tonight and you could tell he feared the worst.

The England squad for Rome was announced at 12.30 pm and the stewards at The Cliff told Phil and I we'd been picked as we came out of the meeting. Robbie Fowler and Steve McManaman were back in the squad, which was no surprise given their ability. Gazza, Adams and Seaman, who didn't play in the Wembley defeat against Italy, are also back in. Alan Shearer will be out for a while yet with the injury he sustained in pre-season, but Seaman, Adams, Ince and Sheringham are all certainties to play. They are the backbone of the team.

We played a practice game in the afternoon. The team that won't be playing in the match is known as the Bomb Squad. They had the difficult task of playing like Juventus!

Later on, Phil and I had a word with my dad. We were told a week ago that we'd been released from our boot contract with Pony. We were disappointed, because we signed a three-year contract just sixteen months ago and now they tell us that they want to stop it on 13 October, which leaves us high and dry during the season. My dad went to see Nike today.

Phil and I haven't got an agent. There's no good reason for us to pay a significant percentage to a third party on club and boot contracts; we know what we should be paid anyway. Take wages for example. There are enough experienced players around to advise us so we can work out a realistic offer. It would upset me if I ever had to give a penny to an agent on my club or boot contracts.

If an agent rings my Dad and wants to offer us a job and we are interested, we will run it past the Gaffer. If he says OK, then the agent gets his percentage because it was he who brought in the work. That's fair enough, but we'll never sign with an agent. The manager's always advised against it, but in any case we see no benefit. They tie you down and they take a big cut. Does an agent deserve that much money for sitting down for a couple of hours with a chairman to do a club contract? No way.

I agree that some players do need agents because they have so many offers coming in, but not Phil and I. The best agents are the ones you never hear or see. The ones who work behind the scenes and leave their lad to play football.

Tuesday 30 September

GARY: Marcello Lippi, the Juventus coach, has been saying very complimentary things about Andy Cole. He rates Andy as our most dangerous player and I think everything he says is true. Andy is always great to play with; his movement is brilliant, and he has an unbelievable scoring record that sometimes gets ignored. Not many United strikers in history can match Andy's league strike rate of a goal every two games.

Andy Gray commented in the *Sun* today that David Beckham should be dropped for the England v Italy game. "This game has nothing to do with potential... it's about experience, maturity and proven bottle," he wrote. Andy Gray does a brilliant job as a Sky analyst, but I thought his comments were ill-timed considering we play Juventus tomorrow.

Sometimes people misinterpret the word 'experience'. There are players of twenty one or twenty two at United who have won the Double, two Championships, played in a European semi-final and play regularly for England. Most players of thirty four haven't achieved what some of our players have achieved at twenty two.

We had another practice match in training. In the build-up to the Juve game, we've been doing loads of functional work – that is, practising the way the back four play together, set pieces, the movement of the front players. I've always done a lot of more functional work with England. At United, it's difficult to find time, with games nearly every Wednesday and Saturday. Brian Kidd's training is absolutely magnificent. It's always interesting – possession, crossing, shooting exercises and things like that – and it's all based on technique work.

PHIL: I asked Henning Berg recently how United's training methods compare with what he was used to. He said, "You probably train for less time at United, but what you do is quality work."

GARY: The Gaffer told me I will play in as one of three, not as a conventional full-back. Usually, I'm allowed to overlap, but he told me specifically to pick up Del Piero when we go forward. He has often said that the biggest problem English teams have in Europe is that they get caught on the break. It happened last year in Turin. I went forward to take a long throw-in and Pally went forward for the flick-on, leaving us exposed at the back against Boksic. We got punished.

Wednesday 1 October   Manchester United 3 Juventus 2

GARY: The Gaffer did something that I've never known in my time here. He brought us in at three o'clock for massages. We all wondered what was happening. Usually he has us in three hours before kick-off, which is long enough to sit around in the players' lounge, but to have us in five hours before! Later on we found out that, in his wisdom, he didn't want us lying in bed and feeling lacklustre.

Keano wasn't in, and we heard the bad news about his cruciate injury. I asked Denis Irwin, who is Roy's closest friend at the club, how he is. Denis says he's taking it brilliantly, but it is a huge blow to the team.

Compared to last season's match with Juventus, I felt good in the tunnel. I was confident. I know we are as good as them.

So much for confidence! They scored in the first minute. It was unreal. I just looked and thought, "No, they've not scored!" As I walked back to the centre circle, I saw Giggsy stood there with his arms in the air and a look on his face as if to say, "What the hell have you done?" The forwards are funny like that. If we concede a goal, they stand at the half-way line with their arms in the air as if they don't belong in the same team.

It was so important for us to score. We didn't score once against Borussia Dortmund or Juventus in four games last season. After Teddy scored, I was sure we would win. At half-time, the Gaffer was pretty relaxed with the 1–1 scoreline. He said, "You are better than this lot. Now go out and show it."

Phil came on in the second half. I said, "What's happening?"

"I'm in midfield," he said.

I thought, "Oh no, here we go!"

Phil's last midfield performance was at home against York in 1995. We lost 3-0 and he got subbed at half-time! Phil used to play in midfield as a youngster, but he hadn't played there for a few years. To be fair, he did an unbelievable job tonight.

Deschamps got sent off, but it was Montero who was throwing his weight around and he didn't get booked. I don't understand it. Nowadays, you can get sent off for throwing the ball away but get away with a two-footed tackle. Despite the provocation, we try to keep our comments to a minimum. The Gaffer fines us if we get booked for dissent. Silly yellow cards can cost you in later games.

Giggsy was flying after the break. I love watching him when he's like that. He scares the life out of defenders. Italian defenders have a reputation for being the best, but Ryan made them look as beatable as the rest of us. It was fitting that he scored the match-clinching goal.

When we got back to the dressing room after the game, it was full of directors. If we lose, they usually wait five minutes to let Alex Ferguson have a chat. We were all delighted to win this game. We could see that the Gaffer's mind was always on Juventus over the past fortnight.

Champions' League / Old Trafford / Att: 53,428

Manchester United 3
Schmeichel, G Neville, Irwin, Pallister, Berg, Beckham, Butt (Scholes), Johnsen, Giggs, Solskjaer (P Neville), Sheringham
Scorers: Sheringham, Scholes, Giggs
Juventus 2
Peruzzi, Birindelli, Ferrara, Montero, Dimas, Pecchia (Luliano), Deschamps, Tacchinardi (Pessotto), Zidane, Inzaghi, Del Piero (Amoruso)
Scorers: Del Piero, Zidane

Thursday 2 October

GARY: The atmosphere at training was decidedly happier than last Thursday after we drew at Chelsea, or Sunday after Leeds. Everyone's happy. The mood of the whole club is based around the first-team results.

Friday 3 October

GARY: Trained in the morning and then went to have something to eat with Becks at a restaurant in Manchester. We always used to go for a meal: me, Becks, Chris Casper and Ben Thornley, every Friday before a game. If we've got nothing on, we still try and do it.

I see Martin Edwards, the club Chairman, is quoted in the papers in favour of re-introducing some terracing at Old Trafford. I'd like it if the lower tiers on all sides of the ground were standing areas. People do say the atmosphere is variable. Perhaps some limited safe standing areas would improve it, who knows. But the law doesn't permit terracing.

Saturday 4 October   Manchester United 2 Crystal Palace 0

GARY: An hour and a half before kick off, the Gaffer spoke to us.

"You did really well on Wednesday," he explained, "but if you want to lift yourself on to a higher level, you must perform Wednesday and

Saturday." We can't have listened to him – we didn't perform at all today! It was Peter Schmeichel who saved us with two brilliant one-on-one saves against Lombardo. Peter is the best footballer in his position that I've ever played with. You talk about Eric Cantona, Bryan Robson, Roy Keane, Paul Ince and all our players playing now – great players, but Peter is untouchable in world football in his position.

Teddy scored. He's had trouble with rib injury, and forwards at United are put under big pressure to score, so it's great that he's got two in two games now.

Arsenal beat Barnsley 5-0. Bergkamp is flying. If they keep that up till the end of the season, they'll win it, but even in my short experience, that doesn't happen. When we won the Double, Newcastle were brilliant until February, but their bad spell came at the end. You're better off coming good on the home straight and that's the habit we've got. It puts extra pressure on the likes of Newcastle and Liverpool when they see us hitting form, because they know we've won the Premiership before.

In the evening, Phil and I went out for a meal with Mum, Dad and David Beckham's family.

Premiership / Old Trafford / Att: 55,143

Manchester United 2
Schmeichel, G Neville, Berg, Pallister, P Neville (Irwin), Beckham, Johnsen (Poborsky), Butt, Scholes, Sheringham, Giggs
Scorer: Sheringham, Hreiderson (own goal)
Crystal Palace 0
Miller, Edworthy, Linighan (Freedman), Roberts, Hreiderson, Gordon, Lombardo (Zoher), Fullarton, Rodger, Ndah,
Warhurst

Sunday 5 October

GARY: I got up late. Ex-Man City pro Paul Lake's testimonial kicks off at two o'clock and I was relaxing. My match preparation consisted of eating a couple of bacon butties. I deserved it – I've had a tough week.

The Boss included five England lads in the side – me, Becks, Scholesy, Butty and Phil. The Gaffer likes to put out a good side for ben-efit matches. The game finished 2-2. Alex Notman, our young Scottish striker, scored. He's a really good prospect and plays in a similar position to Paul Scholes – who also scored, with a great scissors kick.

The England lads came off after twenty-five minutes as planned and headed for Manchester Airport for a four o'clock flight. We checked in at Burnham Beeches at six.

The FA has put me in the same room for the past two and a half years as I'm superstitious. I used to share with Becks, but I could never get on the phone and I like my early nights. Becks is the worst one for using the phone – he's frightening! I shared a room with him in Georgia for a whole week. Three weeks later, I picked up my wage slip at the club. It had an £800 deduction under "FA telephone bill", though I hadn't used the phone, so I phoned the FA to complain.

"Your room telephone bill for the two of you for that week was £1,600," they said

"There's nothing I can do about it this time," I told them, "but next time will you put me in a room on my own."

God knows where he was ringing that week. The Outer Hebrides or somewhere. To be fair, he's away from his girlfriend and family a lot and it's the only way he can talk to them. Becks and I laughed about it, but since then my England stays have been a lot cheaper and I've had my full nine hours.

Monday 6 October

GARY: Seventeen-year old Michael Owen trained with the England squad today. Rio Ferdinand and Frank Lampard have joined us a couple of times in the past. Glenn Hoddle's policy is to give young players with potential some valuable experience.

Given the way he's performing, I'm sure Michael will make his debut before his next birthday. His pace is frightening. He's apparently just signed a £10,000-a-week contract. I was on £39.50 at that age!

At a press conference afterwards, I said that man for man we've got better players than Italy. For their Zola, we've got Sheringham; for their Casiraghi, we've got Wright and for their Albertini we've got Beckham.

In the afternoon Becks, Teddy, Butty, Scholesy and I played golf – a sixball! We got a good telling-off from the golf club secretary afterwards.

Tuesday 7 October

GARY: Me, Pally, Butty, Scholesy and Phil crammed into the security guard's car and went to Sainsbury's this morning. We all got loads of sweets, chocolate and magazines for Italy. Experience tells us you've got to get stocked up when you go abroad.

My press conference comments have made the headlines today. Some players have what I call a 'camera talk', but I think you are better off just telling the truth. I said what I feel. We are as good as Italy in every department and if we perform to our ability, we will win.

Wednesday 8 October

GARY: Before leaving Burnham Beeches for the training ground, we had a team meeting. On the way I saw the Boss in reception and had the feeling he was waiting for me. I started to sweat – I knew it wasn't good news. Glenn beckoned me into his room and just said, "I'm leaving you out." He explained that he felt Gareth Southgate was more suited to deal with their aerial threat, and reassured me that I'd done nothing wrong. In a strange way I wish he'd just told me I wasn't playing, full-stop. Neither Alex Ferguson nor Glenn Hoddle need to apologise for leaving me out.

I walked down to the team meeting, sat down next to Philip and told him. Glenn hadn't had a word with Phil, so I thought he must be in the side. But when the team was announced, neither Phil nor Scholesy were in. You can't afford to show your disappointment because there are thirteen other disappointed players. If you whinge, people start to question your character. After all, the whole squad has a common aim – to qualify.

The choice of Paul Ince as captain was a surprise only in that the Gaffer didn't go for Tony Adams. Tony's presence before, during and at half-time in a game is amazing. Having said that, Paul is someone I look up to. He helped me considerably when I first made the Manchester United team. He is one of the best midfielders in Europe.

We were told to be very discreet about the selection. Before the

Switzerland game in Euro '96, Terry Venables announced the team on Tuesday and it was in the paper two days before the game. Sometimes players tell their agents the team and the line-up gets out. I know one player has been been warned about that.

PHIL: I was gutted I wasn't in the team; I had been looking forward to this game for ages. Glenn had a word with Scholesy and I after the meeting, which was nice of him.

I've never seen anyone run out of a team meeting in tears when they aren't picked, but some people need half an hour on their own to gather their thoughts and get back to normal. On the coach to Bisham Abbey, Gary, Scholesy, Nicky and I were all a bit quiet at first, but there was still a chance of us getting on as subs so we weren't too downcast.

In training, us subs had a half-hour practice game with Glenn Hoddle. We had to whip our bibs off ten minutes before the press arrived so as not to give away the team.

GARY: We arrived in Rome in the afternoon. The hotel was on the outskirts where no one could get at us. Gazza said he used to come here for three days when Lazio lost. It was like a prison camp. The intention is to focus our minds for the game, but it's a fine line between that and boring us to death, stuck in a hotel for thirteen hours a day. There weren't enough rooms for us to have our own, so I shared with Phil. He complained!

We have brought our own chef with us even though we are in Italy, of all places. I suppose it's to make sure they don't poison our food!

Thursday 9 October

PHIL: In training, the subs impersonated Italy and attacked England's back five of Beckham, Southgate, Campbell, Adams and Le Saux. We paid particular attention to how to cope with Italy's danger man Zola (played by Scholesy) dropping off deep.

In the evening, we watched video 'highlights' of Italy's 0-0 game against Georgia and our game against Italy at Wembley. Clearly, they like to play a lot of diagonal balls over the right centre back. Ironically, the Wembley footage showed Gary had headed all the high balls clear!

Friday 10 October

PHIL: We trained at the Olympic Stadium. John Gorman was snapping at everybody because the players were moaning and not training properly. The lads were probably just a little uptight.

Before the session, Glenn Hoddle told us to smile and show the Italians we were in relaxed mood. Glenn also said to Becks, who's had a cold but is now almost completely over it, "Look, we're only training for forty-five minutes. After half an hour we'll give you a shout and you just go in and get your shower. We'll say you're struggling with the flu." During the session, Gareth Southgate just walked around the pitch, though he'd passed a fitness test that morning with flying colours. It was pure kidology.

Saturday 11 October   Italy 0 England 0

GARY: At the lunchtime team talk, Glenn Hoddle said he was confident we would get the result. He told Gazza, "I know it's going to be difficult for you, going back to Italy and wanting to prove yourself., but just play the game and don't get involved."

On the tactical side, we know we can't defend all night because eventually they will break you down. The Boss encouraged us to make blindside runs behind their full back or wing back and pass the ball. I expect the Italians will match our three in midfield, with Zola in a central role.

PHIL: Glenn Hoddle's talk is more to do with motivation than football. It's strange when you hear Glenn Hoddle giving a "Land Of Hope and Glory" speech, but he got everyone fired up. Glenn comes across as a very thoughtful person – I've rarely seen him get angry, and even when he has he's still totally under control.

The Boss ends by saying, "Right lads, go in and enjoy it." Gazza always has to have the last word. He stands up and shouts, "Come on England."

GARY: On the coach, I sat next to David Beckham as usual. It's a bit of a superstition. At United, I've sat in in the aisle seat with David at the window for about three years. The best way to relax if you are feeling nervous before a big game is by talking to your best friends to take your mind off it. This coach journey was much quieter than usual. Even people like Gazza and Ian Wright were quiet.

PHIL: When we got in sight of the stadium lights, we started to see the England fans and that was probably when I felt most disappointed. My mum, my dad, my girlfriend and her parents had all come over and I wasn't playing.

We were jeered as we got out on to the pitch to have a look around, so we walked towards the England fans. It was boiling, a really muggy night, and the atmosphere was brilliant. I turned to Nicky Butt and we both spoke at the same time: "I'm gutted."

GARY: Because I wasn't in the team, I felt more relaxed than I normally would before such a big game. You've got to prepare the same way, but I didn't have quite the same nervous tension inside. The Boss tapped me on the shoulder about ten minutes before the lads went out. "Make sure you're tuned in," he said. Even at half-time he came up to me and said we might have to go to back four.

Just before we went out for the kick-off, Tony Adams clicked his fingers and started shouting, "Let's be winners out there, let's be winners." It really got everyone focussed. Tony is a real leader. When we're playing at Wembley, Tony will shout, "It's our turf, don't let them come here and enjoy it!" The first time I heard him, I didn't know whether to be scared or laugh, but now I appreciate that it helps you to concentrate.

All the lads put in great performances. In the first half, I was off the bench when Becks went close. If there is one person on the team you want the ball to fall to outside the box, it's him. Afterwards, he told me it had bobbled as he was about to hit it and the ball just cleared the bar.

On the bench, I was sitting next to the team doctor, John Crane, a lovely bloke of about sixty five. When Incey came off needing four stitches in a head wound, he and John ran down to the changing rooms, which were at least two hundred yards away. A minute later, the Doc came running back gasping for air. He'd forgotten the dressing room key – the kit man was sitting on the bench with it! The Gaffer was going mad, snapping at the kit man about the key, and at the doctor because he didn't have any stitches with him on the bench.

Eventually, Incey came back on the pitch with his head bandaged. Soon after, the doctor reappeared looking blue. I thought he was going to have a heart attack if he didn't relax, so I gave him a drink.

Sometimes when you're a sub, you don't want to get on. 0-0 with ten minutes is such a time. If I went on and didn't adapt immediately to the pace of the game, it could have cost us a place in the World Cup Finals.

PHIL: I never thought I was going to get on, once I saw how well we were playing. Our back five were superb. I always felt we were comfortable, even when Italy were on the attack.

I can't deny I felt a little bit on the outside, but when we won I couldn't have given a damn. When the final whistle blew, Butty was standing near the bench so I hugged him and then Teddy and the manager. Like Gary, I made a point of congratulating everyone who played. They deserved all the credit. In the dressing room, Ian Wright just collapsed on the floor in floods of tears. No one laughed. He's thirty three years old and it means the world to him.

GARY: When the game ended and the lads were running over to the fans, I felt that I should take a back seat. There was no jealousy at all on my part. I was just happy that I've got a chance of playing in a World Cup Finals tournament.

Euro '96 was the best three weeks of my life. It was just the most unbelievable feeling. Stuart Pearce said to me at the time, "You'll never get that again. I've played in a World Cup, but it was nothing like that, because it wasn't in England." Unless England gets the World Cup in 2006 (and it's touch and go whether I'll still be involved then), Euro '96 was probably my only chance to play in a major championship in my own country.

Later, I knocked on the Italians' dressing room door. A lad opened it and I asked if he could get Maldini to sign the Italy shirt I'd swapped with him at the final whistle. Instead, Paolo Maldini waved at me and said, "Come in". He shook my hand, said "Well done" and his Dad, their manager, came over and did the same. He signed the shirt "To Gary" and shook my hand again.

Maldini sets the standard for defenders around the world. He's twenty nine, he's got eighty-four caps and he's played in something like three World Cups. He's got three European Cup medals and four Italian championships. When you say Italian, you think Maldini.

I thought to myself, "He wouldn't have been let into our dressing room if we had lost." A different mentality completely. Even when we were waiting by the coach, the Italian players were walking past and congratulating us. Philip asked Angelo Di Livio for his Italian cap and he gave it him, no problems. You just think to yourself, "Deary me, so relaxed!" We seem to be more despondent in those situations. I suppose this match wasn't their last chance saloon. There are still the play-offs.

We shouldn't get too carried away, either; I believe England should always be in the World Cup Finals. The great achievement will be to reach the final or win the competition. Then we can go barmy.

The coach was a lot noisier on the way to the airport. Gazza was making us laugh with stories about his time in Italy. He was delighted that he'd come back to Rome and proved a point.

PHIL: When we got on the plane, the press, the Under–21s and the FA delegates were already there. We usually have to wait for the press as they file their reports, but this time they'd got there first and drunk all the beer. There were a few unhappy players, until the champagne started flowing. We didn't act like fools on the flight home though. When Rio Ferdinand was dropped for drink-driving, it was a warning to all of us.

Glenn wasn't involved with the celebrations on the plane. Most managers like to keep themselves to themselves when travelling, but John Gorman came down and had a laugh with us.

World Cup qualifer / Rome

Italy 0
Perruzi, Costacurta, Nesta, Cannavaro, Maldini (Benarrivo), D Baggio, Albertini, Di Livio, Inzaghi (Chiesa), Zola (Del Piero), Vieri
England 0
Seaman, Campbell, Adams, Southgate, Beckham, Batty, Ince, Le Saux, Gascoigne (Butt), Sheringham, Wright

Sunday 12 October

PHIL: Thinking back to last night's game, the Italians' tactics were all wrong. Despite knowing that we would play three in midfield, they only put two in there for a large part of the game. Terry Venables and Alex Ferguson drum it into you that you must match man for man in midfield or you're never going to control the game.

There seemed a little bit of a worry on the bench among the coaches that Beckham was isolated against Zola early on, because David's not the most defensive player in the world. Actually I felt that was a blessing in disguise. As long as Zola, their best player by far, was out on the left wing, he wasn't going to be firing balls into the back of our net. What could he do on the left wing? Even if he beat Becks, our three centre halves were able to handle crosses all night. It was the equivalent of the United of two years ago playing Eric Cantona out on the right wing. Italy took away their biggest threat by playing him in a position where he couldn't do maximum damage.

GARY: The other headlines today concern the trouble on the terraces in Rome last night.

I watched the terraces more than the actual game in the first half. It looked like the police were just laying into the English fans with batons. The Italian fans were throwing things at the England fans, but if you start charging the police, which I saw a number of our fans doing, you're asking for trouble. I was thinking to myself, "You're going to get a good beating there." They let the other England fans down. If they had just stood still and said, "What are you doing to us?" I don't think the police would have lashed out.

Probably only fifty people go looking for trouble, but 12,000 English fans get tarred with the same brush. On the other hand, probably only about twenty Italian police were actually hitting out, and the whole Italian police get a bad name.

It wasn't the worst situation I've seen. That was in Porto last March. There were 10,000 Man United fans in Porto, but when we went out for our warm-up there were just a thousand sprinkled around the away end. I went over because I'd not seen my dad and he's always in the ground twenty-five minutes before kick-off. I always wave to my dad before every game; it's a superstition. When I reached the perimeter fence, I found grown men crying. They were shouting, "They're beating us to death outside." I saw Eric Cantona's dad and shouted Eric over. He physically pulled his dad out.

Even when the game started, my head was full of what might be going on. Finally, I saw Dad in the main stand, which reassured me, but when we got on the coach afterwards, we heard a rumour (which turned out to be untrue) that three people had died. I felt sick. You think to yourself, What does it matter whether we've qualified for the European semi final?

3
Goal glut

Monday 13 October

GARY: Thankfully, I won't be going to Ipswich for the Coca-Cola Cup match. With an injury, a five-hour coach ride is not what you want.

We've finalised our compensation deal with Pony and we're out of contract as of today. In the evening, the Adidas rep finally rang up to say that they don't want to offer us a boot contract. Their budget won't allow them to do it this year.

They came to us last Tuesday and said they'd be interested in a five-year contract, but the guy said he'd need authorisation from Germany. He said he'd call us back later in the week, but he's avoided my dad's calls since Thursday night. I don't like it when people hide behind their secretaries.

When I was seventeen, I signed my first contract with Adidas for £300 worth of wholesale clothing and boots. The year after they came to me with the same contract, but they wanted two match tickets per game so I moved to Asics. They've lost me twice now.

David Beckham endorses Adidas. He was surprised they were offering us a contract in the first place. "I thought I had taken all their money!" he said.

Phil and I were disappointed. Adidas would have been a good choice. Now we are switching our attention to Diadora and Nike, who have both made good offers. Kappa have also told us not to sign with anyone until we speak to them, but I can't get past the fact that they sponsor Man City!

Philip and I tend to get offered joint contracts, because we're easier to market as "the Neville brothers". Though if either of us is ever offered individual work, we consider it.

Tuesday 14 October   Ipswich Town 2 Manchester United 0

PHIL: The Coca-Cola Cup's stature seems to be falling. I think players like Karel and Ben Thornley were the most disappointed that we lost. Now we're out of the Coca-Cola Cup, they'll have fewer opportunities to play in the first team.

Coca-Cola Cup Round Three / Portman Road / Att: 22,173

Ipswich Town 2
Wright, Stockwell, Taricco, Williams (Stein), Mowbray, Cundt, Dyer, Holland, Matthie, Dozzell, Petta (Milton)
Scorers: Mathie, Taricco
Manchester United 0
Schmeichel, Curtis, P Neville, May, McClair, Johsen (Irwin), Poborsky, Mulryne (Eric Nevland), Cole, Cruyff, Thornley (Scholes)

Saturday 18 October   Derby County 2 Manchester United 2

GARY: Despite being 2-0 down at half-time, it wasn't as if Derby hammered us. Giggs had a goal ruled offside and Teddy missed a penalty. At half-time, the Boss said that if we got another penalty Denis Irwin would take it.

Baiano scored from a rebound after Peter made a great save from Wanchope's header. It was the same as the goal we conceded against Leeds. We need to practice defending against free-kicks played deep to the far post.

I made a bad mistake for Wanchope's goal. He pulled my shirt first and spun me round. I ended up diving in near the half-way line and, to make it even worse, he went all the way through and scored. The manager blasted me at half-time for not getting goalside. Wanchope is awkward to play against; he's very gangly and his arms flail about all over the place. He scored a great goal last year at Old Trafford on his debut.

Andy Cole came on and grabbed an equaliser and everyone was happy for him. He looked really sharp and I think he will play against Feyenoord on Wednesday.

PHIL: I feel sorry for Teddy. It's a difficult job following Eric Cantona, especially when it comes to penalties. Eric had the best penalty technique I've ever seen. His trick was to wait until the goalkeeper moved and then put it the other way. No matter how late the goalkeeper left it, Eric never panicked. To concentrate on the goalkeeper and the ball at the same time is so difficult – I tried it and it seems impossible. To be fair to Teddy, the new rules allowing goalkeepers to move about on their goal-line before the kick is taken has made penalty-taking even more difficult.

Premiership / Pride Park / Att: 30,014

Derby County 2
Poom, Rowett, Dailly, Laursen, Powell, Van Der Laan (Hunt), Carsely, Trollope, Sturridge, Baiano (Burton), Wanchope / Scorers: Baiano, Wanchope
Manchester United 2
Schmeichel, G Neville, Berg, Pallister, Irwin (P Neville), Beckham, Butt (Johnsen), Scholes (Cole), Giggs, Sheringham, Solskjaer / Scorers: Sheringham, Cole

Monday 20 October

GARY: Describing my performance against Derby County, the *Guardian* reporter wrote: "Gary Neville spent the first half striking attitudes reminiscent of those confronted by papier maché aliens in The Outer Limits." I think he means I got roasted by Wanchope.

The Boss went to see Feyenoord play on Sunday and reported back that they weren't anything special. He told us not to fall into the trap of playing too slowly at the back. We did that against Fenerbahçe last year and lost, though we had dominated possession. We're to play it like a Premiership game, keep the tempo high and get the ball forward quickly. If you win a few corners and free-kicks early on, you get the crowd excited and make the most of home advantage.

Wednesday 22 October   Manchester United 2 SC Feyenoord 1

PHIL: Just like the day we played Juventus, we went in for massages from three o'clock, but the atmosphere was more relaxed. Ronny Johnsen had failed his fitness test which meant I was playing. In the team talk, the Boss joked that all our centre-halves had gone soft and that he wasn't going to buy any more Norwegians.

I was very confident we were going to win. With Scholes and Giggs in midfield, I thought we'd be too strong for them. Sure enough, we dominated the game, but we missed too many chances. At least the goals are going in more freely than last year, but it got a bit nervy in the last ten minutes when they got it back to 2-1.

Just before we went out, the Boss said to Ryan, "I think you can drift a bit tonight and tuck in behind the strikers." As instructed, Ryan came in off the left wing where he wasn't getting much joy against big Van Gobbel. Ryan is experienced enough now to adjust his tactics.

Gary played centre-back alongside Pally tonight. I think that is definitely his best position and Pally enjoys playing next to him. My brother organises everyone and, although people talk about his lack of height, no one won headers against him tonight.

Our aim now is to win our next two European games and make the result in Turin irrelevant.

Champions' League / Old Trafford / Att: 53,188

Manchester United 2
Schmeichel, G Neville, Irwin, Pallister, P Neville, Beckham, Butt, Scholes, Giggs, Cole (Solskjaer), Sheringham /
Scorers: Scholes, Irwin (pen)
SC Feyenoord 1
Dudek, Picun, Van Gobbel, Schuiteman, Van Wonderen, Graff, Bosvelt, Van Gastel, Van Bronckhorst (Korneev),
Sanchez (Boateng), Connolly (Vos) / Scorer: Vos

Friday 24 October

PHIL: According to press reports, Feyenoord players are claiming that David Beckham tried to 'do' Van Bronckhorst. That is absolute rubbish. If you set out to kick people you wear studs, but David wears moulds. Eric Cantona did too and if you get tackled by moulds it's not as severe. David Beckham wouldn't know how to attack a player.

We wore Nike boots on Wednesday and today there is a story in the papers saying the Neville Brothers and Paul Scholes have signed a contract with them. Not true – and the figures quoted in the paper were far from accurate.

Played a five-a-side Olds v Youngs. There were so many young ones and so many injuries that Ryan had to play for the Olds. He's always sworn he'd never do that, but judging by his performance, he was still on our side in spirit. He kept missing chances on purpose. The Olds won't have him back now!

| Saturday 25 October | Manchester United 7   Barnsley 0 |

GARY: A great win, and not just because of the scoreline. When Pally went off, the back four was made up of me, Philip, John Curtis and Ronnie Wallwork who are all twenty two and under. In midfield were Beckham, twenty two, Giggs, twenty three, Butt, twenty two, and Scholes, twenty two. Up front we had Cole and Solskjaer at twenty six and twenty four respectively. Only Peter Schmeichel at thirty three lifted the average age to twenty three. That's got to be one of the youngest Premiership teams ever. It's not far off our Youth team line-up of three years ago.

I was next to League debutant John Curtis in the dressing room before the game, and he asked me about my debut. It was in the last League game of 1993/94 against Coventry, Bryan Robson's final game for United. I had been in the crowd the day Robbo signed, and to make my debut in my hero's last game made it even more memorable. Actually, I don't think the Gaffer was too impressed with my first performance – I didn't even train with the first team for the first two months of the next season! I wondered if I had done something wrong. Eric Harrison, the Youth team coach who I always went to for advice, said I wasn't training with my usual effort at the start of 1994/95. I didn't agree, but I just worked even harder. Within three weeks I was back in the first team squad and I ended up playing thirty games that season.

I count my real League debut as Crystal Palace at home in November 1994, because I wasn't really picked for the Coventry game on merit. United had already won the League and the Gaffer was just resting players for the Cup Final the following week.

When I joined United, I wasn't the kind of lad of whom you'd say, "He'll make a first-team player," but a game against Sunderland in the 1992 Youth Cup was vital. The Youth Cup is a massive trophy for apprentices and I knew that game could trigger two good years or make things difficult for me if I played badly. Luckily, I played really well. I felt that this Crystal Palace game was the same – I had to produce or it would put more doubts in my mind (and the manager's) about whether I'd make it.

I just told John Curtis to go for it and he had a dream debut. He made a couple of crunching tackles which got the crowd on his side, and that's important. The fans play a massive part at Manchester United. If they don't take to you, it affects your confidence and eventually it will reach the manager. But John has seen me, Philip, Butty, Scholes, all of those lads he played with in the youth team, establishing ourselves in the first team. That must give you the confidence that you will cope.

PHIL: Andy Cole was razor sharp today. If I could pick one person to score every game, I would choose Andy Cole just to shut everyone up. We've won two Championships and an FA Cup with Andy Cole in the team and you can't achieve all that by carrying players. His scoring record for Manchester United is one goal in two, which any other striker would be happy with, but because it's Andy Cole they expect three in two.

He got some terrible stick after the Feyenoord game. In the papers this morning the headlines all said Cole would be axed. I think that made the Boss even more determined to play him. He would never desert a player like that and Andy repaid him with a hat-trick.

Ole Gunnar Solskjaer didn't score, but he set up three good goals today. Ole and Andy Cole always play well together. Some players just have an understanding. Maybe Andy and Eric Cantona didn't, nor Brian McClair and Mark Hughes, but Ole Gunnar and Andy just click. Their movement is the key; they're both so quick and take up dangerous positions.

Last season Southampton beat us 6-3 and at the end of the game their fans were jeering our every pass. You don't forget things like that. Even at 7-0 today, we were still professional, and I think Barnsley's players appreciated that.

GARY: Teddy Sheringham was rested today. The Gaffer will chop and change the team at this stage. In the two months at the end of the season, if you aren't picked for a big match it means you're dropped. He can't say he's resting you for a European Cup quarter final.

At Man United, you have to accept that you won't play in every game. Only the likes of Schmeichel and Pallister are certain starters if they are fit. Eric Cantona was another player you couldn't leave on the bench. Ironically though, Eric's retirement has given us more flexibility. We've got more balance, we're maturing and there's plenty of pace in the team. I think we'll be a better side this year, although we've still got to prove it.

The Gaffer said well done afterwards, but not much else. He doesn't say too much when we win. It's when he feels we aren't giving our best, win, lose or draw, that he has a few things to say. The experienced players say he's calmed down a lot and we've got him at his best. I tell them it's their own fault he was like that. Us young lads have calmed him down, because we don't give him any trouble!

Premiership / Old Trafford / Att: 55,142

Manchester United 7
Schmeichel, G Neville, Pallister (Wallwork), P Neville, Curtis, Butt, Beckham (Poborsky), Giggs, Scholes (Cruyff), Solskjaer, Cole
Scorers: Cole 3, Giggs 2, Scholes, Poborsky
Barnsley 0
Watson, Eaden, Sheridan, De Zeeuw, Redfearn, Thompson (Bosancic), Bullock, Hristov (Hendrie), Krizan (Moses), Barnard, Ward

PHIL: In the evening, I took my girlfriend to a fish and chip shop I like in Blackpool. We were waiting for a table when I noticed twenty kids looking through the window and screaming because they'd seen me! I had some photos in my car so I went outside and said, "Look, if I give you my autograph will you be quiet and mind my car?"

So while we were eating our fish and chips, I had twenty kids outside surrounding my car. That's what I call a car alarm!

Monday 27 October

GARY: Day off. I played golf with Phil, Scholesy and Butty. The manager doesn't always like us to play. I think it started when players had injury problems after playing a lot of golf. The Boss banned it for the last three months of last season, but it's all right this early on.

Personally, I can't see the problem with playing a nice, relaxing round on your day off. Some footballers go out and drink and gamble. Golf doesn't really tire me out because we usually use buggies. I would never play within four days of a match.

Tuesday 28 October

PHIL: We had a practice match at The Cliff for trialist Salou Lassisi, a French central midfielder, so the Boss and Kiddo could have a look at him. Alex Ferguson brought him into in the dressing room a few days ago and everyone was thinking, "Who's that?" The Gaffer introduced Salou to everybody and we all shook his hand. The next day, Salou came into the changing room alone and started to walk round and shake everyone's hand again. He thought it was our daily ritual!

Trialists tend to just appear without warning. I've heard very confused messages about Salou. Apparently, he has signed for both Parma and Juventus! I think he's only nineteen, but he's really muscular – his calves were the size of my thighs. He was not as quick as I thought he might be, but he was very composed on the ball.

GARY: Philip is one of the most welcoming people to new players – he's foreign-daft. Scholesy is sure Phil's a foreigner himself. He went out with Jordi Cruyff last night. I'm sure they bored each other to death!

PHIL: In the afternoon, all the players went out to a bar in Worsley for a 'team meeting'. It's basically a chance once a month for the first team and reserve lads to go out together and have a drink and a laugh together – a bonding session! There were only a couple of absentees, including Roy Keane. I talked to him this morning and he's going in for some operations on his knee next Monday. He has quietened down recently. I think it's starting to hit him now, especially with Ireland playing tommorrow night and the European Cup matches coming up. I wouldn't wish what's happened to Roy on anyone.

Wednesday 29 October

GARY: Phil did a horrendous tackle on Nicky Butt during the prac-

c Cantona: "Eric's name has not been mentioned once among the players. Never.
's gone and the club's moved on." *Gary*

mily and friends' support: (left to right) Ted Beckham, dad Neville, mum Jill, Sandra Beckham
d sister Tracey.

Early promise: Can you spot Gary Neville, Nicky Butt and Paul Scholes in this Boundary Park Juniors line-up?

Captaining United's Youth team to victory in the 1995 FA Youth Cup Final

September 1997, England v Moldova: "Standing in the tunnel listening to Elton John's 'Candle in the Wind', I felt overwhelmed by it all – I was shivering." *Phil*

Vicky and Becks listen to some good advice on a Slovakian airstrip!

11 August 1997: "I went to Old Trafford this morning and bumped into Henning Berg in the toilet. 'All right there, have you signed for us or something?' 'Yes, I've just done it. It's all been hush-hush,' he replied." *Phil*

13 September 1997 v West Ham (h): "David Beckham was on the end of some disgusting chant from the West Ham fans about his girlfriend... After Keaney equalised, Becks, Roy and I ran over to them as if to say, 'Have some of that!' *Gary*

Ken Bates: "He's been quoted as saying that we are just a club from the slum-side of Manchester. To me, Chelsea could move their stadium to the middle of Harrods and win 15 championships on the trot, and even if you moved Old Trafford to downtown Beirut, they still wouldn't be as big as us." *Gary*

October 1997 v Juventus (h): "Giggsy was flying after the break... Italian defenders have a putation for being the best, but Ryan made them look as beatable as the rest of us." *Gary*

1 October 1997 v Juventus (h): "We were all delighted that we won. We could see that the Gaffer's mind was always on Juventus for the past fortnight." *Gary*

11 October 1997, Italy v England (a): "When the game ended and the lads were running over to the fans, I felt that I should take a back seat. There was no jealousy at all on my part." *Gary*

20 October 1997 v Derby (a): "Describing my performance, *The Guardian* reporter wrote: 'Gary Neville spent the first half striking attitudes reminiscent of those confronted by papier maché aliens in The Outer Limits.' I think it means I got roasted by Wanchope!" *Gary*

October 1997: England coach John Gorman and some of us United lads relax before the big game against Italy.

5 October 1997 v Barnsley (h): "If I could pick one person to score every game, I would choose
ndy Cole just to shut everyone up." *Phil*

28 October 1997:
"Roy's going in for some
operations next Monday on
his knee. He has quietened
down recently. I think it's
starting to hit him now,
especially with Ireland
playing tomorrow night and
the European Cup matches
coming up." *Phil*

5 November 1997 v Feyenoord (a): "Their striker, Cruz, intentionally elbowed me in the head. I got up and went face-to-face with him, which is unusual for me, but I was really annoyed." *Gary*

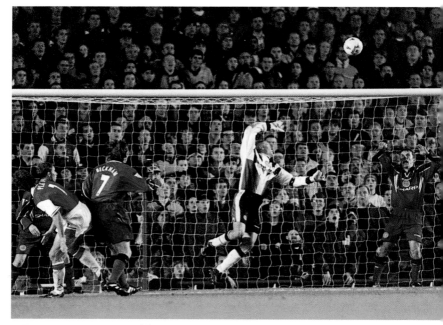

9 November 1997 v Arsenal (a): "David Platt grabbed the winner for Arsenal. I jumped on the line but the ball went over my head... It was agonising. Maybe I should have stopped it with my hand, but that would have been cheating." *Phil*

tice match this morning. It put them both in the treatment room, but they're OK now. The Gaffer stopped the tackling after that.

Phil was feeling a bit guilty. When I went into the treatment room, I told Butty, "You don't mess with the Nevilles!" It's a good job he had two bags of ice on his leg or he would have hit me.

In the afternoon, Phil, my dad and I had a chat about Nike's boot deal proposal. Nike are very interested, but the terms of the contract are very restrictive. We've come to realise that we want to go with a company where we have more personal input.

Afterwards, we rang Diadora and arranged a meeting with them tomorrow. We've said that if we can iron out a few things in the contract we will sign it. My Dad has been impressed with Diadora all along, and he thinks we should go with them. When it looked as if we were going to sign with Nike, Diadora told us that they understood, but if for any reason the deal fell through they would still be keen to have us. That sort of attitude made me sit up, because if I was in their position I would have said, "On yer bike".

Thursday 30 October

PHIL: The lads were winding up Becks today, saying that Denis should start taking our free-kicks again. Denis scored a beauty last night for Ireland. I asked Denis why he was hitting the ball so well again. He told me that two years ago, he had a problem with his knee and it stopped him whipping into the ball, but he's fine now. It's good to have one more option.

My shin was still a bit sore after yesterday, but both Nicky and I trained. Nicky was blaming me and promised to 'do' me. He was only joking ... I think.

GARY: Later, we met with Diadora. It's a relief finally to agree a deal. We will do a press conference next Friday.

We informed Nike, who told us not to sign anything and that they will get back to us, but by now nothing they could do would change our minds.

for club and country

Friday 31 October

PHIL: The issue of footballers betting on games is in the news again. Funnily enough, when we were playing golf at Rossendale on Sunday, the pro said they take bets on who gets the first throw-in in a game. He joked, "Tell Teddy to kick it out and we'll go fifty-fifty on the winnings!"

Saturday 1 November   Manchester United 6 Sheffield Wed 1

PHIL: Dave Fevre, the club physio, told me that Roy Keane won't be coming to many games because he finds it too hard to watch. Roy's in the gym every morning at half nine. He's working his tripe off.

Nicky Butt isn't pleased to hear that we've signed for the same boot company as him. "They shouldn't be signing dufus defenders like you," he said. "You'll bring the company name down!"

Sheffield Wednesday started really brightly. We played three up front and their full backs were pushing on. Because we didn't play with any wingers, their full backs got too much space, but moving Ole over to the left wing solved that. After the second goal, the two Italians up front, Carbone and Di Canio, started moaning. They were both taken off at half-time which was still a shock because they are probably Wednesday's best players. They've got all the skill in the world, but they like it purely to feet and when the going gets tough you need a target man.

It was nice to be 4-0 at half-time. The Boss came in and said, "Don't do anything silly, keep going for goals." Then he went to find out the other half-time scores. It was that relaxed, the same as for the Barnsley game. At the moment it feels like no one can beat us, but you mustn't take the opposition lightly.

Premiership / Old Trafford / Att: 55,202

Manchester United 6
Schmeichel, G Neville, P Neville, Pallister, Berg (Curtis), Beckham, Butt (McClair), Cole, Sheringham, Solskjaer, Scholes (Poborsky)
Scorers: Sheringham 2, Solskjaer 2, Cole, Newsome o.g.
Sheffield Wednesday 1
Pressman, Nolan, Pembridge, Newsome, Walker, Whittingham, Carbone (Nicol), Di Canio (Humphreys), Collins (Poric), Magilton, Rudi
Scorer: Whittingham

Monday 3 November

PHIL: When we arrived at The Cliff, we were told there was a meeting. That meant the team was going to be announced for Wednesday's game at Feyenoord, and Denis was fit so I wasn't confident. When Kiddo came down and said, "Ole, the Gaffer wants to speak to you," I thought, "He's not told me, so I should be all right." Then Kiddo came back and said, "You as well, Phil" so I knew I was gone.

I walked into the Boss's room and we just looked at each and burst out laughing. We both knew the score. He said how well I've been playing recently and not to worry about anything, I'll be back in.

"I just need to play Denis in the big games when he's fit," he said.

Even though we've won the last couple of games 6-1 and 7-0, and the team has put in some great performances with me in the side, I've just got to accept it. But it doesn't make it any easier. Although I'm only twenty, I've got more experience than many older Premiership players and I always want to play. But I understand the Boss's problem.

Tuesday 4 November

PHIL: We are staying in the same Rotterdam hotel that the team stayed in for the 1991 European Cup Winners' Cup Final. The Boss must think it's lucky.

We trained at the De Kuyp stadium. We always train about the same time of day as the match will be played, in order to get used to the flood-lighting and conditions. The night before an away European match is probably the best training session ever, because everyone is so excited and the ground is always good.

Unfortunately, I embarassed myself. I went to cross the ball with my left foot but my right foot touched the ball first, so I completely missed. Everyone collapsed on the floor laughing. The club video magazine guy was filming and he said it was his duty to show it. So I threatened him with legal action.

for club and country

Wednesday 5 November   Feyenoord 0 Manchester United 3

GARY: On the way to the stadium, our coach was halted by the police on the motorway. They said there was trouble outside the ground. I was worried about my dad so I rang him on my mobile, ignoring the rule about not using phone on the coach to games. Dad was already safely inside the ground. The Gaffer turned round: "Oi, Neville get that phone off! That's a fine." Close to a big game is not the time to start questioning him so I went quietly.

We finally arrived forty-five minutes before kick-off, which is almost unheard of. Phil, David and I always go out on to the pitch when we arrive and we didn't want to break our routine, so we nipped out there quickly. The ground was full and very hostile.

Coley's first goal gave the game a better look after a drab opening twenty-five minutes, during which the Boss yelled at us to up the tempo. From that moment they were struggling, because they had to come at us. The best teams I've played against, like Brazil and Juventus, keep it slow at the back but once they move it up into your half, their forward players are so quick and sharp. Feyenoord were sluggish and predictable.

There was a little luck involved in Andy's first goal, but the other two were classic moves. Simple, accurate passes opened them up. For the third, Giggs ran through on to Pallister's pass. The keeper rushed out but Ryan got there first. At the time I thought, "Go over Giggsy, go over," sure the ref would give a penalty. But he stayed on his feet, played the ball across goal and Andy was in the right place again. Coley thoroughly deserved his hat-trick; his all-round performance was fantastic.

Sadly, Andy's hat-trick was overshadowed by Feyenoord's brutal play. In the second half, their left back booted Becks up in the air. I ran over to David.

"Look out," I said. "I can tell by the way he kicked you there he wasn't going for the ball. If there's a fifty-fifty ball, don't go in for it. It's not worth getting injured."

"He's already told me, 'You've put two of our players out of the game, and now it's your turn,'" Becks replied.

Their striker Cruz intentionally elbowed me in the head. I got up and

56

went face-to-face with Cruz, which is unusual for me, but I was really annoyed. I was a bit naughty when we scored the third goal. I was standing next to Cruz and shouted "3-0" right in his face. He spat at me. The referee turned round and there was spit running down my face and Cruz was the only one near me, but the ref did nothing.

When Cruz was substituted, three of us gave him a wave on the way off and Cruz turned round and said, "See you in the tunnel." He wanted a fight afterwards! That's Sunday league stuff! I said to Nicky, "Hey, Butty. It could go off in the tunnel, I'm staying next to you!" Nicky doesn't cause trouble, but he'll always stick up for you.

I just don't understand why there were no sendings off all night. Bosvelt's tackle on Denis Irwin was scandalous, a leg-breaker. His injury put a dampener on the whole game. At the final whistle, the Gaffer was shouting, "Get off the pitch! Don't swap shirts with them! They don't deserve to wear the United shirt!" But I'd swapped with their number eleven before I heard him.

We are now as confident as we've ever been in Champions' League matches. We're learning how to play in Europe, with two sitting in midfield at all times, not over-committing and leaving us open to the counter-attack, unlike previous years.

I think we are looking a better team in Europe this year. Before, everyone was always looking to Eric Cantona to produce that bit of magic. Now we are all taking more responsiblity.

Champions' League / De Kuyp / Att: 45,000

SC Feyenoord 1
Dudek, Van Gobbel, Van Wonderen, Van Gastel, Schuiteman, Bosvelt (Zwijnenberg), Boateng, Van Bronckhorst, Graff (Claeys), Korneev, Cruz (Vos)
Scorer: Korneev
Manchester United 3
Schmeichel, G Neville, Irwin (P Neville), Pallister, Berg, Beckham, Butt, Giggs, Sheringham, Scholes (Poborsky), Cole (Solskjaer)
Scorer: Cole 3

Friday 7 November

GARY: The Gaffer called me into his office before training this morning. He said, "Every time I pick up a paper, you're in it!" I'm to stop talking to the press for a while. He also said not to speak to the media about Feyenoord or the Arsenal controversies of the past at our press conference today. He didn't want us to stir up old news before Highbury. I asked the Gaffer what I should do if they ask me a question like that.

"Just refer them to me from now on," he replied.

He's fined me again, but not for talking to the press. We trained at Littleton Road today and he gave me a lift back to The Cliff in his car. On the way, his mobile phone rang. "I thought that was yours for a minute, Neville. You're fined!" he laughed. "The staff Christmas party's coming up and I need some money for it!"

After training, I went over to Old Trafford for the Diadora boot deal press call. Ken Ramsden, the club's assistant secretary, confirmed that eight of us had been selected for the England squad including Andy Cole. The more the merrier.

At the Diadora do, we did that photo with loads of boots hanging around our necks – the one I'd said I'd never do because it's so corny!

Saturday 8 November

PHIL: In training we played Young v Old and we won 3-2, but Kiddo was playing for us so the oldies claimed it was a false victory. Kiddo was a help: an experienced old man at the back – and he gave us most of the decisions because he was the referee as well.

We were leaving for London at two o'clock. We packed enough for a week, because after the Arsenal game we are joining the England training camp. Because we'd organised a game of golf at Wentworth, Nicky, Scholesy, Gary and I took our golf bags as well. Fortunately, the Gaffer was away watching Wimbledon's game, so we got away with it.

Sunday 9 November   Arsenal 3 Manchester United 2

PHIL: Highbury has got a bit of character, with its marble entrance hall, and the pitch is perfect if a bit narrow. The dressing rooms even have a heated tile floor, so your feet feel boiling!

It was a weird game.

We went 2-0 down in the first half but we were battering them. Peter was unsighted for both of the goals; Anelka's shot went through Gary's legs so Peter didn't see it until very late, then Vieira's second also went through a crowd of bodies.

We got back into the game with two goals from Teddy. His second was a classic half volley. Teddy is genuinely growing to love the club and relishes the chance to play on the biggest stage. Once you put on that Man United shirt, other teams fear you, and that definitely helps.

At 2-1, we had a clear penalty when Scholesy was tripped in the box, but it wasn't given. I was also disappointed to get booked for a foul on Parlour, my fourth booking of the season. One more and I'm suspended.

At half-time, the manager said, "It's there for the winning, don't take your foot off the pedal." But for some reason that is exactly what we did and David Platt grabbed a winner for Arsenal. I jumped up on the line, but the ball went over my head. I was thinking, "I'm there, I'm there," but I just couldn't reach it. It was agonising. Maybe I should have stopped it with my hand, but that would have been cheating. Peter said to me after the game that he could have saved it, but he thought I had it covered.

The Boss wasn't happy that we sat back. He said that wasn't Man United. After our rivalry with Arsenal over the last couple of years, it is a bitter pill to swallow.

Premiership / Highbury / Att: 38,205

Arsenal 3
Seaman, Dixon, Winterburn, Vieira (Bould), Adams, Platt, Wright, Anelka (Wreh), Overmars, Parlour, Grimandi /Scorers: Anelka, Vieira, Platt
Manchester United 2
Schmeichel, G Neville, Pallister (Johnsen), P Neville, Berg, Butt, Beckham, Giggs (Solskjaer), Scholes, Sheringham, Cole Scorer: Sheringham 2

GARY: My hamstring felt tight. I went into the Arsenal physio room to see their physio, Gary Lewin, and Doc Crane, who do the same jobs for England. Gary Lewin examined me and said, "If I was an Arsenal player, I would want you at the club for a week getting treatment." The message was relayed back to Glenn Hoddle who had been at the game, but he had already left.

Twenty minutes later, we got a message back saying Glenn wanted us to report to Bisham Abbey, which was fine by me.

I said to Gary Lewin, "If you want me to report, I will report, no problem with that. If I can train, I'll train."

PHIL: It had been a heavy couple of weeks and Scholesy, Nicky, Gary and I fancied a night out to unwind. Teddy invited us to a private function at Epping Golf and Country club, but when we got there it was closed. We thought he'd stitched us up. We ended up getting a McDonalds and coming back to the hotel.

Monday 10 November

PHIL: As usual, the papers are full of controversy over an Arsenal v United game. They are even trying to hype up a feud between the Boss and Glenn Hoddle over Gary and Teddy being called up to the training camp.

Glenn wanted Gary and Teddy to meet up because on the Tuesday he was taking us all out for a meal to celebrate qualifying for the World Cup. He certainly wasn't demanding that they train with England if they are injured. I don't think Alex Ferguson knew about the celebration dinner to start with, but it was soon sorted out.

Golf at Wentworth was called off because Nicky took a bang on his shoulder at Highbury. So we dropped our bags off at Burnham Beeches and went shopping in London instead.

GARY: The police received a complaint from an Arsenal fan about Teddy Sheringham kissing his shirt after scoring yesterday. Ridiculous. Listen to the stick players get off fans. Can you imagine Teddy going to the police station after the game at Spurs in August and saying, "Excuse me, I'd like to make a complaint against the White Hart Lane crowd"?

Tuesday 11 November

PHIL: At breakfast, Teddy got slaughtered about Sunday night. He explained that he was in the golf club and we'd gone to the wrong door.

We had a brilliant meal and a few drinks at an Italian place in Slough in the evening. Les Ferdinand came along, but it was basically for everyone in the squad plus the admin and management team. Gazza ran the show. He sang and danced, but nobody else really got up. We left him to it.

Wednesday 12 November

GARY: In the morning, I had a phone call from Alex Ferguson asking me to come back to Manchester if I was still injured. I spoke to Glenn Hoddle, who immediately rang the Gaffer back to discuss the situation. Glenn explained that he was putting no pressure on me whatsoever to stay down and they eventually agreed I should go back to Manchester. Alex Ferguson was just protecting his players. He said to Glenn that if it was a World Cup qualifier he would have no qualms with me or Teddy staying down until Friday, but because it was a friendly match, he wanted me back. I got a flight back to Manchester with Teddy in the evening.

PHIL: I rang my mum, who told me that one of my closest friends, David Johnson, was moving from Bury to Ipswich in a £1 million deal. David and I went through the United youth system together until a cruciate injury stopped him in his tracks. His recovery was helped by his move to Bury and I think he's good enough to be in the Premiership now.

Dave's totally changed since his United days, when he was Jack the Lad, always going out. Now that he's married and has a kid, he goes home and does the housework.

Thursday 13 November

PHIL: John Curtis gave an interview to the *Daily Star*. He's away with the Under-21s and that's when the press try to catch you away from Alex Ferguson. He sounded very confident of ousting Gary from the United team. I wouldn't think Gary has any problem with it. He knows journalists can ask loaded questions, and that they get away with them with the inexperienced ones.

GARY: Youth players do receive some media skills training at United. I remember Jimmy Wagg, a presenter with local radio station GMR, coming in and talking to all the eighteen year olds. We did mock interviews for a game that we had lost. You had to pick your worst game ever for Man United and then Jimmy asked some awkward questions. It was nerve-racking – the rest of the lads were behind a partition in the room watching it on the screen – but it was a lot of help.

PHIL: In training at the England camp, we did an eleven v eleven. I was playing left wing back in the team without bibs, so although the Boss said not to read anything into it, I'm quietly confident that I'm in.

Scholesy joined our team in the second half and Andy Cole came in for Robbie Fowler. It looks like we'll play one up front with McManaman and Scholes just behind, so it's between Robbie and Andy for the striker spot. Glenn Hoddle hasn't said too much about Cameroon. I think he wants us to show that we can adapt to whatever they do.

Friday 14 November

PHIL: The team was announced in the afternoon. I was pleased to be picked in, but disappointed for Andy and Nicky who missed out. We all want to play. In training, we walked through a few set pieces, defending and attacking. The lads that haven't been picked just have to sit behind the goal and watch. You can see the disappointment on their faces. It's difficult for them when they've trained all week.

Later we watched a video of Cameroon. They looked a team with bags of talent, but disorganised. I'm very confident.

GARY: An article in the *Express* today claimed that for all the fuss about the use of 'social' drugs, like cannabis, in football, the thing the football authorities should really clamp down on are painkilling injections given to players by their clubs.

Our Manager would never put pressure on you to have an injection, but if it is a big game in the European Cup or World Cup, I would risk it. However, I would never have an injection in a muscle injury because you could rupture the muscle and do long-term damage.

I played in our European Cup quarter-final second-leg against Porto last year with a pain-killing injection. I'd had two stitches in my ankle the previous Saturday and the night before the game, it felt too sore to play. But I wanted to play so badly. Our Doctor said that he would be willing to give me a pain-killing injection because it wasn't a muscle injury so it wouldn't deteriorate. But I did find that I was running differently during that game and I developed another minor injury which meant I missed the following game against Everton.

The reporter gave examples of players who played in Euro '96 on painkillers and the problems they've had since. They probably felt the risk was worth taking, because it was a unique opportunity to play in a major tournament in England.

Saturday 15 November   England 2 Cameroon 0

PHIL: As the coach got close to Wembley, Glenn Hoddle put on a motivational video. It includes the Three Lions song and highlights from our previous games. It gets you pumped up.

There were 40,000 at the game, including Mum, Dad, Gran, Grandad and my girlfriend. Cameroon had some nice touches but didn't really threaten us. We gave the ball away sloppily at times, but scoring two goals just before half-time killed them.

At half-time, Glenn Hoddle said we had tried to take people on instead of just passing it easy in the first twenty minutes. When we played one- or two-touch football, we got past them with ease. Rio Ferdinand came on and made a great debut. He's an ice man. Nothing fazes him.

I was playing more like a winger than a wing back. Scholesy put me clean through, but my shot nearly hit the corner flag. I turned around and he was laughing at me! I'll have to watch a video of Paul's goal to see how he does it. His goal tonight was such a cool finish.

The one disappointing aspect of the match for me was when I heard the crowd sing, "Stand Up If You Hate Man U". What a load of rubbish. At the end, Becks asked me, "Were they singing what I thought they were singing?" There seemed to be a lot of West Ham fans in the crowd, because when Rio came on he got the biggest cheer of the night. That might explain it.

International friendly / Wembley

England 2
Martyn, Campbell, P Neville, Southgate (Ferdinand), Hinchcliffe, Beckham, Ince, Gascoigne (Lee), McManaman, Scholes (Sutton), Fowler
Scorers: Scholes, Fowler
Cameroon 0
Ongadze, Kalia, Song, Mimboe, Elchi, Foe, Ipoua (Bilong), Etame (Olembe), Wome, Mboma (Njitap), Job

Monday 17 November

PHIL: I asked Gary last Thursday to slip Kiddo the idea that I might have a day off today after all my international exertions. Kiddo sent the message back that the Gaffer was away and I should come in with a smile on my face, because we would be running. He's a fitness fanatic, Kiddo.

There are some rave newspaper reviews about Paul Scholes' performance on Saturday. Paul's class. He just comes in, does his job and goes home. No fuss whatsoever. He never mentions anything about his play unless you ask.

Glenn Hoddle has said there is no player like Paul in the world. He can play in five different positions with no bother. He even played a disciplined holding role against Feyenoord. He has such a clever football brain and people often don't realise how quick he is. Maybe not over fifty or sixty metres, but if we had a race over twenty yards he'd be one of the fastest.

Wednesday 19 November

PHIL: The news that Bosvelt will not be punished for his tackle on Denis Irwin came out today. It's amazing that UEFA received five reports about the match and not one of them mentioned it. That happens, and then some little incident like taking your shirt off when you are celebrating gets reported and you get suspended. Bizarre.

GARY: My ankle injury seems to have cleared up. I resumed normal training on Monday morning.

Kiddo thinks our defeat at Highbury was due to not having enough left in the tank in the last twenty minutes of the match. So this week, he's been running the socks off us. Today was the hardest we've worked this season, but we need it. United's success over the past few years is based on work done on the training pitch.

Thursday 20 November

PHIL: Alex Ferguson was back today. He's been away looking at a Chilean striker called Marcelo Salas. The papers are full of it, and I just read about it like everybody else. Fans often ask who we are going to sign, but we're always the last to know. Andy Cole has signed a new contract. I remember talking to him about it at Ipswich, saying that everyone else had got extended contracts and that he must be due soon. He laughed at me, because he still had two years left on his current one.

We are all on long contracts now. With the Bosman ruling, clubs are scared of players leaving for free. It's good business, and the players want it, because there is nothing better than having that security of a four- or five-year contract. Not many jobs can offer such security.

In the evening, Becks and I returned to The Cliff to coach the Under-13s. Paul McGuinness, who runs the School Of Excellence, asked us last week if we'd help out, and it was something we both wanted to do. Becks and me played on opposite sides. At first I was just fannying around but then I had to take it seriously because I was embarassing myself.

We did a questions and answers at the end and a few cheeky kids took the mickey out of my shot at Wembley on Saturday! I don't know, you do them a favour ...

Friday 21 November

GARY: After training I went shopping in Manchester with David Beckham. He tried to persuade me to buy a £8,500 Rolex watch. No chance – I've never worn a watch in my life! We spend our money on different things. He said I should live a little! I went back to Dave's house and met his two new rotweiler puppies. He's named them Snoop and Puffy after his favourite rap stars.

PHIL: We flew down to Wimbledon at 2.30. All the players and Kiddo have rooms on the same level in the hotel, and the Gaffer has his own suite – the Royal Suite, I think! It's the worst hotel for autograph hunters. There must have been at least twenty there. The hotel security tried to keep them in Reception, but most of them jumped in the lift with us.

There are a bunch of 'trainspotters' who follow us to hotels all around England. Wherever we go, they seem to be booked in there, the same faces. You don't mind kids, but these are grown men. They just wait outside your rooms with thick files of all the different team photos – they've got more magazines than my mum and dad – and it takes a quarter of an hour at a time to sign all their stuff. They don't seem embarassed to ask at all.

I don't sign autographs anymore. I don't mind signing one, but when one person wants you to sign twenty five or thirty, that's taking the mickey. I don't know whether they're just building up an autograph collection or making a career out of it. You see them at breakfast the next morning, so they must be getting something to afford an overnight stay. The manager is getting wise and usually asks the hotel staff to keep them away.

Saturday 22 November   Wimbledon 2 Manchester United 5

PHIL: 0-0 at half-time and the Boss had a bit of a go. He was not pleased with what we were doing defensively. We defend as a team so the criticism was directed at everyone. He also thought the service up to the front men was poor.

Our only excuse could be that the grass was really long. It resembled a rugby pitch and it was hard to get our passing game going. Also, Wimbledon are a very good side and very hard to play against. Their two big lads up front, Carl Cort and Marcus Gayle, caused us problems.

After the break, it was totally different. We went 2-0 up quickly. Becks came on and scored with his first touch. Paul Scholes was Man of the Match by a long margin, and set up that goal brilliantly with a burst of acceleration over ten yards. People wouldn't believe he'd been up coughing all the night before. The only down side is that he was booked and now he's suspended for the next three games.

Within two minutes, Wimbledon were level again. They shoved four men up front in the second half, and teams like that deserve credit. Wimbledon play their own game and I think that's why they've produced so many good players over the years and sold them on for loads of money. I really admire what Joe Kinnear has achieved. Becks's deflected shot for the third goal was the turning point. I guess we were lucky there, but a Scholes backheel and a Cole rocket finished it off.

The Boss was much happier after the game.

GARY: I had an absolute nightmare from start to finish! I didn't make any mistakes, but my distribution was non-existent. Every time I got the ball, all I could see was blue! I had a shooting chance in the first half and I thought, "Right, here we go!" My shot went miles wide.

At half-time the Gaffer wasn't happy. He turned to me and said, "Gary Neville, do you know we're playing in red? And when are you ever going to score from thirty yards?"

We had training the next day, so everyone flew back that night except Teddy, who was allowed to stay down and see his son. I sat across from the Boss on the coach back to Gatwick and he was joking with me. Even when he has had a go at you, he'll always talk to you afterwards.

Premiership / Selhurst Park / Att: 26,309

Wimbledon 2
Sullivan, Cunningham, Jones (Earle), Blackwell, Thatcher, C Hughes (Clarke), Gayle, Perry, M Hughes, Ardley (Solbakken), Cort
Scorers: Ardley, M Hughes
Manchester United 5
Schmeichel, G Neville (Beckham), Berg, Pallister, P Neville, Butt, Johsen, Giggs, Scholes, Sheringham, Cole
Scorers: Butt, Beckham 2, Scholes, Cole

GARY: The lads like it when we fly, because we are back in Manchester by 8.30. I just went out for a quiet meal with the family. I was going to go out with Becks and Ryan, but I hate going out when I've played badly. It just does my head in. In the last couple of games I've felt really sluggish. The physio thinks it's because I did no pre-season work and I'm out of condition. They're sending me for scans on Tuesday.

PHIL: At night, I was a judge for the North West talent show at the Willow Salford Rugby League Club. The other judges included the Battersbys from *Coronation Street* and Tiffany Chapman, who plays Rachel Jordache in *Brookside*. It was an enjoyable night. A sixteen-year old called Jamie Metcalf won. Remember the name.

Tuesday 25 November

PHIL: Gary and I went to the Tag Heuer watch warehouse. A friend of mine invited us to have a look round. They let us into the vault where all the watches are kept. This evening, a new Mappin and Webb store opened in Manchester. Andy Cole, Nicky Butt and I did the honours and each received a nice present for twenty minutes' work.

GARY: My dad rang the Gaffer this morning to arrange a meeting about our contracts. They're meeting on Wednesday at 8.30 am.

Up at seven, because I was due in Manchester at 8.30 for scans on my back. Our physio Dave Fevre was a little bit worried that the problems I am getting with fatigue in my hamstrings and calves may be coming from my back, which is really stiff. Happily, the scans didn't show any abnormalities.

The Gaffer is not at The Cliff again. Lucky for me too, because I picked up the *Express* and there is another article full of quotes from me. They must have saved them up from when I was last away with England.

Wednesday 26 November

GARY: Dad met the Gaffer this morning. We're always a bit worried, but on past experience we shouldn't be. The Gaffer agreed straight away that we should be brought into line, and said he would ring the Chairman that afternoon to arrange a meeting to discuss new contracts.

PHIL: Henning has been left out of the team for tomorrow. The Boss feels that Ronny Johnsen needs games now. I think he's got something in mind for Liverpool, because Scholesy's out suspended for that one.

Denis has received a fax from the Feyenoord defender Bosvelt to apologise for that tackle. I don't think Denis bears any grudges. I suppose the club could have taken action, but that would leave the door open for players to sue each other for any tackle that went on the pitch. I think the club is right to leave it alone.

GARY: In fairness to Bosvelt, I know other people who've done terrible tackles – I've even done a few myself in the heat of a game which I've regretted afterwards. In my first full season, I did a horrific tackle on Jason Dodd at Southampton. Afterwards, I couldn't believe I'd done something so out of character. I still don't know why I wasn't sent off.

Thursday 27 November   Manchester United 3 Kosice 0

PHIL: In Old Trafford at three o'clock for our massages. Since the Juve home game we've stuck to the same routine. Meet at three, pre-match meal at 4.45 pm and team meeting at 6.15 pm. We spend most of the time chatting in the players' lounge. Juventus's 2-0 defeat by Feyenoord last night was mentioned.

We were confident about tonight's game because our result out there was quite convincing, but on Monday, the Boss said how much Kosice had improved. That fired us up.

The game turned out to be quite comfortable. In the first twenty minutes they were bright and more organised than Feyenoord through-out. We still should have been three up at half-time. Teddy had a couple of easy chances and I had a horrible shot. My only excuse is that I was dazzled by the floodlights ... honest! Fortunately, Ryan had an even worse effort so everyone forgot about mine.

Coley scored another good goal after a great Beckham pass.

I got a bang in the teeth and an elbow in the eye and had to go off with blurred vision, so I didn't see the last two goals – an own goal and

Teddy's great strike – until the highlights programme.

As I walked off the pitch with the Doc, he said, "Did you have blurred vision when you took that shot?" Very funny.

Champions' League / Old Trafford / Att: 53,535

Manchester United 3
Schmeichel, G Neville, Johnsen, Pallister, P Neville (Berg), Butt (Solskjaer), Beckham, Giggs (Poborsky), Scholes, Sheringham, Cole / Scorers: Cole, Sheringham, Faktor (own goal)
FC Kosice 0
Molnar, Semenik, Kozak, Spilar, Toth, Sovic, Dzurik, Zvara (Faktor), Janocko (Rusnak), Ljubarskij, Kozlej (Bochnovic)

Saturday 29 November

PHIL: Kenny Dalglish's son Paul was released by Liverpool recently. Kenny signed him for Newcastle and immediately loaned him out to Bury for the rest of this season. My Dad says he has really impressed them at Bury. He's the spit of his dad apparently, and walks and runs just like him.

Everyone is really looking forward to the Blackburn game. At training, the Boss repeated this week's message: no slip-ups. After all the talk in the papers about Blackburn's new manager, their new methods and how fit they are, I think the Boss wants us to prove we are still the best.

My Mum went to watch my twin sister Tracey at the England netball training camp. They are preparing for the game against Australia next Saturday. They have the Commonwealth Games in Kuala Lumpur this summer, and she toured to Canada and South Africa last year. Diadora supply her with gear too. Any deal we've ever had, they've always been willing to look after Tracey as well.

Paul Gascoigne was interviewed on *Grandstand*. He was saying that he regrets some of the silly things he did earlier in his career because they cost him the chance to captain his country. He said Bryan Robson was always his hero and when asked why, Gazza replied, "Anyone who can drink sixteen pints and still train the next day as if it's the World Cup Final is top man in my book!"

Everyone who has played with Bryan Robson admires him. He typified English football with his determination to win and the way he battled back from every setback. He's always been nice to me, and he's always there for advice even now.

Sunday 30 November   Manchester United 4 Blackburn Rovers 0

GARY: Our best performance of the season so far.

Henning Berg played like a man possessed against his old team. We said at half-time that Chris Sutton was going to get sent off because he looked frustrated at not getting any support. He'd already done a bad tackle on Henning.

I got on quite well with Chris when we were away with England, but I was going mad after his tackle on Nicky Butt. I don't usually go up to the referee, but if somebody goes over the top, that's very dangerous. I don't think Chris is a malicious player, but this time he deserved to be sent off – Nicky has a gash all the way down his shin.

Strangely, Blackburn played their best after they went down to ten men, but their centre halves seemed very nervous. I wouldn't want to play against our front four at the moment.

PHIL: Ole caused Blackburn problems playing as a sort of left-winger and scored two great goals. He's now scored five in six – impressive , considering his injury problems. Before the game, while Ole was having his massage, the Boss came up to him and said, "How do you feel?"

"I'm very, very, very, very fresh!" Ole replied.

The Boss said, "Good, because you might be needed today."

But Ole didn't really seem to get the hint that he would be starting until the team was announced at 1.30 p.m.

Liverpool won at Highbury later with a great goal by McManaman. It should be a good game against them next week.

Premiership / Old Trafford / Att: 55,175

Manchester United 4
Schmeichel, G Neville, Pallister (Poborsky), Berg, P Neville, Butt (Johnsen), Beckham, Giggs, Sheringham (McClair), Solskjaer, Cole
Scorers: Solskjaer 2, Henchoz (own goal), Kenna (own goal)
Blackburn Rovers 0
Flowers, Kenna, Sherwood, Pedersen, Ripley (Bohinen), Sutton, Wilcox (Duff), Flitcroft, McKinlay (Gallacher), Croft, Henchoz

Wednesday 3 December

GARY: It's Mum and Dad's twenty-fifth wedding anniversary today. They had told us they didn't want any presents, but today Dad said he thought we might be throwing a surprise party for them. I said, "You must be joking!" We took them out for a meal instead.

The Gaffer rang and said the Chairman would contact us next week about our contracts.

Peter Schmeichel said today that he thinks England have a great chance of winning the World Cup, if Glenn Hoddle picks the Manchester United players. Obviously he's biased, but looking at our midfield he has a point. I wouldn't swap Beckham, Scholes and Butt for any midfield three in Britain.

4

The best team in Europe?

Thursday 4 December

PHIL: The Cliff is still frozen, so we had a light training session at Old Trafford and worked on corners and set-pieces for the Liverpool game, just like we did before our last Anfield visit. Giggsy and Becks were whipping in crosses and Teddy worked on getting across in front of the keeper at the near post to blur his vision.

According to the newspapers, UEFA have decided that Sandor Puhl, who refereed our game in Feyenoord, won't be used in any more Champions' League games. It's strange, because when Andy Cole, having scored a hat-trick, asked him for the match ball at the end of that game, Mr Puhl said, "I'm retiring. It's my last game and I'd like to keep it." He gave it to Andy in the end, but it still seems a bit odd.

GARY: I finally got planning permission for my barn conversion today. We knocked down a wall we shouldn't have, so we had to go through the whole planning stage again after a complaint from the guy I bought the house from, who had been involved in a long-running feud with the planning authority. It would have been a huge financial loss if I hadn't got it. Now I'm looking forward to moving in next summer.

At six o'clock it was time to watch the World Cup draw.

Group A: Brazil, Scotland, Morocco, Norway

Group B: Italy, Chile, Cameroon, Austria

Group C: France, South Africa, Saudi Arabia, Denmark

Group D: Spain, Nigeria, Paraguay, Bulgaria

Group E: Holland, Belgium, South Korea, Mexico

Group F: Germany, USA, Yugoslavia, Iran

Group G: Romania, Colombia, England, Tunisia

Group H: Argentina, Japan, Jamaica, Croatia

I wouldn't have minded getting Norway's draw in Group A. There would be a chance to look at Brazil, and I'd expect England to beat Scotland and Morroco. I thought ours was a great group, until Colombia were drawn out rather than Japan. If Colombia hit form, they could be dangerous. But the fact that we have Tunisia in our first game will work in our favour. I don't look at the next best team in a group, but at the two poor ones, because they are the teams you have to beat to get through. On that basis, Italy and France should qualify easily too.

After the draw, Alan Hansen said he thought England had their best chance of winning the World Cup since 1970. There's a lot of dangerous talk about England's chances; you're always better off going in as the underdogs. After the group stages in France, it's one-off matches, do or die. If we have an off-day, there are teams which can beat us. We could play a team who get eleven men behind the ball, play for a 0-0 and beat us on penalties.

Friday 5 December

GARY: The team was announced for Liverpool. The Gaffer had to tell Ole Gunnar he was out. "I'd like somebody else to pick the team for me," he said. It must be hard to drop someone who scored twice and won us our last game, but you can't leave Andy Cole out at the moment. No way.

Saturday 6 December   Liverpool 1 Manchester United 3

GARY: Breakfast at 8.15 a.m. We always eat three hours before the game. I could only stomach some cornflakes and toast.

I enjoy playing in the morning. A lot of us used to play for the A team at 11.00 a.m. on a Saturday, and it helps when you are playing away from home. There's less time to hang around.

Before the game, the Gaffer told us, "If you don't score goals against this Liverpool defence, you can forget it." Their Norwegian defender

Kvarme didn't have a good game against us in April and he looked really nervous again today. Andy Cole exploited that for the first goal.

I haven't played in many games where we have gone one up and lost. The first goal is usually a killer, but then came the downer of Liverpool's penalty. Fowler scored, and it sinks you a little bit after working hard to get in front. Fortunately, Becks came up with an unbelievable free-kick. In the A team, he used to score about one in three. Now he's scored I'm sure he'll keep banging them in.

The third goal proved that practice pays. We did the same preparation before the Anfield game last season, when Pally scored two. It worked again. Liverpool are definitely weak down the middle, not in terms of football ability, but in height. Only Matteo is quite big. We have Sheringham, Johnsen, Berg and Pallister, who are all brilliant in the air, so if we delivered the right corner, we felt we'd score. Giggs delivered it, Sheringham got the header and Cole poked it in.

In the last month we have played unbelievable attacking football, the best since I've been in the team. Giggs, Beckham, Scholes, Butt, Cole, Solskjaer and Sheringham are all buzzing.

Teddy has made a difference. He always seems to be within working distance of Andy Cole. Eric Cantona was extraordinary for United, but he used to drift to the left and to the right and detach himself from Andy, which left Andy up front on his own.

Teddy is also more convincing in the air than Eric. Not only does he win a lot of headers, he usually guides the ball to a red shirt. Klinsmann and Shearer have both said that Teddy is the best strike partner they've had, and I can see why.

Anfield is the best place in the world to win a game of football. I grew up as a United fan sick of Liverpool winning trophies. I had a great childhood, but the one blip was Man United's lack of success. There were always players in the team about whom you thought, "They aren't good enough and don't work hard enough to wear the United shirt." Alex Ferguson has changed all that. He won't suffer any prima donnas at the club. Whether you're in the first team or in the youth team, you work 110 percent or you are out.

PHIL: The Boss was really happy after the game. He loves winning at

Anfield. When we came in the dressing room he shook everyone's hand and hugged everyone. We are normally in on a Sunday before a European game, but we asked, "Boss, do we get a day off tomorrow?"

"No way, you've done nothing yet," he said, and brought us back down to earth.

As we got on the coach, the Gaffer asked our masseur Jimmy Curran how the B team had got on against Man City that morning. He was ecstatic when Jimmy said they had won 3-2. That just sums him up. Even when the first team wins at Anfield, he's still looking to the future. He doesn't want to lose at any level.

GARY: Chelsea hammered Spurs 6–1 today. Chelsea are the best team we've played so far in the League. They've lost five games out of seventeen and they've still got thirty points. People say Chelsea have lost too many games already, but they've won as many as us so we are only three points clear.

Went out with David Beckham tonight to celebrate.

Premiership / Anfield / Att: 41,027

Liverpool 1
James, McAteer, Kvarme (Berger), Matteo, Bjornebye (Riedle), Carragher, Leonharsen, Redknapp, McManaman, Owen, Fowler
Scorer: Fowler (pen)
Manchester United 3
Schmeichel, G Neville, Pallister, Berg, Johnsen, P Neville, Butt, Beckham, Giggs, Sheringham, Cole
Scorers: Cole 2, Beckham

Sunday 7 December

PHIL: Very light training session. The pitch was heavy at Anfield and the Boss wanted us to rest. It was our Nan's 70th birthday, so after wards we went to her house for something to eat and then I went to my girlfriend's. Julie wanted a picture of her and me for her mum's Christmas present and she'd invited Jordi Cruyff's girlfriend Noemi, who is a photography student, to take it. She did a nice job.

GARY: I'm a little bit wary at the moment. We've qualified for the Champions' League so convincingly, we're top of the League and everyone thinks we are going to walk it. If we carry on playing like this for the rest of the season then there's no stopping us, but we know it's not going to happen like that.

We all realise it's dangerous to get ahead of ourselves, especially over the European Cup, given there are three German teams and one Italian team still in the competition. They win these tournaments every season while English teams haven't in recent years. We could turn up at Bayern Munich in the quarter-final; a team like that can beat anybody on the day.

Monday 8 December

PHIL: Normally on the Monday before a European game, the Boss names the team, but today we went straight over to Littleton Road. I don't know why. Maybe because we've already qualified.

We only trained for an hour but it was short, sharp stuff. Nicky Butt pulled out injured with a tight hamstring after the warm-up.

Tuesday 9 December

PHIL: We arrived at our hotel in Turin at lunchtime – apparently it used to be a Fiat Factory. I didn't go last year so it was my first time. We trained at the Stadio Delle Alpi at night.

I started to feel ill when I went to bed. That famous Italian food had given me food poisoning!

Wednesday 10 December   Juventus 1 Manchester United 0

PHIL: Woke up feeling rough. The Doctor gave me some tablets, but I was still feeling a bit lethargic come match time.

Although we wanted to win and improve on last year, there wasn't the same tension in the build-up as for Juventus at home. I think if it had been a Cup Final, Nicky Butt and Andy Cole would have played, but there is no use risking players of that calibre for nothing.

Zidane caused us a lot of problems. He's one of the best I've played against. Ronny Johnson was marking him, but when Ronny was pushed back into the back three, the midfield (minus Nicky Butt) were left to deal with him. At the back of our minds we knew we were already through, but we were all gutted after the game. It was not just that we'd missed a chance to knock them out; it's not nice losing, especially when you see the other side all jumping up and down. When I got back to the dressing room, I was physically sick. It hadn't been a good night.

GARY: We were absolutely gutted after the game for two reasons: one, we didn't score again and two, we've never really gone away and got a good result against these top teams. Although we're doing better than last season, we've got to express ourselves more away from home. We can't lose in the away leg in the quarters, because if they score at Old Trafford we'll be knackered.

Against Juventus, it might have looked like we were taking it easy, but the truth is we never got going. In the first half we handled it OK, but there was more at stake for them in the second half and it showed.

I wasn't particularly happy with the way I played. I was average and my passing was poor. I gave it away needlessly two or three times, but Juventus pen you back in your own half, and there is less time on the ball.

The Gaffer could see we were gutted. "You'll learn one day," he told us.

Champions' League / Stadio Delle Alpi / Att: 47,786

Juventus 1
Peruzzi, Birindelli (Dimas), Ferrara, Luliano, Torricelli, Di Livio, Conte, Zidane, Tacchinardi (Pecchia), Fonseca, Inzaghi / Scorer: Inzaghi
Manchester United 0
Schmeichel, G Neville, Pallister, P Neville, Berg, Beckham, Johsen, Giggs, Poborsky (McClair), Solskjaer (Cole), Sheringham

Friday 12 December

PHIL: Marcello Lippi said in the papers that Manchester United would become one of the world's best teams over the next ten years. In the past, Italians have beaten us and then slagged us off, so it shows we are improving.

The Boss is not scared of anyone. He told me, "We will take anyone in the quarter finals and beat them." I think if the final was United v Juventus, we would be quietly confident

Today, Gary drove me in to The Cliff, but I didn't train. I felt a lot better but still a bit groggy. While I was waiting for my brother, I had my body fat measured. I'd lost four pounds and my body fat had gone down from 9.8 percent last week to 8.3 percent. Because I'm below my fighting weight, the physio has told me to eat more than usual to fight off the virus.

Monday 15 December   **Manchester United 1 Aston Villa 0**

PHIL: I set up Villa's best chance of the game for Gareth Southgate. I was innocently running out of the six yard box when Peter threw the ball out at me, it hit the back of my legs and went straight to Gareth. Fortunately, he missed. Then Peter had a go at me.

"Are you stupid or something!" he bawled.

Unbelievable – it was obvious that it wasn't my fault! Peter's like that on the pitch, but he'll come up to you in the dressing room afterwards and apologise and we'll have a laugh about it.

Villa play five at the back and the last few games against them have been 0–0, so we'd have taken a 1–0 win before the game. Unfortunately, Teddy missed his third penalty this season. Later someone went down injured and I was chatting with Ole Gunnar. He was annoyed.

"I wanted to take that penalty," he said.

"Well you should have grabbed the ball then!" I replied.

When we watched the replay after the game, we all had a laugh at Teddy. He took it well. He can laugh at himself.

Andy Cole was in a bad mood for most of the game. In the first five minutes, he'd made a challenge on Gary Charles. Charles turned round and said, "You tried to do me there." I think Andy took offence because he's never done that in his life. Later he got tangled up with Ehiogu, but they had a drink in the players' lounge afterwards and it was all forgotten.

Premiership / Old Trafford / Att: 55,151

Manchester United 1
Schmeichel, G Neville, Johnsen, Pallister, P Neville, Beckham, Butt, Giggs, Sheringham, Cole, Solskjaer (McClair)
Scorer: Giggs
Aston Villa 0
Oakes, Charles, Ehiogu, Staunton, Southgate, Wright, Draper, Taylor, Grayson (Hendrie), Collymore, Milosevic (Joachim)

Tuesday 16 December

GARY: I met Ben Thornley's lawyer in the morning to talk about the civil action he's taking against Nicky Marker. After Nicky's tackle in a reserve game four years ago, Ben was out injured for two years. I might be a witness.

Becks, Paul, Nick, Phil and I have always been treated as a five since we broke through into the first team, but we've been playing together for United since 1992 when we won the FA Youth Cup. In 1991/92 though, as a first-year apprentice Ben looked a better player than all of us. He was quick, he could dribble and shoot with both feet. In our Youth Cup run, he was by far our best player, setting up or scoring the important goals in every game.

In the afternoon it was our Christmas do, and about forty of us went. Roy Keane was there. He's lost a lot of weight and seemed in good spirits, although deep down I suspect he must be quite low. The party was spoilt slightly by the press following us around. When we left the first pub we went to, a photographer came up and shoved his camera in our faces.

"Where are you from?" we said.

"The *Star*. Just give us a group shot and we'll leave you alone."

"No deal, mate."

That's not the shot they want anyway – they want one of us drunk and sprawled on the pavement.

We went to Bill Wyman's Sticky Fingers for a meal and the press got a table opposite, which really annoyed us. How could we relax at our Christmas lunch with the press staring at us? So one of the senior players put in a call to the United security staff. They came down and had a quiet word and we never saw the press again.

A woman came up to our table while we were eating and asked Becks for a kiss. When he said no, she asked me and I refused as well.

"I'm not going to go tell the News Of The World, you know," she said.

"Has it occured to you that it might not be the fact that you're going to go to the *News Of The World* that's bothering us?" I replied. "It might just be that we don't want to kiss you."

She screamed and stormed off.

We didn't have anything planned for the evening, but last Saturday Becks overheard some shop assistants talking in Kendalls department store about their party at Royal's, so he asked if we could gatecrash it. They gave us forty-five tickets.

PHIL: It's the one day of the year when the manager actually gives his blessing for us to go out and have a drink, so you've got a license to kill! But no one got really legless. You know that people are going to be looking at you so you tend to be sensible about it. I didn't last the full night. I wasn't drunk, but I'd had enough so I went home. Only Nicky, Roy, Denis, Giggsy and Ben stayed the course.

Wednesday 17 December

PHIL: In the evening, I went to see the premiere of *Spice Girls: The Movie* at the Nynex cinema with my girlfriend and sister. The Boss, Peter, Teddy, Jordi, Ole, Pally and Ryan were there as well.

I got a little bit bored, but the little kids really, really enjoyed it and that's probably the audience they're aiming at.

GARY: Flicked on Teletext when I got home from training and saw the European Cup quarter-finals draw. Monaco: it could have been worse. But on the other hand, given the way Monaco played against Newcastle last year, it's going to be a really difficult tie. They've sold four players since then, including Sonny Anderson who went to Barcelona, but they won their group and Thierry Henry was top scorer in the qualifying stages, so they're obviously a good side.

We still have everything to prove. If they only beat you 1–0, like Dortmund in last year's semi-final, you go into the second-leg knowing that if you concede another goal, you've got to score three.

Thursday 18 December

PHIL: Kiddo worked us very hard in training this morning. He's quite clever, because he disguises running exercises as something else. For instance, we did some crossing practice, but you had to run forty yards before crossing the ball. At the end your legs are knackered.

Paul Parker signed for non-league side Farnborough today. He pops in the players' room every two or three months. In the early 1990s he was the best man-marker around and the player who looked like stopping Gary and I from ever getting into United team. Paul should still be playing League football. He's a nice lad and we all feel for him.

Friday 19 December

GARY: My Dad got a call from the Chairman. They had a discussion about the timing of a new contract. The Chairman said he would raise the matter at a forthcoming board meeting and come back to us on 5 January.

Saturday 20 December

PHIL: Watched the A team at The Cliff. It was Jordi's first comeback game after injury. He scored two goals and looked really sharp. The Boss has given him permission to play for Catalonia in a friendly match in Spain on Tuesday night.

Jordi has become a good friend and I chat with him virtually every day. He's the type of player who will make sure he is 100 percent fit before he plays in a game. Most of the other lads would probably play if they were 95 percent fit.

Sadly, David May injured a knee during the match so he's back on the physio room. He's hardly played a first team game this year. It must be getting quite worrying for him although he doesn't let it show.

GARY: In an interview with the *Daily Mail*, Peter Beardsley was expressing his belief that Eric Cantona, while brilliant for United, was not so good for his team mates, especially Andy Cole. I understand what Peter's saying, but I think having Eric Cantona on our side only did us good. Opposition players were in awe of him.

Chelsea won 4–1 at Sheffield Wednesday today. Chelsea and Blackburn seem our main challengers at the moment. People wrote Blackburn off after we beat them at Old Trafford but, with hindsight, that isn't fair. If they'd just played their normal game it would have been tough for us. They changed their tactics, and if you play in a way that's foreign to you, it's impossible to perform to your best.

I'm not sure whether Blackburn will be there at the end of the season, but like Liverpool and Arsenal they are still in with a shout. The headlines saying no one can catch us when we are just four points – a win and a draw – ahead are just ridiculous.

Sunday 21 December   Newcastle United 0 Manchester United 1

PHIL: St James' Park is one of my favourite grounds. There isn't the same hatred you feel at Anfield and other places. I'll never forget in 1996 when we won 1–0. As we were walking off the pitch, the Newcastle fans applauded us. They are a real football crowd.

Nonetheless, they gave me some stick today during my battle with my old team-mate Keith Gillespie. We both got booked for tackles on each other. I was only one game away from having one yellow card wiped off my record, but now I'll be suspended for our FA Cup match at Chelsea and the League game against Tottenham.

Peter Schmeichel saved us yet again with two incredible stops from John Barnes and Stuart Pearce. The amazing thing about Peter is his concentration. He can go two or three games without having much to do, but he's always ready for action.

Our winning goal was brilliant. End-to-end in twenty seconds, a great cross from Beckham and another fantastic finish by Andy.

We were in the dressing room congratulating each other when the Boss walked in and said sternly, "That wasn't good enough, boys." He said we had given the ball away far too easily and our defending at set pieces had been unacceptable in recent games. Given the standard we set ourselves over the past few seasons, he has every right to be angry.

A few seconds later, Tony Blair came in. He seemed like a really genuine bloke. He and his eldest son are Newcastle fans, but his youngest has switched to Man United. As the Prime Minister was walking round, Giggsy was having a laugh muttering under his breath, "Lower the taxes, lower the taxes." I don't think Mr Blair heard.

Premiership / St James' Park / Att: 36,767

Newcastle United 0
Hislop, Watson, Peacock, Pearce, Albert (Barton), Pistone, Beresford (Ketsbaia), Batty, Gillespie, Barnes, Asprilla

Manchester United 1
Schmeichel, G Neville, Pallister, P Neville, Johnsen, Scholes (Solskjaer), Butt, Beckham, Giggs, Sheringham (McClair), Cole / Scorer: Cole

Monday 22 December

GARY: The Gaffer told us to keep a few afternoons free to work on set pieces. We have been all to pot on defending corners and free-kicks recently. Barnes and Pearce both had free headers against us yesterday and we had problems at Highbury too.

Wednesday 24 December

PHIL: Jordi came in at lunchtime with bad news: he got injured playing for Catalonia. He thought he'd ruptured a thigh muscle. I spoke to the physio Dave Fevre later who said it was just a dead leg. Jordi does tend to exaggerate these things!

Thursday 25 December

PHIL: We opened our Christmas presents before training. Gary and I don't give each other presents, but we spoil our Mum, Dad and sister. Dad's present of a mobile phone/fax gave him something to play with all day.

Training was heavier than usual for the day before a game.

I couldn't believe how many autograph hunters there were at The

Cliff today. It's Christmas Day, for chrissakes! There was a Sky TV film crew there as well, to follow training.

The team was announced for tomorrow. Ryan and Teddy are being rested and Kevin Pilkington comes in for the injured Peter Schmeichel.

Mum had made a buffet lunch. I stuck to the healthy stuff, but I probably ate a bit too much.

Friday 26 December   Manchester United 2 Everton 0

PHIL: Like a practice game. It was all over by the second half and we should have scored more. Everton are going to struggle if they keep playing like that. I didn't have much to do, which was good because I still felt sluggish. I just had to hold my position and play simple passes.

Andy Cole scored a brilliant goal, a 25-yard chip that reminded me of Eric's goal against Sunderland last season.

In the dressing room afterwards, Gary Pallister said that Karel Poborsky was about to go over to Benfica for talks.

GARY: It was one of the easiest games I have ever played in. Even though we put seven past them, Barnsley were a better football team.

Uriah Rennie refereed this one. He gave me my first yellow card of the season and seemed to be on to me throughout the match.

Premiership / Old Trafford / Att: 55,167

Manchester United 2
Pilkington, G Neville, Berg, Pallister (McClair), P Neville (Curtis), Beckham (Poborsky), Johnsen, Scholes, Butt, Solskjaer, Cole
Scorers: Berg, Cole
Everton 0
Myhre, Barrett (Allen), Hinchcliffe, Short, Watson (Jeffers), Tiler, Oster, Ball (Thomsen), Farrelly, Cadamateri, Barmby

---

Sunday 28 December   Coventry 3 Manchester United 2

PHIL: While we were having dinner, the Boss leaned over and told me I wouldn't be playing today because he needs to look at the options in case Denis doesn't make it for the Chelsea game. When we got to the ground I was even more shocked to discover I wasn't even on the bench, so Ben Thornley and I went up to the director's box and sulked!

We didn't play particularly well and threw the game away in the last five minutes. I went into the dressing room afterwards and was surprised to find the manager quite calm. He just wanted to know whether it was a penalty. Henning claimed that Darren Huckerby had dived. Huckerby had been doing it all game and the referee had ignored it, so I was surprised the penalty was given.

The journey home wasn't too bad. Whatever is said in the dressing room is left there. The Boss got on the bus after a game and played cards with Teddy, Peter and Pally. I've seen him have a go at people and then play cards with them on the way home.

None of our nearest challengers took advantage of our defeat. I can't see Blackburn winning the League but I still think Liverpool could put together a dangerous run.

Karel has signed for Benfica. All the lads were moaning that he hadn't bothered to say goodbye.

Premiership / Highfield Road / Att: 23,054

Coventry City 3
Hedman, Nilsson, Shaw, Williams, Burrows, Telfer, Boateng (Boland), Whelan, Hall (Soltvedt), Dublin, Huckerby
Scorers: Whelan, Dublin (pen), Huckerby
Manchester United 2
Pilkington, G Neville, Pallister, Berg, Johnsen (Curtis), Beckham, Scholes, Giggs, Solskjaer (Butt), Sheringham, Cole
Scorers: Solskjaer, Sheringham

Monday 29 December

PHIL: Karel came to The Cliff this morning to say goodbye before he left for Portugal. Unfortunately, the first team had been given the day off so only the injured players, me, Roy, Denis and Maysie, were in. Karel was disappointed, but everyone there shook his hand and wished him well. He just smiled at us because he speaks very little English. In fact, I don't think anyone ever had a real conversation with him. He was still one of the most popular players, because he never moaned even though he wasn't getting in the team.

Karel's move wasn't a great surprise. It was unlikely his work permit was going to be renewed, and Becks was always going to be first choice for the right side of midfield. To be fair, we never really played to Karel's strengths. He is a direct player who likes the ball over the top, whereas we build up slowly.

In the evening we went to a party at Ryan Giggs' house. It was a house warming for Ryan's mum, who is moving in when he moves out. The party's theme was for the boys to come dressed as girls and the girls to come dressed as boys, but Gary and I thought it was a wind-up. When we arrived we were the only ones in men's clothes.

Giggsy was in a nurse's dress and frankly, he looked good. Nicky Butt was in a full-flowing floral dress, but he ruined it by wearing big boots. His excuse was that he couldn't find any high heels to fit! He had a massive chest as well, stuffed full of tissues.

Wednesday 31 December

PHIL: After two days off we normally do a three-hour running session so everyone was fearing the worst. Kiddo wanted to run us ragged but luckily the manager took pity on us.

The Gaffer warned us not to be silly tonight, and told us that training starts at 11 am tomorrow, so we've got an hour extra in bed.

5

Sublime to the ridiculous

Thursday 1 January

PHIL: We were allowed to come in an hour later today because of the excesses of last night! Everyone looked knackered as they swapped stories. Fortunately, the manager didn't carry out his threat to smell each player's breath. Kiddo trained us hard, not as a punishment but to work off the drinking from the night before. He took pity and stopped the session after an hour, but we'd done enough to get a sweat on.

Sunday 4 January   **Chelsea 3 Manchester United 5**

GARY: This was one of the greatest United performances I have been involved in. Before the game the manager said, "Chelsea can be beaten easily, get out there and do it." We absolutely battered them.

Our game plan was to exploit what we reckoned to be a weakness in Chelsea – Frank Leboeuf. A week before, we decided to play a lot of high balls into the area where Leboeuf plays, a tactic that worked well when we played at Stamford Bridge last season. Leboeuf is an excellent player when he's given space at the back – he can put 50-yard passes on to a sixpence. We put Teddy on top of him to make sure he didn't get time on the ball. The plan worked brilliantly and Frank started getting frustrated and losing his temper. Like a lot of foreign players in the Premiership, Leboeuf is built up to be a player we should learn from, but English defenders with similar qualities don't seem to get the same recognition.

Becks opened the scoring after great work from Coley, then got a second from a free-kick whipped in quick and low. De Goey is a good keeper, but because he's so tall, it's difficult for him to get down low.

To be two goals up away from home is great, but we knew that if they got one back it could leave the match on a knife edge. Then Coley got the third just before half-time and after that we were never going to lose. In the dressing room, the manager told us to make sure that we kept up the pressure in the first 15 minutes of the second half. We were aware that last year in the Cup Liverpool had been 2–0 up and Chelsea had come back with four goals. We got the fourth and the fifth and could have scored more. Then we backed off a little bit and they got three goals. It made it look a lot closer than it was.

Mark Hughes gave me a pretty rough time. His finger caught me in the eye, which wouldn't open for a couple of minutes. It was an accident, though. Sparky is a great player and honest with it. He always goes for the ball and would never "do" a player.

There seems to be this impression that we aren't bothered with the FA Cup, but today's performance proves that wrong. We would have been gutted if we lost today. We wanted to prove a point to Chelsea.

After the game, David Beckham did an interview in which he called Frank Leboeuf "a baby". Leboeuf must have seen it because he had a go at one or two of us in the tunnel later as we were waiting to get on our coach. It all got a bit silly.

PHIL: I was particularly pleased for Coley today. His two strikes took him to the brink of 20 goals and we're only halfway through the season. I put it down to confidence. In training he's banging everything in. The more goals he scores the better he plays all round.

Even during the bad times he never hid himself away. If anything, it brought him out of his shell and made him more on for having a laugh with us. When he was getting loads of stick off the press he would always come into training with a big smile on his face. It didn't seem to affect him, or if it did, he never let it show. He won a lot of respect from the lads for the way he battled through those tough times.

FA Cup Round Three / Stamford Bridge / Att: 34,792

Chelsea 3
De Goey, Leboeuf, Clarke, Petrescu, Le Saux, Duberry, Di Matteo, Nicholls (Myers), Flo (Vialli), Zola, Hughes
Scorers: Le Saux, Vialli 2
Manchester United 5
Schmeichel, G Neville, Pallister, Johnsen, Irwin, Beckham, Butt, Scholes (Solskjaer), Giggs, Sheringham, Cole
Scorers: Beckham 2, Cole 2, Sheringham

Monday 5 January

GARY: My dad, Phil and I met the chairman at Old Trafford today to discuss our contracts. He offered us both seven-and-a-half-year contracts, the longest United have ever given to anyone. We were delighted.

I have always preferred dealing directly with the club about my contracts. Agents might tell you not to sign long-term agreements and to hold out for more money, but the club has never let us down. If we fall behind the other players we have always been brought back into line. We're going back on Friday to sign on the dotted line.

Wednesday 7 January

PHIL: We told Butty, Becks and Scholesy about our contracts this morning. We have always been open with them. There is no point in hiding anything. They looked pleased – it's made it easier for them to go in and see the chairman now themselves.

GARY: After the Tottenham game on Saturday we have nine days until our next game, so the lads are arranging a golfing trip to The Belfry for next week. The manager has yet to enforce his usual late-season ban on golf.

Roy Keane is back in training this week and I've seen him running and jogging. He's doing really well.

Friday 9 January

GARY: After training we went to sign our new contracts in the chairman's office at Old Trafford. It took us about 15 minutes as we have to do three copies, one for the Premier League, one for us and one for the club.

I am more than happy to commit myself to United for the next seven and a half years. In fact, I want to spend the rest of my career here. Italy and Spain aren't the same draw they were five years ago. United are now proving they are as big as any club in Europe. I realise that since the Bosman ruling people say that you shouldn't sign long-term contracts, but I think that only comes into play when you are at a club that you want to leave.

Butty, Becks and Scholesy are going to follow us in. I hope all the young players will be here for the rest of their careers. We have grown up together for nearly a decade and we get on with each other now as well as we ever have. As apprentices it was just football that brought us together, but now we socialise away from the club as well.

I first met Becks when he came to United's School Of Excellence as a 14 year old. He was already very confident and liked to show off all his United gear. At that time David was really thin, but he could still kick the ball miles. Only Becks could have scored that goal from the halfway line against Wimbledon. Most players couldn't kick that far and make it look that sweet. They could probably leather it after a twenty-yard run up, but David struck it after just one step.

Becks and I became close friends even though we are very different people. It means we complement each other –he tries to make me live a little bit more and I try to make him calm down a bit.

I first came across Butty and Scholesy when I played for my Sunday team, Bury Juniors, against their team Boundary Park Juniors (which Phil and I later joined). They used to kick lumps out of us. We were beaten before we got on the pitch because they were so much stronger. Scholesy and Nicky were difficult to play against. They were both as hard as nails.

Saturday 10 January   Manchester United 2 Tottenham Hotspur 0

GARY: Against Tottenham today we played well enough to win the game. A couple of times this season we have dropped down a gear. If we had played at our full tempo, as we did a week ago at Chelsea, I'm sure we would have scored five or six.

I was surprised at how little drive Tottenham had. It seemed like they were happy to get beaten 2–0 and had no desire to get back into the game. Klinsmann has come back, but looked ineffective. Then again, he was up against Ronny Johnson and Gary Pallister, who were outstanding. Nevertheless, Tottenham have too many quality players to get relegated.

The manager came into the dressing room afterwards and said, "You lot will get football banned if you carry on playing like that, it was terrible to watch!" He was laughing.

Fortunately, unlike at the game against Everton two weeks ago, none of the problems over our fans standing boiled over today. I can understand why fans want to stand, but it's not something I would risk losing my seat over. It would be more important to me to be able to watch United than bang on about standing, get chucked out and lose my season ticket. I would rather just sit down and accept it.

PHIL: When I arrived at Old Trafford for the game and parked, there were about 2,000 people just staring at all the cars. I've never witnessed anything like it – the crowd was four deep round the railings. I spent about half an hour signing autographs.

It was a bit of a dull match. We were never in trouble, never had to get out of second gear. The one bright spot was Giggsy's performance. He played everywhere – midfield, scored two goals up front and was probably our best defender as well. Ryan is the complete player now. I noticed it at Chelsea where he was roasting their full back and then about 15 seconds later was tackling at left back. He's no longer just a winger.

I went into the dressing room afterwards and you could tell Giggsy was in a good mood. He laughed at my new shoes, and said they were too big and I looked like I was about to go skiing.

I went into the Players' Lounge to have a chat with Sol Campbell who was a bit down. A few Spurs players have publicly criticised Christian Gross and his training methods, but Sol told me how much he rates him. He admitted that Gross doesn't come across that well on television, but that he has really enjoyed playing under him.

Premiership / Old Trafford / Att: 55,281

Manchester United 2
Schmeichel, G Neville, Johnsen, Pallister, P Neville, Beckham, Scholes, Giggs, Sheringham, Solskjaer, Cole
Scorer: Giggs 2
Tottenham Hotspur 0
Baardsen, Carr, Campbell, Vega, Wilson, Fox (Brady), Calderwood, Berti, Clemence (Sinton), Dominguez, Klinsman

Premiership (top) *at 11 January*	P	W	D	L	F	A	Pts	GD
Manchester United	22	15	4	3	51	16	49	35
Chelsea	22	13	3	6	49	22	42	27
Blackburn Rovers	21	11	8	2	38	21	41	17
Liverpool	21	12	4	5	38	19	40	19
Arsenal	21	10	7	4	37	24	37	13
Leeds United	22	10	5	7	31	25	35	6

Monday 12 January

GARY: Giggsy, Butty, Becks and I had a round of golf at The Belfry today – Scholesy was invited too but he was injured. Meanwhile, the Norwegian lads had a training day at Blackburn with the national squad and Philip played for the Reserves.

Thursday 15 January

GARY: I'm impressed with a lad called Matt Jansen who's on trial here from Carlisle. In the practice match we staged especially for him, he looked really sharp and scored twice. I believe United have been quoted £2 million for him and he would definitely be worth it.

In the evening, Becks invited me around to his house for dinner. He made a chicken stir-fry – I think it's the only thing he can cook!

Friday 16 January

GARY: In training this morning we practiced on a narrow pitch like the one at The Dell. We've been thrashed on our last two visits there, so hopefully this will help.

The FA has sent me some World Cup promotions they would like me to contribute to, but I'm slightly reluctant. There are still a lot of people fighting for squad places. What if I get injured or lose form and don't make it to France? I'd look ridiculous in all these World Cup adverts.

I've not missed selection for the squad for two and a half years so it would be a huge shock not to go, but I have to accept it could happen.

There are plenty of quality players who can play on the right side of defence: Campbell, Southgate, Becks, Philip, Le Saux and Watson.

Saturday 17 January

GARY: No game for us, but an eventful day in the Premiership. Dennis Bergkamp has attracted a lot of criticism for going down when he was through on the Coventry goal. I thought he was touched by the defender, Paul Williams.

This is a grey area in football. There have been times when I've seen a player coming in at me and I've jumped up in the air. He's not touched me, but I know that if I carried on he would have hurt me. It looks like a dive, but I'm just getting out of the way of a challenge. There seems to be more diving in the game now, which is a shame. Del Piero could have cost England our World Cup spot with his blatant dive in Rome last year.

PHIL: We never seem to play well at The Dell. Two seasons ago they beat us 3-1 when we were going for the title and we changed our kits at half-time. Then last year Keano got sent off, Butty got injured and they thrashed us 6-3.

The manager is desperate for us to win a game there. In the practice match he asked us to get the ball forward earlier. Coley and Ole practised running into space with the ball played to them. Ryan has been given licence to roam and try to make some runs through the middle.

The manager thinks Ostenstad and Hirst will play instead of Kevin Davies, who has been subbed and rested a lot recently. I've known Kevin since we played for England Under-18s together. He's always been a handful; now he's added a lot more to his game and he's seeing the benefits. He may look soft but he's a hard player – though not in a nasty way.

Monday 19 January   **Southampton 1 Manchester United 0**

PHIL: We flew down in the morning and checked into a hotel in Southampton. I shared a room with Erik Nevland. He's a quiet lad, but

I'm sure he's going to be a great player. Our fans may expect him to make the same impact as Ole Gunnar Solskjaer, but Erik is younger and it will take him longer. There is this assumption that Ole is really young but it's just down to his famous baby face. He's actually older than most of us.

In the team talk, the first thing the manager said was, "It's going to be a hell of a game tonight." He reckoned Southampton were going to play this one like a Cup tie and really battle.

We had a nightmare start. Butty slipped while marking Kevin Davies for a corner in the third minute, allowing him a free header. 1-0. It's going to be one of those Southampton days again, we thought.

Southampton didn't have a shot on goal after they scored, but then we never looked like scoring either. Everything we did was rushed and panicked instead of our usual slow build up.

Even though we were losing, the manager was still in a good mood. Gary was 66-1 in the programme to score the first goal, and in the second half he had a shot that went miles over. The manager turned around to us and said, "More like bloody 166-1!"

GARY: We were fired up for this game, but ended up getting nothing from it. It's always difficult when you give the opposition something to hang on to. Southampton put ten men behind the ball to protect their lead and at one point were just hoofing it away. Teams playing us rarely try to build on their lead; I think the only time we've won a game this season after going a goal down was at home to West Ham in September.

A strange thing happened during the game. At one point I went to take a throw-in and a fan shouted, "Stop spitting at us, Neville!" It wasn't a kid winding me up, it was an older guy who seriously thought I was spitting at him! These people are dangerous.

There's no doubt we missed Teddy tonight. He has really helped us this season by winning so many balls in the air and the way he flicks it on for Coley or the midfield is brilliant. Even when you don't think he is going to win the ball, he pulls it off by timing his jump so well. I remember when we had Mark Hughes – whatever ball you gave him, he would bring it down with his chest. Teddy performs the same role.

It's very disappointing to have lost four games away from home. As the Gaffer says, if you lose more than six you make it tough for yourself. It means that with 15 games left we can only really afford to lose two more and we've still got to play Blackburn, Villa, Liverpool, Chelsea, Arsenal and Leeds. The losses against Coventry and Southampton could come back to haunt us.

Giggsy and Butty were both sick on the flight home. A bad night all round.

Premiership / The Dell / 15,241

Southampton 1
Jones, Dodd, Monkou, Lundekvam, Benali, Oakley, Palmer, Le Tissier (Slater), Richardson (Spedding), Davies (Ostenstad), Hirst
Scorer: Davies
Manchester United 0
Schmeichel, G Neville (Nevland), Irwin, Pallister, Johnsen, Beckham, Butt (McClair), Giggs, Scholes, Solskjaer, Cole

Tuesday 20 January

GARY: After their win over Newcastle tonight, Liverpool may be our main challenger for the title. With Owen, McManaman, Ince and Fowler, they look strong and they've got the second best defensive record after ours. They are capable of hitting a purple patch and going on an unbeaten run of 15 games.

Saturday 24 January   Manchester United 5 Walsall 1

PHIL: I was looking forward to playing Walsall. Actually, I was a bit nervous as it was my first game for a month. I didn't know how my fitness would hold up.

The manager warned the defence that we shouldn't take their forwards for granted and start pushing up just because they're Second Division. We were told to leave the attacking to our midfield and forwards.

The game was played in a really good spirit. Their lads talked to us all the way through. Clearly, they had come to enjoy their day; I think they were just happy to be on the same pitch.

I know the Walsall lads were upset that we wouldn't swap shirts with them at the end, but we've never been allowed to. The manager and the kit man don't like it. I don't really understand the objection when it comes to one-off games like this, when the Walsall players would love to have our shirts as keepsakes.

But it's club policy, and a bit of a standing joke among us. Teddy even had to get permission to give his shirt to Jurgen Klinsmann two weeks ago. If we ever want to wind up Albert, the kit man, we threaten to swap our shirts.

The 8,000 Walsall fans really improved the atmosphere. Gary and I think they should let in that many away fans each week.

That night my girlfriend and I stayed in a nice hotel in Manchester to celebrate my 21st birthday.

FA Cup Round Four / Old Trafford / Att: 54,669

Manchester United 5
Schmeichel, Irwin (Clegg), Berg, Johnsen, P Neville, McClair, Beckham, Scholes (Mulryne), Thornley (Nevland), Solskjaer, Cole
Scorers: Cole 2, Solskjaer 2, Johnsen
Walsall 1
Walker, Evans, Marsh, Viveash, Mountfield, Peron (Blake), Boli, Porter, Keates, Watson, Hodge
Scorer: Boli

Sunday 25 January

GARY: Before we went out on to the training pitch, Becks told me that yesterday he asked Victoria to marry him. He showed me the ring, which looks very impressive. He asked me to be best man, which of course I agreed to straightaway. I remember watching Victoria on Top of the Pops when we were away with England. Becks turned to me and said, "I have to be with her!" Now, just eighteen months later, they're getting married. Victoria is lovely and so well suited for Becks. It's been difficult for them, what with all the media attention and being apart for such long periods, so they deserve this happiness.

Becks and Victoria were all over the news after announcing their engagement this afternoon. If they hadn't given a press call there would have been photographers camped outside David's house for days. I thought the two of them handled it perfectly.

Monday 26 January

GARY: All the lads shook Becks' hand to congratulate him. Apparently, as best man I'm organising the stag night, but the lads said they expect me to book the snooker club in Bury and that they'll not bother coming. Then they took bets on how long it would be before people fell asleep during my speech.

The manager wasn't in today, but he's always happy when his players settle down. I remember when I first came into the squad he was always coming in and saying to certain players, "When are you going to get married?" He believes it gives a player more stability.

Tuesday 27 January

PHIL: The manager wasn't in again today. The word is that he's on a scouting mission for a player he wants to buy before this week's Champions' League transfer deadline.

We all try and mine Kiddo for information, but he only ever gives hints and never spils the beans properly. He just fobs us off by saying the Boss has gone to watch some horses.

As ever, when the manager isn't here we have to train harder.

Wednesday 28 January

PHIL: The pitch was frozen in the morning so we had to settle for a head tennis competition. It was me, Gary and David Beckham against Ole Gunnar, Henning and Ronny – England v Norway. We lost. The manager was the referee and he was biased towards them. He's softening them up before the World Cup.

Yesterday our old youth coach Eric Harrison, who's now retired, asked us why we no longer do any extra training in the afternoons. We felt a bit guilty so we asked him to come in to do some. It started with a kicking drill where we had to put the ball on to a sixpence. The other lads – Becks, Butty, Scholesy and Giggsy – saw us doing it and liked the idea, so they joined us for the rest of the session.

Along with my dad, Eric Harrison has been the biggest influence on my football career. I don't think anyone outside the club fully appreciates how much Eric has contributed to United's success. Eric always pushed me and had the guts to play me in the Youth Team when I was only 15 years old. Only Norman Whiteside and Ryan Giggs had managed that before. As far as he was concerned, there wasn't a youth structure to adhere to. Instead his policy was, "If you're good enough, I'll pick you. I don't care how old you are."

From day one, Eric was preparing me for the First Team. When I was in the Youth Team and he saw me try things he didn't like, he used to pull me to the side and say, "If you had done that in the First Team, you'd get roasted."

Later on yesterday, Diadora's United players – me, Gary, Maysie, Roy and Butty, plus Stan Collymore – did an appearance. The Diadora reps showed us the boots they want us to wear in the World Cup. Every player will have boots in the colours of their national flag, so the England lads will get red, white and blue ones. They also want us to wear red boots when we play for United, but there's no way the Boss would have it.

GARY: If it wasn't for Eric Harrison, I wouldn't be a footballer.

When I arrived at United he was the man who really guided me. I needed someone to tell me how to become a pro, because I didn't have a clue – I hated tackling! Eric laid it on the line: "Look, you're a defender, if you don't tackle, you won't make it." He was very strict, but in a way that made you respect him, not fear him. If he shouted at me, I would want to bury myself in the ground feeling I'd let him down, but in the same way a "Well done" from him was a massive boost.

Even now, although he's semi-retired, he's still around. He scouts for the club, but he belongs on the training field. I feel sorry for the young players who are missing out on his expertise. Eric still has a special relationship with the young First Teamers.

And I've never heard anyone say a bad word about him, which in football is rare.

Thursday 29 January

GARY: Tonight, Ryan and I went with Alex Ferguson to St Luke's church in Salford. The Vicar there, who is a good friend of the Gaffer, had asked if we could come along and present trophies to the St Luke's football team who practise next door to the church.

It was a good evening, but Giggsy and I got totally stitched up. A local artist called Harold Riley, another friend of the Gaffer, was also there. Harold does sketches for The Belfry Golf Club and the first thing he said when he came up to us was, "When you were playing golf down at the Belfry last week ..."

Our anti-golf Gaffer shot Ryan and I a disapproving look.

Later on, the Reverend's speech only made matters worse. He said the greatest thing that Alex Ferguson had brought to Manchester United was team spirit. The girls who work behind the bar at the pub "where the players regularly go for their team meeting" had told him that they couldn't believe how well we all got on.

Uh-oh! The Gaffer isn't supposed to know about our "team Meetings". He looked round at Giggsy and me and said, "The pub, eh?"

"Yeah, Gaffer. Great food!" replied Ryan.

Friday 30 January

PHIL: Kiddo came out on the training pitch today and handed green bibs to the team who would play as Leicester in the practice match. I thought I had escaped, but I was the last one he gave a bib to. Soon after, the manager came up and told me not to worry, that I would get plenty of games before the end of the season. It gets harder to accept, but I suppose I have to appreciate the fact that he tells me personally because he doesn't do that with everyone.

In the practice match, the bibs beat Saturday's team 1-0 and I scored the winning goal. From a corner it hit my chest and went in, but they said I'd handled it. Giggsy blasted the ball at me and called me a cheat. Big Peter wasn't happy either. We do shooting practice every day and that was the first I've ever put past him! I think he only really tries when Gary or I are shooting. I enjoyed rubbing it in, celebrating like it was a Cup Final winner.

John O'Kane left for Everton today in a £400,000 deal. I think they have got an absolute steal. I honestly believe that if John fulfills his potential he could become an England regular, maybe even make the World Cup squad. I suppose when he saw John Curtis and Michael Clegg jumping the queue for the First Team he realised it was time to leave.

Saturday 31 January	Manchester United 0 Leicester 1

PHIL: The manager asked us to start off really quickly and make it like a Cup tie, but we did the opposite! We were really lethargic, played too deep and just fannied about. The crowd didn't help; they were really quiet, expecting us to slaughter the visitors. We were grateful to get in at half-time only a goal down and the manager rightly said that it was the worst half of football he had seen all season.

"I want a 100-per-cent change in the second half," he said. "You're playing for Manchester United. No team should should come here and work harder than you. No one doubts your skill, it's just your desire to win games like these." After that we raised our game and I think we did enough for a draw, but they held out for their win.

GARY: We were absolute garbage in the first half, the worst I can remember in a long time. In the second half, we missed some absolute sitters and pumped high balls into the area which didn't really work. Leicester have a good defensive unit and just kept heading the ball away.

We were all gutted at our first home loss of the season, but we're still four points clear. By now we really should have an 11-point lead. We should have kept our lead at Coventry and beaten Southampton and Leicester.

Premiership / Old Trafford / Att: 55,156

Manchester United 0
Schmeichel, G Neville, Irwin, Johnsen (Berg), Pallister, Beckham, Butt, Cole, Giggs, Scholes (P Neville), Solskjaer (Sheringham)
Leicester City 1
Keller, Savage, Guppy, Kaamark, Elliott, Walsh (Prior), Izzet, Lennon, Parker (Campbell), Cottee (Wilson), Heskey Scorer: Cottee

6

Munich Remembered

Sunday 1 February

GARY: Sulked all day.

Phil and I were meant to have a game of golf but we even cancelled that. You just feel depressed until you get another game.

Monday 2 February

PHIL: The newspapers made for strange reading this morning, packed with articles about why United are in disarray. Sure, the lads are all gutted about Saturday's performance, but at The Cliff everybody was saying, "Crisis, what crisis?" We're four points clear at the top of the Premiership, we've made it to the European Quarter Final and we're still in the FA Cup.

Scholesy picked up his fifth booking on Saturday, which means he joins Nicky Butt on the suspended list. Ronny Johnsen got injured in the same game, so I might move into midfield for the next couple of games.

At United, we believe there is only one way to get over disappointment and that is to work even harder. Gary, Jordi and I stayed behind in the afternoon for extra training with the Under-19s, who are going to Viareggio in Italy next week to play in the prestigious Coppa Carnevale Youth Tournament.

I was in the squad that entered last year, when I was recovering from glandular fever. It was good for my rehabilitation, but we lost all three games. The pitches out there are really bad and they use such a light ball that it is impossible to pass properly, so coach Jim Ryan is preparing his lads to play a more direct style.

Us First Teamers played in a team against the XI who will start in Viareggio. It was enjoyable because we were allowed to play our own formation and we won 3-0.

At The Cliff, all the players were all talking about last night's TV documentary on the Munich tragedy.

GARY: As I've said before, the mood in training depends on First Team results and today it was all work and not too much banter.

I gave David Beckham a lift home at lunchtime. When I dropped him off, we found out the England squad for the forthcoming Chile game. All the usual United players are in.

PHIL: I was apprehensive about my chances of making the England squad as I haven't played much in recent weeks, so it was a relief to be selected. I was surprised that Gary Pallister wasn't in either the A or B squads because, for me, Pally is still the best centre-half in the country. However, I'm delighted Dion Dublin's in the squad. When he was at United, he was in the reserve side when all the young players were coming through. He was top scorer for us in 1993/94. We got all the attention, but we wouldn't have won the League that year without him. In fact, he probably helped us more than anyone else. Talk to anyone at United – we all love Dion.

GARY: We watched a video of that Munich documentary when we finally went home. It's hard for any United fan to watch, but I'm glad I did.

In the evening, we went to Eric Harrison's testimonial dinner in Rochdale. It was a brilliant night. The whole First Team squad were there, along with ex-players like Bryan Robson, Steve Bruce, Norman Whiteside and Kevin Moran. It was a great turn-out and all the proceeds went to Eric. He definitely deserved it.

Our former B-Team coach Nobby Stiles made an after-dinner speech. He's only five foot four and seven-and-a-half stone and, he told us, even at his peak he couldn't see properly, his sight was so poor! To play centre half at that size is incredible. He must have been a hard man and a great player.

He's a down-to-earth person, no edge to him at all, and the lads love him.

Tuesday 3 February

PHIL: After training yesterday, Kiddo flew to Italy to visit Udinese's training camp. He is looking for things to include at our proposed new training ground at Carrington. Kiddo's been to both the Milan clubs, Juventus and Real Madrid. He's always looking to improve his knowledge.

It is rare nowadays for the Gaffer to take training as he trusts Kiddo to look after that. Kiddo usually goes over to the training pitch fifteen minutes before we get there and divides it up with plastic cones.

GARY: The Gaffer had a long chat with us before training. He felt we hadn't worked hard enough in the first half against Leicester. He said that it should be part of our professional pride that we can always say, Well at least I worked hard – even in defeat.

He took six or seven lads including me aside during the morning and talked to us individually. He's always trying to improve us.

Wednesday 4 February

GARY: Alex Ferguson rang up my dad this morning to say that we must cancel the two personal appearances booked for the FA tomorrow. We were supposed to open a garage in Stretford and then attend an exhibition at the G-Mex. The Gaffer probably feels that players are doing too many off-pitch activities at the moment.

In training, we did some shooting and crossing practice. The Gaffer asked two of the groundsmen to keep score. It turned out that I had the most assists, but scored the fewest goals! I only scored two, while Denis Irwin came top with 15. When the assists and goals totals were combined, the overall joint winners were Ole Gunnar, Nicky Butt and Scholesy.

PHIL: Tony Cottee, who scored Leicester's match-winning goal against us, was quoted in today's papers calling United players "arrogant". I don't know why he should say that, as he was talking amicably to most of us in the tunnel before Saturday's game. Tony is really good friends with Teddy, so I don't think he was being malicious.

Everyone, including Wenger and Gullit, is saying United can now be caught in the title race. Over the weekend, Harry Redknapp said he thought Liverpool would win the League. They are all entitled to an opinion, but no one at United has ever said we are walking away with the title. Back in December when we beat Newcastle, the media said we'd already won it. We were four points ahead then – the same gap as now – so what's changed?

Tonight I watched the replay of the FA Cup game between Stevenage v Newcastle. To be honest, I was hoping that Stevenage would get absolutely hammered. Stevenage players have been a bit cheeky, saying Alan Shearer and the other Newcastle players aren't that great in the first game. I just think they have got too much to say for a small club. They should be delighted that they are playing Newcastle. They've got too big for their boots and they're showing a complete lack of respect.

Thursday 5 February

PHIL: Chris Sutton has withdrawn from the England B squad. He must be upset that he wasn't picked for the full squad. Glenn Hoddle probably thought he would get a better look if Chris played 90 minutes for the B Team than from a couple of days training followed by the subs' bench at Wembley.

At training, the Gaffer named the team for Saturday. Gary is in for Henning Berg – when Gary went to centre back against Leicester, the Boss said it was his best game for the club. The Gaffer said that given the occasion, commemorating Munich and the Busby Babes, he needed the young lads to play.

Practice games are normally slow affairs, but today's was very competitive. Everyone is really fired up for the weekend.

There has been talk among the players about whether the Bolton fans will observe the minute's silence for the Munich dead. Apparently Bolton have only sold seats to season-ticket holders and anyone who misbehaves will lose their season ticket at the Reebok Stadium. My grandad, who lives in Bolton, told me there's a big campaign there appealing for everyone to stay quiet. When Sir Matt Busby died the Everton fans were magnificent. I just hope the Bolton fans follow suit.

GARY: The crowd always seem to rise the occasion after a bad spell. They were unbelievable at the Arsenal home game last year after we'd lost to Newcastle five, Southampton six and been beaten by Fenerbahçe at home. The Gaffer thinks the crowd will be like that again on Saturday and wants that passion reflected in our play.

Friday 6 February

GARY: The fortieth anniversary of the Munich tragedy.

At 7 pm we met up at Old Trafford to get the coach to Manchester Cathedral for the Munich Memorial Service. Every single current United player and every Munich survivor attended and there were representatives from all the families of the people who died. I was particularly moved when Duncan Edwards' mum, with tears in her eyes, got up to light a candle for her son.

PHIL: It was a really moving service. I'd met one or two of the Munich survivors before, including Bill Foulkes and Harry Gregg. In fact we stayed in Harry's hotel in Ireland on a pre-season tour.

Alex Ferguson, Sir Bobby Charlton and Frank Taylor, a journalist who survived the crash, all spoke during the service. Wilf McGuiness, a Busby Babe who had been injured and missed the trip to Belgrade in 1958, also made a speech. His humour brightened the atmosphere.

Saturday 7 February   **Manchester United 1 Bolton 1**

GARY: At Old Trafford, there were wreaths of flowers under Sir Matt Busby's statue. Sir Bobby Charlton came into the Players' Lounge before the game. He said, "Forget about all this and concentrate on the game." It was a nice gesture.

We all put our arms around each other during the minute's silence. It was something I'd suggested to Peter Schmeichel in the Players' Lounge before the game. I wanted us to show everyone that we were together and that we cared. Every player was happy to do it.

I had expected two or three of Bolton's fans to let them down, but they were magnificent. 55,000 people stood in total silence. The build-up before the game may have been different because of the occasion, but I can't use that as an excuse for playing badly. Nathan Blake caused me problems with his strength and I didn't feel comfortable until I went to right back in the second half.

After half-time, I was involved in a penalty incident. I knocked the ball past Gudni Bergsson; he's a big lad and he kind of stood in my way. I probably shouldn't have fallen down and a couple of Bolton players were on to me saying I dived. But if you stay standing, the ref just waves it off. I thought it was an obstruction and deserved at least an indirect free-kick.

At the press conference afterwards, I blamed myself for their goal, but looking back I'm not so sure. It was a goalmouth scramble between Taylor and me. The ball was too far away for me to get my leg round it to clear it wide so I went to put my leg over the ball, but he put his foot up, stopped me making the clearance, and then squirmed it over the line.

I also had two late chances to score myself, but I snatched at both of them. I've now had three great chances in the last two games and I should have scored each time. It's unacceptable. I'm a Manchester United player and I should be able to handle any situation put in front of me.

Even finding out that Liverpool and Blackburn had both lost couldn't raise my spirits after the game. I felt we had let ourselves down on such a special day. The club's Assistant Secretary Ken Ramsden asked me to speak at the post-match press conference, but at first I refused because I was so low. In the evening, I was so depressed – the worst I've felt after a game this season.

PHIL: Like a lot of the players, I was close to tears when the referee blew his whistle to signal the end of the minute's silence. It was an extra-ordinary feeling.

I've never felt so up for a game, but strangely we didn't play that well in the first half. We lacked cohesion, especially in midfield. With our ball-winners Keane and Butt out, Scholesy was forced to sit in midfield instead of going forward. He has a lot more to offer than that.

At half-time, the Gaffer was as angry as I've seen him all season. He criticised our passing and the lack of care we'd taken in the last third of the pitch. After Bolton took the lead in the second half, we bombarded them. He moved me into midfield, which allowed Ryan and Paul Scholes to run free without having to worry about defending. Gary was also bombing forward from right back, supporting Becks, and together they caused havoc. We always seem to play better with Becks and Giggsy out wide in a 4-4-2 formation.

Ole Gunnar, Coley and Gary all had good chances to score the winner, but it didn't happen.

Premiership / Old Trafford / Att: 55,156

Manchester United 1
Schmeichel, G Neville, Irwin, Pallister, P Neville, Scholes, Beckham, Solskjaer, Sheringham (Berg), Giggs, Cole
Scorer: Cole
Bolton Wanderers 1
Branagan, Bergsson, Fairclough, Cox, Todd, Pollock, Sellars, Frandsen, Thompson, Blake, Taylor (Holdsworth)
Scorer: Taylor

Sunday 8 February

GARY: Still depressed. We've now won just one game in five and the dreaded 'blip' word has resurfaced for the first time since autumn 1996. I can think of five home games this season – Coventry, Crystal Palace, Tottenham, Southampton and Villa – which we've won without playing very well. But in the last three league games we've scored just one goal, and you aren't going to win many like that. The longer we go without scoring at Old Trafford, the more our opponents' confidence grows. We aren't scoring early enough.

I watched a bit of the Arsenal v Chelsea game before leaving for Burnham Beeches to prepare for England v Chile. Arsenal won 2-0. A good result for us, although Arsenal may turn out to be our strongest challengers because they have players with experience of winning the title. But at this point it's still in our hands. If we play to our capabilities, we will still win the Premiership.

I bumped into Mark Hughes at Heathrow and we had a laugh about our battle at Stamford Bridge in January. "I'd kick my own grandmother if she was in my way on a football pitch," laughed Sparky.

PHIL: In the Sunday papers, there's a story claiming David Beckham is refusing to sign a new contract for United. Utter rubbish. David hasn't even talked to the chairman yet.

The weekend's results have been amazing for us – we're still five points clear. Looking back, if we had won all the games we should have done, we might have had the title sewn up by now. The Boss's theory is that we always keep our fans on the edge of their seats at United.

We met Scholesy, Nicky and Michael Owen at Manchester airport for the journey to Burnham Beeches. Mike's a nice lad and he's got a great chance of making his debut on Wednesday. David Beckham didn't come with us. He's had a tight hamstring for three weeks and aggravated it on Saturday.

Les Ferdinand has also withdrawn from the squad. Chris Sutton might have been drafted in if he hadn't refused to play for the B Team. I admire Chris in a way, though I wouldn't have done what he's done. He could have come out of Saturday's game with a bogus injury, but he was honest enough to say, "I can't accept this."

Monday 9 February

GARY: The team wasn't named at training this morning, but the practice match pointed to a front three of Cole, Sheringham and Owen.

I spoke to Teddy about the finishing problems I had on Saturday. He said, "You've just got to slow everything down in your mind when you go through on goal. You always have more time than you think." His advice made a lot of sense.

Matt Jansen, the young striker who had a trial with us recently, has decided to join Crystal Palace. I don't know whether United actually bid for him, but I would be surprised if he turned United down. You only get one chance to play for this club. Matt looked a good player and although he might not have got in the team straightaway, I feel that ten games for

United are worth 50 somewhere else.

PHIL: In the afternoon Gary, Graeme Le Saux, Gareth Southgate and I had our pictures taken for a Snickers promotion. Meanwhile, Coley and a few others did a TV commercial for a washing powder which involved diving around in mud. Like United, England has a players' pool. The players are all expected to do a little work for the team sponsors during the year and every six months, we each receive a players' pool cheque.

Gary and I also took £150 off Nicky Butt and Paul Scholes at snooker. £25 a frame – we were flying! But Scholesy is flying home tomorrow. The knee problem he's had for a while hasn't responded to treatment.

Tuesday 10 February

PHIL: At a 9.45 a.m. meeting Glenn Hoddle announced the team. Gary and I were in. Coley and Nicky Butt were getting a chance too. Michael Owen will also start, the youngest player to be capped for England this century, beating Duncan Edwards' record.

We went straight out for a practice match against the Bomb Squad and got hammered. Glenn Hoddle and Glenn Roeder were playing for them, so to get thrashed wasn't a good sign. To be fair, their team also included Gazza, McManaman, Southgate, Dublin and Shearer.

In the afternoon, we watched a video of Paraguay v Chile. Chile lost 1-0 (they lost to Iran, New Zealand and Hong Kong Select on their recent tour), but they were fielding a side so weakened it was practically their B Team. I'm a bit worried we might be overrun in midfield. Nicky Butt joked, "I'm going to wear running spikes instead of football boots tomorrow night!"

The Boss was saying that Teddy and Michael could drop in and pick up one of Chile's midfielders. It will be tough for Michael to do a job that is foreign to him. At 18 years old, it's enough responsibility just to play for your country.

GARY: Our main problem in the practice match this morning was that we only had two players in midfield against their three. Steve

McManaman was absolutely killing us. Tony Adams, myself and couple of the other lads turned round to John Gorman and said, "Look, we are going to get annihilated if Chile play this system."

John said, "Don't worry, they don't have anybody like McManaman."

Sadly, Andy Cole had to pull out of the session with a back injury. He looks doubtful for tomorrow.

My dad rang the chairman on Monday suggesting we should announce that we'd signed our new United contracts, to discourage media speculation. Today, Alex Ferguson rang Dad back and said they will be getting Nicky, Becks and Scholesy in to discuss their contracts soon and announce all five deals at the same time.

After dinner, I watched England B v Chile B on TV. Although we lost 2–0, Paul Merson played superbly and probably earned a place in the next full squad.

Wednesday 11 February   England 0 Chile 2

GARY: Coley's bad run of luck with England continues. His back injury hadn't eased and he was sent home this morning. The United lads were gutted for him, but delighted for Dion who would replace him.

Up front, Dion and Michael Owen both did well for us. To put Michael's performance in context, I was playing in United's Youth Team at his age. Mike is wafer-thin but he's like Giggsy – his strength, balance and speed makes him hard to shake off the ball.

The Chilean striker Marcelo Salas, who United almost signed, was outstanding tonight. He has quick feet, he was sharp and his first goal was world-class. I was marking him, but when the ball came in, David Batty shouted, "I've got him". David was only a yard off him, which shows how quickly Salas controlled the ball and shot. A great finish.

Salas produced great skill to get the penalty. We never got to grips with him and it didn't help that Chile always had a spare man going forward. Glenn Hoddle told us after the game that this result would bring us down to earth after all the hype. He warned us that Colombia, whom we play in the World Cup, are better than Chile.

PHIL: There were 70,000-odd supporters at Wembley and the atmos- phere gave us an extra buzz. Chile played well and deserved to win, although the result was partly down to tactics. Nicky Butt was probably our best player on the night, but he was outnumbered in midfield.

I was surprised to be substituted at half-time. All that the Boss said was, "I'm making one change, Graeme Le Saux for Phil Neville." I was gutted. All my family had come down to watch the game and at first I thought I'd let everyone down. But sitting on the bench in the second half I started to think, "I didn't have a beast ... I didn't deserve to brought off."

After the game, neither John Gorman nor Glenn Hoddle explained their decision to me. I wouldn't have minded if they'd told me before-hand they were going to give Graeme and me a half each, or if a mid-fielder had come on for tactical reasons. I was disappointed.

The press have built us up as potential World Cup winners. In the long-run, I don't think this defeat will do us any harm, but it will keep every player on their toes. These things happen. Brazil lost to USA recently.

International friendly / Wembley

England 0
Martyn, G Neville, Adams, Campbell, Lee, Batty (Ince), Butt, P Neville (Le Saux), Owen, Dublin,
Sheringham (Shearer)
Chile 2
Tapia, Reyes, Fuentes, Margas, Vilarbell, Acuna, Paraguez, Rojas, Sierra (Valenzuela), Barrera (Carreno), Salas
Scorer: Salas 2

Thursday 12 February

PHIL: Back in Manchester. Alex Ferguson walked past me in The Cliff dressing room. I was rubbing my calves and he said, "Is that why you came off?" I said no and he sounded shocked.

GARY: In training, Phil, Teddy, Nicky and me did a loosener while the rest of the squad trained together. We chatted about the Chile game as we stretched. Although we had been outnumbered in midfield, we all agreed that we couldn't use tactics as an excuse. We just didn't play that well, full stop.

Afterwards the other lads told us that the Gaffer had spoken to them. He doesn't want anyone playing golf until the end of the season. He also wants us all to cut down on our commercial commitments – personal appearances within two days of the game are out. He will be selecting his best team for each League match until the end of the season. There will be no resting of players from now on. It was a rallying speech: the slump has gone on too long. Let's start winning again.

PHIL: I spoke to Andy Cole. He's still struggling with his back. He had no luck with England, but he was pleased for Dion. Coley is 26 now and experienced enough to take setbacks in his stride.

I've watched the video of last night's game three times today. I still don't know what I did wrong.

In the afternoon, I flicked on Teletext and saw the news that Ruud Gullit has been sacked and Gianluca Vialli will take over at Chelsea – an unbelievable move at this stage of the season. One of the deciding factors seemed to be that Gullit was demanding £2 million in wages ... "netto". That adds up to £3.5 million gross. He was clearly still categorising himself as a player-manager, but if that figure is correct, Chelsea were right not to pay it.

Jordi explained to me once that because the first year he was in England he paid 56 per cent in Spanish taxes, he is actually better off paying 40 per cent in England. If he moved back to Spain, he would only pay 40 per cent in the first year, so he'd cash in.

Chelsea have a Continental-style management system with a general manager to deal with contracts and paperwork, which left Gullit to get on with the coaching alongside Graham Rix. With Rix still there, the transition may not be so difficult, but we'll find out over the next few weeks.

GARY: This money dispute highlights the gap between top players and the man on the street. The fans only tend to comment about how much money we earn when results are bad. If a United fan ever criticises me for what I earn, I respond by pointing out that I don't set the pay structures. All I do is play to the best of my ability.

Friday 13 February

PHIL: The Gaffer wasn't in today. He's in Monaco on a spying mission.

With Scholes and Butt suspended, there is talk of me playing in midfield against Barnsley in the FA Cup on Sunday. The Gaffer spoke to Choccy, Pally, Denis Irwin and Peter Schmeichel yesterday and suggested playing five at the back against Barnsley. The senior players told him that hadn't worked well in the past. The Gaffer said he'd go away and think about it.

This afternoon, John Gorman phoned our house. I wasn't in. He said he'd call again tonight. Dad said it would be good to speak to him to clear my mind. I rang him back, but by then he was in a meeting with Glenn Hoddle. In the evening, John phoned back. He explained that I'd been taken off because I was cutting in onto my right foot too often. It's something I've always done because I favour my right peg slightly.

John said he'd like me to play more for United, but that's out of my hands. I told him Alex Ferguson had promised me a decent run in the side in the next few weeks, and John said to keep practising getting to the byline and crossing with my left foot. I took the point.

Saturday 14 February

PHIL: Kiddo named the team. Ole Gunnar is in, but Gary and Becks will be rested.

The Boss was still in Monaco, but he has obviously listened to his senior players because we aren't playing a sweeper. I was a bit worried about playing right midfield. I've never done it before.

In the afternoon, we went to Maine Road to see Bury beat Man City 1-0. When Bury scored, my dad and Tracey jumped up to celebrate and Gary and I dived under our seats so we wouldn't be spotted by any City fans! With about 20 minutes left, a City fan ran on to the pitch and ripped up his season ticket. He got a standing ovation and the City fans started singing, "We're shit and we're sick of it." Gary and I decided it was time to leave.

Three years ago, you couldn't even imagine Bury playing at Maine Road, but there are massive problems now at City. The quality of their football was dire today. I feel sorry for their fans, because 28,000 people turn out every week and for that alone they deserve to be in the Premiership. It's also one of my favourite grounds and I'd love to play in a derby match again, but I can't see it happening for a while.

Sunday 15 February   Manchester United 1 Barnsley 1

PHIL: Ole Gunnar had to withdraw from the team with a stomach upset an hour before kick-off so Erik Nevland, another Norwegian striker, made his full debut.

We were playing badly in the first half. Then Peter took his eye off a back pass and miss-kicked to gift Barnsley striker John Hendrie with a goal. Incredible – Peter is probably the best in the Premiership at dealing with the back pass rule. Fortunately, we responded immediately with Teddy's equaliser just before half-time. But overall our passing was poor again. We had a makeshift midfield and it took us the whole of the first half to get into our stride.

In the second half, Becks came on and gave us more width on the right and we dominated them from then on. Pally went up front for the last 20 minutes as the Gaffer went for the win. As Giggsy said to me afterwards, we've been playing long ball for the final 20 minutes of our last few home games. That's not our usual game, but teams are putting ten men behind the ball against us at Old Trafford. A visit to Villa Park on Wednesday may do us some good.

Full back Michael Clegg was our Man of the Match today. His passing was accurate and he nearly scored with a great header as well. Michael is really athletic, perhaps unsurprisingly as his Dad owns a weights gym. Mike's brother Steve also plays for United, in the Under-17s, and he's 100 per cent into it. He'll do well too.

When we beat Barnsley 7-0 in the League, I said they weren't a bad team but everything went in our favour that day. Today, they played good football and defended better.

15 November 1997, England v Cameroon (h): "Scholesy put me clean through, but my shot nearly hit the corner flag. I turned round and he was laughing at me! I'll have to watch a video of Paul's goal to see how he does it." *Phil*

January 1998 v Chelsea (a). "This was one of the greatest United performances I have been involved in... We absolutely battered them." *Gary*

6 February 1998, Munich Memorial Service at Manchester Cathedral: "I was particularly moved when Duncan Edwards' mum, with tears in her eyes, got up to light a candle for her son." *Gar*

7 February 1998 v Bolton Wanderers (h): "I was close to tears when the referee blew his whistle to signal the end of the minute's silence." *Phil*

February 1998: "Three Barnsley MPs are raising a motion in the House of Commons about the
or standard of refereeing following the 'non-penalty' when I tackled Andy Liddell of Barnsley
st Sunday. I might have to go down and debate that one with them face-to-face!" *Gary*

ex Ferguson: "For the first year I was a professional, whenever the manager walked into
e room I shut up and sat up straight as if I was at school... My initial fear has turned into
omplete respect for him." *Phil*

18 February 1998 v Aston Villa (a):
"When Becks scored in the
82nd minute, he dived into
the crowd to celebrate and the
whole team followed. It wasn't
an ordinary celebration.
That goal was a release." *Phil*

28 February 1998 v Chelsea (a). My first goal: "Ole Gunnar Solskjaer came up to me three times in the hour before kick-off and said, 'You're going to score today, Phil. Remember what I say.' I just laughed." *Phil*

3 March 1998: Taking a break in the Monaco sunshine before the big game

⁴ March 1998 v Arsenal (h): "I was already in the dressing room when my dejected
am-mates started to arrive after the final whistle. The door was open and we could hear
e Arsenal boys screaming and shouting." *Phil*

18 March 1998 v Monaco (h):
"After the game, people said to me, 'You
were unlucky' and 'Don't worry, you'll win it
next year', but I'm sick of hearing that." *Gary*

⁴ March 1998 v Arsenal (h): "We couldn't
·lieve that a player of Peter's importance had
·t injured so close to the Monaco game." *Gary*

28 March 1998 v Wimbledon (h): "When Ronny Johnsen scored, I went barmy – I even kicked a advertising board Ketsbaia-style!" *Phil*

28 March 1998 v Wimbledon (h): "Ben Thornley came on and clinched the game for us." *Phil*

April 1998 v Blackburn Rovers (a): "We were in debt to Andy Cole for drawing us level. His goal won us the match because, until then, our heads had been down." *Phil*

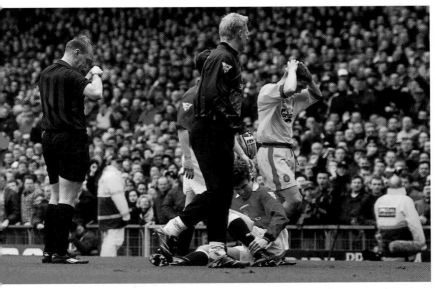

O April 1998 v Liverpool (h). Michael Owen's sending off: "Roy Evans tried to excuse these ackles, saying we had been winding Michael up. That is the biggest load of rubbish I have ever eard. No one said a single word to him." *Phil*

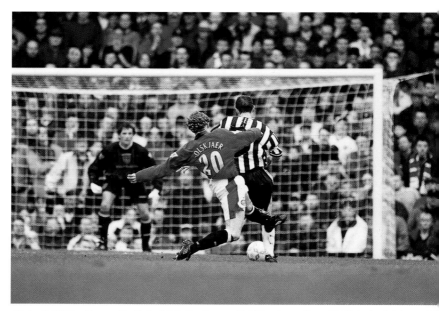

18 April 1998 v Newcastle United (h). Ole Gunnar Solskjaer's sending off: "If he hadn't brought him down, our title hopes could have ended there and then – he had to do it." *Gary*

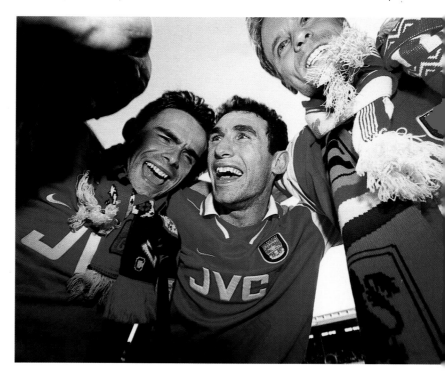

3 May 1998: "Arsenal are Champions... At first I felt quite bitter. 'They're going a bit over the top, aren't they?' I thought. But then you remember what a great feeling it is." *Phil*

GARY: I really wanted to play today, because I wasn't particularly pleased with my England performance. But I wasn't picked. People might think the Boss isn't taking the FA Cup seriously, but that's unfair. Against Chelsea in the Third Round he played our strongest team, but he felt that we could win against Walsall and Barnsley by changing the team a bit. He wants to win the FA Cup but at the same time give a rest to the players who need it. After the game, one of the Barnsley players said our line-up showed a lack of respect, but our starting eleven today was packed with internationals.

I came on as sub and nearly threw it away. Andy Liddell went through in the penalty area and I thought he'd score if I didn't make a tackle. Try as I might, I couldn't reach the ball. As I fell to the ground I listened out for the ref's whistle to signal a penalty. After a couple of seconds I thought, "He's not going to blow."

Liddell came up to me and said, "I can't believe this. You never got the ball, did you?"

I certainly wouldn't have argued if the referee had given a penalty. That incident may be a turning point for us. It's the first piece of luck we've had for a while.

The Gaffer had a little go at Andy Gray during his post-match interview on Sky for implying we get loads of penalties at Old Trafford. The fact is we've had eleven in nine years – the Gaffer often jokes that we don't get any penalties.

It has been said that Alex Ferguson likes to engineer a siege mentality at the club, but that's not unusual in football. Before Euro '96, the England players all had a sense that the media were against us, and we used that to strengthen our determination.

Anyway, it's a fact that a lot of people hate Manchester United. It's not just a complex we've got.

FA Cup Round Five / Old Trafford / Att: 54,700

Manchester United 1
Schmeichel, Irwin, Berg, Pallister, Clegg, P Neville, Johnsen (Beckham), McClair (G Neville), Giggs, Sheringham, Nevland (Cruyff)
Scorer: Sheringham
Barnsley 1
Watson, Eaden, De Zeeuw (Appleby), Moses, Morgan, Krizan, Redfearn, Bosancic, Bullock, Hendrie (Liddell), Ward
Scorer: Hendrie

Monday 16 February

GARY: At The Cliff today Andy Cole came up to me laughing. He'd seen the TV replay of my tackle yesterday.

"It was a Twickenham job," he chuckled.

PHIL: At training, a few players moaned that the last thing we need at the moment is a FA Cup replay.

"How many games have you all missed this season?" the Boss asked.

We told him. Teddy's missed eight, I've missed ten, and Denis hasn't played in fifteen. It's only Pally, Peter, Becks and Gary who have been virtually ever-present. We still have loads left in the tank and tiredness shouldn't come into it.

The Gaffer thinks that when I play in midfield, I'm receiving the ball with my back to our opponents. He arranged an exercise just for me to practice receiving passes on the half-turn.

Tuesday 17 February

PHIL: The Youth Team have returned from Viareggio. They won their first game, then got disqualified for not showing their passports to the referee before kick-off. Daylight robbery!

GARY: No practice match today. We've played practice games the day before the last five or six matches and each time the team selected for the match has had a nightmare.

After training, the Gaffer got us all into his office to watch a video. It showed the techniques the British Lions used to build team spirit and confidence before their victorious South African tour last year.

"You already have these qualities, but you don't seem to believe it," Alex Ferguson said. "Monaco are a good side, but make no bones about it. Your objective this season is to win the European Cup."

That's the first time he has ever said that. What with last Thursday's talk with the lads and today, the message is clear: we've got to start performing.

Monaco is only a fortnight away.

Wednesday 18 February   Aston Villa 0 Manchester United 2

PHIL: I was disappointed to be dropped for the Villa game. Brian McClair was chosen ahead of me in midfield. Choccy hasn't played many full games this year and he said to me, "Get a good warm-up. I'll be knackered after 70 minutes!"

Savo Milosevic was booed in the warm-up but the Villa fans got behind him after the first ten minutes. He's a decent player and he set up good chances for Grayson and Taylor. When we saw his name on the teamsheet beforehand, we knew he had a point to prove so we marked him that little bit tighter.

At half-time the Gaffer said, "You've got to take a risk to win games." He put me on as sub for Choccy and told Ryan and Butty to get into the box. I was to sit in and pick up the pieces. In the second half, we were less direct and started to pass the ball. If it's 0-0 with 20 minutes to go at home, the crowd start baying for goals and you find yourself playing desperate long balls. Our travelling fans are more patient and just get behind you.

When you've got Giggsy and Beckham in the side, you need a ball-winner in midfield so they can concentrate on attacking and Nicky Butt's return to the side helped us. When Becks scored in the 82nd minute, he dived into the crowd to celebrate and the whole team followed. It wasn't an ordinary celebration. That goal was a release.

We had to win tonight. In the dressing room afterwards, it was as if we'd won a Cup Semi-Final. Now we are seven points clear of Liverpool and eight points clear of the rest. It was a happy coach journey home.

I watched the highlights of the Chelsea v Arsenal Coca-Cola Cup Semi-Final when I got in. There were some great goals and Vialli got his first win as manager. When someone new takes over, players always seem to lift themselves. Hopefully, their Cup run will take the Chelsea players' minds off the League.

Middlesbrough also produced a shock to beat Liverpool 2-0 and reach the Final.

GARY: The Gaffer told us before the game that we were playing Villa at the right time. He had seen them play against Coventry and said the fans were turning on their players and they were losing confidence and making mistakes.

Nevertheless, Villa probably had the upper hand for an hour and our own lack of confidence showed through. When I blasted a shot over the bar, my dad heard one fan shout, "Neville, when are you going to get it into your dumb head that you aren't a goalscorer?" One day, I'm going to bang it in the top corner and jump into the crowd after him!

At half-time the Gaffer said we were trying to play it forward too quickly. Earlier in the season, we had had a lot of success playing more direct football, but we've maybe lost a bit of variation in our game. In the last half hour, we passed it really well and reaped the rewards.

I wasn't sure whether to celebrate or not when I heard the results from the Coca-Cola Cup. Most United fans would be pleased to see Liverpool and Arsenal lose, but you can look at the Premiership race in two ways. If Liverpool or Arsenal had gone on to win the Coca-Cola Cup, it could have taken the pressure off them in the League, because they'd already have a trophy in the bag. On the other hand, both teams can now concentrate all their efforts on the League. All the hype surrounding a Wembley final means an extra mental strain in the fortnight building up to it, and that's how tiredness sets in. One thing is for sure: neither Liverpool nor Arsenal are going to have a fixture problem.

I hope Middlesbrough do well at Wembley and come straight back up to the Premiership.

Premiership / Villa Park / Att: 39,372

Aston Villa 0
Bosnich, Scimeca, Ehiogu, Southgate, Wright, Joachim, Taylor, Grayson, Nelson,
Collymore, Milosovic
Manchester United 2
Schmeichel, G Neville, Berg, Pallister, Irwin, Beckham, McClair (P Neville), Butt, Giggs, Sheringham, Cole
Scorers: Beckham, Giggs

Thursday 19 February

PHIL: If we lose a match, the lads don't get into The Cliff the next day until five minutes before training. But everyone was in early today, talking about last night. There was a good atmosphere.

It was Gary's 23rd birthday yesterday and we had a belated celebration meal this evening at a local Italian restaurant. On my birthday, Gary told the waiters who got the whole restaurant to sing "Happy Birthday", so I threatened to do the same for him. He hates things like that. As soon as we sat down at our table, they put the 'Happy Birthday' music on. Gary stormed, "If that's for me, I'm leaving!" In fact, it was for someone on the next table. I couldn't stop laughing.

Friday 20 February

GARY: It's the time of year when all the lads fill in forms for the Professional Footballers' Association awards. I've been named as full back in the winning eleven for the past two years. You get a medal and I treasure that, because it's your fellow players who vote for you. You aren't allowed to nominate players in your own club, so this year my team was:

Tim Flowers

Lee Dixon   Tony Adams   Sol Campbell   Nigel Winterburn

Steve McManaman   Paul Ince   Marc Overmars

Gianfranco Zola   Dennis Bergkamp   Alan Shearer

Some of the lads slaughtered me for picking Shearer because he's been injured, but over the years Alan's proved himself to be the best around. My Player Of The Year is Sol Campbell. He's an unbelievable defender and, with Dennis Bergkamp, the most popular choice in our dressing room.

Not surprisingly, Michael Owen got my vote for the Young Player award. He should walk it. My own best showing in that category was two years ago, when I came second to Robbie Fowler by about fifty votes. Brian McClair hands out the forms; he's our PFA rep. Among his other duties, Brian signs our players' pool cheques and it's my job to countersign them. When he hangs up his PFA boots, I'd expect Peter, Pally or Denis to take over, but maybe I'll do it in a couple of years time.

PHIL: Played a Young v Olds five-a-side with benches for goals.

David May is back playing for the Olds so Jordi transferred to our side. We went 4-0 up in about two minutes so Kiddo switched the teams around. Pally and Peter didn't fancy it this morning and just stayed up front, so they had no defence. Forwards usually play as defenders and vice-versa in these games.

After training, the manager gave us each a video to watch at home of two Champions' League games involving Monaco.

GARY: I got home from training and flicked on Sky News. Three Barnsley MPs are raising a motion in the House of Commons about the poor standard of refereeing following the "non-penalty" when I tackled Andy Liddell of Barnsley last Sunday. I couldn't believe it. I might have to go down and debate that one with them face-to-face.

PHIL: I wonder if those MPs would have bothered if the penalty had been at The Dell? It's laughable, really. Andy Gray commented after the Barnsley game that the penalty would have been given at the other end. I think there is some truth in what he said, but that's also true of any intimidating ground. If a Liverpool player goes down in front of the Kop, that's a penalty. It's not just Old Trafford.

Saturday 21 February   Manchester United 2 Derby County 0

PHIL: The Boss stuck with the team that finished the game against Villa. In the second half of that game, we played our best football since the FA Cup match against Chelsea in January.

I was happy to to play in midfield again; it was only at Villa that I felt I was getting the hang of it. Teddy said to me before kick-off, "You're in there to win the ball, leave the silky skills to Giggsy and Becks." That took the pressure off and today's midfield performance was my best yet.

GARY: We knew Derby would be really tough opponents. Before today they'd never lost against us in the Premiership. I was up against Wanchope again, who left me lying on the ground when he scored against us at Pride Park. Before the game, I decided that I was just going to sit back and make sure that I defended well against him.

PHIL: Derby's front three of Wanchope, Baiano and Sturridge are as good as any in the League. But today we didn't give them a chance to shine. It wasn't a good game to watch and despite the importance of the match, the atmosphere was quiet.

We were devastated when Giggsy pulled his hamstring. He scored a fantastic goal set up by Andy Cole with a perfect cross – but only for Giggs, because no one else would have the pace to get there. Ryan didn't have to break stride. And it was Ryan who was tripped for the penalty. As soon as he went down, I shouted to Denis Irwin to grab the ball. I feel so safe when he takes them. The new penalty law allows goalies to move on their line, but Denis doesn't get ruffled and he has great technique.

In the dressing room afterwards, the manager's first question was, "How's Ryan?"

GARY: Ryan was sitting down and he said his leg felt sore. Five minutes later, he got up and limped, which is a bad sign. On a minor hamstring strain, you can usually walk around OK.

It's a huge loss. We haven't got another midfielder of Ryan's type.

PHIL: A hamstring pull takes three to four weeks to recover. It will have to be life or death for him to risk the second leg against Monaco. The Boss was gutted because Ryan's been playing so well and he gives us balance; we play best with a 4-4-2 with Becks and Ryan out wide.

GARY: Jordi was also injured, thanks to a dreadful two-footed, over-the-top tackle by Dean Sturridge. A few of our players ran over to the referee shouting, "That was a bad one, ref." He told us to go away and then booked Sturridge. I just don't understand it. You can get booked for pushing an opponent nowadays, and you're not going to hurt anyone by pushing them, and yet you get the same punishment for a leg-breaker. It was a terrible thing to happen to Jordi; he's had enough trouble with injuries this year. What's more, Jordi and Ben Thornley are the only people who could fill Ryan's role on the left side of midfield.

PHIL: Sturridge's tackle on Jordi was one of the worst I've seen all season. Strangely, the United players on the bench hadn't seen how bad it was, but I was right next Jordi when it happened.

Derby manager Jim Smith said afterwards that he thought we

were cruising and I agree. We put in a good professional performance, but we can still go up a couple of gears. We'll need to over the next couple of weeks.

Playing midfield knackers me. At left back or wing back, you can cheat a bit and get a breather, but in midfield you never stop. I nearly collapsed in the shower. I said to Coley, who was standing next to me in the shower, "I'll never give a bad pass to a midfielder again!"

Premiership / Old Trafford / Att: 55,170

Manchester United 2
Schmeichel, G Neville, Berg, Pallister, Irwin (Clegg), Beckham, P Neville, Butt, Giggs (McClair), Sheringham, Cole (Cruyff)
Scorers: Giggs, Irwin (pen)
Derby County 0
Poom, Rowett, Stimac, Dailly, Delap (Willems), Eranio, Carsley, Powell, Baiano, Wanchope, Sturridge

PHIL: Elsewhere today, Chelsea lost, Blackburn lost, but Arsenal won. Arsenal are in the best shape because they have two games in hand, but they've got to go to West Ham on Monday night and that'll be a tough one. I'd rather have the points in the bag.

The Boss always stresses the importance of goal difference and that's an extra point for us over Arsenal, too. A lot of the credit goes to Peter and a more settled defence – Gary and Pally have played virtually every game.

Premiership (top) *at 22 February*	P	W	D	L	F	A	Pts	GD
Manchester United	27	17	5	5	56	19	56	37
Arsenal	25	13	8	4	45	26	47	19
Liverpool	26	13	8	4	45	26	47	19
Chelsea	26	14	3	9	52	29	45	23
Blackburn Rovers	26	12	9	5	44	30	45	14
Derby County	27	12	6	9	41	34	42	7

Sunday 22 February

PHIL: Day off today. I rang Jordi in the morning to see how he was. He'd had an X-ray on his ankle and the injury was diagnosed as a hairline fracture. He won't be fit again until mid-April and he's virtually resigned to his season being over. He's had horrendous luck this year.

Monday 23 February

PHIL: Went straight up to the medical room to see how everyone was. Not a pretty sight. Giggsy and Ronny were there, Denis had a slight strain, and Ole had picked up a virus and was having a blood test.

The Boss wasn't in, but the team Kiddo put in bibs for the practice match looked like the team for Wednesday. Gary was at left back, Pally and David May in central defence, Michael Clegg at right back, with me, Nicky and Choccy in midfield. Andy Cole was the lone striker with Erik Nevland and Ben Thornley on either wing. We played this 4-5-1 formation for twenty minutes, then chopped and changed, but nothing seemed to work. Barnsley play wing backs, and the Bomb Squad's wing backs were constantly getting on the ball and attacking us.

Tuesday 24 February

PHIL: The Gaffer heard about the problems in yesterday's practice match and called a meeting before training. He suggested we should go 4-5-1 or something similar, with Ben and Erik as out-and-out wingers. Then he asked for our views. Peter Schmeichel said he thought the proposed line-up was asking a lot of Erik, who usually plays as a striker and has never played a full First Team game. Gary said he thought the system was too negative, because Andy would be up there on his own with three defenders on him. After some debate, the Boss decided we should try a few things out. Soon after we started the practice game in a 4-5-1 formation, Butty had to pull out with a tight calf, so Becks came on our side. He moved to the right side and we went to a 4-4-2. That worked better, but we still weren't getting enough possession.

Wednesday 25 February   Barnsley 3 Manchester United 2

PHIL: The Gaffer decided to go for 4-4-2. We found out in the morning that Butty couldn't be risked, so Becks played in the middle and

I was in right midfield. Erik Nevland and Coley were put up front with Ben Thornley on the left wing.

GARY: It was a frustrating game. When Hendrie scored, I was looking right down the defensive line and I couldn't believe it wasn't given as offside. I ran over to the linesman and said, "Who was playing him on?"

"Somebody over there," he replied, pointing. He was shaking like a leaf. Then the referee arrived on the scene and got his book out.

"What are you booking me for?" I asked.

"You've just run over thirty yards to complain," replied the ref.

"Hang on, aren't I allowed to run over and ask who played him on?"

He didn't answer. It's amazing that you get the same punishment for something like that as you get for a two-footed tackle. The other two goals we conceded were down to poor marking from set pieces. I was nearest to their goalscorer Scott Jones for the second, but I wasn't supposed to be marking him on free-kicks. It was my job to mark Jones on corners though, so I was to blame for his second and their third. It was a good header, but bad defending to let him get round the back of me.

At half-time, the Gaffer announced that if Choccy was substituted I would be moved into midfield. Half the players in the dressing room started laughing!

PHIL: Before the second half kick-off, Becks looked round and said, "I can't believe this. I'm surrounded by Nevilles. I never thought I'd see the day!"

Gary's been saying he could do a better job than me since I started playing in midfield. He did well today, though he was running round like a headless chicken at times, much to Becks' amusement. At one point Gary tried a crossfield pass which went straight into touch. "Leave that to Beckham," I told him.

GARY: With 25 minutes to go, a couple of Barnsley players were shouting "3-1" to their fans. The same two players also said "You're going out!" to us for the last ten minutes of the game. I couldn't believe they were gloating during the game. It's something I've never come across before. When we beat them 7-0 back in October, we could have showboated, but we didn't. Having said that, we are due back at Oakwell on the last day of the season and that could be interesting.

Michael Twiss came on as sub tonight and looked the part. He's a local lad, strong, with a thunderous left-foot shot. I've seen him in training and he probably hits it as hard as Becks. I hope it comes right for him at United because he's a nice lad.

When we got it back to 3-2, I've never felt so desperate to equalise in my whole life. In the last few minutes, Barnsley were dead on their feet and I was sure we'd beat them if it went to extra time. I had a shot blocked on the line and Ben Thornley nearly became a hero in the last minute. To be fair, it wasn't an easy chance and I think Ben played well overall. He's worked hard on his fitness and now he's getting First Team games under his belt the match sharpness will follow.

PHIL: Anyone who thought we didn't care about the FA Cup this year should have seen us in the dressing room afterwards, or on the coach home. The likes of Teddy and Ole haven't played in a FA Cup Final and it's the best feeling in the world to walk out at Wembley. We were devastated.

FA Cup Round Five replay / Oakwell Ground / Att: 18,655

Barnsley 3
Watson, Markstedt, Jones, Moses, Appleby (Sheridan), Bullock (Marcelle), Redfearn, Bosancic, Barnard, Hendrie (Liddell), Ward
Scorers: Hendrie, Jones 2
Manchester United 2
Schmeichel, G Neville, May, Pallister, Clegg (Twiss), P Neville, McClair (Irwin), Beckham, Thornley, Nevland (Sheringham), Cole
Scorers: Sheringham, Cole

Thursday 26 February

PHIL: The manager came in and said, "I was proud of you all last night. Every player out there wanted to win and I love teams like that." He told us to put the defeat behind us and to get plenty of rest before Saturday's game against Chelsea.

Today, Robbie Fowler confirmed that his cruciate injury would force him to miss the World Cup. Everyone at United was gutted for him. Roy Keane said he wouldn't wish a cruciate injury on his worst enemy. Robbie's young though, and I'm sure he'll play in more World Cups.

Rumours are going round Manchester that Roy is almost fit

enough to play. He is training with us now and doing everything except tackling, but he's at least six weeks off full fitness.

GARY: We watched the Monaco tapes this afternoon. We are in for a really tough game. Their front three of Ipkeba, Henry and Trezeguet are all rapid, they defend in numbers and in midfield they have Ali Bernabia, a dangerous Beardsley-type floater.

Thierry Henry often plays out on the left, on my side, and he looks like an Olympic sprinter. I'll have to give myself a couple of yards.

Friday 27 February

PHIL: Paul Scholes trained with us today. For the past ten days, all he's had is physio treatment. I don't think Scholesy would even be considered for Chelsea if Ryan was fit.

Most of the lads came in wearing their club blazers this morning, then had dinner at The Cliff and went straight to the airport. We've got a new chef called Tom at The Cliff and he's making a real effort. He leaves a big plate of fruit slices in the dressing room for when we arrive in the morning and he's putting on three-course meals. Loads of First Teamers are staying for lunch now. It's good for team spirit and means that Trevor Lea, the club nutritionist, can monitor each player's eating habits.

In London for the away game against Chelsea, we are staying in an amazing hotel. Our room has its own lounge, TV and video and the bedroom overlooks all the yachts docked in Chelsea Harbour.

In the evening, the Boss named the team. It has a solid look about it with Scholesy and Butt back together in midfield. He stressed we mustn't get involved in any nastiness and he was really confident we'd win.

7

A little miracle

Saturday 28 February   **Chelsea 0 Manchester United 1**

PHIL: I can't believe it, I actually scored! My first goal in ninety League and Cup games!

Strangely, Ole Gunnar had a premonition that I was going to do it. He came up to me three times in the hour before kick-off and said, "You're going to score today, Phil. Remember what I say." I just laughed.

It all happened so fast. Teddy played the ball through and there was no one near me so I thought I was miles offside. In a one-on-one situation with the goalie, I've probably got the worst record in the League, but this time I caught my shot perfectly on the half-volley. It was the type of situation Kiddo makes us practice in training all the time. As soon as I hit it I knew it was in.

I'd always thought I'd cry like Ketsbaia if I scored, but when it finally happened I didn't know what to do. I ran over to the corner full of Chelsea fans and thought about doing that thing Becks did last time with the ears, but decided against it. Soon, all the lads were diving on top of me and laughing. Gary and Nicky were saying, "Phil, do you know what you've done?" Unfortunately my Dad wasn't there to see it, because Bury were at home today. He'd had another £20 bet on me to score last week, but after yet another blank day, he'd given up on me.

I was pleased for my old friend Grant Brebner, who has a fiver on me every week and was set to cash in at 33–1 ... or so I thought. Grant's on loan to Hibernian at the moment. Today he made his debut against Celtic. I rang him in the evening and Grant said he was so fired up for his game that he forgot to put the bet on! So everyone who bets on me is still in debt!

As soon as I scored, I wanted the ref to blow the whistle so I could march off with the match ball. As I was walking back to the centre circle, I heard the United fans singing my name for the first time ever.

At half-time, every player I spoke to just seemed to laugh. Ole Gunnar shook my hand, and I said, "Will you tell me that before every game, please!"

GARY: It's brilliant that Phil scored. The only downside is that after scoring just one goal, he now has a better strike rate than me – I've played over 100 matches for my one goal. It was an excellent finish and Phil's overall performance in midfield was very good. Having played there in the second half against Barnsley, I know how difficult it is to adjust!

Although there was the odd flashpoint, I thought the game was played in a decent spirit overall. You expect to be tackled hard when you go to a place like Chelsea, but they have some superb players.

PHIL: We defended as well today as we have all season. Chelsea hardly had a chance all game. Once we had a lead, we sat back and hit them on the break and we never looked in danger because they kept bumping in high balls. Ronny Johnsen was outstanding for us. We call him the Ice Man, not for his temperament or because he's from Norway, but because he always has an ice pack on his legs after a game. Ronny's one you don't want to take on in training. He quick, strong, almost unbeatable.

The Boss was really happy after the game.

It was nice travelling home and listening to the other matches on the radio, with everyone else under pressure. Blackburn won, but Liverpool lost 2-1 to Villa. John Gregory has taken over at Villa and players always seem to raise themselves for a new manager. Stan Collymore scored two and when he's on that sort of form, there's no better striker in the country. When he runs at people with the ball, he's unstoppable.

GARY: Other results may be going our way, but you don't start punching the air. You feel inwardly happy, but you don't gloat at another team's misfortunes because it could come back to haunt you. We are in a strong position now, but I still guard against any thoughts that the title race is over. Arsenal now look the likeliest challengers and if they win their games in hand and beat us at Old Trafford, they'll be level with us. And we also have tough games against Leeds and Blackburn ahead of us.

PHIL: In the evening, I went out with Paul Scholes and our girl-friends but we were both knackered. I'm loving it in midfield, it's good fun. I'd like to stay there and hopefully score a few more goals. People want to talk to you when you score.

Premiership / Stamford Bridge / Att: 34,511

Chelsea 0
Kharine, Petrescu, Leboeuf, Clarke, Vialli (Flo), Hughes, Wise, Duberry, Le Saux, Di Matteo, Zola
Manchester United 1
Schmeichel, G Neville, Irwin, Pallister (Berg), Johnsen, Beckham, P Neville, Butt, Scholes, Sheringham, Cole
Scorer: P Neville

8

Monte Carlo and bust

Monday 2 March

GARY: When we arrived at our hotel in France, the manager called a team meeting. He announced the team and told us how we would play. He was very clear about what he wanted. "Don't be be fooled into thinking you've come here to play any football," he said. "There is going to be no football in this game, you won't be able to get it down to pass it. The pitch will not allow it. It's going to be very difficult."

PHIL: I will be playing in midfield. The Gaffer told me that my main job will be to keep an eye on Monaco's little number eight, Ali Bernabia. I'm to stay within ten yards of him when we are attacking. Basically, it's a man-to-man marking job and if Bernabia scores, it will be my fault.

Tuesday 3 March

PHIL: No sightseeing today. If the Boss caught us out, he'd go barmy, so I just stayed in. I had some precautionary treatment on my swollen shin instead. If I get kicked on it, it's going to be really painful.

In the evening, we played an eight-a-side possession game at the Stade Louis II. Before we started, the Boss came up to me and quietly told me to play for the team in bibs, so that it would look like I'm not playing tomorrow and Ole Gunnar Solskjaer is. It was kidology designed to fool the French press, but it fooled our team as well – half of them came up to me saying, "Has he bombed you?"

The Gaffer only let us train for 25 minutes, because he didn't want any of us turning ankles on this uneven surface so close to such a massive game.

GARY: On the Monaco videos we watched, their pitch looked like a bowling green, but up close it was in a dreadful state. It was rock hard and they've had to paint large patches green where there were cracks and the grass was missing. Apparently, because the pitch is built on top of a car park, the roots don't have a chance to grow properly.

Wednesday 4 March   Monaco 0 Manchester United 0

PHIL: We all had a gentle stroll around the hotel grounds in the morning and then watched Monaco v Sporting Lisbon on video to refresh our memories. Monaco may have some good attacking players, but we were certain they wouldn't be able to show anything on this pitch. It was always going to be a midfield battle. The Boss said if we kept it tight, got stuck in and played it forward early, we'd be ok.

Even when we got to the ground, nobody knew what kind of boots to wear. The pitch had been watered, but it was still bone-hard underneath. In the end, I opted for a stud. As a defender at United, if you wear moulds and you slip, the Boss will kill you.

It was a bit tense in the dressing room, but the United fans made us feel at home when we walked out on to the pitch. Although it must have been the worst match ever to watch, the game plan worked perfectly. We minimised their chances. Sometimes you have to curb your instincts in order to get a result.

Monaco substituted Ipkeba, Henry and Bernabia in the second half, so maybe they were satisfied with 0-0, too. Monaco have an excellent away record so they must be confident.

In the dressing room and back at the hotel, the Boss, Bobby Charlton and the directors were delighted. I know it's important to score an away goal in Europe nowadays, but when I saw the Boss was buzzing I thought 0-0 must be a good result.

GARY: We stuck to the plan, which was to keep it tight. Having lost 1-0 to Dortmund in the first leg last season, perhaps because we were a little naive, we were desperate not to make the same mistake again by conceding a goal. I was marking Thierry Henry. His touch wasn't very good, but he was lightning quick, so I gave myself two yards and did all right against him. Monaco had a few chances, but we always kept it tight at the back.

Although in this respect it was a good defensive display, we just couldn't create enough pressure on them at the other end. Conceding a goal would have made it tough, but by keeping a clean sheet we've given ourselves a clear task in the second leg: to win! We're all hoping Giggsy will be back.

Champions' League Quarter-Final first leg / Louis II Stadium / Att: 15,000

Monaco 0
Barthez, Sagnol, Dumas, Konjic, Leonard, Legwinski, Djetou, Collins, Benarbia (Carnot), Henry (Lefevre), Ipkeba (Spehar)
Manchester United 0
Schmeichel, G Neville, Johnsen, Berg, Irwin (McClair), Beckham, Butt, Scholes, P Neville, Sheringham, Cole

Thursday 5 March

GARY: In the morning, we did a loosener at a local sports ground and the manager gathered us around to have a few words about last night's game. He said he was pleased that we had kept a clean sheet, but thought we might have been a little more adventurous going for that crucial away goal. I think everyone agreed with him, but in the back of our minds we were also thinking that if we had been more attacking, we may have conceded a goal.

As if to reinforce the Gaffer's point, that evening I watched Chelsea score two away goals in Spain. It made me wish we'd done the same. The manager told us at the start of the season that if we scored in every game, we'd win the European Cup. Not scoring in Monaco could still hurt us.

Friday 6 March

GARY: Peter injured himself in Monaco, so the lads told me I would be captain tomorrow for the game at Sheffield Wednesday. No chance. Brian McClair, Teddy or Maysie would be selected before me.

Saturday 7 March   Sheffield Wednesday 2 Manchester United 0

GARY: Kiddo came up to me 45 minutes before kick-off at Hillsborough and told me I would be captain for the game. I didn't smile, I just nodded, but inside I was happy. To lead out United is a huge honour.

The manager told us that if we win our next three games, against Sheffield Wednesday, West Ham and Arsenal, we will clinch the League. But by half-time we were 1-0 down and the manager said to me, "You'd better do something about this Neville. You don't want to lose your first game as captain!" We were poor. After they scored we were always chasing the game. I know a lot of the lads had tight calves and hamstrings after the game in Monaco.

PHIL: Rai Van Der Gouw, who has just recovered from a knee operation, came in for Peter Schmeichel. Of course you notice the difference when Peter's not playing, because he's the world's best. But we train with Rai every day and when the Gaffer names him in the the team, nobody bats an eyelid.

The pitch was sandy and heavy today, but for the first 20 minutes we played really well. Then we conceded the goal from a corner and after that we never looked like getting back into it. Maysie held his hand up in the dressing room at half-time to take the blame because Atherton was his man, but it was a great cross by Carbone.

Since we beat them 6-1, Wednesday have raised their game under their new manager, Ron Atkinson. I still think we would have won if we hadn't conceded a goal before half-time, but the goal seemed to knock the stuffing out of us. When things aren't going well tiredness affects your performance. Ronny Johnsen got a knock on the head and threw up at half-time, so I moved from midfield back to left back. I made a couple of runs, then all of a sudden my hamstring started cramping so I had to go off. The physio, Dave Fevre, examined it and said, "It's a good job you came off or you would have pulled it like Giggsy."

The Gaffer didn't say much afterwards. He was upset that we gave another goal away from a corner, but he could see there was no lack of effort. In a farcical finish to a bad day, the water in the showers was boiling hot, so the whole squad had to take turns to wash in two sinks.

Premiership / Hillsborough / Att: 39,427

Sheffield Wednesday 2
Pressman, Barrett, Newsome, Walker, Hinchcliffe, Carbone, Atherton, Stefanovic, Pembridge (Whittingham), Di Canio (Oakes), Booth /
Scorers: Atherton, Di Canio
Manchester United 0
Van Der Gouw, G Neville, May, Johnsen (Scholes), Berg, Beckham, P Neville (Curtis), Butt, Solskjaer, Sheringham, Cole (McClair)

Sunday 8 March

GARY: Frank Leboeuf was quoted on the back of the News of the World slagging off almost the entire United team. Beckham was a "spoilt child", Schmeichel made "big blunders", Irwin was "getting old", Cole "made everyone laugh with his misses", Sheringham "uses his elbows" and I'm "anonymous". We've played Chelsea four times this season, and he obviously doesn't think we are that good a team!

Monday 9 March

PHIL: Everyone is a bit down about our crippling injury situation. The Gaffer pulled Ben, Casp and John Curtis out of tonight's Reserve game because there aren't enough fit First Team regulars left.

The physio had a word with all the injured players to tell us to stay positive. Recovery from injury is psychological as well as physical and Dave wants to brighten the mood. Today, he let Ryan go out for a jog despite his hamstring, just so that Ryan will feel he's making progress. At the same time, Peter and Pally were allowed to do some stretching.

Tuesday 10 March

PHIL: The First Team trained at Mottram Hall today for a swim, a jacuzzi, lunch, and a change of scenery. I had to stay at The Cliff for a fitness test to see if I was ready for the West Ham game. I was made to do an intense couple of minutes of backward running to test my

for club and country

hamstring. It still didn't feel right. The Boss doesn't want to take any risks, so I had to be honest and declare myself unfit. I was a bit gutted because I've had a good run of games recently.

When the squad travelled to London tonight, I was left behind.

Wednesday 11 March   **West Ham United 1 Manchester United 1**

PHIL: A quiet day at The Cliff. The physio had Terry Cooke, Jordi, Giggsy and me playing basketball in the gym. Giggsy isn't bad and Jordi at least thinks he's good.

I went to Julie's house to watch the game on TV. I felt physically sick when West Ham scored and then went mad when we equalised. It's at this stage of the season that you start getting those sorts of emotions during games. I rang my brother afterwards and he told me that Nicky had pulled his calf and will be out for two weeks. But Nicky is the tough type who gets back quickly and he'll be desperate to play against Monaco.

Gary told me he felt he should have scored in the last minutes, so I gave him a bit of advice about how to hit it into the bottom left corner.

"Oh scored a goal, have we? Now you know it all," retorted Gaz.

GARY: We didn't play well again, particularly in the first half. Our injury situation was so bad that I ended up having to play in midfield and I'm certainly no midfielder. I blew a chance to win the game right at the death. I can't keep on doing this. My finishing is disgraceful.

West Ham have an excellent home record, so a draw isn't a terrible result, but we should be winning games now. On the coach back to the hotel we listened to the last bits of Arsenal's game at Wimbledon. We were gutted at the final whistle because their 1-0 win puts them mathematically level with us. We're in a real race now.

Premiership / Upton Park / Att: 25,892

West Ham United 1
Lama, Impey, Potts, R Ferdinand, Pearce, Lazaridis, Lampard, Berkovic, Lomas, Abou, Sinclair
Scorer: Sinclair
Manchester United 1
Schmeichel, G Neville, Berg, May, Irwin, Beckham, Butt (Curtis), McClair (Thornley), Scholes, Sheringham, Cole (Solskjaer)
Scorer: Scholes

Thursday 12 March

PHIL: I still felt my hamstring a bit in training but each day it gets a little better.

John Gorman telephoned today to ask about my injury. I told him I would be fit for Monaco and he said, "Well, that's good, because we're naming the England squad on Monday and you'll be in it." He was happy that I'd been playing more regularly and getting some experience in midfield and he asked me how Nicky was.

"He's OK," I replied.

"Oh, I spoke to Nicky earlier and he said he'd pulled his calf," said John.

Arsenal physio Gary Lewin does the same job for England and naturally the Boss doesn't want him to know which of us is fit or unfit before the Saturday game against the Gunners.

Friday 13 March

PHIL: I had a bit of treatment before training. Dave Fevre told me that the Boss wasn't going to risk me tomorrow against Arsenal, but my leg felt fine doing a box in training so I went up to the Gaffer.

"Look, Boss. I am fit to play tomorrow," I said.

He looked surprised. "Oh right, but I need you for Monaco."

"Honestly, Boss. I'm OK for tomorrow."

I'm probably a bit stupid because I didn't really test the hamstring with any strenuous exercises, but I'm desperate to play.

Later, Gary told me his leg injury has been diagnosed as muscle fatigue. It's pure tiredness. The schedule of non-stop playing and travelling we've had over the past couple of months does catch up with you.

Saturday 14 March   **Manchester United 0 Arsenal 1**

PHIL: Arrived at Old Trafford at 8.30 a.m. for massages and breakfast. As I was getting my rub-down from Jimmy Curran, the Boss wandered past and asked me if I was fit. When I said yes, he replied, "Ah good, I've got a new position for you today," and walked away laughing. It turned out that I was playing left midfield. The Gaffer wanted me to keep a track on Parlour.

We started the game fairly well and both Coley and Teddy probably should have scored, but Arsenal were creating chances too. During the first half I was switched to right back to deal with Overmars. He's the quickest player we face in the League and when you are marking him, you have to make a decision: either you get a good tackle in straight-away or stand off him deep. If he turns you, you just won't beat him for pace. I managed to put in a couple of good tackles on him and he didn't really cause me too much bother until I went off.

During the second half, I tackled Dennis Bergkamp and he screamed. I thought he was making a meal of it and told him so. It was all just in the heat of the moment, though. I think he is a great player.

My hamstring had tightened up and I had it massaged at half-time. The Boss wanted to take me off, but I was desperate to carry on. After about 70 minutes, it started to cramp up again. I signalled to the bench and came off at the same time as Ronny Johnsen was substituted. When you lose two defensive players, it takes time for the players coming on to get into the game, and during that period of uncertainty Overmars scored.

I was already in the dressing room when my dejected team-mates started to arrive after the final whistle. The door was open and we could hear the Arsenal boys screaming and shouting.

"The title's not over yet, not for them or for us," Denis Irwin said.

Then Kiddo came in. "We're still six points clear. Some crisis!" he exclaimed.

GARY: Manchester United always raise themselves for the big game. In my time with United we've always got a result when it has mattered most, so it was disappointing that Arsenal left Old Trafford with all three points today. We desperately missed the experience of Pallister, Keane, Giggs and Butt.

It seems odd that since we destroyed Chelsea just two months ago, we haven't recaptured that form. I can't put my finger on what's happened, but there were no excuses today. Arsenal undoubtedly deserved to win this one. I was surprised at the improvement in their play since we last came up against them. Overmars was outstanding, a constant thorn in our side.

Up until they scored, I was quite happy with my own performance. But looking back at the goal on TV afterwards, I thought I should have sat back and kept my position rather than going up for that first header with Anelka. It was a split-second decision and maybe I got it wrong. I felt I had to challenge for it, but when Anelka won the ball it left me in no-man's land. To make things worse, Peter went up for a corner in the last minute and injured himself trying to get back. We couldn't believe that a player of Peter's importance had got injured so close to the Monaco game, especially with Pally and Giggsy both looking very doubtful.

We are still confident we'll win the League. Arsenal have to play a lot of games in a short space of time and they're in the FA Cup as well. I know the Gunners control their own destiny, but I honestly believe that if we rediscover our form we'll still win the title.

Premierhsip / Old Trafford / Att: 55,174

Manchester United 0
Schmeichel, G Neville, Berg, Irwin, Curtis (Thornley), Beckham, Scholes, P Neville (Solskjaer), Johnsen (May), Sheringham, Cole
Arsenal 1
Manninger, Dixon, Adams, Keown, Winterburn, Parlour (Garde), Petit, Viera, Bergkamp, Overmars, Wreh (Anelka)
Scorer: Overmars

Premiership (top) *at 15 March*	P	W	D	L	F	A	Pts	GD
Manchester United	31	18	6	7	58	23	60	35
Arsenal	28	15	9	4	47	26	54	21
Liverpool	30	14	9	7	51	32	51	19
Chelsea	30	15	3	12	59	35	48	24
Leeds United	30	14	6	10	45	30	48	15
Blackburn Rovers	29	13	9	7	49	38	48	11

Sunday 15 March

PHIL: Yesterday's morning kick-off allowed me to rest up in the afternoon, so I felt totally refreshed when I woke up today. The Boss made us come in to The Cliff for breakfast. He wants to monitor what we are eating and when.

Peter Schmeichel said his hamstring didn't feel so bad today and he hopes he will be fit for Wednesday. It's easy to be wise after the event, but Peter has gone up for corners before and scored for us. Perhaps the only thing he did wrong was to challenge Bergkamp rather than sprinting back to goal. But basically the injury was just down to fatigue. Peter told us he's never felt so tired. He said recently that he's even finding it hard to kick it as far as normal – and that's coming from a keeper.

Nevertheless, the mood is really upbeat. Nicky now looks a cert for the Monaco game and Giggsy is still hopeful.

The News Of The World broke the Freddy Shepherd/Doug Hall story today. There was a fair bit of discussion about it at The Cliff, especially the "revelation" that Newcastle sold Andy Cole to United despite knowing he had a bad injury. Andy told us that was absolute rubbish. He was fit when he joined us.

Monday 16 March

PHIL: The Boss reckoned rest would do us more good than training today, so we watched videos of Monaco against Lierse and Bayern Leverkusen. The videos proved they are not invincible.

The general view in today's press seems to be that our injury problems could beat us on Wednesday, but I think the injury setbacks have only made our team spirit stronger. My feeling is that we'll batter them.

"If we win on Wednesday, we'll win the European Cup, because everyone will be fit for the Semi-Final," said the Gaffer.

The manager didn't reveal his team selection, except to say that David Beckham would play central midfield with Ole Gunnar on the left side, which made me think I wouldn't play. Ole, Coley and Teddy will all start, because he wants lots of legs up front to create chances. There is still a slim chance that Peter and Giggsy will play.

The Gaffer spoke to Glenn Hoddle this morning and told us which of us were in the England squad to play Switzerland. He'd agreed with Glenn that Coley, Scholesy and me won't join up with the squad because of our injuries.

GARY: When I woke up yesterday morning my ribs were in agony. When I sneezed, it felt like my insides were going to explode. I must have hurt myself when I collided with Anelka on Saturday. This morning I tried to train, but I couldn't run properly and had to drop out. They sent me for X-rays which showed nothing broken, but severe bruising on my ribs.

Tuesday 17 March

PHIL: The team to face Monaco was announced and I was in. Unfortunately, Peter Schmeichel isn't fit after all and Giggsy failed a fitness test this morning. Alex Ferguson told the press Ryan had trained today, but I think that was just a ploy to scare Monaco.

In the evening, I watched the Arsenal v West Ham FA Cup tie on television. Bergkamp got sent off for elbowing Steve Lomas. From our point of view, his three-game suspension is very significant. I was also happy to see the game go to extra time. I then caught the last ten minutes of Aston Villa's game against Athletico Madrid. Villa looked to have played really well, but it's the same old story. The continental team score an away goal and get the win.

Wednesday 18 March   Manchester United 1   Monaco 1

Phil: I woke up to read Arsene Wenger calling Rai Van Der Gouw "a jinx" in the papers. That is just rubbish. Everyone says Alex Ferguson plays mind games, but he hasn't said anything in public about any other team this season. Norway's boss Egil Olsen was also in the papers questioning Ole Gunnar Solskjaer's World Cup chances. Ole hasn't played for them since last April. Again, the timing of the comment was poor.

When we went in for massages several hours before our biggest game of the season, the mood was brilliant, everyone was confident.

Unfortunately, we got off to a disastrous start.

GARY: I was right next to Trezeguet when he struck his 96-mile-an-hour shot to give them the lead after five minutes. If I had been fully fit, I might have been able to get across to him. I'd had a pain-killing injection before kick-off and just two minutes into the game I had to sprint for the ball, but I was too slow. I tried to run my injury off, without success, so I signalled to the bench and Henning Berg replaced me.

Trezeguet's strike was frightening, the hardest shot I have ever seen. The ball was aimed only two yards to the side of Raimond, but it was hit with such power that he didn't have any chance. The goal was a sickener. My first thought was that it was a re-run of last year, when Dortmund took the lead in the first ten minutes. It meant we now had to score twice, which I still thought we could do.

I watched the rest of the game in the dressing room. Scholesy, who had to come off injured at half-time, watched it with me. I really fancied us to do it, especially when Ole Gunnar scored only eight minutes into the second half, but we just couldn't get the second goal.

The lads trooped back in and all just sat down in silence. It was a similiar mood to when we lost the League at West Ham three years ago. When the manager came in, he praised our effort, but he was obviously upset as well.

After the game, people said to me "You were unlucky" and "Don't worry, you'll win it next year," but I'm sick of hearing that. We had the chance to do it today. It's not just bad luck that sees us fail in Europe. I've played against European teams since I was sixteen. When I was in the Youth Team, we got to the final of a youth tournament in Zurich three years running and lost to Barcelona each time. That's not luck; European teams just know how to win. We need to find that extra something.

It makes it worse that some of us genuinely believed this was going to be our year. We won our first five games and, most importantly, the win over Juventus showed we could beat the best.

PHIL: The fact that Monaco's goalkeeper hardly had a save to make over the two games and Rai Van Der Gouw did brilliantly for us tonight tells the story. We just didn't create enough chances.

Monaco were strong, but injuries caught up with us. Becks, Coley, Nicky, Teddy, Gary, Scholesy and I were all carrying knocks. Our injury situation was so severe that we had four defenders on the bench tonight. We couldn't even bring on two extra attackers to win us the game.

Teddy got a bit of stick from the fans, but we all love Teddy and he doesn't deserve any abuse. What some people don't realise is that he hasn't been getting the service recently and it's totally unfair to make him a scapegoat for this defeat.

In the dressing room afterwards, I felt as low as I ever have in my time at United. Naturally, the Boss was gutted. No one said a word until Kiddo came in, saying, "Come on, let's win the League now." He's brilliant like that.

The Boss has already pulled Gary (ribs), Coley (back), Scholesy (knee) and me (hamstring) out of the England squad to play Switzerland. As a compromise, Becks (calf), Teddy (Achilles) and Nicky (calf) will all join up with the squad, despite their injuries.

Champions' League Quarter-Final second leg / Old Trafford / Att: 53, 683

Manchester United 1
Van Der Gouw, G Neville (Clegg), P Neville, Johnsen, Irwin, Beckham, Butt, Scholes (Berg), Solskjaer, Sheringham, Cole
Scorer: Solskjaer
Monaco 1
Barthez, Sagnol, Dumas, Konjic (Da Costa), Leonard, Djetou, Colllins, Diawara, Bernabia (Carnot), Trezeguet, Ipkeba (Henry)
Scorer: Trezeguet

Thursday 19 March

GARY: The inquest has begun.

The media's main theory seems to be that our squad is too weak, which is laughable. Six weeks ago we were called the best British team ever, but now all of a sudden we're not good enough for anybody. The simple fact is that we played against Monaco without the spine of our team. I know it's a well-worn excuse, but we really were decimated by injuries. No Schmeichel, no Keane, no Giggs, no Pallister. What's more, we had Butty, Becks and Phil all playing with injuries and Scholesy and I actually had to come off. I can say without a shadow of doubt that a fully fit United would have beaten Monaco.

Again, thoughts go back to the first leg in Monaco when maybe we were too cautious. The manager told us then that if we had been a bit more cavalier we might have taken a step into the Semi-Finals. What this has taught us is that we need to be more positive on our travels. In recent years we've twice failed to score at Juventus and Galatasaray, and got nothing at Porto, Monaco, Dortmund and Barcelona. This team still hasn't won a big European game away from home.

Our determination to win the League is now stronger than ever. We have to get our heads down and make sure we do it.

PHIL: As you might imagine, the atmosphere at The Cliff was very bad. We'll probably have a meeting when the Boss is next in, but today we didn't go over the defeat.

Being without Schmeichel, Pallister, Keane and Giggs is the equivalent of Juventus losing Peruzzi, Ferrara, Zidane and Del Piero. Even Juve wouldn't be able to handle that. It might be fate. It just wasn't to be for us this year.

The Gaffer has given us the weekend off, so I've decided to get away from it all. I booked a trip to Paris with Julie.

I watched Chelsea beat Real Betis in the Cup Winners' Cup tonight and I was delighted to see them go through. I want all English sides to do well in Europe.

9

Slipping away

Friday 20 March

GARY: I bumped into the Boss showing Jonathan Greening and his parents round the club. We've just signed him from York City for £350,000.

Monday 23 March

PHIL: Peter, Pally, Ryan, Gary, Scholesy, Nicky and Becks were all receiving treatment today. The physios are working overtime and the Monaco pitch takes most of the blame. Schmeichel didn't play in the Sheffield Wednesday game because of a back injury linked to the hamstring damage he sustained in Monaco; Becks and Butty both picked up calf injuries there, and I've felt tightness in my hamstring ever since.

Glenn Hoddle is concerned about the number of absentees from the England squad for the Switzerland game on Wednesday. He says even if players are injured they still need to be present, to watch videos and take tactics on board. There are new rules coming into force for the World Cup, and we need to get used to them. For instance, tackling is a fine art and my brother is one of the best at sliding in and tackling from behind. Every time Gary does that in France, he will risk being sent off.

Tuesday 24 March

PHIL: It's no surprise that Paul Gascoigne has chosen to sign for Middlesbrough, as Bryan Robson is his hero. Contrary to popular belief, Gazza is probably the most fitness-conscious player I've ever come across. He'll be sat talking to you, and then the next minute he'll be on the floor doing sit-ups. I think he will play in the Coca-Cola Cup Final on Saturday. Some reckon he won't last ninety minutes, but he'll work harder than anyone else while he's on the pitch. Middlesbrough are a good team and with Gazza in the side, I'm sure they'll be promoted.

Ryan Giggs and Roy Keane trained with us today. Roy has the all-clear to resume full training. We weren't allowed to tackle him, but he joined in everything else. It's now just a matter of regaining his own confidence to tackle. He's been out for seven months, so there must be doubts in his mind. He has said that he's still a bit wary about what would happen if someone came in and tackled him from behind, but he looks good.

Scholesy and I stayed behind to do some extra shooting practice with Rai Van Der Gouw. I supplied the crosses and Paul banged them in.

In the afternoon, I drove my sister to the airport. Tracey's going to Kuala Lumpur for ten days and then on to Sydney with the England net-ball team. It's an acclimatisation trip before the Commonwealth Games.

Wednesday 25 March   Switzerland 1 England 1

PHIL: The Boss wasn't in, so Kiddo had free reign with us. Since Monaco, we haven't really trained properly, so we did various stop-start-jump-turn-rollover running exercises. It was the most tiring running session I've ever done.

Gary was back in training. Scholesy should also be alright for Saturday, which is important given that Teddy is suspended.

There was surprise at Glenn Hoddle's comments about Michael Owen today. Among other things, Glenn said he's not sure if Mike's a natural goalscorer. I think it's just a ploy to keep Mike level-headed as all the media hype closes in on him. If he ends up scoring the winning goal in the World Cup Final, it will have been good management. I can't see Mike as a starter in the early games of the Finals, but he's one who'll get thrown on at the end of games, score a goal and become a star.

I watched tonight's game against Switzerland at my girlfriend's house. The pitch looked bad and we didn't play too well in the first half.

McManaman played right wing back, which isn't his best position, but when Teddy came on in the second half I thought he gave us more presence up front. With so many changes to the team because of the injury withdrawals, it looked like it took the lads 45 minutes to get into it. But they'll be really pleased with their second half performances.

International friendly / Wankdorf Stadium

Switzerland 1
Corminboeuf, Yakin, Vega, Henchoz, Vogel, Sforza, Wicky (Lonfat), Fournier, Sesa (Kunz), Grassi, Chapuisat
Scorer: Vega
England 1
Flowers, Ferdinand, Keown, Southgate, Ince, McManaman, Hinchcliffe, Lee, Merson (Batty), Owen (Sheringham), Shearer
Scorer: Merson

Thursday 26 March

PHIL: The Boss was back at The Cliff today. He went to see Germany v Brazil last night and said Ronaldo was class. Brazil won 2-1 through his last-minute goal.

The injury situation here is pretty desperate now. There were only ten of us in training today and five of those were reserves. It looks like Giggs, Becks, Butty, Pally and Schmeichel will all miss Saturday's game. Peter trained and was diving about, but he can't kick or throw the ball yet. Ryan pulled out of the session with his hamstring again.

Today was transfer deadline day, but it wasn't really a surprise that we didn't make a signing. Since the Bosman ruling the days of deadline-day panic are gone. Players don't want to be rushed into a move if their contract expires in the summer and they can get a free transfer. In any case, very few quality players are available because they are all tied up on long-term deals. Clubs can end up paying up to six or seven million pounds for a good player with three years left on his current club's contract.

Friday 27 March

GARY: The manager usually talks about the opposition and the dossiers he's compiled from their last three performances, but for our match against Wimbledon tomorrow he said he wouldn't bother. "It's not about tactics or team work, I want you to go out there and enjoy yourself," he said. "The title is still in our hands, it's still in your hands. There is no way Arsenal are going to win nine games. You have one game a week until the end of the season. Tiredness isn't an excuse."

PHIL: It was Becks' first day of training this week, but the Gaffer still wants him to play against Wimbledon tomorrow. We spent half an hour practising set pieces. Wimbledon have some big players and the Gaffer wants us to compete for every ball in the air.

Teddy was back at The Cliff. He told me that considering the poor state of the pitch, he was surprised at the reaction to England's draw in Switzerland. Glenn Hoddle was getting nothing but praise up to the Chile game and now he's getting slated and linked with the Monaco manager's job, which is just ridiculous.

Peter Schmeichel asked the Boss for permission for us all to go paint-balling next Wednesday and go out afterwards for our "team meeting".

"Yes," replied the Gaffer. "But only if you use real bullets instead of paint!"

It's the first chance we've had to arrange anything since our Christmas party, so it was nice of the Gaffer to let us go. He was in a great mood, which really lightens the pressure before a big game. He's been the same since the morning after we were knocked out of the European Cup. You would have thought he'd still be upset, but instead he's been amazingly positive. In the team talk today, he said that we will win the League if we can score twice in every remaining game. He expects Arsenal to win at Bolton tomorrow, but they have a tough run-in and that's when they may drop points.

Saturday 28 March   Manchester United 2 Wimbledon 0

PHIL: We started off with a midfield three of Ronny on the right, Becks in the centre and me on the left, with Scholesy playing further up behind Cole and Solskjaer. But Michael Hughes and Robbie Earle were getting too much time on the ball and midway through the first half, the

Boss pulled Scholesy back into midfield. The 4-4-2 formation worked better, but we started getting a bit nervous when it was still 0-0 with time running out. Against Leicester, if anyone made a bad pass late in the game the crowd really got on their backs, but today the fans were as good as they have been for any Saturday match this season.

Towards the end of the game today, Brian Kidd was on the side of the pitch egging us on. It reminded me of the old Sunday League days. I thought it was class; it showed what the game meant to Kiddo.

When Ronny scored I went barmy – I even kicked an advertising board, Ketsbaia-style! It was just such a release from all the tension that has built up over the past two months. After that goal, Wimbledon put us under immense pressure – four corners in a row, a free-kick on the edge of the box – and I found myself thinking about last year's FA Cup match when they equalised with the last kick of the game. But this time Ben Thornley came on and clinched the game for us. He made a great run and cross for our second goal. At the time, I thought the scorer Paul Scholes was offside and TV replays later confirmed it. Needless to say, Joe Kinnear was not happy and I sympathise with him. We would have felt aggrieved as well if we'd worked hard for eighty minutes and got nothing from the game.

Not only that, but three of our players, including Andy Cole, were standing in an offside position for our first goal. I think the referee would have given offside if the keeper had palmed Ronny's shot away and Andy put it in, but the rule is that if you aren't interfering with play the referee has got to give the goal. Neither the Wimbledon defenders nor, more importantly, Neil Sullivan complained at the time. We haven't had much luck recently, so maybe our fortunes are changing.

At the final whistle, Kiddo grabbed Ben Thornley to congratulate him. Ben's been doing extra fitness work with him to improve his match sharpness. The reserves didn't have a game for two months after Christmas and when Ben played in the FA Cup clash against Walsall, he struggled to keep up with the pace. Ben showed glimpses of his best form at West Ham and now he's won us a match. His contract runs out in summer, and with Ryan Giggs around it will always be hard for him to hold a place. Speaking to Ben this season, he's often said it might be better for him to try elsewhere – even though he'd love to stay at United.

David Johnson, who is doing so well at Ipswich now, was in the same position as Ben. He thought there's no way I'm going to get in here and decided to go elsewhere. Leaving United is a massive wrench but it's proved the right career move for Jonno. Ben is 23 now and he can't afford a couple more years like his last two.

In the dressing room, everyone was high-fiving. The Boss hugged everyone and said, "That's going to be a great result for you."

Premiership / Old Trafford / Att: 55,306

Manchester United 2
Van Der Gouw, G Neville, Berg, May, Irwin, Beckham, Scholes, Johnsen, P Neville, Solskjaer (Thornley), Cole (McClair)
Scorers: Johnsen, Scholes
Wimbledon 0
Sullivan, Cunningham, Thatcher, Perry, Kimble, Hughes, Ardley, Roberts, Earle, Leaburn, Gayle (Euell)

Sunday 29 March

PHIL: I stayed over at my girlfriend's house last night. When I saw the newspapers this morning, I told her not to look at them because there was this embarrassing photo of me going mad after Ronny's goal. When Julie saw it, she couldn't stop laughing.

I watched the Coca-Cola Cup Final on television. I wanted Boro to win, but Chelsea created more chances and deserved their victory. I thought Gazza might change things when he came on, but Middlesbrough looked tired. I hope they get promoted now – mainly for Bryan Robson's sake. I've got a soft spot for him. He's a legend in my eyes.

Monday 30 March

PHIL: We've got until next Monday before we play again. The likes of Ryan, Nicky and Peter will all be able to get a full week's training before then, and we should have our full team out to play Blackburn.

This morning, a journalist rang my dad to ask whether we had signed new contracts. We've all been sworn to secrecy so Dad didn't say anything. Then in the afternoon, when the club's annual reports were revealed, the Chairman announced our new deals.

The Boss has got the flu and we had a light five-a-side at The Cliff in his absence.In the evening I went to watch the Reserves at Preston. There was a crowd of 10,000 and a brilliant atmosphere. We won 6-1 – Michael Twiss and Alex Notman both scored two, and Jordi and Ben Thornley completed the rout.

Tuesday 31 March

PHIL: Woke to the news that the aeroplane carrying the Leeds team home after their game at West Ham was forced to make a crash landing. Apparently, they dropped 150 feet. Thankfully, they all got out alive.

A few of the lads in our team, such as Ryan and Pally, don't like flying. They either close their eyes and try to sleep or play cards to take their minds off it. Ryan in particular likes the window shutters down until we are above the clouds.

The club made an important appointment today. Mick Brown, who used to be Ron Atkinson's number two at United, is joining us from Blackburn as Chief Scout. United's current Chief Scout Les Kershaw is moving across to look after the academy at our new training ground.

Later on, I started listening to Arsenal v Bolton on the radio, but turned off after Arsenal scored. They have such a strong defence, I knew they wouldn't lose after that. I thought to myself, "I'm not going to get depressed tonight."

Wednesday 1 April

PHIL: There was an obvious April Fool's in this morning's newspaper claiming Adidas have created a shin pad that sends an electric shock up your leg to warn you when an opponent is approaching from behind. Pally and Teddy obviously fell for it – they both asked Becks if he had been sent a pair!

GARY: In the afternoon we went paint-balling. Thirty five of the lads, First-Teamers, Reserves and Youth came along – every player in the club was there except for the apprentices. The rules of paint-balling involve one team defending their flag while the other has to try to capture it. We all got kitted out with army gear, protective masks and a gun, before splitting into two teams.

My finest effort was when I shot Butty right in the head from point-blank range. I was jumping about screaming and Nick rubbed his head, going barmy. It was a great laugh, good for team spirit.

It's strange to think we were paint-balling on the day we might have been preparing for a European Cup Semi-Final. Tonight, Juventus annihilated Monaco 4-1. Juventus always seem to peak at the right time. They have great players, but they work too. Everyone thinks players like Del Piero just waltz up the pitch, do a few tricks and look good, but they work so hard it's untrue.

Friday 3 April

PHIL: Kiddo ran us hard today. He said we need to be a little bit fitter to win the League and some tough training would help to add a little to our tanks. He does it the clever way, with short fifty-yard bursts rather than slogging our guts out over long distances. Kiddo measures everything, and compares what we do now to last season.

His main asset is that he's not stuck in his ways and is always willing to add new things to training. He travels all over the world researching the latest methods. He has become one of football's most respected coaches, and now people from other big clubs come to him for advice.

GARY: The first time I was coached by Brian Kidd was at United's Centre Of Excellence when I was thirteen. When Kiddo joined, the whole set-up improved immeasurably. He put so much time into the job and made it fun as well, always laughing and joking. He also brought in Archie Knox and Nobby Stiles to coach us. At the same time, Alex Ferguson started to come to watch regularly, and suddenly we all really felt part of the club. Brian Kidd was responsible for bringing through so many talented young players, some of whom have gone on to play for the First Team. Paul Scholes and Nicky Butt were spotted by Kiddo and he played a major role in Ryan Giggs' development too.

Kiddo rarely joins in with our training at The Cliff; instead, he's constantly encouraging us, with an eye on the stopwatch, monitoring exactly how long we take over each exercise and the rest periods in between. That's just what you want: short, intensive sessions. Sometimes when we're training with England, sessions can drag on. I suppose it's because we only meet up every couple of months and there's so much to cram in.

PHIL: There were rumours recently that Barcelona wanted Kiddo, but we were all relieved when the chairman announced that Kiddo had a job for life at United. Brian loves United and I don't think he would ever be interested in leaving. You only had to see him urging us on against Wimbledon last Saturday to understand what the club means to him.

Saturday 4 April

GARY: At last, the Gaffer has a full complement of fit players to choose from, and he announced the team to play Blackburn today. It's good to have Peter, Pally and Giggsy back. Their presence gives the side a stronger look.

In training, we worked on switching play from one side to the other. Last Tuesday, Kiddo watched Blackburn v Barnsley and said Blackburn looked really quick and strong for the first 40 minutes, but had nothing left in their legs in the second half. We plan to make them work hard through Denis and I getting forward and supporting Becks and Giggsy on the flanks.

PHIL: I was surprised to be in the team for Monday's game, as I thought he would have brought Butty back into midfield. It's a great confidence booster for me.

Ole Gunnar is in. The Gaffer said he wanted to play him because he's got a great goalscoring record against Blackburn.

Sunday 5 April

GARY: More preparations for Blackburn, including working on defending set-pieces. We've been weak in this area. When we lost to Barnsley in the FA Cup, we were marking different people depending on whether it was a free-kick or a corner. Now we are all going to stick with one man.

The PFA awards ceremony took place tonight. I've never actually been in person, because of clashes with our fixtures. When I came second to Robbie Fowler in the Young Player category in 1996, I couldn't go because we were playing Chelsea in the FA Cup Semi-Final. I watched on TV and was delighted to find out I'd been voted in as right back in the Premiership Team Of The Year. Nevertheless, I think it's an absolute travesty that Peter Schmeichel wasn't picked. No disrespect to Nigel Martyn, but Peter is not only the best goalkeeper in the Premiership, he's the best in the world. Congratulations were due to Andy Cole on coming second in the Player Of The Year category, even though I found it strange that he didn't make the Team of the Year.

Monday 6 April   Blackburn 1 Manchester United 3

PHIL: On the coach to the game, I congratulated Andy Cole on coming second in the PFA Player of the Year awards. "I hope it's the only time you come second this year," I told him.

GARY: The first half tonight was probably the worst United First Team performance I've ever been involved in. It reminded me of Turin in 1996, when Juventus battered us for 45 minutes. We didn't play well today mainly because Blackburn didn't allow us to, but we didn't show any flair at all either.

What's more, I gave away a stupid penalty. The way I brought down Damien Duff may have looked like a mauling, but in fact I just lost my balance. I put my hand on Duff's shoulder to stop myself falling over and just fell right on top of him. It was bad defending and a definite penalty.

When we trudged into the dressing room at half-time, the Gaffer immediately told Nicky he was coming on as sub, before addressing our poor performance. The message was simply to start playing properly. We hadn't made a tackle or had a shot on goal in the whole of the first half. The Gaffer told us in no uncertain terms that we needed to make amends in the second half. I realised I'd defended disgracefully for their goal and the Boss told me so.

Early in the second half, I had a chance to redeem myself. I got myself into a good shooting position, my first touch was good, but on the strike I almost missed the ball entirely and it just rolled through to Fettis. Another shooting nightmare.

PHIL: We all knew that we had 45 minutes to stay in the title race. We were in debt to Andy Cole for drawing us level. He pulled off an unbelievable finish from a tight angle, a shot that Ronaldo would have been proud of. His goal won us the match because until then our heads had been down.

GARY: The equaliser was an absolute killer for Blackburn. They'd been all over us and then suddenly the scores were level. Having felt lethargic the whole match, all of a sudden I felt a bit of bounce in my legs and the energy seemed to drain away from Blackburn. Kiddo's homework had been spot on.

Damien Duff's legs had completely gone and I couldn't believe he was kept on the pitch for the whole game. For our second goal, I got in front of him, touched the ball to Becks (although I was actually trying to play myself in!) and he delivered the perfect cross which hit Paul Scholes' hip and went in. Afterwards, Denis Irwin said to me, "Scholesy's touch was the first bit of luck we've had all season in a game where we've played badly." It's true that against Bolton, Leicester and West Ham –the sort of tight games we've won in previous years – we haven't nicked the vital goal.

The refereeing decisions also went our way in the second half. Blackburn should have had a second penalty when Pally made a tackle in the box, but it wasn't given. Phil was probably the luckiest person on the pitch though. He was tackling like a maniac!

PHIL: To be honest, I was lucky not to be sent off. Straight after I was booked for a tackle from behind on Flitcroft, I did a similar tackle on

Kevin Gallacher. The referee Gerald Ashby told me, "If this was the World Cup, I'd have to send you off now."

GARY: We didn't even play our best in the second half, but we fought hard and took our chances (five shots, three on target, three goals). Becks sealed the game with an assured finish.

After the match came a feeling of pure relief. Especially for me, because the goal we conceded was totally my fault.

PHIL: At the final whistle it was as if we'd won a Cup Final. Everyone gave each other high fives and went over to the supporters to celebrate. All the lads were buzzing in the dressing room. Pally was so tired he was lying on the floor. He could hardly speak.

This win has given us a six-point lead, but Arsenal have three games in hand. I think we need seventy-eight points to win the League. If we beat Liverpool on Friday, we'll be nine points in front and Arsenal have two difficult games coming up against Newcastle and Blackburn .

Premiership / Ewood Park / Att: 30,547

Blackburn Rovers 1
Fettis, Kenna, Sherwood, Hendry, Gallacher, Sutton, Wilcox, Flitcroft, McKinlay, Henchoz, Duff
Scorer: Sutton
Manchester United 3
Schmeichel, G Neville, Irwin, Johnsen, Pallister, Beckham, Cole, Giggs, P Neville, Scholes, Solskjaer (Butt)
Scorers: Cole, Scholes, Beckham

Premiership (top) *at 7 April*	P	W	D	L	F	A	Pts	GD
Manchester United	33	20	6	7	63	24	66	39
Arsenal	30	17	9	4	49	26	60	23
Liverpool	31	15	9	7	54	34	54	20
Chelsea	31	16	3	12	60	35	51	25
Leeds United	32	15	6	11	47	34	51	13
Blackburn Rovers	31	14	9	8	52	42	51	10

Tuesday 7 April

PHIL: After our first-half performance last night, I expected some Fergie fury in the dressing room, but he was remarkably calm. He just walked around telling us that he expected better from us.

In fact, I have rarely seen the Boss lose his temper. When I was younger I read about him throwing tea cups and the like, so I went into the First Team thinking that if we were drawing 0-0 at half-time we would get all sorts thrown at us. But he has never done that. I'm told he's mellowed, but he has always been the same calm man to me. For the first year that I was a professional, whenever the manager walked into the room I just shut up and sat up straight as if I was at school. And when I was an apprentice I was scared of him, there's no other way to put it. If I heard him coming down the stairs at The Cliff, I would turn around and flee back to the dressing room.

But since then I've got to know him better. You can have a laugh with him and you learn what you can get away with. My initial fear has turned into complete respect. I enjoyed seeing him on the touchline questioning the linesman in the second half last night. It gets the whole team going to see the manager's passion, how desperate he is to win the League.

GARY: It's still doubtful whether Roy Keane will play again this season. If we've won the title, he'll definitely come on as a substitute against Barnsley so he gets his winner's medal – he needs to play just one more game to reach the minimum requirement. Roy is tackling in training now and the coaching staff have to hold him back.

We did a signing session for Diadora in a shop in Preston today. I had a word with the Diadora rep about my blue, white and red World Cup boots. I'm still not sure about wearing them.

Thursday 9 April

PHIL: It looks like we're on the brink of signing Jaap Stam. Our two Dutchmen, Jordi and Rai, both speak really highly of him and say he's the next Franco Baresi. Although I haven't seen Jaap play, I'm already impressed – in the interviews I've read, he sounds desperate to play here.

GARY: The Gaffer has named the side for tomorrow's game against Liverpool. It's the same eleven that ended the game at Blackburn.

The Boss explained his tactic for dealing with Steve McManaman, who he sees as their main threat. Steve is great at running the ball out of defence, so we'll have someone marking him when we attack. We are also planning to get plenty of early crosses in. I've played Liverpool five or six times now, and we've always created chances against them in the air.

Friday 10 April   Manchester United 1 Liverpool 1

PHIL: The manager had a word with me and Nicky But before the game. "Don't let Paul Ince bully you," he told us. "He'll want to prove a point to us, but don't allow him to."

Liverpool's visit has been hyped up as Paul Ince's return to Old Trafford. He was in the morning papers saying that United stabbed him in the back when the club sold him to Inter Milan.

GARY: I felt really confident for the first half hour of the match. It was the best we've played for a while. Our plan to deal with Steve McManaman was working a treat; he hardly got on the ball and Liverpool couldn't get any rhythm at all. We were causing them major problems in the air as usual and Ronny scored with a free header from a corner.

PHIL: Michael Owen equalised after a misunderstanding between Pally and Peter. After the game Peter admitted it was his fault, that he should have come out. Even so, Michael showed exceptional pace as well as the composure to finish.

GARY: For Michael Owen to be playing this way at eighteen is simply frightening. The way he kept his cool as he went through on goal was amazing, but he definitely deserved the sending off for his two tackles on Peter and Ronny. You never want to see an opposing player get a red card, but it was a relief for us because Michael was causing us constant problems.

PHIL: Roy Evans tried to excuse Owen's tackles by saying we had been winding Michael up. That is the biggest load of rubbish I've ever heard. No one said a single word to him, it's not in our players' natures. Butty and Scholsey aren't talkers, they just get on with the game. Pally and Ronny have never attempted to wind up opposition players. It was just an attempt by Liverpool to shield Mike from any criticism. I know him from the England set-up and those lunges were out of character, but it's not fair to start blaming us.

When I came off after sixty-five minutes, I saw Michael was coming out of the medical room where Ronny was receiving treatment, so he must have apologised.

GARY: As it turned out, the sending-off didn't do us any favours – in fact I thought the ten minutes before half-time when they were down to ten men was their best period of the game. When teams are down to ten men, it gives them a siege mentality. To start with, Leonhardsen, McManaman, Murphy and Owen were all concentrating on attack. Once Owen was sent off, they tightened up to two banks of four defenders with Murphy, who played superbly, alone up front and McManaman used as an outlet to ease pressure.

The only half chances we had were from blocks or high balls launched into the box. We couldn't argue with the result because we just hadn't done enough to win. To be honest, I don't think our form has been there for a while; probably our last decent performance was the 1-0 win at Chelsea back in February. It was an unhappy dressing room after the match today. The Gaffer said, "You're making it difficult for yourselves," and he's damn right there.

Premiership / Old Trafford / Att: 55,171

Manchester United 1
Schmeichel, G Neville, Pallister, Johnsen (May), Irwin, Butt, Beckham, Scholes, P Neville (Sheringham), Giggs (Thornley), Cole
Scorer: Johnsen
Liverpool 1
Friedel, Jones, Babb, Matteo, Harkness, Leonhardsen, McManaman, Ince, Redknapp, Murphy (Berger), Owen
Scorer: Owen

Saturday 11 April

GARY: Today's media reaction to Michael Owen's sending off was totally over the top. The lad mistimed a couple of tackles, but what footballer hasn't? No one mentioned the fact that Michael saved the game for Liverpool with his goal.

Arsenal beat Newcastle 3-1 today to trail us by just four points with three games in hand. Watching the game live, I thought Newcastle had a chance of a 0-0 draw, but once Arsenal scored I couldn't see any way back for them. Viera and Petit were brilliant, and Anelka scored two great goals.

In the evening I went to the Spice Girls concert at the Nynex Arena in Manchester with Becks, Ben, Casp, Hannah, my mum, dad and sister.

The girls were on for two hours and they were excellent. At one point, Ginger Spice shouted out, "We've got Gary Neville in the house, the best man at a certain wedding!" Becks had had a word beforehand – I was so embarrassed.

Becks threw a party for all the girls and his close friends at his house afterwards. Phil and Julie came over and I met all the Spice Girls for the first time. After watching the concert and seeing the excitement on the kids' faces, I don't see how the Spice Girls can be criticised. Meeting them in person, I thought they were nice people, too.

Sunday 12 April

GARY: Today we made front page of the People! Apparently, Phil, Giggsy and I went round to Becks' house on Tuesday night with baseball bats to protect him from a stalker. The only truth in the story is that Becks is looking to move house and there was some bloke who kept knocking on David's door. The story made it sound like Becks was in fear of his life! And can you imagine the Neville brothers going around with baseball bats? Scary stuff!

PHIL: We were all disappointed with comments in the News Of The World today claiming Peter Schmeichel had made a meal of Michael Owen's challenge to get him sent off. Peter couldn't believe the accusation. He didn't say anything when Owen lunged at him, he just span away with his arms in the air.

GARY: We've got to wait until next Saturday for our next game against Newcastle, then it's another nine days before we play Crystal Palace. We've had no problems with fixture congestion this season, but now I wish the games would come more quickly. When results are bad you just want to play again straightaway to put things right.

Arsenal now have to drop points at Blackburn if we are to be in with a fair chance. Blackburn's defence was very hard to break down earlier this season, but they are on a poor run of results now and I'm worried they may run out of steam in the second half, as they did against us. Everyone was raving about Blackburn's fitness levels last year, and the fact that they trained mornings and afternoons. I know that is the Continental way, but I'm not sure if you can do that throughout an English season. Once tiredness sets in, you can't shake it off and I wonder whether Blackburn have enough strength to cope physically with an Arsenal team bubbling with confidence. If Arsenal lose, I would rather be in our position, because they won't win their last six games. If they beat Blackburn, they will be just one point behind us with two games in hand and therefore in the driving seat. However, their last two fixtures – away to Liverpool and Villa, two teams chasing a place in Europe – will be very tough for them.

We've got to hang in there. If we win our last four games, my feeling is that we will be Champions.

Monday 13 April

PHIL: Alex Ferguson gathered us together this morning to give us a stern talk about our problems in recent games. He was angry that Andy Cole has been starved of support up front. He wants two of us to run from midfield when we're on the attack. At this stage of the season you don't need people just sitting in midfield.

GARY: The Gaffer concentrated on functional work in training. He wants us to pass the ball more in the last third instead of just lumping in high balls. We don't have a lot of height up front and the way we've been playing recently doesn't make sense. The Gaffer wants our midfielders to break forward into the box more often to support the strikers.

Later on I watched Arsenal v Blackburn on television. Arsenal were awesome in the first half, but I was surprised at the level of Blackburn's performance compared to the way they played against us last week. They seemed a different, far inferior side.

Blackburn have been on a bad run, and that can drain your energy. But I was worried about them collapsing in the second half, not in the first quarter of an hour. We had booked a table at a restaurant for eight o'clock, but we rang up and moved the booking to seven. I couldn't bear to watch any more. 4-0 at half-time. It was all over.

Tuesday 14 April

PHIL: Peter Schmeichel is still convinced we'll win the League. I talked to him about Arsenal's game against Blackburn last night and he said from past experience we should be used to teams raising themselves when they play us.

It's when you play as Champions that you find out how good you really are. In recent years, when Leeds and Blackburn won the League they couldn't cope the next season with teams raising their game against them every week. If Arsenal do win, it will be interesting to see how they cope.

The manager was upbeat too.

"If you win your last four games you'll win the League," he said. "You can't worry what Arsenal get up to because if you do, you'll slip up. Arsenal will struggle once the pitches start to dry and get bare."

GARY: I still believe we will win the League, but Arsenal's confidence must be growing by the day. If they go unbeaten to the end of the season, then they deserve to take the title. The way they are playing at the moment, I can't see where the loss will come from, but nobody at Old Trafford will give in. We must stay in touch until their last two away games. Our goal difference is still far superior to Arsenal's and that extra point may still be crucial.

Glenn Hoddle announced a large England squad today for the Portugal game. He said that anyone not included can book their summer holidays.

England squad

David Seaman, Nigel Martyn, Ian Walker, Tim Flowers, Kevin Pressman, Gareth Southgate, Gary Neville, Phil Neville, Sol Campbell, Tony Adams, Martin Keown, Rio Ferdinand, Graeme Le Saux, Andy Hinchcliffe, Stuart Pearce, Dominic Matteo, Jamie Redknapp, Paul Ince, Paul Gascoigne, Paul Scholes, Ray Parlour, David Beckham, Nicky Butt, Robert Lee, Steve McManaman, Teddy Sheringham, Andy Cole, Alan Shearer, Dion Dublin, Michael Owen, Paul Merson, Les Ferdinand, Ian Wright.

These thirty-four players will be trimmed to twenty two before France, so there'll be a few hearts broken yet. It certainly puts you on edge; there are eleven defenders in this squad and only seven will go to France.

He's also picked twenty-two players for the B Team match against Russia. It was nice to see John Curtis and Michael Clegg in there, along with our old team-mate David Johnson.

PHIL: The biggest surprise today was the omission of Gary Pallister. For me, he's the best central defender in the country and would certainly be in my top twenty two, never mind thirty four. The only reason is that Hoddle might be put off by his injury problems. It was Pally's misfortune to get injured at such a critical stage of the season. I think Pally was expecting to be left out, because he's booked a holiday already.

Wednesday 15 April

PHIL: We received a letter this morning confirming our places in the England squad. There was a note attached from Glenn Hoddle telling us that unless we were in plaster or in hospital he expects us to report.

GARY: Our functional work is showing signs of paying off. Today, the Gaffer played what looked like Saturday's team in a practice match on a half-size pitch and it looked really good. We won the game something like 15–1, the passing was sharp and the team was linking up well.

PHIL: I watched the Champions' League Semi-Finals feeling just a little bit jealous. It could so easily have been us. Monaco beat Juventus and looked a far better side than the one we played. It was Juventus' third loss of the competition; strange to think we only lost once, in Turin, when it didn't matter.

Thursday 16 April

PHIL: The manager phoned up from Newmarket and told everyone to put a bet on his horse, Queensland Star, which is running in its first ever race. Everyone ignored him, then regretted it when it won!

GARY: Tonight, Chelsea beat Vicenza to reach the European Cup Winners' Cup Final. 1 wanted Chelsea to win. If they'd lost, the old moan about English teams not being able to beat Italian sides would have come up again. Mark Hughes came on as sub and scored a brilliant winning goal. It was typical of him. 1 remember Sparky as really quiet off the pitch at United, but he was great to have in your team. You could knock a bad ball towards Mark and he would make it look good. He's built like a brick wall, with legs like tree trunks. Even if he had a defender right behind him, he'd always keep possession.

PHIL: When Sparky was still at the club 1 was too young to approach him. 1 felt intimidated because he was such a legend – his nickname was The Ledge.

Friday 17 April

GARY: 1 don't know whether it was something 1 ate, but from six o'clock 1 was, to put it politely, constantly on the toilet. 1 felt really rough.

Saturday 18 April   Manchester United 1 Newcastle United 1

GARY: Throughout the build-up to the game 1 stayed close to the loo!

By half-time, thanks to my stomach bug, 1 had absolutely no energy. 1 was getting forward OK, but 1 wasn't getting back quickly enough. The boss said to give it ten minutes, and 1 was happy to do that, but soon 1 felt dizzy and light-headed and decided to come off.

As in the Liverpool game, we started off well, demonstrating some of the passing and teamwork we've showed in our training sessions this week. But yet again we couldn't keep it up, and then we gave away a bad goal. At first, 1 thought it was offside, but it turned out not to be and Andersson had all the time in the world to put the ball in the net.

Before the game, Peter Schmeichel said that he wouldn't be able to take the goal-kicks because of a hamstring problem and he had to go off after only seventeen minutes. Nicky Butt was also substituted with double vision. Everything seems to be going against us at the moment.

PHIL: Uriah Rennie gave Gary a hard time back in December and now it was my turn. He kept turning to me and saying, "Shut up you prima donna!" I think he got fed up with me telling him to watch Newcastle's time-wasting. The manager often reminds us to keep on to refs about time-wasting. Shay Given kept taking ages swapping sides for his goal kicks, so I made sure the referee was aware of it. The Boss doesn't like dissent – we get heavily fined if we're booked for that – but making sure we play the full ninety minutes isn't dissent.

Alan Shearer was guilty of a really late tackle which caught my ankle. As I lay on the floor in agony, I was sure the ref would send Alan off, but he only booked him. I was really angry about it at the time, but seeing the incident on television later, maybe the referee was right.

At 1–1, with only minutes remaining, Rob Lee sprinted free with just the goalkeeper to beat. I thought we had had it, but then I saw Ole Gunnar chase back and bring him down. Quite rightly, Ole was shown the red card, but the crowd gave him a standing ovation as he walked off. In Ole's position I would have done the same. He sacrificed himself so we wouldn't lose the game. "That tackle could win us the League," I told him afterwards. Everyone appreciated what Ole had done, but we still had a laugh at his expense because he isn't exactly a hard man.

GARY: I watched the last part of the game on the television in the dressing room with Peter Schmeichel. Pally was pushed forward to play up front in the last few minutes and we were throwing hopeful punts into the box. That isn't us. We aren't playing well.

This result left me totally dejected. The immediate feeling was that the title had gone, especially as Arsenal won so convincingly 5-0 against Wimbledon. On the way home, I listened to a local radio phone-in and all the callers were having a go at us. I had to turn it off.

Premiership / Old Trafford / 55,194

Manchester United 1
Schmeichel (Van Der Gouw), G Neville (Solskjaer), Pallister, May, Irwin, Butt (Scholes), Beckham, Sheringham, P Neville, Giggs, Cole
Scorer: Beckham
Newcastle United 1
Given, Barton, Batty, Lee, Pearce, Albert, Dabizas, Pistone, Speed, Andersson (Ketsbaia), Shearer
Scorer: Andersson

Sunday 19 April

GARY: The media reaction to Ole Gunnar Solskjaer's sending off yesterday, saying that what he did was immoral, is a load of rubbish. Ole Gunnar had to make a split-second decision. It wasn't malicious; he was just doing what he thought best for Manchester United. Even though Rai Van Der Gouw had already made some excellent saves, there was still a fifty-fifty chance that Rob Lee would score and with only a minute remaining, there's no way we could have got an equaliser. If Ole Gunnar hadn't brought him down, our title hopes could have ended there and then – he had to do it. Even Newcastle's manager Kenny Dalglish agreed with that in his post-match press conference.

Ole Gunnar was actually very unselfish, because people outside Manchester United won't think well of him. He did it for his team-mates and the club. He saved us a point and the fans were right to give him a standing ovation as he walked off the pitch.

PHIL: Gary, Scholesy, Coley and I flew down to Burnham Beeches. We talked happily about Crystal Palace's first home win of the season yesterday. We're praying they win before we go down there at the end of the month – it would have been just like us to give them their first home win.

As soon as we arrived at the England camp, we took part in the World Cup song video with the Spice Girls. Then we trained, though Gary only joined in with the warm-up. He hasn't eaten for two days and is absolutely knackered.

The United lads were pleased to have a change of scene. It's taken our minds off slipping up in the title race – everyone seemed a lot more relaxed here. I spoke to Martin Keown and he certainly doesn't think it's over yet. I said to him, "Oh, we've blown it," to try and make him complacent, but I don't think it worked!

Glenn Hoddle told us that a faith healer called Eileen Drewery would now be an official part of the set-up. "She's there if you want to go and see her, but there is no pressure," he told us. "If you don't want to, that's fine. Personally, in my twenty years in the game I've found her very helpful and I'm sure you will too."

A lot of the players have been to see Eileen already. I would say at least twenty have had a session with her, but to my knowledge, so far no one from United. I'm not against the idea, there just isn't any reason for me to try it at the moment.

I know Tony Adams has talked about how good she is. He says he can be feeling miserable, go in and see her, and come out feeling like a different person.

Monday 20 April

GARY: We had blood tests this morning so the England nutritionists can design a specific diet plan for each player. The way I feel today, the results should be interesting! In the past, blood tests have shown I have a low blood-sugar level and I've had to change my diet to compensate. We won't get the results for a week or two.

I trained today. Although I'm still not a hundred per cent, I felt better as I got going. We played a practice match and I was in the team that looks likely to play on Wednesday. If I can get some food inside me by then, I should be all right.

PHIL: There is a real excitement in the air with the World Cup so close now. Today, Glenn Hoddle said, "There are only forty-three days to go, so for the moment forget about the title race and the FA Cup Final and just concentrate on the World Cup."

You could see everyone looking around thinking, "Who isn't going to be here next time?" Later, we got measured up for our World Cup suits, but only twenty two of the players here will get to wear them in France.

Tuesday 21 April

GARY: There's been a bit of a stir in the press about Eileen Drewery. Glenn Hoddle knew he would get some stick, so he probably thought it was better to get it out of the way now before we go to France. I know that Wrighty, Gazza, Merse and Darren Anderton have benefitted from

Mrs Drewery's help and others may have visited her room without anyone knowing. She has definitely helped players. If it works for them, I don't see anything wrong in it.

PHIL: We trained on a pitch surrounded by massive speakers pumping out music. Someone forgot the proper tape, so we had to listen to Take That, which didn't go down well!

GARY: We had a meeting at 1.45 p.m. and Glenn Hoddle announced the team. I was delighted to be picked. He said he was playing his strongest side, so it makes me confident about my chances of being among the twenty two to go to the World Cup. Phil was among the subs, which is a good sign too.

England B beat Russia 4-1 tonight; the highlight was Le Tissier's hat-trick. Only two or three of the lads playing will get into the squad and Matt, Les Ferdinand and Darren Anderton have the best chance.

I had severe stomach pains this evening and called the doctor. I've been visiting the toilet all too frequently for four days now, so the doctor gave me some tablets.

Wednesday 22 April   England 3 Portugal 0

PHIL: Strangely, no one mentioned the England B game or Matt Le Tissierís hat-trick today.

I was one of the subs that Glenn Hoddle named this morning. Andy Cole and Nicky Butt were very disappointed not even to make the bench. I was surprised about Coley as he was absolutely flying in training, but I donít think he or Nicky has to worry. They should be certainties for the World Cup.

GARY: I felt fine in training this morning as we worked on set pieces. The Boss videos every training session and he felt we hadn't been paying enough attention to free-kicks and corners.

The original plan had been to play a 4-4-2, but the Boss had heard Portugal were going to switch their system so he changed tack to a back three with two wing-backs. I was moved to right centre back and Becks will play at wing-back. Glenn Hoddle said to us before the game, "I want you to put your World Cup heads on now."

Five minutes into the match, the message came from the bench to revert back to 4-4-2, because Portugal were playing three up front. With three against three at the back, it may have given us extra men going forward, but there were a few frightening moments in defence.

After half-time, I was one of the first England players to run out of the tunnel ... and the first to run back in. A severe case of the runs meant I had to dive into the disabled toilet. The kick-off was held up for a few seconds until I ran back out.

We weren't positive enough in the first half, but the second half was a completely different matter. We took control and could have scored more. Everyone was delighted to win against a decent Portugal side.

PHIL: I came on as sub for Gary. The other lads reckoned we had planned it between us in order to get me another cap. Becks was also brought off for Paul Merson. It was a similar situation to the one I had faced in the Chile game – neither Glenn Hoddle nor John Gorman explained to him why he was substituted.

GARY: Alan Shearer scored two. I was right behind the line of his second goal and thought he would take the ball on. Instead, he just belted it first time into the top corner from twenty-five yards. A normal player would have controlled the ball and tried to get nearer the goal, but Alan just has confidence in his ability to finish from that distance.

It's strange for a goalkeeper to be Man of the Match when you win 3-0, but David Seaman was forced to make some great saves.

International Friendly / Wembley

England 3
Seaman, G Neville (P Neville), Adams, Campbell, Beckham (Merson), Le Saux, Ince, Batty, Sheringham (Owen), Scholes, Shearer
Scorers: Shearer 2, Sheringham
Portugal 0
Vitor Baia, Xavier, Couto, Beto, Dimas (Barbosa), Santos, Figo, Calado, Sousa (Oceano), Pinto (Capucho), Cadete

Thursday 23 April

GARY: Paul Ince was punched in the Wembley car park last night by an "England fan" who still hasn't forgiven him for leaving West Ham –

nine years ago! At Old Trafford, two security men stand either side of you and whisk you to and from your car on match days. I've always felt a bit embarrassed by that, because it might give the impression to fans that I'm unapproachable. But at Wembley, you come out from the steps near the Twin Towers then walk a few hundred yards to your car with no security presence at all. I've never given it a second thought until now. I left at eleven o'clock last night, and at that time it would be easy for someone to come up and have a go at you.

Like on Saturday, I was completely drained after last night's game. Dad drove us back to Manchester, but I hardly got any sleep. This illness has been going on too long now, so this morning I went to the hospital for tests. I had to give a urine sample and I'll get the results in a few days.

PHIL: There is speculation about a young Danish goalkeeper called Jimmy Nielsen joining United. Our scouts have been out to watch him a couple of times and he's trained with us at The Cliff. He's built just like Peter and looks a great prospect.

Friday 24 April

PHIL: Roy Keane received the all-clear today, but he's been advised to enjoy a summer off and come back fresh for next season. There was a chance he could play in an A Team game at The Cliff, but the surgeon advised against it. The physios at United are all relieved that Roy's fine.

Saturday 25 April

GARY: Today, I was well enough to train for the first time since England camp. During the session, the Gaffer pulled me aside to say he was leaving me out of the team to play Crystal Palace. "I can't see how you can be all right if you can't keep anything down," he said.

We went to watch Bury v Ipswich at Gigg Lane this afternoon. During the game, when David Johnson was within earshot, I shouted, "Score and you're dead, Johnson." Dave looked around, saw me and started laughing. I don't care if he's scored thirty goals this season, I won't have him scoring against Bury!

PHIL: I kept in touch with Arsenal's score at Barnsley today. I was praying Barnsley would win, but as soon as Arsenal went 1-0 up I knew it was very unlikely. Arsenal don't concede goals any more. The manager told us this morning he was hoping for a draw, but this win puts them four points clear. It's looking grim.

GARY: I got terrible stomach pains during the night, worse than ever.

Sunday 26 April

GARY: I telephoned the hospital this morning. The diagnosis is a virus.

When I arrived at The Cliff, the Gaffer called me into his office and said, "I think you are better off going home to rest rather than train."

"If I feel better tomorrow, can I come down to London?" I asked.

"What, to watch?" he inquired.

"No, to play."

He laughed and said he'd ring me tomorrow morning. It might seem daft, but if we win tomorrow we can still put pressure on Arsenal. On Wednesday, they play Derby, who are still going for a place in Europe. Everton will also battle like mad next Saturday to avoid relegation. Arsenal can tie it up in the next two games and I wouldn't be surprised if they did, but I still have a feeling that there might be a twist. When we've won the title, although we've always had long unbeaten runs, we've still dropped the odd point here and there. Arsenal have now won eight on the trot. They keep snuffing out our increasingly desperate hopes.

Monday 27 April   Crystal Palace 0 Manchester United 3

GARY: I felt a lot better today and I told the doctor at The Cliff that I wanted to play. He spoke to Dave Fevre and then rang Kiddo. The message came back that I should stay where I was. I was gutted, because this will be the first League game I've missed since last August.

PHIL: The manager hasn't been saying much to us before games recently, but today he gathered us together for a chat. He talked for about half an hour. Usually there is a bit of joking from the lads, but this time everyone was silent.

"The League has almost gone," he said. "We have to face the fact that Arsenal have been on a brilliant run and if they win the League, they will undoubtedly deserve it. The only thing you can do now is play for pride and keep the pressure on by winning. Never forget that you play for the greatest club in the world, never forget that 55,000 people come and watch you at Old Trafford every other week.

"It's hurting them like hell to lose the League. You've played some magnificent football this year that will live long in the memory. Injuries have hurt us," he continued, "but we haven't helped ourselves at all. I remember after we lost to Coventry after Christmas, I turned to Kiddo and said, 'If we don't win the League, then this will be the game that cost us.' I couldn't believe that we could throw away a 2-1 lead at Coventry. That's just not what Manchester United do."

His talk had everyone fired up for the match. We played our normal game for the first time in ages: quick passing to feet rather than hoofing it into the area. All our goals came from good passing moves.

Against Liverpool and Newcastle we became too desperate and started just pumping high balls into the area. The crowd at Old Trafford can become restless, pressurising us to get the ball into the box quickly, but tonight we felt a release of pressure and the freedom to play.

Premiership / Selhurst Park / Att: 26,180

Crystal Palace 0
Miller, Smith, Ismael, Edworthy, Gordon, Lombardo (Hreidarsson), Brolin (Fullarton), Curcic, Bent, Padovano (Dyer), Shipperley
Manchester United 3
Schmeichel, P Neville, Irwin (Clegg), May, Pallister, Butt, Scholes, Beckham, Giggs, Sheringham, Cole / Scorers: Scholes, Butt, Cole

Tuesday 28 April

GARY: Went into The Cliff, but could only do some cycling in the gym. I'm not taking any tablets. With a virus like this, the best cure is rest.

One thing all the newspaper reports missed today is that last night's win secured our place in next season's Champions' League. Although Arsenal will probably go in as Champions, we may be better prepared than them because of the experience we've picked up in recent years. If we finish second, we'll have to play a qualifying round in August and already the Gaffer has that in his mind. He came up to me and Becks today and asked, "When do you meet up with England?"

"17 May," I replied.

"When are you going to get any rest, lads?" he grimaced.

Wednesday 29 April

GARY: A few weeks ago, I was given a quote for a fitted kitchen for my barn. It seemed expensive, so my dad sent someone who works for him at Bury to another outlet in the same company's chain. He was quoted £10,000 less for the same job and we ordered the kitchen at the cheaper price.

Today, Dad and I went over and confronted the head of the kitchen company over the huge difference between the two quotes. He confirmed that the original quote I had been given was way over the top and he apologised. Later, I rang the woman who had surcharged me for having a famous face and told her I didn't appreciate being ripped off. I was angry, as she'd done a lot of work for me and I'd trusted her.

Thursday 30 April

GARY: Arsenal stepped closer to the title by beating Derby last night. We felt they had to drop points in that game. Now there is an air of inevitability and our players are just living in hope.

We trained at Old Trafford today. It was a long session and a really tough one for me, as it was my first proper session since my illness.

Afterwards we did a photo shoot for the cover of this book at the players' tunnel. A lot of the lads were still around and giving us stick. When he saw me in the England kit, Ryan walked past muttering, "Has the World Cup squad been picked yet?" Then as he disappeared up the tunnel, we heard him chanting, "Ke-own, Ke-own!"

Friday 1 May

GARY: Paul Scholes and Nicky Butt have both put their names to new seven-year contracts. That means Ryan, Phil, Paul, Nicky and I have all committed our futures to United. Becks is negotiating to sign an extended contract, too. I'm glad we're all sticking together.

Dennis Bergkamp was named the Football Writers' Player Of The Year tonight, with Tony Adams in second. They thoroughly deserve the honours.

Saturday 2 May

GARY: I can't believe that the incident in which Alan Shearer was accused of kicking Neil Lennon is still front- and back-page news, four days after the game. If it had been Neil Lennon and someone else, there wouldn't be paid anything like this amount of attention.

Alan Shearer is a tough player in the mould of Mark Hughes, who takes a lot of punishment. Who cares if he kicked somebody? Does Alan moan every time someone kicks him? On the TV, they are replaying close-ups of the incident and in one newspaper, they printed all the statistics on how many tackles and fouls he's committed since he came back from injury. It's ridiculous.

Sunday 3 May

PHIL: Arsenal are champions.

It was hard to watch them lifting the Premiership trophy. At first I felt quite bitter. "They're going a bit over the top, aren't they?" I thought. But then you remember what a great feeling it is.

We were the best team in the Premiership, and possibly Europe, until just after Christmas, but we peaked too soon. We found it difficult to recapture our lost form and didn't cope well with injuries, whereas Arsenal seemed to deal with the absences of Wright and Seaman very well.

I reckon our home form cost us the League. Everything went wrong from our Old Trafford defeat by Leicester; after that match, we failed to beat Bolton, Arsenal, Liverpool and Newcastle. If we had won those games, we would have won the League. We've been accused of complacency in the League, because of our desire to win the European Cup, but we've all been trying our hearts out.

GARY: After the first half of Arsenal v Everton, I knew it was all over so I went down to Greenmount to watch my local cricket team instead. For weeks I've been saying Arsenal must slip up, but ten wins on the trot says they haven't! What's more, they've conceded just two goals in that time. It's a remarkable run, something I've never seen before, and fully deserves the Premiership title. I can only congratulate them.

Watching the highlights later, I saw Steve Bould set up Tony Adams to smash in Arsenal's fourth goal. It was fitting that Arsenal's leader should complete the job. It reminded me of Pally scoring from a free-kick against Blackburn in 1993, when United clinched the Premiership title. It's destiny. Sometimes things are just meant to happen.

The key to Arsenal's success has been their outstanding back four. What's more, to even get to their defence you have to get past Viera and Petit. Meanwhile, the lads up front have scored the vital goals. Since Christmas, they've just had a purple patch.

It's going to be difficult to pick up a newspaper or watch TV for a couple of weeks, because every time you do, you'll see Tony Adams lifting the Premier League trophy. It was the same with Alan Shearer and Blackburn three years ago. Blackburn didn't really go forward after that success, but Arsenal definitely have more about them. Their defence will last another one or two years and Arsene Wenger is bringing in new blood.

As for United, there's been talk of the turning point after which our form started to fall away. For instance, our loss at Coventry back in

December: we were playing so well, then we got over-confident and threw it away. I've even heard the FA Cup game at Chelsea cited, when we let a 5-0 lead carelessly slip to 5-3. But I think the crucial game was when Arsenal came to Old Trafford. If we'd beaten them, it might have put doubts in their minds about whether they were good enough to win the title. In the last six years, none of the teams competing with us for the title have come here and won. That game must have been a big psychological boost for Arsenal.

We've got to play Leeds tomorrow. Right now I'm thinking the fans won't be happy, we won't be happy, and it won't be a whole lot of fun. At the same time, some of our fans waited twenty-six years for our first League success, so they've tasted disappointment before. But as the Gaffer has said to us, we're playing in front of a new type of fan now. There seem to be 10,000 now who are up for it every game, but 45,000 who need inspiring. When I used to go as a fan to watch United play, there was a sense of anticipation, but now it's more tension than anything else. Some of the fans who've started supporting us in recent years come expecting that we will win and just wait for it to happen.

I remember being a spectator at United v Wimbledon in 1986/87, Alex Ferguson's first season as manager, and there were only 31,000 at Old Trafford. We have got to make sure it never goes back to that.

If you take a wider view, in six years we've won the title four times and come second twice, which is a record to be proud of. All the same, it hardly eases the disappointment we're feeling right now. But the great thing about playing at this level is that after every disappointment, there is always something else to go for. Now I've got the World Cup to look forward to, then we can come back next season trying harder than ever.

Bury won 1-0 at QPR and avoided relegation. It was the only bright spot on a bleak day. It's a great achievement for Bury to stay up and something I couldn't have forseen when they sold David Johnson at Christmas. At the time, I told Bury's chairman Terry Robinson, who lives next door to me, that I couldn't see where the goals would come from to save them. In fact, they haven't scored many but their defence is absolutely brilliant and the work they put in is phenomenal. Bury may not have a Kinkladze, but they make up for that in sheer commitment.

Unbelievably, Man City were relegated despite winning 5-2 at Stoke. At Palace last week, our fans were singing "City versus Macclesfield" and now it's actually going to happen. I've always been a United fan, but I'm still shocked at what has happened at Maine Road. It's strange to think that City are now going to have 27,000 people watching Division Two football; then again, maybe that means they're big enough to bounce back. Yet Burnley had a 22,000 crowd yesterday. It just goes to show that being a massive club doesn't guarantee good results.

Monday 4 May   **Manchester United 3 Leeds United 0**

GARY: Jaap Stam, our new £10.75 million signing from PSV Eindhoven, was at Old Trafford to watch the match today. Jaap has a reputation as the best defender in Europe. I didn't meet him, but a few of the lads saw him in the medical room and told me that he looks a hell of a big fellow. In the press recently, the Gaffer has indicated that he will be bringing in other new signings and there's a lot of speculation about Marc-Vivien Foe, the Cameroon midfielder who plays in France with Lens.

In the dressing room, the Gaffer told us to go and put on a show. Wes Brown, our eighteen-year-old central defender, came on as a substitute in the second half and made it look easy. He has the same sort of abilities as Rio Ferdinand: aggressive, quick, good on the ball and a fine reader of the game – he seems to have the lot. I think he's going to be a great player.

With the title no longer at stake, the first half felt a bit dead, but our fans were excellent today. The taunts from Leeds fans helped to fire us up, too. When Becks scored, all the lads ran over to the Leeds fans; we don't particularly like their style of abuse. Considering they only needed a point to get into Europe, Leeds were very dour. They came to defend and tried to catch us on the break. We were pleased with our performance and the fact that we finished at home on a good note. After the dejection of yesterday, I hope the fans went home with their spirits raised a little.

for club and country

PHIL: The lads just wanted to get this game out of the way. It felt very odd playing in a game which meant nothing. It's the first time since I broke into the United First Team that I've been in such a situation. I would never have predicted that our last home game of the season would be meaningless.

Premiership / Old Trafford / Att: 55,167

Manchester United 3
Van Der Gouw, G Neville, Irwin (P Neville), May (Brown), Pallister, Butt, Beckham, Scholes, Giggs, Sheringham (McClair), Cole
Scorers: Giggs, Irwin (pen), Beckham
Leeds United 0
Martyn, Kelly, Haaland, Radebe, Wetherall, Hasselbaink, Bowyer, Halle, Kewell, Harte (Robertson), Hiden (Hopkin)

Tuesday 5 May

PHIL: The manager had a chat with us today. He said he felt that Becks, Scholesy, Gary and I needed a rest and told us today's training session would be the end of our season.

It makes sense to give us a break now, because pre-season training begins on 9 July, three days before the World Cup Final! At first I thought the Boss had got his dates mixed up, but then he told us that the Champions' League qualifiers begin on 12 August, and that we have to prepare properly for them.

GARY: If we do well in the World Cup, I won't have time for a holiday. I now haven't had a free summer since way back in 1995. All the matches I've played in have been massive games, so I wouldn't have it any other way, but sometimes I think it's all going to catch up with me. By the end of next season, that will be five straight years of football with about three months off in total. That's just not enough rest. I will definitely have to take next summer off.

Thursday 7 May

PHIL: I was saddened to hear today that Brian McClair has been released. He's been a great help to all the young players, giving us

23 May 1998, England v Saudi Arabia: "Phil and I went straight out to have a look at the pitch and were greeted by a chorus of 'Stand Up If You Hate Man U'. We've had this abuse before, but over the last year it's got worse." *Gary*

1 June 1998: "There is no case for questioning Glenn Hoddle's choice... He can't afford to listen to anyone else. He must have the players he thinks can win the World Cup for England." *Gary*

29 May 1998, England v Belgium (a): "What a time to play badly... I would go as far as to say it's the worst game I've ever played." *Phil*

Tony Adams: "When we're playing at Wembley, Tony will shout, 'It's our turf, don't let them come here and enjoy it.' The first time I heard him, I didn't know whether to be scared or laugh. Now I appreciate it helps you to concentrate." *Gary*

31 May 1998. Phil is left out of England's 22 to go to France '98. "I've always said that when it comes to football, the fact that Phil and I are brothers must not come into it. But at this moment, it's exceptionally difficult to seperate football and family." *Gary*

31 May 1998: "Somebody told me that Gazza had been left out. I just could not believe it. I'd never once doubted that Gazza would make the final squad." *Gary*

10 June 1998: "It's starting to drag a bit... There is talk that Ian Wright may come out to La Baule to be with the squad, and he's the sort of bubbly character the lads like." *Gary*

15 June 1998, England v Tunisia: "As usual, Scholesy didn't say anything about his performance. No matter how well or badly he plays, he never talks about his game unless asked." *Gary*

June 1998. Becks, Alan and me at Brazil v Morocco: "For a while I just watched Ronaldo and didn't seem to move, but then he scored one and set up another! It's just as if he pulls the trigger and explodes into life to win games. He has amazing ability." *Gary*

22 June 1998, England v Romania: "When Michael Owen scored with about ten minutes left, we had to make a decision whether to go for the winner or sit back. We did neither and instead got hit with a sucker punch."

26 June 1998,
England v Colombia:
"What a time for Becks to
score his first goal for
England! After his problems
of the last week, it was a
great way to respond." *Gary*

June 1998, England v Argentina: "I saw the referee produce the yellow card for Simeone, so thought Becks was going to be all right. He then called Becks over, but put away the yellow rd. 'Oh God, no', I thought." *Gary*

June 1998, England v Argentina: "I felt sick and numb... Back at the hotel, Becks, chael Owen, Rio Ferdinand and I played pool and chatted until five in the morning, just ing over the game again and again." *Gary*

2 June 1998: "Now, I've got a month off to prepare for what I want to be the best season of m
life. I want to prove a few people wrong and make sure I'm never left behind again." *Phil*

advice when we had problems, not just with our football but also with our contracts.

There had been an expectation among the fans that he would get a coaching job, but I never heard any talk of that myself. There simply isn't a vacancy. In the past, Bryan Robson and Steve Bruce have both left the club to do their managerial apprenticeships, and that's probably the case with Choccy now as well. Anyway, I've heard he wants to play for a couple more years yet.

GARY: Ben Thornley and Chris Casper have also been in to see the Boss and they've agreed it's time to move on. They are both excellent players and they need First-Team football. I'm sure the manager will help them find good clubs. He's fond of all the young players who have come through the ranks, especially the ones who don't give him any trouble. Ben and Chris have trained as hard as anyone, but just haven't had the luck here. Given the opportunity, they will prove to be top players. I hope they find local clubs, because they are good friends of ours.

Sunday 10 May   Barnsley 0 Manchester United 2

GARY: I only caught the highlights of our win today on TV. It's nice to go out on a high note, especially with so many youngsters playing. It shows there's nothing wrong with the structure of the club.

Premiership / Oakwell / 18,694

Barnsley 0
Watson, Appleby (Eaden), Barnard, Sheridan, Moses, Redfearn, Bullock, Jones, Hristov (Fjortoft), Ward, Morgan
Manchester United 2
Van Der Gouw, Clegg (Higginbotham), May, Berg, Brown, Curtis, Mulryne, Butt, Cole, Sheringham, Giggs
Scorers: Cole, Sheringham

Although I'm sure they eased off a little, Arsenal did lose their last two Premiership matches at Liverpool and Aston Villa. I've always said they would be tough games for Arsenal and it's a shame we didn't manage to stay in touch until the last weekend.

Alex Ferguson will now reflect on the season, and each player has to look hard at himself too. In a recent interview, the Gaffer said there were a couple of players who haven't shown the hunger that the coaching staff and fans deserve and that there will be changes this summer. I just hope I'll be here next season. The last time we lost the League, Kanchelskis, Hughes and Ince were all sold, so no one can assume they are safe.

I've got to look at ways to improve my game. This season, I've probably done fewer extra training sessions than ever before. I used to stay behind regularly after team training sessions for extra technical training, but there didn't seem to be time this year. Eric Harrison always instilled in us the importance of individual exercises to work on technique. Next season I intend to put an afternoon aside every week next season to focus on my weak points. I'll ask Eric if he'll help me out.

The Boss has also said that we've missed Roy Keane, who would have helped us during those tough end-of-season games. Roy is one of only two or three genuine leaders in the team who let their feelings be known. I think I need to improve my communication skills on the pitch. I want to get back to being as vocal as I was when I played in the Youth Team, although it's difficult when you are playing with more experienced footballers.

The greatest players I've played with – like Beardsley, Pearce, Adams, Bruce, Robson, Ince, Schmeichel and Keane – are all regarded as born winners. It's no coincidence that they always speak their mind. I prefer to know when I go wrong; those players will certainly tell you when you fall short of the highest standards.

Monday 11 May

GARY: Today the first of 150 wagon-loads of Old Trafford top-soil arrived at the site of my barn.

They are laying a new pitch at Old Trafford this summer and a couple of weeks ago I asked Keith Kent, our head groundsman, if he could spare any soil. They started digging up the old pitch today and giving out lumps of turf as mementos to thousands of United fans.

Apparently, the rest of the top-soil is going to Haydock and

Cheltenham racecourses. It will be nice to have a bit of Old Trafford in my garden!

Tuesday 12 May

PHIL: The squad list was announced today for the pre-World Cup friendlies against Saudi Arabia, Morocco and Belgium.

England squad

David Seaman, Ian Walker, Nigel Martyn, Tim Flowers, Gary Neville, Phil Neville, Gareth Southgate, Tony Adams, Martin Keown, Sol Campbell, Graeme Le Saux, Andy Hinchcliffe, Rio Ferdinand, David Beckham, Paul Ince, Rob Lee, Paul Gascoigne, David Batty, Nicky Butt, Jamie Redknapp, Paul Scholes, Darren Anderton, Paul Merson, Steve McManaman, Alan Shearer, Teddy Sheringham, Michael Owen, Dion Dublin, Ian Wright, Les Ferdinand.

I was on the golf course at Mottram Hall when Nicky Butt phoned to tell me that Andy Cole hadn't made it. Glenn Hoddle phoned Andy with the news that he wasn't in the squad. Gary and I were very disappointed for Coley and he himself was gutted, but he's at an age where he can deal with it and at least he's got the summer off. He's had a great season, scored more goals than anyone else, but that doesn't seem to have been enough.

GARY: I thought Andy was a certainty for the preliminary squad, with a good chance of getting into the the final twenty two. Another surprise was the omission of Ray Parlour, who had his best-ever season.

Glenn has picked thirty players to join up at Burnham Beeches next Monday, a figure that will be whittled down to the final twenty two on 2 June. There are going to be eight inconsolable players that day. The next four weeks are going to be crucial. For most of us, it may be our only chance to go to the World Cup Finals.

I reckon three goalkeepers, seven defenders, seven midfielders and five strikers will go to France. It's important you have a versatile squad. There will be a couple of midfielders who can also play in defence and a couple of attackers who can drop into midfield, so players like Scholes, McManaman and Becks, who can play different positions, will be very valuable.

I'm the only specialist right back in the squad, so I'm confident of getting into the final twenty two. Philip should be too, because he can play on the right or left of defence.

The selection of Darren Anderton may have surprised some because of his lack of match practice, but I think he will be go to France if he proves his fitness. I played behind him in Euro '96 and he's a great foot-baller. I'm sure Glenn Hoddle already knows his final squad, barring injuries. He's had two years of build-up and France is only weeks away, so if he doesn't know now, he never will. The only question is about the fitness of Wright, Anderton and Redknapp.

PHIL: I knew that Glenn was going to pick a thirty-man squad, but I wish it had just been the twenty two he was taking to France. If I'm not going, I would rather know now than play three games and then be told I'm not selected.

10

The worst day of our lives

Monday 18 May

GARY: This morning, Phil and I went down to Burnham Beeches to join up with the England squad with the prospect of just three more warm-up games before the World Cup. I've spent most of the past fortnight resting, but I went into The Cliff last Friday to do a training session with Ben Thornley and Chris Casper, and on Saturday and Sunday I went out jogging in order to get going again.

At the hotel, we congratulated the Arsenal lads on completing the Double by beating Newcastle in the FA Cup Final on Saturday. There are four Arsenal players in the squad and they are very confident going into the summer.

Paul Gascoigne is in the news again for going out to have a late-night kebab. It's a total non-story. If you went through the whole squad of thirty, you would probably find that twenty-five players had had a couple of nights out since the season ended. The way the press are treating Gazza, you'd think he'd committed a crime. They should be getting behind him. He's one of England's most important players.

PHIL: After Middlesbrough's season finished, Gazza was given two weeks off and probably thought to himself, "This is going to be my only break this summer, so I am going to enjoy it." I don't think a couple of nights out will do him any harm. He deserves a chance to relax after helping Middlesbrough to promotion.

I love Gazza. He has always been brilliant to me. Since I got into the squad, he's made me feel more welcome than anyone. He likes having a laugh and a joke, but he becomes more serious when he gets on the training pitch. I would say he is one of the best trainers in the camp, going at each session as if were his last. We could be away for six weeks at the World Cup, and having Gazza around to have a laugh with is definitely going to lift the boredom.

GARY: The first training session was a light one, but it didn't go that well for me. I felt like I was starting pre-season again. We did a long warm-up with plenty of stretching and then a possession game. You have to build up slowly; you can't just go back in whacking balls everywhere.

We all took blood tests and started on a course of vitamins, potassium and iron tablets to balance our dietary system, as prescribed by Dr Yann Rougier. Rougier has worked with Fabio Capello at AC Milan and with Arsene Wenger at Monaco, in Japan and at Arsenal. When Glenn Hoddle played for Monaco, he was introduced to Rougier by Wenger.

At this moment, I'm a little bit sceptical about taking five tablets a day, but the Arsenal players swear by it and the Boss has asked us all to give it a go.

Tuesday 19 May

PHIL: Glenn Hoddle has invited Paul Durkin, the only Englishman refereeing at France '98, to Burnham Beeches to tell us about FIFA's new rules for the World Cup. It seems a strange time for FIFA to introduce them. It would have been more sensible to let us get used to anything new in our domestic leagues for a season.

Glenn Hoddle showed us a video of Tunisia, our first opponents in the World Cup. Paul Durkin watched it with us and pointed out seven examples where, under the new rules, a player would be sent off. He told us that if you win the ball first from behind but get the man as you follow through, you'll get a red card. As a defender, it looks frightening. We'll see a lot of teams finishing with nine men if referees follow these directives.

There are other rules to be wary of, too. If you jump over the advertising boards to celebrate a goal, you'll get booked. Even letting your socks roll down will cost you a yellow card. It looks like you'll get booked or even sent off for dissent. Anyway, Glenn Hoddle's has been saying that all year: don't talk back to referees because you get nowhere.

It's going to be hard to adapt. At least we're the last team to play, so we have a chance to gauge what players can get away with.

GARY: Paul Durkin watched us train. When I did a fairly innocuous tackle from the side on Nicky Butt, Paul stopped the game and I was amazed to be told that the challenge would get me a yellow card in France. I don't think the people who make up these rules know what a bad tackle is. If you slide in from the back, you rarely hurt your opponent, whereas a two-footed tackle from the front can break an opponent's legs.

Wednesday 20 May

GARY: All the players took part in a pro-am golf day at Mill Ride golf course near Ascot. We were each given a set of brand-new golf clubs to play with by the competition sponsor. Becks and I played in a group with European Tour pro Paul Broadhurst.

Derek Lawrenson, a Liverpool-supporting journalist who was playing in a group with Paul Ince and Steve McManaman, got a hole-in-one. He did it at the par three fifteenth hole and won a £189,000 Lamborghini Diablo!

In the evening, Glenn Hoddle called a meeting and told us he sincerely believes we will win the World Cup. He said that we've got to believe in ourselves.

"You mustn't be frightened of anyone, not even Brazil," he said.

Thursday 21 May

PHIL: Our players' committee – Alan Shearer, Tony Adams and David Seaman – met Phil Carling, the FA Commercial Director yesterday to discuss team endorsements. Today, it's back page news that there is a huge rift between the players and the FA. If there is, I know nothing about it.

The FA has found a group of companies willing to pay £4 million a year to sponsor "Team England". That's a lot of money to split among the squad. I can understand that some players are concerned this arrangement may affect their own commercial income, and I presume that's what the discussions are about. The issue will probably be left until after the World Cup now. You don't earn the same sort of money playing for England as you get at club level, but playing for your country is all about pride. I would play for nothing.

Paul Durkin refereed an eleven v eleven practice game to get used to the new rules. It didn't really work, because all our tackles were a bit soft. The team hasn't been announced yet. I had Gascoigne and Campbell on my side, so I don't think the Boss was playing Saturday's side. At least I hope not, because I wasn't in it!

GARY: The side I played for looked like it might be the starting eleven. But the Boss seems to be changing things. I think there are fourteen certainties for the final squad, but I struggle to pick the last eight. There are players coming into the reckoning with late surges of form.

Paul Ince is the only injury worry at the moment. Graeme Le Saux didn't train today, but he should be all right for Saturday.

Friday 22 May

GARY: A big disappointment today: Jamie Redknapp pulled out of the World Cup squad. I was surprised, because Jamie looked really sharp in training yesterday, pinging long passes all over the pitch. Maybe he was trying to test his ankle fully one last time and hid the pain. Jamie has had nightmare luck with England. He came on against Scotland in Euro '96 and turned the game but got injured and missed the rest of the tournament. Then last year, he was selected to go to Le Tournoi, but broke his ankle playing against South Africa at Old Trafford the week before. Everyone was gutted for him.

The team to face Saudi Arabia was announced at this afternoon's training session. It was the same team that played together yesterday. I was disappointed for Phil, who was named as substitute. It's getting a bit twitchy now for the players who feel they are on the fringes of the squad. There will be so much pressure during these next three games.

In preparation for tomorrow's game, we worked on set-pieces and watched Saudi Arabia v Brazil on video. The Saudis lost 3-0 but they opened Brazil up two or three times early on and should have taken the lead. We could see they are a decent side.

Saturday 23 May   England 0 Saudi Arabia 0

GARY: When we arrived at Wembley, Phil and I went straight out to have a look at the pitch and were greeted by a chorus of "Stand Up If You Hate Man U" from thousands of England fans near the players' tunnel. We've had this abuse before, but over the last year it's got worse. Around 15,000 were singing and the rest of the crowd stood up. I thought it was a disgrace. At Euro '96 we all got a standing ovation from the crowds at Wembley before each game, and I remember the boost that gave us, so it's very sad.

The no-score draw was a disappointing result. We missed a few good chances, but I don't think that is a concern at the moment. The way Saudi Arabia got at us on the break is more of a worry. They opened us up a couple of times and created good chances. Their number nine, Al-Jaber, was quick and skilful and caused us the most problems.

We did two-hour sessions morning and afternoon on Thursday, which is far more than you'd usually do two days before a game. That probably took the edge off us. The Boss and John Gorman admitted as much after the game, but told us that it's all about reaching peak fitness in France. It's as if we are doing a mini pre-season with all the heavy training now, and all the short, sharp stuff will kick in later.

United players weren't the only ones to get abuse: Darren Anderton was also targeted. Darren got booed when he had the ball, he passed it to Ian Wright, and Ian got wild applause. Darren had a really good game, especially when you consider he's only played a handful of times for his club this season. To boo him was disgraceful.

Because it was our last Wembley appearance before the World Cup, we did a lap of appreciation for the crowd at the end. I was happy to do it for the 40 or 50,000 people there who supported us. It was mainly the fans near the tunnel who gave us all the stick.

PHIL: This wasn't the best send-off for the World Cup. We didn't play that well and crowd gave us some terrible abuse.

Glenn Hoddle wasn't too down after the game. I think he was reasonably pleased with our performance, but said there was room for improvement. I think we treated the game like a practice match. The days of beating teams like Saudi Arabia 10-0 are over, but we should still have scored. If we had got a goal in the first ten minutes, I'm sure we would have hammered them.

The lap of appreciation afterwards was something I'd normally enjoy, but this time I wondered if the spectators who had constantly abused the United players deserved it. On the other hand, I knew that the large majority of the crowd were true English football fans, supporting every player representing their country. It was to those people that I showed my appreciation.

I came on in the second half at left wing back and thought I did well. The manager told me afterwards, 'The position is there for the taking."

International friendly / Wembley

England 0
Seaman, G Neville, Adams, Southgate, Hinchcliffe (P Neville), Anderton, Beckham (Gascoigne), Batty, Sheringham (Wright), Scholes, Shearer (Ferdinand)
Saudi Arabia 0
Al-Daye, Al-Jahni, Al-Khlawi, Zebramawi, Amin (Al-Dosary), Al-Sharani, Al-Jaber, S Al-Owairan (Al-Temiyat), Solaimani, Al-Muwalid, K Al-Owairan

Sunday 24 May

GARY: We were given the day off before we set off for our week in La Manga, where Glenn Hoddle will make his final decision about the World Cup squad. After staying in a hotel, I was happy to spend a quiet day at home.

PHIL: Glenn Hoddle has been quoted as saying that he's made up his mind about twenty of his squad. I hope I'm included in that. It's getting very tense at the moment. I have always thought I was a definite, but being with England for the last week, little doubts have been creeping into my mind. I don't know why, but I have a bad feeling.

Monday 25 May

GARY: Woke up early for the flight down to Luton, where we picked up our bags and caught the flight to Spain.

Our home for the next week is a superb hotel and golf complex. My room overlooks the eighteenth green of La Manga's championship golf course. The weather is perfect and the food is magnificent.

Ten minutes after we arrived, we had a tough two-hour training session. I must have left my legs on the plane – I wasn't at the races. It amazes me how Gazza and Wrighty can be so hyperactive after a flight. They're always buzzing and never shut up. They may be years older than me, but I wish I had their enthusiasm.

Ian Wright and Paul Ince bumped into Chris Eubank later on. Chris, who is good mates with Ian, is on a charity hitch-hike and somehow he's ended up in La Manga!

The results of our blood tests came through today. I've got a build-up of lactic acid in my body which is making me feel tired and I'm also low on iron. All the players have now been given a personal programme for taking vitamins. In addition to the tablets we were given last week, we are now taking creatine. According to Doctor Rougier, creatine helps to replenish essential energy reserves in the muscles footballers use for sudden energy bursts; for example, when you make a five-yard sprint for the ball. Doctor Rougier gave a talk on the effects of creatine, telling us about experiments he had done with three rats. One rat was fed a little less food than normal, the second was fed normally and the third was put on a high-vitamin and creatine diet. In races, the creatine-taking rat performed up to thirty per cent better than the rat on a normal diet.

The reason we have not taken creatine before now is that you need the right base of vitamins and minerals in your body before creatine can take effect. It feels a bit unnatural to take all these pills, but I'm told it will be worth it.

The overall mood in the camp may seem relaxed, but the battle is on for places in the final squad. I think Philip is a certainty to go to France, but Andy Hinchcliffe playing in the Saudi game has put doubt in Phil's mind. Like Nicky Butt, he just wants a game, and he will be hoping to be in the team against Morocco tomorrow. The Boss has said he will make changes, but no one yet knows what he has in mind.

We play Morocco on Wednesday and Belgium on Friday at the King Hassan International tournament in Casablanca. We fly to Casablanca at 10 a.m. on the morning of each game, kick off at 4.30 p.m. and fly back to La Manga at midnight after each match. It's a tough schedule.

Tuesday 26 May

GARY: Loads of England fans are turning out to watch us training, which makes for a good atmosphere. This morning's session was just a loosener for the benefit of the press, which pleased me because I'm quite tired. I think it's just because we are training so hard at the end of a long season. The four-day break after this tournament will be my chance to relax and get my sharpness back.

There was no respite today, though. The afternoon training session was a long one, especially for the day before a game. Glenn Hoddle then went through a video of the Saudi Arabia game with us. He was quite happy with our performance apart from the finishing, and also said that the midfield needed to be closer to the defence for us to play more as a unit.

As usual, we watched an edited version of the game as seen from the gantry camera. Some of the movement looked really good, but the Boss pointed out some bits of bad defending. He was concerned that the Saudi midfield were allowed to break on to the back three and that we backed off instead of one of us getting in a tackle.

The eleven starters for tomorrow's game were announced later. Me, Phil, Becks and Nicky Butt were all left out.

PHIL: So close to the World Cup, it's a bit worrying not to be selected, even though it was understandable that Glenn Hoddle chose Graeme Le Saux who hasn't played for three weeks. I would have been more concerned if he had picked Andy Hinchcliffe ahead of me. I think it's between me and Andy for a place in the squad as back-up for Graeme.

Wednesday 27 May   England 1 Morocco 0

GARY: On the plane to Casablanca, the air stewardesses presented Gazza with a cake and we all sang "Happy Birthday". He's 31 today.

John Gorman walked down the aisle naming the subs for today's game. He told David and I that we weren't among them.

We took our seats in the stands to watch the match, which was pretty dull, but it taught us an important lesson. If anyone had been complacent about our first game in the World Cup against Tunisia, Saudi Arabia and Morocco have proved these "lesser" teams can play a bit. Overall, we gave a pretty tired performance, which is quite understandable given the heavy training we've been doing and the fact that we travelled on the day of the game.

The twenty-three-degree heat was a killer. Added to the tension of players going for a World Cup spot, plus the experimental team selection, it was never going to be a classic performance. The worst aspect of the game was the injury to Ian Wright. To pull a hamstring so close to a major tournament is desperately unlucky. We were all worried for him.

Michael Owen came on to replace Ian and became the youngest player ever to score in an international. He took the goal brilliantly. Seeing him every day in training, it's hard to believe the temperament and ability of a lad so young. Michael is always on his toes, very lively and very, very quick. He will be a danger to any opposition team.

There was an 80,000-strong crowd and I was amazed how the Moroccan supporters turned on their team when we scored. They ended up cheering us and booing their own team. Despite our bad experience at Wembley last Saturday, I'm glad I don't play for Morocco!

After the game, Glenn Hoddle told the lads he was pleased with the second-half performance, but he didn't see why they waited 45 minutes to start playing.

We hung around for an hour and a half before the journey to the airport. Then the flight home took an hour and 20 minutes and finally we had the coach ride back to our hotel. We got in at 2 a.m. and fell straight into bed.

for club and country

England 1
Flowers, Keown, Le Saux, Campbell, Southgate, Ince, Anderton, McManaman, Gascoigne, Wright (Owen), Dublin (Ferdinand)
 Scorer: Owen
Morocco 0
Benzekri, Saber, Rossi, Negrouz, El Hadrioui, Chiba, Tahar, Chippo, Bassir, Quakill, Rokki

Thursday 28 May

PHIL: I didn't see Ian Wright this morning, but word got round that he was out of the World Cup and had gone home. He was offered the chance to stay until we all left on Monday, but after saying goodbye to Les Ferdinand and Paul Ince, his closest friends in the squad, he headed straight back to England. I would have done the same. Wrighty's departure is a real loss. He's a fantastic striker, but just as important is the role he plays in the camp, helping lift team morale. On the coach, his is always the loudest voice, laughing and joking with everyone.

Glenn Hoddle called a meeting before training and announced the team for the tomorrow's game. I was relieved to be in it. This will be my chance to shine.

John Gorman took me to one side in training and dropped a big hint that I was in the squad.

"Philip, look me in the eye," he said. "You haven't got anything to worry about concerning the squad. You can play in any position, so just enjoy these next few days."

I took that as being a hint, but for some reason I'm not convinced. Obviously, I would have preferred to have heard it from Glenn Hoddle. I still have a bad feeling in the pit of my stomach.

GARY: I thought the Boss would select near enough his strongest team against Belgium, but instead he opted for a very experimental side with Phil and I as full backs in a 4-4-2 formation.

Again, it was a long practice session for the day before a game. I'm feeling pretty tired at the moment. We're training hard in hot weather and we've got the prospect of another long day tomorrow.

the worst day of our lives

Friday 29 May   England 0 Belgium 0 (lost 4–3 on penalties)

PHIL: What a time to play badly! I have never felt so bad on a foot-ball pitch in my life. I couldn't move my legs. The fact that I hadn't played for a month didn't help. I would go as far to say it's the worst game I've ever played.

My heart sank when Glenn Hoddle took me off at half-time. All through the second half I replayed my performance over and over in my head, re-living how bad it was. My only consolation is that I'm sure Glenn Hoddle isn't going to decide about me on the evidence of forty-five minutes. We are due to be told the squad on Sunday night. It's going to be a horrible two-day wait.

GARY: We played really badly in the first half. The system wasn't working and it was easy for Belgium to get at us.

At half-time, Glenn Hoddle came in and spoke for three or four minutes about the team's poor performance. "I can't believe you lads," he said. "You do things in training, but you're not doing it out there. Now, go out and express yourselves."

Then, out of the blue, he said, "Gary and Phil, you'll be coming off."

I looked at the Boss in disbelief. I know neither of us were having the best of games, but I didn't feel we deserved to be substituted.

When the players went out for the second half, Philip and I were left on our own, not knowing why we'd been substituted. I had all sorts going through my mind. Was the Boss taking me off because he'd planned to before the game or, more worryingly, was it because I'd played so badly that he felt he had to substitute me? The difficult thing was not knowing why I had come off, as I'm the type of player who would rather be told directly. Maybe I'll find out tomorrow.

Glenn went for three at the back for the second half. There's no doubt that the lads played better, but the different system seemed to help.

In the dressing room afterwards, the Boss said he was pleased with the improvement but warned, "I don't want to come in at half-time in France and have to tell you to start playing. You can say it's a friendly match, but I don't want it to become a habit."

for club and country

King Hassan International Cup / Casablanca

England 0
Martyn, G Neville (Owen), Keown, Campbell (Dublin), P Neville (R Ferdinand), Lee, Gascoigne (Beckham), Butt, Le Saux, Merson, L Ferdinand
Belgium 0
Van Der Walle, Deflandre, Van Meir, Verstraeten, Borkelmans, Verheyen, De Boeck, Scifo, Boffin, Goossens, L Mpenza
Belgium win 4–3 on penalties

Saturday 30 May

GARY: Again, it was a long trip back from Casablanca last night. We didn't get back until 2 a.m. and training this morning was limited to a light stretch in the gym. But this afternoon we got our first chance to play golf. La Manga is a beautiful course and I enjoyed the game, but everyone is getting edgy because the squad is announced tomorrow. I was drawn to play with Darren Anderton against Glenn Hoddle and the ex-QPR and Arsenal defender Terry Mancini.

Before the game of golf started, I thought there would be an opportunity during the round for the Boss to tell me why he substituted me yesterday, but football wasn't mentioned at all. Without being over-confident or wishing to tempt fate, I'm certain I will be in the Finals squad. Anyway, it was an enjoyable game and Darren and I managed to take £50 each off the Boss and Terry.

PHIL: The tension is unbearable. There are about ten players who look relaxed because they're assured of their place in the squad, like Alan Shearer and David Seaman, but it's a nightmare for the rest of us. I played golf with David Seaman and Ian Walker, but we didn't talk about the squad, although I know Ian and I were thinking about nothing else.

In the evening we had the hotel's piano bar to ourselves. The windows had been blacked out, so we could really have a good time and forget about the outside world. Everyone was merry and a few of the lads tried out the karaoke or gathered around the piano for a sing-song. After two weeks of hard training, it was good to let our hair down and have a few drinks.

Glenn Hoddle joined us for a little while. but generally he likes to keep himself slightly detached from the players. When the team goes out for a meal he sits on his own table. John Gorman mingles a bit more with us, but tonight he was away watching Germany play Colombia.

GARY: It wasn't really a fun night. There was a lot of tension about the squad being announced tomorrow; it might have been better if there had been other hotel guests in there to relax the atmosphere. Although we had a few laughs, we were with the same people we had been talking to for three weeks. By one o'clock, only about fifteen people were left in the bar and we were told to go to bed.

PHIL: Nicky Butt and I had a chat about our worries. Nicky thinks it's between him and Rob Lee for a place in the squad. Of the players at risk, Nicky's the only one I know well enough to approach for a chat. I'm not really close to Andy Hinchcliffe, so it's not like we can have a joke about our fight for a place.

The night before I find out my fate, I think I'll be in the squad. I believe I have proved myself over the course of the season with both Manchester United and England, so I'll be shocked if I'm left out. At the same time, I have got a really bad feeling about tomorrow. Maybe it's just nerves.

Sunday 31 May

PHIL: I woke up with a sick feeling in my stomach, which stayed with me all day. At breakfast we were each told the time of our appointments with Glenn Hoddle to hear our fates. There were five-minute gaps between each player's meeting; I was down for 4.35 p.m.

Before that, we played another round of golf. Once again, I was with David Seaman and Ian Walker, only this time we were joined by Gazza. He was his usual bubbly self, treating everything he did as a joke, but such is the man's talent, he won the golf tournament.

No one mentioned the squad.

GARY: Darren and I were drawn to play golf with Glenn Hoddle again, and we were in the first group teeing off at 10.36 p.m. Glenn obviously wanted to try and get his money back, but Darren and I won again.

The conversation was all about golf during the round. Just like yesterday, nothing was mentioned about football in general or the Belgium game in particular.

We finished our round at 2.30 p.m. and Terry Mancini gave us all a lift back to the hotel. There was just time for a bite to eat in the dining room before it was time to make our down the corridor to the Boss's room to get the verdict.

David Seaman was the first man in at 4.15, Darren was second. They set off while we were still eating. I was third on the list so I wandered down with Ian Walker a few minutes later. When we got there, David Seaman was still in with Glenn. John Gorman and Peter Taylor were in the room next door with the door open. They were there to comfort those who don't make the cut.

'Bad news, eh?' I joked when David came out. He smiled and punched me playfully.

Then Darren went in and he was with Glenn for about ten minutes. Even though Darren was widely regarded as a borderline case, I always felt he was a certainty if he could prove his fitness. When Darren re-appeared, I made a thumbs-up sign.

"Yeah," he said.

"Well done," I told him, and shook his hand.

Even though I was confident, I still felt a pang of nerves as I walked into the Boss's room.

"This is one of the easy ones," Glenn said. "You're obviously in. Have a seat."

Straight away, I was relaxed.

"You've done well," he continued. "You play in that right-sided centre back role, and we know you can also play as right back in a flat back four. I'm going to go with three at the back with two wing-backs, so if we come up against a team with a flying left winger, you may have to play right wing back ... "

Immediately, it hit me: Phil wasn't not in the squad. I thought, there's no way he'd ask me to play at right wing back if Phil was in the squad. Phil's been chosen ahead of me in that position and he's better than me in that role.

Glenn continued talking, but for a while I couldn't concentrate on what he was saying. Eventually I snapped out of it.

"It's time for you express yourself more in an England shirt," Glenn said. "You've played a lot of games for England now and you should be more adventurous, especially with your long-passing."

I said that if I saw David Beckham five yards away from me, I usually banked on him to hit those passes with more consistency. But I agreed that it was something for me to work on. When I came out, Ian Walker congratulated me as he went in.

Phil was the only person left in the corridor.

"Did he say anything to you?" he asked.

"No," I said. I could see in Phil's eyes that he was really nervous, but I couldn't tell him my fears because I didn't know for sure that he wasn't in.

PHIL: I had the fifth appointment after Seaman, Anderton, Gary and Ian Walker. I walked to Glenn Hoddle's room on the third floor with my heart beating really hard, then waited outside his door with Gary and Ian Walker.

When Gary came out and told me he was in, as soon as I saw his eyes I knew I wasn't. He should have been thrilled to be going to the World Cup, but instead he looked as if he was going to cry. He didn't stop to talk, but went straight back to his room. I was distraught but I tried to compose myself.

Minutes later, Glenn Hoddle showed Ian Walker out saying, "There'll be plenty of World Cups. Keep your chin up son.' Ian went straight into John Gorman's room next door for a chat, without looking at me.

Glenn called me in to his room. He had two chairs facing each other by the window and I sat down opposite him. My heart was thumping and my palms were all sweaty.

"I'm sorry, I'm not taking you to the World Cup," he said.

My head just dropped and my eyes filled up with tears. I couldn't look at him. I stared at the floor as he told me why I wasn't going.

"I was really pleased with you at Le Tournoi last year, but you haven't taken the chances I've given you since," he explained. "Constantly switching positions at United hasn't helped your cause either.

"Would you like to say anything?" he asked.

But I was speechless. Even if I had wanted to say something I wouldn't have been able to. I just stood up and shook my head. I shook his hand and left without saying a word. I wanted to rant and rave, but that would have been pointless. It was better to show a bit of dignity.

John Gorman was waiting for me outside when I left. "Do you want to speak to me, Philip?" he said, but I just ignored him and walked past. As I went down the corridor I heard him say something about it probably not being the best time. I was so upset, I didn't want to speak to anybody at that moment.

Back in my room I just cried my eyes out. Within seconds Gary knocked on my door. I can't remember the last time I cried and normally I would have felt embarrassed in front of Gary, but he just put his arm around me and said all the right things.

I phoned my dad and my girlfriend, while Gary kept coming in and out of my room with up-dates on the squad. Nicky Butt came to my room after his meeting, and from the look on his face when I opened the door I knew he had been left out as well. We didn't say anything, but gave each other a big hug, both with tears in our eyes. Nicky's usually such a tough lad, but even he showed his emotions.

GARY: After my meeting, I went back to my room and rang my dad immediately to tell him I was in.

"What about Phil?" he asked.

"I'm really nervous, Dad," I replied. Dad later told me it was the first time I'd ever sounded doubtful about Phil's chances. He'd been nervous about Phil getting in for a while, and after he'd spoken to me he didn't have a good feeling at all.

Next I rang up my girlfriend. "I've not told my dad yet because I don't know for sure," I told her, "but I don't think Phil's going to be in." I was still on the phone to Hannah when I heard Phil's door slam. I told Hannah I had to go.

When I walked to Phil's room, he'd broken down and the worst few hours of my career followed. To be chosen to play in the World Cup should be the greatest thrill of any player's career, but I didn't feel any excitement whatsoever.

Phil was inconsolable. He was sitting on the bed in tears. I just said, "I can't believe it" and put my arm round him. Even though my meeting with Glenn Hoddle had made me fear the worst, I still couldn't take it in. We sat there for a few minutes without saying a word.

Eventually I said, "Who's he taking then?"

Phil turned round and said, "It must be Andy Hinchcliffe."

I told Phil I'd go next door and ring Dad. When I got through, Dad was broken-hearted. He couldn't believe it, especially after John Gorman had told Phil he had nothing to worry about.

It was back in my room that I discovered the news about Paul Gascoigne, whose room was next door to mine. I was sitting there upset about Phil when I heard shouting in the corridor. I went outside to find out what was going on and somebody told me that Gazza had been left out. I just could not believe it. I'd never once doubted that Gazza would make the final squad.

Everything was happening at a hundred miles an hour; it was hard to take it all in. First Phil had been left out and now Gazza. Before we came out to La Manga, Glenn Hoddle had said he had already chosen twenty players for the final twenty two, but I feel the squad may have changed this week. When I heard that Andy Hinchcliffe, whom I assumed was Phil's only competitor for the second left back slot, had not been picked either, I wondered who was in the squad instead. By now, I was adding and subtracting names and trying to work out the final twenty two in my head. I supposed that Rio Ferdinand, a centre back, must have been selected instead of Phil or Andy Hinchcliffe. Rio is an excellent player, but his selection would mean five centre backs and only two specialist full backs, myself and Graeme Le Saux, with no cover if either of us are injured or suspended. I thought Glenn must be planning to play five at the back with Graeme, Darren Anderton, Becks and I competing for places at wing back.

PHIL: When I left Glenn Hoddle's room, he gave me a piece of paper which said we were due to leave for the airport in forty-five minutes. That was a good thing. I didn't want to hang around. I quickly packed my stuff and waited outside Gazza's room to go down with him to reception. While we were standing there, one of the coaches, Glenn

Roeder, who's known Paul since he was a youth player at Newcastle, came out. He looked absolutely gutted and had tears in his eyes. The day seemed to be getting to everyone.

Teddy, Scholesy and Becks all came up gave me a hug as I waited to leave the hotel. They couldn't believe it.

There was silence in the cars all the way to the airport, but on the flight home we chatted to each other a bit. We were all completely shocked. None of us thought we would be on our way home so soon. Gazza said he knew he was going to be marked man over the next week. He expected the press to hound him.

I felt most sorry for the stewardess. At one point, the five of us were sitting there with tears rolling down our faces. It must have been difficult for her.

There were six cars ready for us at the end of the runway when we landed at Birmingham airport. It made us feel like high-security prisoners, but at least we avoided any press. My dad and girlfriend were at the bottom of the steps when I got off the plane. Gazza was really kind – he hugged them both and told them what a special lad I was.

On the drive home, the first person to phone me on my mobile was Alex Ferguson. "I'm devastated for you, Phil, I really am," he said. "I never thought this would happen. But I want you to know that whatever happens with England makes no difference at United. You've nothing to worry about, your future is secure." He told me he had once been dropped an hour before a Scottish Cup Final and though it had hurt like hell, it had made him stronger. He told me I had to do the same.

GARY: I managed to keep my emotions under control until the moment I had to say goodbye to Phil and Nicky. I couldn't handle it anymore and broke down.

After Phil left, I went to Scholesy's room and Teddy and Becks came down for a chat. I don't think anybody could believe the squad – not that we disagreed with it, we were just in a state of shock.

When the squad for Euro '96, was announced I was rooming with Jason Wilcox of Blackburn, who missed out. I remember how bad I felt for him. But this is the worst night of my football career. The biggest disappointment before this was when Ben Thornley got his cruciate injury.

I wish the people who say footballers are selfish and don't care about their profession had been in our hotel today. I'd experienced every emotion from nervousness to happiness and relief, then anxiety for Phil and finally complete devastation.

I felt totally drained and ended up falling asleep on the spare bed in Scholesy's room.

Monday 1 June

PHIL: I am still really upset. I still don't know why I'm not in the squad. John Gorman had told me all week I'd been training brilliantly. I listened to Glenn Hoddle's press conference in Spain for some clues, but it made me even more confused. He said I had lost form at the wrong time.

It saddened me that this was the reason given; I thought my form for United and England had been good. I played in many positions for United last season, but for England I played in my more accustomed wing back position against Moldova, Cameroon, Chile and for twenty minutes against Saudi Arabia, before the game against Belgium, which was a nightmare for me.

I really feel I did nothing to harm my chances. I proved myself in Le Tournoi against Italy, Brazil and France, the best teams in the world. And with United I've been playing in the Champions' League for most of the season.

Gazza's exclusion has been all over the papers, so the press haven't bothered me too much. They were on to my dad first thing this morning wanting a quote. He issued a statement saying I had already gone on holiday and that I would be cheering on Gary during the tournament. Alex Ferguson told me not to speak to anyone.

I'm still shocked Gazza isn't going to France. I realise he didn't show his fitness in the Casablanca friendlies, but in training he was looking good. You need someone like Paul Gascoigne in a major tournament, even if you just bring him on for the last twenty minutes, because he can get you a goal or do something special.

GARY: I woke up and went down to my own room to shower and change into my kit, even though I didn't feel like training. As I left, Glenn Hoddle walked past.

"Gary," he said. "I know it was a massive disappointment for you yesterday. It's something I didn't enjoy doing. You've got to make sure that you get yourself right now, that you don't let it affect you."

"Right," I replied, and he is. I've always said that, when it comes football, the fact that Phil and I are brothers must not come in to it. But at this moment it's exceptionally difficult to separate football and family.

On the way to breakfast, I knocked on Scholesy's door and then John Gorman came past. He called me to one side. "I'm absolutely devastated," he said, and I could see on his face that he was.

"So am I, John," I replied. "Phil was told he had no worries."

"I know," John said. "He was in, Gary."

The Boss must have made his mind up after the first half against Belgium on Friday. There is no case for questioning Glenn Hoddle's choice, though. To my mind, Phil is the best full back in Britain along with Denis Irwin, and he would be in my twenty two every time, but I'm not burdened with these difficult decisions. Glenn Hoddle is the Boss, he can't afford to listen to anyone else, and the overriding factor is that he must have the players he thinks can win the World Cup for England.

Before training, the Boss sat us all down and said: "Look lads. Yesterday was a difficult day for us all. It wasn't something I enjoyed doing, but it had to be done and there were always going to be lads disappointed. But you are the twenty-two players I have picked to bring that World Cup home and that's what we must focus on now."

The training session lasted for two hours and was quite intensive. The press were watching and the atmosphere was quiet, but it definitely helped me to put my boots on and get straight back into it.

We flew back to England in the afternoon and I was pleased to get back home. Phil and his girlfriend Julie were there when I arrived. I walked into the house wearing my England tracksuit, with all my tickets, information pack and vitamins for France in my bag. I may be going to the World Cup, but it didn't seem appropriate to even think about it, let alone talk about it.

France chose their World Cup twenty two before going to the tournament in Casablanca, and the cruelty of dropping players so close to the start of the competition has been questioned, rather than naming the squad and putting some players on stand-by. In my opinion, Glenn Hoddle went about it the right way because he wanted to keep twenty-eight players interested and fit should they be needed.

Looking back, the only thing that might have been done better was the way players were told whether they were in or out. There is no easy way of doing this, but an afternoon appointment on Sunday meant a very nervous wait. Also, a lot of the meetings overran. Yesterday, after Phil had heard his bad news, I wandered down to Glenn's room to see if Nicky Butt had been in yet. There were five or six lads sitting waiting in the corridor, and I felt for them.

Tuesday 2 June

GARY: Paul Gascoigne's omission from the squad is still massive news. A lot of the press reports centre on Gazza admitting he got drunk on Saturday night. I don't believe this was an issue in his non-selection; the Boss told us all we could let our hair down that evening. We were in a private room, we all had a drink and it would be wrong to single out any one player. I'm sure Glenn Hoddle had already made up his mind about his final squad before Saturday night.

PHIL: John Gorman phoned me today to offer his help and commiseration. I was just getting over the shock of being left out and I felt a bit uncomfortable speaking to him. To be honest, I couldn't get off the phone quick enough. At this point in time, all I want is my own peace of mind.

Looking on the positive side for a moment, I've only had three weeks' rest over the last two years. Now, I've now got a month off to prepare for what I want to be the best season of my life. I want to prove a few people wrong and make sure I'm never left behind again.

11

To win or Toulouse?

Wednesday 3 June

GARY: The squad numbers we will wear in France were announced today. I am to be number twelve. I've been number two every time I've played for England and it's my number at United... I'm not too bothered, but it would have been nice to have kept the same shirt. There is speculation that numbers one to eleven may be the starters against Tunisia, but you can read too much into these things.

SQUAD NUMBERS:
1. David Seaman
2. Sol Campbell
3. Graeme Le Saux
4. Paul Ince
5. Tony Adams
6. Gareth Southgate
7. David Beckham
8. David Batty
9. Alan Shearer
10. Teddy Sheringham
11. Steve McManaman
12. Gary Neville
13. Nigel Martyn
14. Darren Anderton
15. Paul Merson
16. Paul Scholes
17. Rob Lee
18. Martin Keown
19. Les Ferdinand
20. Michael Owen
21. Rio Ferdinand
22. Tim Flowers

Thursday 4 June

PHIL: A back-page article in the Daily Mail today – headlined "Outcast Phil can leave United" – linked me with Middlesbrough. The Gaffer was fuming about the story and asked the club secretary Ken Merrett to phone me to reassure me there wasn't a grain of truth in it. We decided the article was such a load of tripe – there wasn't one quote from anyone at Manchester United – that it wasn't even worth issuing a statement in reply.

Talk about kicking a man when he's down. It must have been a slow day for sports news. Later, Peter Spencer from the Manchester Evening News telephoned to find out if there was any truth in the rumours. After talking to my dad, he realised there wasn't, and they didn't run the story.

It was funny, because yesterday Bryan Robson phoned me up. Bryan only called to commiserate with me for not getting in the squad, but for a while I thought someone must have been bugging my phone!

Never mind. I'm off on holiday tomorrow.

Friday 5 June

GARY: A photo of Teddy Sheringham in a Portuguese nightclub at 6.45 a.m. is all over the front pages today. My view is that a player has got to relax in the way he normally does. I just stayed at home, but every player is different. Teddy was obviously stitched up. He appears in the pictures with a cigarette in his mouth, even though he doesn't smoke. There are two-and-a-half weeks before our next game and Teddy will be fit and ready to play in the World Cup.

Scholesy and I set off early to meet up at Burnham Beeches at 1 p.m. It's the first time in a long while that I've made the journey without Phil, but I know I'm going to have to get used to it over the next few weeks. I've no doubt Phil will be back in the next squad after the World Cup; it's just really unfortunate that he's been left out this time.

We had lunch and then went out to train, practising breaking down teams that defend deep in preparation for Tunisia. They have a Polish coach, and we suspect they will play as defensively as Poland. The Boss was emphasizing the need for our wide players to stay really wide. The idea is for our wing backs to overlap and pull two defenders out wide, in order to create gaps in the middle.

It was a fairly long training session again, but we've been told that we will be gradually easing down over the next week. We play Caen next Tuesday in our last practice match before the World Cup, and after that we won't be training for more than an hour a day.

Saturday 6 June

GARY: We played an eleven v ten practice match this morning - the uneven numbers are a consequence of having three goalkeepers in the squad. It was really competitive, with plenty of tackles going in, not like a normal practice game at all. I played on the team of ten in the first half and we defended really well to keep the score goalless. At half-time, Tony Adams swapped over to our side. He took my place at centre back and I changed to right wing back. Amazingly, with eleven men we then conceded two goals; even more amazingly, I scored both our goals to grab a 2-2 draw! Two-goal Neville – whatever next!

Glenn Hoddle told me when he selected the Finals squad that I might have to play right wing back, so it was a good test for me. It's not a position I've played in that often. I played there against Moldova in the qualifying game and set up a goal for Nicky Barmby, but apart from forty-five minutes against Italy in Le Tournoi last summer, that's the only time I've played wing back for England.

Tunisia beat Wales 4-0 today, underlining what a tough opening game it will be for us. Saudi Arabia and Morocco have already shown there will be no mugs in France, and clearly Tunisia are a decent side.

In the evening, we went to see the musical "Chicago" at the Adelphi Theatre in London and then on for a meal. To be honest, musicals aren't my cup of tea. After an hour and twenty minutes the curtain came down and I thought it was the end. It killed me when I found out there was another half! But a few of the other lads enjoyed it, and it was a last chance to meet up with wives and girlfriends before France. Unfortunately for me, Hannah couldn't make it because she's doing exams.

When we came out of the theatre, a pubfull of fairly drunk people over the road serenaded us with England chants and songs.

Monday 8 June

GARY: An uneventful training session this morning ... apart from the pitch being invaded at one point by a giant stick of Pepperami!

I was asked to attend the press conference with Paul Scholes afterwards, but decided against it. I knew they would only ask me about Phil's omission from the squad and I felt I'd already said everything I wanted to in my column for the Saturday Times. Every player has to take their turn to meet the press, but it would be better to wait until the games have started next week, when the focus is on football matters.

The Boss told us the team which will play in our behind-closed-doors friendly against Caen tomorrow and I was delighted to be picked. The line-up will be Seaman; in defence, myself, Adams, Southgate, Anderton and Rio Ferdinand at left wing back; Beckham, Scholes and Ince in midfield, and Owen and Shearer up front. I'm hoping it's a guide to what the team will be next Monday.

Tuesday 9 June

GARY: We set off for Heathrow all wearing our beige Paul Smith suits. I like the suits, but I'm not so sure about the blue suede shoes! There was a mood real of excitement during the flight to France. We are finally on our way to the World Cup Finals.

We only had an hour at the hotel in Caen before we set off for the game. In the dressing room, Glenn Hoddle told us to go out and be really professional. It turned out to be a difficult game on a slippery pitch. French teams carry on training after their season finishes through to the end of May, before having June and July off, so Caen were still very fresh and lively. It was 0-0 before Scholesy, our outstanding player of the game, scored the winner with about ten minutes to go.

All our players had a dilemma. On the one hand you were worried about getting injured; on the other, you knew you were playing for your place in the Tunisia game. I thought I defended well, but I wasn't happy with my passing in the first half – though it improved in the second. As a team, we created a few chances without playing at our best. Rio Ferdinand did well at left wing back, considering it was probably the first time in his career he has played there. Graeme Le Saux is ill and we hope he recovers soon, because he's the only specialist left-sided player in the squad.

It was very odd atmosphere playing in an empty stadium. Armed policemen were on guard to keep out prying eyes. I can't really see the point of playing behind closed doors. There were a few VIP guests watching and I'm sure one of them could let the team slip out.

"Don't worry that you haven't put the performances together in the past three or four weeks," Glenn Hoddle said after the game. "We've been working you very hard in training and the preparation for games hasn't been normal. We'll ease it down now and you'll be fresh for the Tunisia game next week."

The flight back from Caen to our World Cup training camp at La Baule in Nantes only took an hour. After a tiring day, everyone was happy to get to what is to be our base for the whole competition.

The England set-up is perfectly organised. It's absolutely amazing how much time and effort people have gone to to make our lives easy – especially the FA team administrator, Michelle Farrer. We never have to wait at airports, we just go straight on to the runway. Our bags are brought to our hotel rooms, and press conferences are spread out evenly so players have to do them only occasionally. We are completely free to concentrate on football.

Wednesday 10 June

GARY: We did very little training today and the Boss told us we will have Friday off. Glenn Hoddle is well aware that all the lads need a rest.

I went to Doctor Rougier for some treatment and told him that my legs felt very tired. He gave me an injection in my arm and told me I would feel fine in three days. We're still taking our course of vitamin pills and creatine powder and he has also given us pills to boost our energy levels before training and matches as well as pills to help the muscles recover afterwards.

The hotel complex where we are staying is the same one we stayed at for Le Tournoi last summer. It is a really nice place with fantastic training facilities and plenty to do. There's a gym, kit room, medical room, an amusement arcade with pinball machines, pool tables ... everything you can think of. As in La Manga, my room overlooks the golf course and I went out to play nine holes this afternoon. The only thing that is not right at the moment is the weather. It was windy, cold and raining this morning. Reminds me of Manchester, anyway!

After training, we all got together in the video room to watch Scotland v Brazil. Scotland were unlucky to lose 2-1. The way the game started I thought they were going to get an absolute battering, but Brazil are very loose in defence and Scotland caused them problems. I don't think Scotland should have been awarded a penalty, but they probably deserved it for the other chances they created.

It was a good game for us to watch. Brazil's attacking play was phenomenal at times – some of the things Ronaldo did were frightening – but the match showed they are human and you can put them under pressure.

Teddy and Alan Shearer were running a book and we all lost money to them. Sampaiao scoring the first goal fooled us all. I had John Collins to score the first goal and Brazil to win 3-1, so I wasn't a million miles away. Teddy and Alan will be back tomorrow for the Italy-Chile game, so I'll try to get my money back then.

In the evening, Norway sneaked a 2-2 draw with Morocco. We got a lot of criticism when we only beat Morocco 1-0 a couple of weeks ago, but their performance tonight showed they are a decent side. Hadgi's goal was superb.

Three of my United team-mates were playing – Ole Gunnar Solskjaer, Ronny Johnsen and Henning Berg. I missed the first half, when Ole

Gunnar had got injured, so I was disappointed that when I arrived he'd already gone off.

I can't wait to get going, but our game is one of the last of the opening matches. It's starting to drag a bit. I missed having Nicky and Phil around because they are good friends. Now Gazza and Ian Wright have gone too, there isn't really a joker in the squad. Of course there are people who are funny in their own groups, but no one like Wrighty and Gazza, who will start telling jokes in front of the whole twenty two. It takes a very confident character to do that. When I was in the Youth Team at United, Robert Savage used to be the joker in the pack. Now, in the First Team David May is the only one who isn't afraid to express himself in front of the whole team.

Naturally, you do miss people like Gazza. When you're with the same lads for weeks on end, it's nice to have that sort of character around. Ultimately, though, that shouldn't affect the football. However, there is talk that Ian Wright may come out to be with the squad, and he is the sort of bubbly character the lads like.

Thursday 11 June

GARY: The press were allowed in to watch us warm up. Once they had left, Glenn Hoddle called us round and said, "Right, I'm going to name the team."

We sat round in a semi-circle as he read out the team. I didn't see how each player reacted – you tend to keep your head down whether you are playing or not. I knew after Glenn Hoddle had read just four names – Seaman, Southgate, Campbell and Adams – that I wasn't in. I'd been confident of playing since I started the Caen game, so I was really disappointed. I was even more surprised that Becks was left out; he'd played in every World Cup qualifying game.

Glenn Hoddle has fallen back on his team from Rome, save for Darren Anderton and Paul Scholes who come in for Becks and Gazza respectively. The back three are Southgate, Adams and Campbell, all great defenders. I guess Glenn Hoddle wants to go with the experienced players who got him a draw against Italy last October.

Back in Rome, the Boss had a word with me to explain why he left me out, but not this time. I don't want to show my disappointment at this stage by asking him. If I do get a chance later on, I've just got to take it. Glenn Hoddle told us to keep the team to ourselves. We aren't allowed to tell anybody (including members of our own families) that the team has even been selected yet.

In the afternoon, I went out and played nine holes of golf on my own to clear my head.

Friday 12 June

GARY: I'm still feeling a little down, but starting to come to terms with the disappointment. I'm glad the team was announced yesterday. It gives me time to get my head round the fact I am a sub and prepare properly for the game. I may have to come on in the first fifteen minutes, as happened against Brazil in Le Tournoi last year.

The rest of the lads played a round of golf today, but I felt tired so I rested up. I love to play golf, but at the moment fitness for the World Cup is my priority.

In the evening, we watched an edited video of Tunisia's strengths and weaknesses. They have very technical players in midfield and are strong attacking down the right wing, but they lack a natural finisher. All the same, if we give them too much time on the ball, they could hurt us.

But Tunisia are vulnerable to the counter-attack. Their centre backs look very immobile and their goalkeeper is extremely erratic when it comes to dealing with crosses. It is an old English tactic, but the plan is to get our wing backs in behind their defence and get plenty of crosses in.

I also watched France's opening game with South Africa tonight and the hosts looked very impressive, the best team I've seen so far. They have an excellent defence, and Zidane and Djorkaeff in midfield create goals for them. Up front they have Dugarry, who isn't very popular with French fans, but I rate him very highly.

Saturday 13 June

GARY: As Doctor Rougier predicted, my legs felt much better in training this afternoon. You might think it's all in my mind, but the transformation is incredible.

It was absolutely throwing down with rain, so the session only lasted half an hour. The team to play Tunisia worked on attacking set-pieces. On free-kicks, Teddy concentrated on drifting into space beyond the far post, because Glenn and John Gorman had identified that as an area which Tunisia don't defend well.

When you do exercises like that you can't help but feel pangs of disappointment, because you are always doing the opposite of what the team selected are doing. When they are attacking, you're defending, or sometimes just watching, which is hard to take. All sorts of different thoughts go through your head, but ultimately you realise you are still involved in a World Cup, which is a dream in itself. I have to believe I will get my chance to play if I hang in there.

South Korea's Ha Seok Ju became the first player to be sent off so far in the tournament. He scored in the twenty-eighth minute and was sent off in the twenty-ninth! Despite my pre-tournament fears, I think the refereeing has been excellent so far. From what Paul Durkin told us back in England, it sounded like the referees wouldn't allow any sort of tackle from behind, but they haven't cracked down as much as we'd expected. The directive that players should be sent off for a tackle from behind, when the tackler gets the ball and then the man, hasn't come into play. Referees seem to be doing their job as before, using their common sense, and the fans have been rewarded with some good, flowing football.

Holland v Belgium this evening gave me my first chance to see Jaap Stam in action. He looked excellent: very strong, comfortable on the ball and good in the air.

At half-time, Tony Adams did a live interview for the BBC from the hotel. The lads have got a bet going on who can drop the most song titles into their interviews. Tony produced a virtuoso performance. "I'm So Excited" he told us, about the Tunisia game, and as for our hotel, he claimed it was like a "Ghost Town".

for club and country

Sunday 14 June

GARY: The team worked on defending set-pieces in the morning, before flying down to Marseilles.

In the evening we went to the Stade Velodrome for an open practice session in front of the press. It looked a good stadium and we heard that they were expecting between 15,000 and 20,000 England fans.

Monday 15 June   England 2 Tunisia 0

GARY: We woke up to the news of trouble caused by some so-called England fans. Apparently, it was going on yesterday near the ground where we trained. It's such a shame that a few idiots can tarnish the reputation of every England fan. It seems that this hooligan element will always follow the England team. Perhaps we should stop reporting on them, putting their photos in the newspapers and making them feel important.

On the coach to the game, we watched a video Ian Wright had sent us of himself. He'd painted the Three Lions on his chest and said how sorry he was that he couldn't be with us and wished us all the best. He's really funny.

In his pre-match talk in the dressing room, Glenn Hoddle said to the lads, "Relax and enjoy the experience of playing in a World Cup Finals. Don't let it pass you by."

The team responded by putting in a solid performance. There was some concern on the bench that we weren't passing the ball enough, then Alan Shearer scored just before half-time. After that the lads relaxed and put in an accomplished performance. Alan's goal was reward for the work we'd done on set-pieces last week. I had predicted Teddy would get a goal from round the back on a free-kick and I was nearly right. If the ball had gone over Alan's head, Teddy was unmarked at the back post ready to knock it in.

Scholesy was outstanding. He has been superb in nearly every one of his eight games for England and he deserves all the plaudits. I thought

Alan Shearer and Teddy held the ball up superbly in attack and our back three were magnificent, with Gareth Southgate running Scholesy close for Man of the Match.

There was a bit of excitement in the dressing room afterwards. It was everybody's first game in a World Cup, so we were happy to have won – though no one was getting too carried away. As usual, Scholesy didn't say anything about his performance. He has a perfect temperament. No matter how well or badly he plays, he never talks about his game unless asked.

It's an excellent start for us. At Euro 96, when we drew our first game against Switzerland we put a lot of pressure on our next game against Scotland. Now I hope we can beat Romania and qualify for the next round.

World Cup Group G / Stade Velodrome, Marseilles / Att: 54,587

England 2
Seaman, Southgate, Adams, Campbell, Anderton, Ince, Scholes, Batty, Le Saux, Sheringham (Owen), Shearer / Goals Shearer 42, Scholes 89
Tunisia 0
El-Quaer, H Trabelsi (Thabet), S Trabelsi, Badra, Boukadida, Clayton, Ghodbane, Chihi, Souayah (Beya), Ben Slimane (Ben Younes), Sellimi

Group G Table	P	W	D	L	F	A	Pts
England	1	1	0	0	2	0	3
Romania	1	1	0	0	1	0	3
Colombia	1	0	0	1	0	1	0
Tunisia	1	0	0	1	0	2	0

Tuesday 16 June

GARY: It was good to get back to La Baule last night. We've got a good set-up here and it feels like home. I'm hoping we'll be here for another month.

We had the morning off and did a sharp five-a-side, attack v defence in the afternoon. Gareth Southgate turned his ankle in the session, but I'm not sure how serious it is. Obviously, with the two of us challenging for the same place in the team, it wouldn't be right for me to ask Gareth. In football, it isn't the done thing to ask about other players' injuries unless you are very close to them.

Scotland were absolutely brilliant against Norway this afternoon.

They deserved to win, and Norway were lucky to scrape a draw. The way they are playing, Scotland still have a great chance of going through.

In the evening, ten of us went with Glenn Hoddle and John Gorman to watch the Brazil v Morocco game at the local team's stadium. I couldn't pass up the opportunity to see Brazil play live. They won 3-0 and played in a way no other team in the world can. I loved it. The Brazilian players are just so relaxed, they don't look like they are working hard – though they are!

Their style of defending is unique to say the least, and there are weaknesses. We defend with three at the back plus two wing backs, but Brazil only play two in central defence! Their two wing backs, Carlos and Cafu, were magnificent. They worked so hard getting up and down. But because they are such a positive team, they do leave themselves open to the counter-attack.

For a while, I just watched Ronaldo, and he didn't seem to move. He did no running off the ball whatsoever, but then straightaway he scored one and set up another! It's just as if he pulls the trigger and explodes into life to win games. He has amazing ability.

You can tell the quality of Brazil's squad by the fact that Denilson is only a substitute. He's incredible at dribbling, but he can't get in the team. Brazil have four or five players who would be the big star of any other international team, and that's why they are World Champions.

PHIL: I got back from my holiday at Puerto Banus in Marbella last Friday. By chance, while I was there I bumped into Keith Gillespie, Clayton Blackmore, Lee Clark, Steve Watson and Nicky Barmby – the place was a footballer's paradise!

I feel fine now, totally refreshed and ready to get back to training. The only thing that gets me down is when people tip-toe around the subject of my omission from the England squad. I think, "Just be normal with me." I thought I'd find it difficult to watch the World Cup on television, but I've enjoyed it. I watched the game at Julie's last night, and I'm going over to see England's next game live.

I spoke to Gary today. He's in good spirits but a bit bored. All the lads who played yesterday are on a high, and Gary is disappointed that he wasn't on the pitch. Even if he doesn't get in against Romania, Gary will definitely play against Colombia, because England are likely to play a back four. If that's the case, Gary is the natural choice at right back.

Wednesday 17 June

GARY: Becks and I did the press conference after training this afternoon. All the questions to me were about Philip being left out of the squad and Becks was pressed on his disappointment at being left out of the Tunisia game. It's normal for any footballer to be down when he is left out, but I don't think Becks is as distressed as the press seem to be making out. We both made the point that it's only the first game of the tournament and we're still in a positive frame of mind.

PHIL: I watched the Italy v Cameroon game in a Venice restaurant tonight. I'm out here for a couple of days as a guest of Diadora. The bar was all decked out with Roberto Baggio memorabilia and the atmosphere was amazing. Out here, they worship the ground Baggio walks on.

I've done a couple of press interviews this week. I wasn't going to speak to anyone during the summer, on Alex Ferguson's instructions, but there have been a few rumours in the papers about what was said and how I reacted when Glenn Hoddle told me I wasn't in the squad. I wanted to put my side of the story.

Thursday 18 June

GARY: The comments Becks and I made at our press conference yesterday are all over the papers, with Becks obviously getting most of the coverage. The idea of speaking to the press was to show that we were not distressed. Judging from the feedback from home, the idea hasn't worked. The papers are still carrying the story prominently.

We do get some of the English papers delivered to our hotel, but not the tabloids. Basically, the idea is that our minds should be clear of the rubbish some of them print. Generally though, the relationship with the press lads out here is quite good and I'm doing a twice-weekly column for The Times. You don't get the publicity that comes with doing a big exclusive in a tabloid newspaper, but The Times are interested not in sensationalism but in doing an informative piece. That's what I prefer to be involved in.

We were given the day off, so it was a choice between playing golf, a trip to the local port, sunbathing or shopping. I decided to play golf with Darren Anderton against David Seaman and David Batty. Darren and I got absolutely hammered. To make it worse I had terrible hay fever.

In the evening, the whole squad went down to a local fish restaurant overlooking the sea. We've been eating at the hotel since we arrived so it was a nice change of scenery, but I couldn't stop sneezing!

We watched the France v Saudi Arabia game afterwards. France looked pretty good, but there were five sendings-off in today's two matches. Since Michel Platini and Sepp Blatter of FIFA commented that referees have been too lenient, it's gone crazy. The Saudi Arabian player who was sent off was very unlucky. He just miss-timed a tackle, and every defender does one of those every two or three games. When you tap someone's ankles from behind and they aren't in a goalscoring position, it should attract only a booking. On the other hand, Zinedine Zidane probably deserved to go for the "stamping incident" in the game against Saudi Arabia. Personally, I might have given a yellow card because it wasn't the worst "stamp" you'll ever see. But if you let him get away with it, other players might try it and it could get more serious.

Up until today, I think every player was enjoying the fact that the changes hadn't been as radical as we'd expected before the tournament. If Platini comes out with more statements in the same vein, he could ruin the World Cup. When somebody in his position criticizes referees, it puts them under too much pressure.

Paul Durkin told us before the tournament that these new refereeing directives will arrive in the Premiership next season. I hope referees will only go by the book for a month or two before they return to a more sensible approach. I don't think FIFA's new rules could possibly last in the Premiership, because controlled aggression and tough tackling is a crucial part of our game.

Friday 19 June

GARY: When we met at 9.30 a.m. in the video room, I thought Glenn Hoddle was going to announce the team, but he didn't. Instead, the Boss showed us an edited video of the Romanians' positive points. I still haven't heard much about Gareth Southgate's injury, so I face an anxious wait before I'll find out if I've been selected. Gareth didn't train again today, so it must be tight whether or not he'll be fit.

There were no clues about the team in the training session. We played possession games with mixed teams taking it in turns to attack each other and finished off with shooting practice.

Eric Harrison came to watch us train. Eric's in France to watch all the games in Nantes. He rang me last night to check if it would be OK to come down. I wasn't sure at the time, because I thought it might be a closed session while we worked on our tactics for Romania. But as the team hadn't been announced, they let Eric in and it was nice to see him.

Saturday 20 June

GARY: Another morning meeting, but this time Glenn Hoddle named the team. I'm in – the only change from the team that played Tunisia. I'm really looking forward to my first game in the World Cup, and my first full game for a month.

In the meeting, the Boss said he was sending Gareth Southgate out to do the press interview today. Our official line was that Gareth was still available for selection. The Boss told them that Gareth had trained for an hour yesterday, which wasn't true. It was just a bit of kidology to keep everyone guessing. In such big games, I think it's the right thing to do.

Before we went out to play a practice match, we watched a video of Romania's negative points and their set-pieces. When I got to the training pitch, Glenn Hoddle came over and told me that I looked sharp and that he was pleased with the attitude I had shown since the Tunisia game. When I don't get picked, there is something inside me that tells me to work harder. If you aren't disappointed to be left out, there is something wrong, but you can't afford to show that you are down for too long. Now I've got my chance through someone else's misfortune and I'm ready to take it.

The Boss also suggested we may have to change the system during the game, with Graeme Le Saux and me playing as orthodox full backs. Romania have got Tunisia in their last group game so they might play for a draw.

In the evening, I watched Holland beat South Korea 5-0. They looked really solid and Jaap Stam impressed again – he's strong, quick and good on the ball too. Edgar Davids in midfield made the Dutch team look far better than they had against Belgium. With his energy, there was a lot more urgency about them. Overmars is having a flier too – in Holland's first two games, his opposing full back has been substituted both times! When Kluivert comes back to play alongside Bergkamp in attack, they will be a great side.

PHIL: I opened the Summer Fair at Martin Edwards' daughter's primary school today. I'd bumped into him at Old Trafford last week and he asked me to do it, probably because I was the only United player in the country! Actually, it turned out to be quite an enjoyable afternoon.

In the papers yesterday, the chairman was quoted as saying there was a major signing on its way after the World Cup, so I couldn't resist asking.

"Honestly, I haven't spoken to the press for a week," he told me.

When I was at Old Trafford, I took a peek inside the stadium. They were rolling out the new turf and it looks perfect, like a bowling green.

Sunday 21 June

GARY: We set off for Toulouse at three o'clock this afternoon. On arrival, we went straight down to the stadium to train. The pitch was patchy and we did just an eight-a-side game for half an hour before the Boss called a halt. Just like the manager at United, Glenn Hoddle doesn't want us to train for too long so close to a game.

Argentina annihilated Jamaica 5-0 tonight. Ortega and Batistuta looked rather useful. We could be playing them in the second round.

Monday 22 June   England 1 Romania 2

GARY: Last night I had the best night's sleep I've had since I got to France. In Nantes, I kept waking up at five o'clock in the morning. I don't know whether it's the beds or all the energy pills we are taking.

As is usual on matchdays, our meals were strictly monitored: bread and unsweetened jam for breakfast. At dinner time, you must start with either yoghurt or poached eggs on toast to get some protein in your body before you take on carbohydrates by eating chicken, pasta or potatoes. Everything is planned meticulously to the last detail.

In the morning, the attackers practised a few set-pieces while we watched. They were working on a few different variations, including the short corner driven low to Teddy at the near post for a first time shot.

PHIL: My dad and I were flown over to Biarritz in a private jet owned by businessman Ron Wood. Ron's a big United fan and we know him quite well. We provided the match tickets, he provided the jet.

Biarritz is a little seaside resort near Toulouse. We stayed there virtually all day, thinking it would be safer after what had happened in Marseilles. Before the game, we bumped into Bryan Robson and stopped for a chat. Robbo's in France commentating for Eurosport ... and scouting too, no doubt.

GARY: At 5.15 p.m., the manager went through our plan for the game. He explained that Gheorghe Hagi was a big danger to us, but also their biggest weakness, because he doesn't defend at all. Adrian Ilie was also mentioned as a lively player. Glenn Hoddle stressed that as soon as Romania lost the ball we should break on them, because he felt they were quite vulnerable to counter-attacks. He also asked us to get good crosses in because their back three, although comfortable on the ball, weren't the bravest.

PHIL: We got to the ground an hour and a half before kick-off because Dad has to see Gary warm up. We had good seats with the rest of the players' families intermingled with England fans. Every supporter who came up to me said I should be in the squad, but I think they were only saying that to get my autograph!

The locals are calling the Stadium Municipal "Mini Wembley", and it looked that way tonight because it was packed with England fans. There were only about 5,000 Romanians there.

GARY: Although it was to be my first World Cup Finals game, I wasn't especially nervous. I never talk much in the dressing room before games. I like to just concentrate and picture in my mind how the game is going to go, what I've got to do and the players I'm up against. However, the England dressing room is a lot louder before the game than at United. Tony Adams, Martin Keown and Gareth Southgate are excellent at getting us going. On the pitch, the national anthem was sung loudly again by the England fans and the atmosphere was unbelievable.

In the first half, Romania controlled the tempo and the slower passing game suited them even if they didn't create a decent chance. I was marking Moldovan and Ilie when he was on my side, and neither of them hurt us.

Paul Ince got injured early on, tried to play through it, but soon had to go off, which gave David Beckham his first chance. He played in central midfield and was exceptional. There's been a lot of talk in the last couple of weeks about David. Becks hasn't made a fuss, but a lot of people have said he should be playing, which put extra pressure on him to perform. Now, Becks has come in and taken his chance.

At half-time, Glenn Hoddle told us to step up the tempo, and Moldovan's goal two minutes after the re-start really got us going. All it took was a slight lack of concentration at the throw-in and the ball was in the net before we could recover. Our performance improved markedly in the next twenty minutes and we created two or three good chances. I got into a shooting position, but tried to pass to Scholesy instead. Listening to the fans' reaction, I immediately realised I should have whacked it first time.

When another substitute, Michael Owen, scored with about ten minutes left, we had to decide whether to go for the winner or sit back. We did neither, and instead got hit with a sucker punch. Petrescu at right wing back took us by surprise when he popped up on the left in the ninetieth minute. He had a bit of luck and put the ball away. It was a killer. Even though Michael Owen hit the post with a great shot, with only a few minutes of injury time left, there was no way back.

We'd conceded two bad goals and lost, though David Seaman hadn't had to make a save all night. There were some disappointed players in the dressing room, but the Boss and John Gorman were very positive: "Come on lads, we have got to prepare for Colombia on Friday." We flew straight back to La Baule and didn't arrive at the hotel until 2.30 a.m.

PHIL: The atmosphere was brilliant, one of the best at any game I've been to watch, but I noticed an anti-United feeling in the crowd. If Gary or Teddy made a mistake, some of the Arsenal fans near me gave them some terrible stick. In the first half, Romania dictated the game. They kept possession better than us but they didn't make any good chances. Hagi had a few shots from long range, but they were all miles off-target.

When Paul Ince went off injured, I thought it upset the balance of the team. Paul's the Guv'nor when it comes to closing down players and after he'd gone, Romania were given too much space in midfield. Once Moldovan scored, I couldn't see us getting back into it because we weren't creating many chances.

When Michael Owen came on and scored, I said, "We're going to win this one." Then Dan Petrescu scored and the fans went silent around me. Although Michael Owen nearly lifted our spirits when he hit the post in the dying seconds, everyone went home bitterly disappointed.

World Cup Group G / Stadium Municipal, Toulouse / Att: 37,000

England 1
Seaman, Neville, Adams, Campbell, Anderton, Ince (Beckham), Batty, Scholes, Le Saux, Sheringham (Owen), Shearer / Scorer: Owen 83
Romania 2
Stelea, Ciobotariu, Petrescu, Filipescu, Gheorghe Popescu, Munteanu, Galca, Hagi (Stanga 73, Marinescu 85), Gabriel Popescu, Ilie, Moldovan (Lacatus) / Scorers: Moldovan 47, Petrescu 90

Group G Table	P	W	D	L	F	A	Pts
Romania	2	2	0	0	3	1	6
England	2	1	0	1	3	2	3
Colombia	2	1	0	1	1	1	3
Tunisia	2	0	0	2	0	3	0

12

Paying the penalty

Tuesday 23 June

GARY: After we all went through a light stretch this afternoon, Glenn Hoddle called a meeting. The Boss said he had always had a funny feeling about last night's Romania game. He felt we didn't give a bad performance, but conceding two sloppy goals was the difference between winning and losing. He's right. Leaking silly goals is pretty new to us because we don't let that many through. Before Romania, David Seaman hadn't conceded a single goal for England since Le Tournoi last summer! Anyway, that's what Colombia will be up against this Friday.

A few of the lads piped up and said that they were disappointed that we had let the Romanians control the pace of the game. David Seaman, Alan Shearer and Paul Ince said they didn't like the way we played so slowly. I agree that in our next game we need to really go after them early on and play an English-style game. The mood wasn't too down because we only need a draw on Friday.

In the evening, Scotland v Morocco was showing in the communal TV room, but I watched Brazil v Norway in my room. I'd said to journalists two days ago that Norway would do much better than Morocco did against Brazil (Morocco lost 0-3) because of their pressing style of play, and they managed to win 2-1.

The team I feel sorry for is Morocco. Scotland have lost two and drawn one, so they don't deserve to go through, but Morocco have beaten Scotland 3-0 tonight and should have won against Norway, so they must count themselves unlucky.

PHIL: Norway's win over Brazil was surprising, but ever since the World Cup draw was announced last December, Ole Gunnar and Ronny have told me that they really fancied themselves to beat Brazil. Norway play a Premiership-style game, and that seemed to upset Brazil's rhythm.

Wednesday 24 June

GARY: Glenn Hoddle has come out and said he feels David Beckham came into the World Cup "unfocused". I just can't agree with that. David is my best friend and all he was talking about leading in to the tournament was his dream of playing in his first World Cup. I know David very well and it meant everything to him to play for England. Nothing else was on his mind.

We played a practice match this morning. There were few clues about the team to play Colombia, apart from Michael Owen playing up front with Alan Shearer. After the match, Glenn Hoddle gathered us round and explained he wasn't going to name the team until tomorrow. Because of Paul Ince's ankle injury he wants to leave the selection as late as possible.

Thursday 25 June

GARY: Glenn Hoddle announced the team for tomorrow down on the training pitch. "There will be two changes: Beckham is in for Batty and Michael Owen is in for Teddy," he said. Gareth is still unfit and I was delighted to keep my place.

Our tactics will be to attack Colombia from the off and try to get in behind them using Michael Owen's pace. Glenn Hoddle has said he'd always planned for Michael to play in this game. Colombia have such a flat back four that his pace will unsettle them.

The eleven playing tomorrow concentrated on set pieces while the other eleven watched from the sidelines with instructions to take everything in. After we had finished, Glenn Hoddle called everyone together and quizzed those who had been watching on our plans for set-pieces. "What's the signal for this corner?" he asked, trying to catch them out. About five players didn't have a clue, which made him angry. They were made to stay behind and do the set-pieces themselves, while the rest of us tried to contain our laughter.

Terry Venables did the same during Euro 96 and a few players were caught out then. When you are not playing, you don't tend to listen to the instructions for set-pieces.

We flew up to Lens at four o'clock and went straight to the stadium for a training session. We did a little bit of passing before going back to the hotel.

All the wives and girlfriends are coming over tomorrow and staying for a night.

Friday 26 June   England 2 Colombia 0

GARY: Glenn Hoddle told us he wanted us to play aggressively for the first half hour and chase them all over the pitch. He said we had nothing to fear from the Colombians, and that Valderrama was completely past it. "If you play properly and go out with the right frame of mind, you know you will have a good night," he said.

There was a mood of real confidence on the coach to the game. We watched a video with all our highlights from the Tunisia game set to stirring music.

The team immediately felt better out on the pitch tonight. We were playing at a higher tempo, which suits our game. Our first goal from Darren Anderton was a huge relief. He was outstanding throughout. His place in the team and even the squad has been questioned, but this performance should silence the critics. Darren hasn't got the credit he deserves.

What a time for Becks to score his first goal for England! It capped a magnificent performance and was a great way to respond to being left out. The goal gave us some breathing space which meant we could relax a bit. At half-time we found out that Tunisia were beating Romania and, if it stayed like that, we would go in to the easier side of the draw against

Croatia. We didn't get too excited, expecting the Romanians to at least equalise. We played some great football in the second half and never gave the Colombians a sniff of the goal. Confidence was running high throughout the side, evidenced in Sol Campbell's amazing run from the back. If he had scored it would have been goal of the century. And Scholesy was outstanding again.

We didn't celebrate too much afterwards, as we've got a tough game against Argentina in four days. Everyone had their partners over and we were put up in a lovely chateau.

PHIL: We flew out to France today with the rest of the players' families on a flight chartered by the FA. Dad, Julie and I were keeping Gary's girlfriend, Hannah, and Paul Scholes girlfriend, Claire, company.

We were dropped off in Lille for the afternoon. There was a twenty-four-hour drinking ban in Lens, so loads of fans congregated in Lille's town centre. I later heard reports of rioting, but I was in the town square and didn't see one ounce of trouble. Yet again, England fans dominated the stadium. I don't know where they get the tickets from.

It was a great game. The Colombians played pretty, fancy-dan football, but everything they did was in front of our defence. They had no pace up front and Valderrama left all the tackling to his midfield partner. All their passes were sideways or backwards, whereas Scholesy and Becks were playing killer passes all the time.

It was a good all-round team performance, highlighted by superb goals from Anderton and Becks. After what he's been through, David's goal was always on the cards. He's a big-occasion player. Glenn Hoddle has said that he felt David needed a jolt, but I don't agree; he'd been looking forward to the World Cup all year. When your manager criticises you, it often makes you step up a level. Whatever the cause, you can't argue with Becks's brilliant performance tonight. I loved watching the game. Naturally, I wished I was playing, but you can learn so much from occasions like these. You understand what the fans go through.

Michael Owen's dad had a seat in a different part of the stadium to the rest of us. He couldn't find the coach afterwards, so we had to just sit there until he found us two-and-a-half hours later! So we didn't get back home until five in the morning.

World Cup Group G / Felix Bollaert Stadium , Lens / Att: 41,275

England 2
Seaman, Campbell, Adams, Neville, Le Saux, Beckham, Ince (Batty), Anderton (Lee), Scholes (McManaman), Shearer, Owen
Scorers: *Anderton 20, Beckham 30*
Colombia 0
Mondragon, Cabrera, Bermudez, Palacios, Moreno, Roncon, Serna (Arisizabal), Lozano, Valderrama, De Avila (Ricard), Preciado (Valencia)

Group G Table	P	W	D	L	F	A	Pts
Romania	3	2	1	0	4	2	7
England	3	2	0	1	5	2	6
Colombia	3	1	0	2	1	3	3
Tunisia	3	0	1	2	1	4	1

Saturday 27 June

GARY: We did a loosener in the morning, then spent some time with our partners before they left at four o'clock. We flew back to Le Baule.

PHIL: England now have a simple route to the final: Argentina, Holland, Brazil, then Italy, Germany or France in the Final!

I'm positive we will beat Argentina. The performance against Colombia was very encouraging. Defensively, we're very strong, and I'm a big believer in the idea that if you play the younger players, you'll get an exciting performance. Even if things are going badly, you always have a chance with people like Michael Owen on the pitch. One incident from last night's game sticks in my mind. Alan Shearer knocked a ball inside their full back for Michael to run on to and I've never seen pace like it in my life. It was like something out of Roadrunner!

I'm going to the England v South Africa Test match at Old Trafford cricket ground on Thursday. As a life member of Lancashire CC, I'm on the automatic mailing list for every Test game there. Football fans who want to go and see the Argentina game are not so fortunate. England have received a measly 2,049 ticket allocation for the game. You can guarantee that 30,000 England fans will travel to Saint Etienne, but they'll have to pay way over the odds for a ticket. Touts will make thousands out of them. It's a farce.

I'm not going to the game, because I'm back in training. I play other sports like golf and tennis to keep me active in summer and I've started doing a bit of jogging.

Sunday 28 June

GARY: After a light training session, the team was announced for Tuesday's game. "Same team for Argentina," is all Hoddle said. Maradona's "Hand of God" goal hasn't been mentioned. As he was heavily involved in that match, I thought Glenn Hoddle might use it to motivate us.

The injections of magnesium and various vitamins and minerals before games have really worked. I was tired coming into the World Cup, but the injections are kicking in and I feel really strong and sharp. All the lads have said the same thing. And after all the pre-tournament fuss about Eileen Drewery, she hasn't once been required to come out to France.

Monday 29 June

GARY: We studied the Argentinians this morning, on an edited video version of their three games in the tournament so far. Ortega and Batistuta are obviously the main threats, while Lopez can be lightning quick. "You might think Argentina look good, but they haven't played anyone decent yet," Glenn Hoddle said. "I'm not convinced they're a great team. They only managed one against Japan and one against Croatia. They might have won three games, but they really haven't been tested yet. If you go at them, I promise you'll find weaknesses at the back."

Our main ploy was for Paul Ince to pick up Ortega, who drops off into the hole behind Batistuta. On the video, we saw that Ortega can cause problems if you give him space, but the Boss stressed that if you get up against him physically, he'll give the ball away.

We travelled down to St Etienne, checked in at the hotel and went straight to the stadium for a quick training session. Back at the hotel there were no further talks from Glenn Hoddle, just dinner and early to bed.

Tuesday 30 June   England 2 Argentina 2 AET
                                    (Argentina win 4-2 on pens)
GARY: I hate the waiting before a big game. We were up at eight in

the morning, so we had to wait thirteen hours before kick off. We bided our time by taking a walk and doing a little stretch. At five o' clock Glenn Hoddle gathered us together at the hotel for his pre-match talk. He reiterated yesterday's message: "Incey must stay tight on Ortega, Becks and Scholesy must make sure they come in alongside Ince, but we must also try to catch them on the break and use the pace of Michael Owen. Darren and Graeme must get forward and put in crosses for Alan, as Argentina haven't got much height at the back."

He took me aside and told me to watch out for the pace of Lopez, who will be coming down my side. I had another injection from the doctor and we left for the ground at just after seven. On the coach, we watched the usual video of our match and training session highlights to gee us up.

"The only thing that will beat you tonight is fear. Respect them, but show no fear," Glenn Hoddle said in the dressing room.

Tony Adams did his usual job of motivating everyone with a rousing speech. There was a lot of talk, everyone psyching each other up. I felt really confident before the game – I knew we would score goals and therefore we could beat them.

In the tunnel we were all buoyant, but the Argentinians standing beside us were completely silent, with looks of steely determination on their faces. Out on the pitch, we had to go along their line and shake them all by the hand. Glenn Hoddle had told us to look each one of them right in the eye to show them we weren't afraid. Some stared back, but some avoided eye contact. There were certainly no smiles.

Five minutes in, and we were a goal down. Simeone collided with Seaman and Batistuta put away the penalty. I felt Simeone dived, but I knew the referee would give a penalty. Simeone had lost control of the ball so he made sure his leg caught Seaman.

We had to get back in quickly. If we didn't score before half-time, they'd shut up shop and make it very difficult for us. Minutes later we were level, after Michael Owen showed unbelievable pace and won a penalty, which Alan put away. To be honest, it was exactly like the first penalty – it shouldn't have been given. Michael burst into the area and obviously thought he could get a bit of contact with a defender and go down.

At 1-1, I thought, "I fancy us here," and then Michael gave us the lead with a phenomenal goal. At 18, I was struggling to get into the United Reserves, and here he is destroying the best defences in the world. Now I knew we could win.

Argentina really hadn't caused us many problems. Tony Adams had a go at me in the first minute after I gave Lopez too much space. I'd made a basic mistake by standing five yards off Lopez, allowing him to turn and run at me. Tony trotted over and grabbed the back of my shirt. "Get tight," he said sternly. From then on I stuck close to Lopez, didn't let him run at me and forced him to lay the ball off all the time.

Scholesy could have made it 3-1 and, from where I was standing, I thought he had. He was gutted with that miss afterwards. Paul's his own biggest critic, but he did everything right, slotting the ball past the goalkeeper. It just missed the post.

We went to sleep for their equaliser just before half-time. They could practice that free kick twenty times on the training ground and it wouldn't have worked as well as it did tonight. The timing of the pass, and of Zanetti popping out from behind the wall, was immaculate. It happened so quickly that no one could get to him.

Their goal was devastating. We were about to go in at half-time a goal up, but suddenly it was level. I looked over at their bench, who were all jumping around, and I was gutted. We should have been winning. We were all a bit shocked in the dressing room, but the feeling was that the game was there to be won. They had only scored from set-pieces.

Minutes into the second half and disaster struck. Becks was sent off! Simeone's barge on him was scandalous and he deserved to go himself. While Becks was lying on the floor I saw him kick out at Simeone and immediately feared the worst. The referee had seen everything. I didn't like the way Batistuta ran up to the referee waving an imaginary card around. Alan Shearer ran up to Batistuta and gave him some serious abuse for that.

When I got to Becks, I said, "What happened there?" Becks didn't answer me. "Stay down, let some time pass," I told him. I hoped that if the referee had some time to think about it he would decide not to send David off.

I saw the referee produce a yellow card for Simeone, so I thought Becks was going to be alright. Then he called Becks over, but put away the yellow card and went for his back pocket. "Oh God, no," I thought. He showed Becks the red card and off he went. I was gutted for Becks.

What Becks did only warranted a yellow card. It wasn't violent conduct. He just flicked his leg out, it was never going to hurt anyone. Violent conduct is elbowing someone in the face or punching someone.

I walked over to Glenn Hoddle and said, "What are we going to do?" He wanted us to go to a 4-4-1, with Darren Anderton coming inside, Michael Owen moving to right midfield and Alan Shearer on his own up front. With ten men, we played with our backs to the wall and didn't give Argentina a chance. For seventy minutes they never looked like scoring. We could see the desperation on their faces as they gradually ran out of ideas. Batistuta and Lopez were substituted.

Ariel Ortega was a constant menace. He is one of the best players I have ever shared a pitch with. I have never seen a player do so many nutmegs in a match. After the game I swapped shirts with him.

With only ten minutes left, we thought we had won it when Sol Campbell headed the ball into the back of the net. Sol and some of the /in the air ... until I heard a shout and turned around to be faced with Veron running at me with the ball. Argentina were breaking on us, four against two! Veron tried to slip it to Ortega, but I won the ball back in a tackle.

The referee was a nightmare and didn't give us anything. The one decision I could not believe was when Alan had the ball punched from the top of his head in their penalty area. How the referee didn't see that one, I'll never know. I saw it from the halfway line, so he's got no excuse.

When the game went into extra time, we all felt strong. There was no tiredness, no question of playing for penalties, just a conviction that we would win. We were all up for it. The defence began to enjoy keeping them out; we got a buzz from it.

The more extra time went on, the more my confidence grew. But with five minutes to go, I thought it was going to go to penalties and became a bit worried when I realised we only had three penalty takers on the pitch: Alan, Michael and Paul Merson.

At the end of extra time, Glenn Hoddle came on and told us who the five penalty-takers would be. The five hadn't been chosen before the game. In fact, penalties had never been mentioned. The regular takers like Alan, Michael and Teddy might practise, but the rest of us never bother. They're not a part of our training sessions and Glenn Hoddle has never told us to practise them in our own time.

There wasn't much to choose between us, so it was just the four lads who had finished extra time in midfield plus Alan. Glenn asked me if I wanted the sixth penalty. There were better penalty-takers on the bench, but I looked around and accepted I was probably the next one in line.

"Just concentrate, pick your spot and whack it or place it. Just don't change your mind," were Glenn Hoddle's instructions.

I stood on my own in the centre circle. When David Seaman saved Crespo's penalty, I thought, "Come on, we're going to win this!" But Paul Ince missed our very next one. I went up to him and patted him on the back. There is little you can say to console someone who has missed a penalty in a shoot-out.

I really fancied Ayala to miss. He was bound to be nervous, but he cooly rolled the ball into the corner. What guts!

As David Batty walked up to take our fifth penalty, I knew that if David missed we were out and if he scored I was up next. I have never been so nervous. I started thinking how I would take my penalty. I decided just to put my head down and whack it, but I never got the chance to put my plan into action. David's penalty was saved and we were out.

Where's the justice? We worked so hard for two years to qualify and then for seven weeks we prepared so well, but it was all thrown away by a penalty shoot-out and some dodgy refereeing decisions.

I felt sick and numb. I clapped our fans, who had been brilliant, but then I couldn't get off the pitch quickly enough. The dressing room was deathly quiet. I've never been in a quieter one. No one spoke.

When Glenn Hoddle came in, he was quite emotional. "You can be proud of yourselves," he said. "You couldn't have given anything more here tonight. You can walk out of here with your heads held high. You were magnificent." He then went around the dressing room patting everyone on the head and saying, Well done.

Becks didn't say anything to me back in the dressing room, but I could see the sorrow in his face. None of us blamed him. It's silly to blame one player. We win, lose or draw as a team, no matter what one player does .

On the coach back to the hotel I sat with Becks, and he was absolutely gutted. He said he felt really empty and that he thought he should release a public apology. I felt that he didn't need to. His team-mates weren't bothered, I told him, so he shouldn't worry.

Back the hotel, Becks, Michael Owen, Rio Ferdinand and I played pool and chatted until five in the morning, just going over the game again and again.

World Cup Last Sixteen / Stade Geoffroy Guichard, Saint Etienne / Att: 30,600

England 2
Seaman, Neville, Adams, Campbell, Ince, Anderton (Batty), Beckham, Le Saux (Southgate), Scholes (Merson), Owen, Shearer
Scorers: Shearer 10 pen, Owen 16
Argentina 2
Roa, Ayala, Chamot, Vivas, Zanetti, Almeyda, Simeone (Berti), Ortega, Veron, Lopez (Gallardo), Batistuta (Crespo) /
Scorers: Batistuta 6 pen, Zanetti 45
Argentina win 4–3 on penalties *(Berti, Shearer, Veron, Merson, Gallardo, Owen, Ayala)*

Wednesday 1 July

PHIL: Last night's game was the best of the tournament. Knock-out games tend to be tense affairs, but the match had end-to-end action plus great skill and technique on both sides.

Our back three of Gary, Tony Adams and Sol Campbell were out-standing, but the whole team defended brilliantly against an excellent opposition side. Ortega looked a great player, but they dealt with him superbly.

I agreed with the referee's decision to disallow Sol's goal for Alan Shearer's foul on the goalkeeper, but we never seem to get those slices of luck you need. It's agonising when you remember Maradona's hand-ball in 1986 and how close England were to scoring a Golden Goal against Germany in Euro '96.

Although we lost in the last sixteen, we were good enough to go further. Argentina are supposed to be one of the top four teams in the world and I thought we were better than them. I didn't think so at the time, but looking back, the defeat by Romania was crucial. If we had won that game and topped the group, I'm sure we would have beaten Croatia.

Of course, it was just another heroic failure, but England haven't won the World Cup since 1966 so we can't just put this defeat down to bad luck. Glenn Hoddle has mentioned that we must learn to concentrate for the whole ninety minutes like the Germans do, and he's right. It's a similar story at United. Over the past couple of seasons, we've looked the best team in Europe at times, but not quite proved it. Every time we've lost, it's silly mistakes that have cost us dear.

English teams do play at a higher tempo and attack more than our rivals. Some say that is our weakness, but I think it's a good thing. England's positive play against Argentina frightened them. All we need to make it at world level is cut out our mistakes, because we have the ability to beat these teams.

Since David Batty admitted he rarely takes penalties in training, many people are asking why he had the responsibility for England. I've only ever taken one penalty in a match in my life, in the 1995 Youth Cup Final shoot-out ... and I missed! I sometimes practise them in training and score ten out of ten, but you can't recreate the feeling you get when the hopes of 30 million fans rest on your kick. The best thing to do is to see who fancies it at the time. At the end of 120 minutes, tiredness is a big factor. The good thing about David Batty and Paul Ince is that they are strong characters and missing a penalty won't destroy them.

Apart from Owen, Shearer and Merson, I didn't have a clue who would take the other two penalties last night. As we were waiting for the shoot-out to start, my sister said, "Don't take one, Gary. I don't want to see you on a pizza advert!"

Overall, I think more good things have come out of the tournament than bad things. On the tactical side, Glenn Hoddle has been criticised for playing three at the back instead of the traditional English 4-4-2, but his system worked well with attacking players like Darren Anderton at wing back. You have to be positive for the system to work. Terry Venables used to play three at the back, and it's been helpful to have continuity since Glenn Hoddle took over.

The players should take a lot of credit. Tony Adams and Paul Ince were both magnificent, and young players like Michael Owen, Paul Scholes, Sol Campbell, Gary and David Beckham have done brilliantly.

It seems to me the whole country is blaming David Beckham for the defeat, but that's totally out of order. If it wasn't for David, we wouldn't have been playing against the Argentinians, because he scored the goal against Colombia that got us to the next round. It's unbelievable how people can change their opinion of someone so quickly.

You'll see a better David Beckham because of this. He will be even more determined. At United, we all know what a great player he is, but he will be hoping to prove a few people wrong now. He will get a lot of stick from opposing fans, but David's handled that before and he will deal with this too. He's got everyone at United behind him.

Watching on television, I couldn't see what Becks had done at first and when I saw the replay, I thought it was a yellow-card offence. Simeone, who's supposed to be a tough-tackling midfielder, went down like a sack of spuds. Obviously, Becks shouldn't have flicked his boot at Simeone, but it's disappointing when an opponent reacts like that. If you compare it to the stamping incident when Dennis Bergkamp escaped without a booking, David was unlucky to get a red card.

If you look at the great players in world football, they've all done similar things. Cantona, Zidane and even George Best used to get sent off for silly things. But when the best players make mistakes, they get magnified. Just because David Beckham did it, everyone is in uproar. I put all the abuse he is getting purely down to jealousy.

It's been said that yesterday's incident proves David isn't focussed on football, but that's rubbish. If you look at his record, he's hardly missed a game in three seasons. When injury forced him to pull out of a midweek international with Switzerland in March, he came to The Cliff on the Friday and declared himself fit for our game on Saturday. He could hardly walk. That's the way David is. He always wants to play.

In France, Paul Scholes learnt that he's up there with the top players in the world. Compared to his rivals, Paul looked a yard quicker, stronger and had the confidence to dribble past players. I love watching Scholesy play. His long passing is outstanding and he can score goals out of nothing. The thing I like is that he's not just a fair-weather player. If it's a game with loads of space, like the one against Tunisia, he can pick his passes, but if it's a tight game, like the Argentina match, he will put his foot in and mark players as well.

Darren Anderton proved virtually everyone wrong. He probably had more help than most in getting into the squad, but he fully justified his selection. I really like Darren as a person and I'm delighted he's been rewarded for all the work he put in to overcome his injury problems.

Michael Owen has shown he is worthy of a starting place for England. The thing that stunned me about his goal against Argentina was that the last defender was twenty yards ahead of him when Michael took David Beckham's pass. The fact that they were defending so deep showed how frightened they were of his pace. They knew that once Michael gets past you, there's no way back. Michael's already drawing comparisons with Ronaldo, but that's unfair to him. Their talent, pace and goal ratios compare, but Ronaldo has produced his form on the world and European stage consistently over the past few years, so Mike's got a long way to go yet.

After the Argentina game, one reporter said that Michael can now go on and join one of the biggest clubs in the world, but Liverpool are in that bracket and I see no reason for him to move. Michael's a level-headed lad and he won't get carried away.

GARY: We flew home on Concorde. The newspapers were laid out for us and it sickened me to read what was being said about David Beckham. He is being absolutely slaughtered. It's easy to apportion blame, but not so easy to sympathise. Becks is a great person, he's a human being, and he's got feelings like everyone else.

My way of dealing with bad press is to read it and use it as motivation. When United lost 3-1 to Aston Villa at the start of our 1995/96 season, the reporters slaughtered all the youngsters in our team. I read the papers the day after that game, and I still remember what each reporter said about me. We went on to win the Double that season.

Seventy-five per cent of journalists are decent lads, but the rest have no shame whatsoever. The next time David wins a game for England, they'll be praising him, but after what some of them said about David today, they should never be allowed to sit in the same press conference room as him again.

I rang up Alex Ferguson from my hotel room in La Baule this morning to ask when I was expected back in training. He's given me four extra days off, but then he wants me back to prepare for our big European Cup qualifier on 12 August.

Another challenge looms.

13

Back home

Monday 3 August

PHIL: After a lot of speculation, Patrick Kluivert has turned down the chance to join United. I've spoken to Jordi who has played with him for Holland and he was very complimentary about him. I played against him in a youth tournament when he was unknown and even then he stood out as a great player.

United fans will start saying again that we can't attract the big names, but I think the Gaffer is doing it right. The team spirit here is excellent, but I don't think that would be the case if you broke the wage structure for one or two players. If a player really wants to join United, like Jaap Stam did, then they will come here whether they could earn more elsewhere or not. Alex Ferguson wants hungry players.

Tuesday 4 August

PHIL: The newspapers are full of rumours linking Andy Cole with Aston Villa. It's funny because within the club everyone knows that he won't leave because of his record here. His performances are getting better all the time and yet everyone outside the club keeps writing him off. He's certainly a player I'd never like to play against.

GARY: Pierre van Hooijdonk's refusal to return to Nottingham Forest has meant that all Premiership players are getting it in the neck. People are worried about the growth of player power, but that's just one man. My bet is it's the first and last time it happens.

Quite simply, it would never happen at United. You can't hold this club to ransom because they would just get rid of you. This club is too big for any player to muck it about.

Thursday 6 August

GARY: Club officials have admitted that Manchester United have been in secret talks about a European Super League. There have been a few rumours flying around, but now it's out in the open. It is something that will happen eventually, so I'm going to look forward to it. The European games are the best ones to play in, so the more of them there are the better, as far as I'm concerned.

I appreciate it might be tougher for the smaller clubs, but my view is that these things are inevitable. My local club, Bury, have a lot stacked against them, but it's up to the people there to pull together and survive. Obviously there will be one or two casualties. I don't think anything is going to stop it, it's the way football has gone over the last four or five years.

PHIL: If you asked me whether I'd rather play in Premiership or Champions' League games, I'd say the Champions' League. They are the ultimate games of the season. But if a European Super League came into being, what would happen to the Premiership, because you wouldn't be able to concentrate on both of them? I like the current format with group stages and a knockout to finish. It's a special competition, but I think a European Super League is probably a step too far.

Sunday 9 August   Arsenal 3 Manchester United 0

PHIL: After losing the title to Arsenal last season, I think we needed to stamp our authority. Instead, we were totally out-played. We've got a crucial Champions' League qualifier in three days' time which took the edge off our performance, but it was still a big disappointment. Towards the end, the Arsenal fans were giving it loads and it's not a nice feeling.

Last year, we were desperate to win the penalty shoot-out against Chelsea because we know that a Charity Shield win can act as a signal to the rest of the League that we mean business.

It was David Beckham's first major game since the World Cup and a couple of idiots in the crowd were holding a "Beckscum" banner up. The stick David's taken since he came back has been ridiculous, but he's handling it well.

GARY: Some might dismiss this game as just a pre-season friendly, but I can tell you we were absolutely gutted to lose it. There were 40,000 United fans there and we let them down with a terrible performance. For the first 20 minutes we were all right, but after Arsenal scored we were out-played. We were never going to score.

It wasn't a happy dressing room afterwards. Players have not regained their full fitness yet, but that's not a good enough excuse. Not a great start to the season.

Charity Shield / Wembley / Att: 67,342

Arsenal 3
Seaman, Dixon, Winterburn, Keown, Adams (Bould), Vieira (Grimandi), Petit (Boa Morte), Parlour, Overmars (Hughes), Bergkamp (Wreh), Anelka
Scorers: Grimandi, Anelka, Wreh
Manchester United 0
Schmeichel, G Neville, Irwin, Stam, Johnsen, Keane (Berg), Butt (Solskjaer), Beckham, Giggs (Cruyff), Scholes (P Neville), Cole (Sheringham)

Monday 10 August

GARY: Headlines about Glenn Hoddle's World Cup diary are splashed across all the newspapers. There are things in there that I would prefer were not. I think if he had the choice again he wouldn't do it until he was no longer England manager.

PHIL: Glenn Hoddle's book includes revelations about how Gazza reacted to the news he wasn't in the World Cup squad. From my own experience, I felt that what was said in that room should have remained private between the players and Glenn Hoddle. In fairness though, Gazza did a piece in the newspapers the day after he was dropped, so the Boss probably felt entitled to put his side of the story.

for club and country

Wednesday 12 August   Manchester United 2 LKS Lodz 0

GARY: It might have been a European Cup game, but it felt like a practice match. Our first half of the season depends on these Champions' League games and it was so important to us to get in there. We were murdering them at 1-0, but we just couldn't add to it, so we were all relieved when Coley nodded in a second. Before a game like this, you worry about what you might come up against, but Lodz were a poor team.

Champions' League qualifier / Old Trafford / Att: 50,906

Manchester United 2
Schmeichel, G Neville, Johnsen, Stam, Irwin, Beckham, Keane, Butt, Giggs, Scholes (Solskjaer), Cole
Scorers: Giggs, Cole
LKS Lodz 0
Wyparlo, Pawlak, Benkowski, Krysiak, Darlington (Jacubowski), Cebula, Wyciszkiewicz, Kos, Niznik (Rodrigo), Wieszczyki, Zuberek (Paszulewicz)

Saturday 15 August   Manchester United 2 Leicester City 2

PHIL: A bad start to our Premiership campaign. After the Lodz game, fans may have thought we'd got it back, but it was an illusion because Lodz weren't very good.

It was a hot, sticky day, but Leicester came out flying and probably deserved to win. At 2-0 down, Teddy came on and really changed the game. He was aggressive and showed the fight the team were lacking. He scored and it was a perfect way to answer those fans who've doubted his hunger to succeed at United.

David Beckham grabbed a last-gasp equaliser with one of his free-kick specials. Even watching from the sidelines, it made me feel happy to see the way United fans supported him today. He was given standing ovations every time he took a corner and I've never heard, "There's only one David Beckham" sung so much before. The way David's been treated since he got back to England must have raised doubts in his mind about his future, but the United fans have played a big part in lifting him.

GARY: We were awful today. Personally, I felt tired and completely off the pace of the game. I didn't know what was wrong with me. I did all the running in pre-season but I just couldn't get my legs going at all.

Premiership / Old Trafford / Att: 55,052

Manchester United 2
Schmeichel, G Neville (Sheringham), Irwin, Johnsen, Stam (Berg), Keane, Butt, Beckham, Giggs, Scholes, Cole
Scorers: Sheringham, Beckham
Leicester City 2
Keller, Sinclair, Elliott (Taggart), Walsh, Savage, Guppy, Izzet, Lennon, Zagorakis, Heskey, Cottee (Wilson)
Scorers: Heskey, Cottee

Sunday 16 August

GARY: We went down to Burnham Beeches for an England get-together. Glenn Hoddle immediately got all the players in a room, stood in front of us and said, "If anyone has a problem with my book, they can come and see me about it. Be my guest and read it."

I don't know who went to see him, but it must have been a difficult thing to do. The Boss killed the issue straight away by doing this.

PHIL: The FA's David Davies told us he would photocopy the bits where we were mentioned. I didn't take up the offer. If there had been anything controversial it probably would have already been in *The Sun*, so I wasn't bothered. It would bring back too many bad memories.

The papers have played up the fact that the Boss believes his biggest mistake was not taking Eileen Drewery to France sooner. I must say that the England squad that went to France were the best prepared team ever. Everything was laid on for the players. The attention to detail was incredible, right down to dental checks. I think Glenn Hoddle probably mentioned Eileen Drewery's absence because everything else was accounted for. Some players had seen her regularly before we went to France, and they will understand what the Boss is saying.

Tuesday 18 August

PHIL: We broke off from the England training get-together for the Munich Testimonial game at Old Trafford. It was Eric Cantona's first time back since he retired and he came into our dressing room before the game and shook our hands. It was special to see him again.

The two teams came out before Eric at the start. When he ran out, the crowd gave him an incredible reception. He's still the King, one of the greatest players ever to play for Manchester United.

The game itself was just what a testimonial match should be. The final score was 8–4 to United and the crowd were entertained, especially by Pascal Olmeta, the keeper for Eric's Invitation team. Olmeta was dancing to the crowd chants, dribbling upfield and nearly scored from a free-kick!

Eric changed sides at half-time and played for us. He's still got the vision. The linesman wasn't too popular when he ruled Eric's goal offside. Fortunately, Eric dribbled past four defenders to score again a bit later, even if the attempted tackles by William Prunier and Joel Cantona were a bit half-hearted!

GARY: I didn't get the chance to speak to Eric, just a hello really. He came in the dressing room and shook everyone's hand.

The atmosphere in the stadium was the best I have ever known at a testimonial. Usually the crowd goes quiet in the second half, but they were buzzing all night. Everyone was excited to see Eric back. He had a special rapport with the fans and no one will be loved as much as he was.

Thursday 20 August

GARY: Dwight Yorke arrived today. His transfer has been rumbling on for ages. We knew the manager would sign a striker after failing to get Kluivert.

Dwight always looked like a Man United player to me – he holds the ball up brilliantly, he has amazing skills and scores plenty of goals. Usually players have their weaknesses, but Dwight really has got it all.

Friday 21 August

GARY: Dwight came in for his first day of training. He was probably a bit nervous, but he didn't show it. He just wore a huge smile the whole time. He was introduced to all the players and fitted in immediately.

Saturday 22 August   West Ham United 0 Manchester United 0

PHIL: At the hotel, before we left for Upton Park, the police told David Beckham not to take a window seat on the coach. There had been all sorts of talk about what West Ham fans would do to him today. It was horrible and you wondered, 'How is he going to play football?' Survival, rather than football, seemed to be the priority.

In fact, the only aggro was getting into the ground where what seemed like the whole West Ham support were waiting for us. Once the game started though, the atmosphere was as flat as the match.

The United fans were chanting "Argentina" which really riled Hammers' fans. In fairness, if West Ham fans are English, they should have been cheering Beckham instead of jeering him, so it was no worse than what they were doing. It's just a way of answering back.

GARY: Early in the game I just didn't feel right. My legs didn't have any energy in them, I felt completely drained. As the half went on, I knew I couldn't continue, so I signalled to the bench and came off. People told me before the World Cup that I would feel like this. I didn't believe them, but they were right.

On the coach back home, the Gaffer said to me, "I don't want to see you for two weeks, come in for your treatment for the next couple of days, but then go on holiday." I took his advice and decided to go to Malta.

The West Ham fans were not as bad as had been predicted. The red cards they were all going to hold up never materialised and the booing was muted at best. It was a lot worse last season. I felt Becks handled the day brilliantly.

The reaction to his sending-off in the World Cup was sickening for me. Some of the things that were allowed to be published in the newspapers were absolutely disgraceful and we can all take strength from the fact that David has come through it. A lesser a person would have folded under the criticism he received and he wasn't helped by certain people along the way who should have been there for him.

Everybody at Manchester United was behind him because he had done nothing wrong. Every footballer at some point in their life reacts on a football pitch. I expected him to get a bit of criticism the day after, but it went on for weeks. The way David was treated has changed my opinion of a lot of people – he could have been helped by a few who basically hung him out to dry. At Manchester United, the manager, the fans and the players were there for him, as well as his family. I admire his character to come through it.

Premiership / Upton Park / Att: 26,039

West Ham United 0
Hislop, Lazaradis, Ruddock, Ferdinand, Pearce, Impey, Sinclair, Lampard, Lomas, Berkovic (Abou), Hartson
Manchester United 0
Schmeichel, Irwin, Berg, Johnsen, G Neville (P Neville), Giggs, Butt, Keane, Beckham, Cole (Sheringham), Yorke

Sunday 23 August

PHIL: Spurs have bid to buy Ole Gunnar Solskjaer. I'm close to him, and I don't think he'll ever go. He could go anywhere else and be top scorer, but the ultimate challenge is to play for United. He trains hard and he knows that if he keeps producing, he'll get his chance.

Wednesday 26 August   LKS Lodz 0 Manchester United 0

PHIL: A really boring game, but qualification for the Champions' League was the only reason for going to Poland. Job done.

Champions' League qualifier/LKS/Att: 8,000

LKS Lodz 0
Wyparlo, Pawlak, Bendkowski, Krysiak, Jacubowski, (Bugaj) Kos, Wyciszkiewicz, Lenart (Pluciennik), Niznik, Wieszczyki, Zuberek (Matys)
Manchester United 0
Schmeichel, P Neville, Johnsen, Stam, Irwin, Beckham, Keane, Butt, Giggs (Solskjaer), Sheringham, Scholes

Friday 28 August

PHIL: We've drawn Barcelona, Bayern Munich and Brondby in our Champions' League group. On paper, it's one of the two hardest groups, but I'm pleased because we tend to raise our game against the big teams.

In the past, we've been too lackadaisical against 'lesser' teams like Galatasaray and Fenerbahce. We beat Brondby 6–0 in pre-season too, so I'm really confident we can progress.

Wednesday 2 September

PHIL: I went down to be with the England squad to prepare for the Sweden game in Stockholm on Saturday.

The serialisation of Tony Adams' book has caused a stir this week and the press are trying to hype up a supposed split between the players and the manager. I don't think the fuss surrounding the book will really affect our preparation, but it might have been better if the serialisation had been next week instead.

When the press are on our side going into games we usually win, but if they are on our backs we don't tend to do as well.

Today, Tony and Glenn did a joint press conference. Journalists seem to think it's a sham, but Tony Adams is not the sort of person who'd do a press conference just to keep the manager happy. There simply haven't been the rows behind the scenes that have been reported in the press.

Thursday 3 September

PHIL: Before we joined up with the squad, Jesper Blomqvist told me that Sweden will give us a tough game, and today the Boss reminded us that Sweden haven't lost to England since 1968. Jesper is still not fully match-fit and isn't playing, and I'm not in the team for Saturday either.

Saturday 5 September   Sweden 2 England 1

PHIL: Alan Shearer gave us the lead after two minutes. Then, twenty minutes into the game, I turned to Tim Flowers on the bench and said: "We'll get three or four here." But they scored two in three minutes around the half-hour mark and their confidence grew. We didn't look like winning after that.

Despite Jesper and Glenn Hoddle's warnings, 1 don't think we expected them to be so good. Darren Anderton went off injured and when Incey got sent off for two bookable offences we were up against it. 1 thought Paul was unlucky with the first booking, and he got the second when we were chasing the game.

European Championship Qualifier / Stockholm

Sweden 2
Hedman, Nilsson, P Andersson, Bjorklund, Kaamark (Lucic), Schwarz, A Andersson (Andersson D), Mjallby, Ljungberg, Larsson, Petterson
Scorers: A Andersson, Mjallby
England 1
Seaman, Campbell (Merson), Le Saux, Ince, Adams, Southgate, Anderton (Lee), Redknapp, Shearer, Owen, Scholes (Sheringham)
Scorer: Shearer

Monday 7 September

PHIL: Since his book, the press have been turning the screws on Glenn Hoddle and after Saturday's game there have been a couple of 'Hoddle quit' headlines.

Some journalists haven't taken kindly to the way Glenn Hoddle keeps his team secret until the last minute. Before Saturday, there were questions about whether Tony Adams would be fit or not and the Boss wouldn't say. But all the fuss surprises me because every manager in Europe does it. Alex Ferguson has a theory that he always expects the opposition to put out their best possible team. Then, if one of their first-choice players gets injured, it's easier to adjust.

Wednesday 9 September   Manchester United 4 Charlton Athletic 1

GARY: Sky's £623 million takeover bid was announced at 3pm today.

1 want United to be the greatest club in the world. 1 want them to be the richest club in the world, to have the best players and the best stadium and 1 firmly believe that Sky's ownership of the club will help

United achieve that. If they don't buy us, they would buy another club, so we should be grateful they've chosen us. Media groups are buying teams all over Europe. It makes sense that we go with Sky.

The fans have their concerns, but I am sure there will be provisions put in place that will safeguard the club. Our best players aren't going to be sold off. I trust the people at the club to make the right decisions, because they want the best for the club and they wouldn't dream of putting it in danger. The fans seem frightened of change, but if we want to move with the times and compete with the Barcelonas and the Inter Milans then we must embrace this deal which can only make us stronger.

The players haven't really talked about it. The whole thing is out of our hands.

PHIL: A Manchester Evening News poll showed that 96 per cent of local fans who voted are against the takeover. If I was a fan, I think I'd be excited that a company was prepared to invest that much money in the club because we'll be able to go out and buy bigger and better players. Some say the club will just be a little dot in Rupert Murdoch's empire, but a club the size of Manchester United is never going be just that. The fans won't allow it. At the moment, no one knows the full facts.

At the press conference, someone asked Sky's Chief Executive, Mark Booth, who plays at left-back for United. He didn't know. I'm sure Denis and I won't be offended! Anyway, if Sky's people thought they knew too much about football, they might start interfering. It's better this way.

Tonight, Yorkie scored his first goals for United. He celebrated the first by jumping into the crowd and I think he's endeared himself to the fans already. There wasn't too much sign of protest against the takeover at the game, apart from a streaker with "Takeover my a****" painted on his back. He had a good sidestep and it took about forty stewards to catch him.

Premiership / Old Trafford / Att: 55,147

Manchester United 4
Schmeichel, P Neville, Stam, Johnsen, Irwin (Berg), Beckham, Keane, Scholes, Blomqvist, Yorke (Sheringham), Solskjaer (Cole)
Scorers: Solskjaer 2, Yorke 2
Charlton Athletic 1
Ilic, Mills, Brown, Youds, Powell, Newton (Mortimer), Kinsella (K Jones), Redfearn, Robinson, Mendonca (S Jones), Hunt
Scorer: Kinsella

Thursday 10 September

PHIL: The club's new television channel MUTV was launched today.

The MUTV crew have been following us since the summer trip to Norway. Out there, they followed us everywhere we went – even into our bedrooms and in the dressing room before the games. Back home, there are swarms of them down at the Cliff every day and the players aren't used to it.

They've got to fill six hours of air-time each day, so they need massive co-operation from the players, but a few of the lads aren't too sure.

Saturday 12 September　　　　**Manchester United 2 Coventry City 0**

PHIL: The Chairman and his deputy, Peter Kenyon, came into the Players' Room before today's game. The Chairman explained that the takeover probably won't go through until next year, because first it must be approved by the Monopolies and Mergers Commission. He said there was nothing to worry about and told us not to read anything in the papers because it's all rubbish.

The game was a bit dull, but Solskjaer and Yorke look a good partnership. It's amazing Andy Cole, our top scorer last season, can't get into the side.

Premiership / Old Trafford / Att: 55, 193

Manchester United 2
Schmeichel, G Neville, Johnsen (Berg), Stam, Beckham (Butt), Giggs (Blomqvist), P Neville, Keane, Scholes, Yorke, Solskjaer
Scorers: Yorke, Johnsen
Coventry City 0
Hedman, Burrows, Shaw, Breen, Huckerby (Hall), Dublin, Boateng, Telfer, Wallemme, Edworthy, Quinn

Wednesday 16 September　　　　**Manchester United 3 Barcelona 3**

PHIL: The Gaffer has said in the papers, "I'll always see demons in Europe... I'll have failed if we don't see them off." Despite all his successes, he desperately wants us to win the European Cup and he's built a big squad to achieve that.

The team played superbly tonight in the first half to take a 2–0 lead, but Barcelona battered us in the second half and in the end a draw was a fair result.

We played a lot of balls forward in the first half to pressurise their makeshift back four. The last thing the Boss said to us before going out for the second half was, "Keep playing the ball forward, don't sit back." So what do we do? We spend the first five minutes playing the ball back to Peter. I was sitting on the bench and the Boss was screaming.

Barcelona were brilliant though. They switched tactics. Giggsy had been killing Luis Enrique in the first half, but Enrique came forward more in the second and caused us problems.

The game had everything: great technique, high skill levels and goals.

Barcelona got two penalties. Rivaldo made the most of a challenge by Jaap Stam to get the first one, but the second one was straightforward. Nicky Butt instinctively hand-balled on the line to stop a certain goal and that's a mandatory sending-off.

GARY: Our first-half performance against Barcelona was one of the best I've played in. We absolutely battered them. We went two goals up and it should have been more. But we just couldn't reproduce it in the second half, which went from bad to worse. We started sloppily, they scored a goal and we then had to play on the back foot. They dictated the whole pace of the game with players who could really open us up. We became timid and started passing the ball backwards instead of forwards. At the end, we were clinging on for dear life. A draw might not be such a bad result.

It was the first time I'd shared a pitch with Rivaldo and he was sensational. He was so quick and was always in areas to hurt us. Did he dive for their first penalty? I don't know, it's something defenders are having to get used to. If you go near a forward in the box they are going down more often now and referees are not seeing through it. I could moan about it, but it's part of the game today.

Champions' League / Old Trafford / Att: 53,601

Manchester United 3
Schmeichel, G Neville, Irwin (P Neville), Stam, Berg, Keane, Scholes, Beckham, Giggs (Blomqvist), Solskjaer (Butt), Yorke
Scorers: Giggs, Scholes, Beckham

Barcelona 3
Hesp, Reiziger, Barjuan, Fernandez, Martinez, Cocu, Figo, Zenden, Rivaldo, Olivera (Creus), Anderson
Scorers: Anderson, Enrique (pen), Giovanni (pen)

Sunday 20 September   Arsenal 3 Manchester United 0

PHIL: This is becoming a habit. Arsenal have beaten us four times in a row now.

The lads were really disappointed after the game. We just didn't play at all. Ole Gunnar Solskjaer was down to play on the morning of the game, but the Gaffer changed tactics and put Giggsy upfront. Ryan's pace has troubled Adams and Keown in past matches, but it just didn't work out today.

Nicky Butt was sent off again. It was a really harsh decision. He brought down Vieira, but he wasn't the last defender. A yellow card would have been sufficient. I feel sorry for Nicky because he's going to miss a few games now.

GARY: Arsenal have been on a good run against us recently. This is the fourth time in a row that they have beaten us and the second time this season they have completely outplayed us. They are a resilient team and Vieira was outstanding today.

Premiership / Highbury / Att: 38,142

Arsenal 3
Seaman, Dixon, Winterburn, Vieira, Adams, Anelka (Ljungberg), Bergkamp, Overmars, Keown, Parlour, Hughes
Scorers: Adams, Anelka, Ljungberg
Manchester United 0
Schmeichel, G Neville, Irwin, Stam, Beckham, Butt, Giggs, Blomqvist, Keane, Yorke, Berg

14

The Cole and Yorke show

Tuesday 22 September

PHIL: A documentary about Alex Ferguson was on television tonight. It was funny to hear all the old Aberdeen players talking about him. He's obviously mellowed since then, but you can imagine he used to be a right old snapper!

The programme featured his team talk before a game against Liverpool (whom we play again this Thursday) where the Gaffer described Paul Ince as a "big-time Charlie". The footage demonstrated his belief that when you play for United, it's us against the world.

I think he's right, because outside of United fans, most people do hate us. So why not use that to motivate the team?

Thursday 24 September   **Manchester United 2 Liverpool 0**

PHIL: The Gaffer has had us working on our defending all week. He was concerned that there hasn't been enough talking in defence. That may have been a factor in him playing Gary in the centre tonight, because Gary's a good organiser, but his pace was also useful against Michael Owen. It was probably Gary's best game to date and our best defensive performance of the season.

We went a goal up through Denis's penalty and then defended tight.

Paul Ince got a rough time. United fans were chanting, "Charlie, Charlie, what's the score?" And, when he had a go at Jaap Stam, Jaap went after him. Incey's a braver man than me, because Jaap's one player in world football I wouldn't mess with!

Jaap's had a lot of criticism since he joined, but he was magnificent tonight. The problems he's had so far have mainly been down to a lack of understanding which you always get when a new player joins a defensive unit. He is an outstanding defender.

GARY: We had to beat Liverpool and I always had a feeling we would. We simply could not contemplate losing to them at home after slipping up against Barcelona and Arsenal. There was an unbelievable atmosphere tonight and we raised our game.

It was particularly satisfying that Jaap Stam and I kept Michael Owen quiet. Some people said it was my best game for United. I don't know about that because I was in awe of Jaap. He was outstanding and it is a pleasure to play with him. He has amazing power, presence and strength. I have no doubt that he'll be a legend for United.

Premiership / Old Trafford / Att: 55,181

Manchester United 2
Schmeichel, P Neville, Stam, G Neville, Irwin, Beckham, Keane, Scholes (Butt), Giggs, Yorke, Solskjaer (Cole)
Scorers: Irwin (pen), Scholes
Liverpool 0
Friedel, McAteer, Babb, Carragher, Bjornebye, Berger, Ince, Redknapp, McManaman, Owen, Riedle (Fowler)

Monday 28 September

PHIL: I've had MUTV installed at my house and every time I turn it on, there's my face on the box! I've been doing interviews virtually every day for them, and I'm going to have to stop for a while or people will start thinking I'm the only one playing for United! Of course, the channel is only in its early stages. I think it's a great idea and the longer it goes on, the better it will get.

Tuesday 29 September

PHIL: We flew to Munich for our next Champions' League game from Manchester Airport. Gary and I were among the first players to arrive at about 10 o'clock. We were on our way to the executive lounge where we were due to meet the others when a security guard said, "Be careful, there are some Leeds fans up there." Leeds are playing a UEFA Cup tie in Madeira tonight.

We walked through the departure gate only to be met by fifty-odd Leeds supporters screaming abuse and singing Munich songs. They looked like your identikit hooligans – all skinheads and scars. It was lucky a policeman was there because I seriously believe we would have got battered. It was frightening. We found out later they should have caught a plane to Madeira at 7.30, but they stayed back just for us. Gary made me laugh because he tried to get away from the fans by walking the wrong way along the horizontal escalator. He wasn't getting very far!

GARY: What a pleasure to bump into those lovely Leeds fans. As soon as they saw us they spat at us, sang about the Munich air crash and threatened to assault us. You'd have thought we'd murdered their families.

Wednesday 30 September   Bayern Munich 2 Manchester United 2

PHIL: It's about time we won in one of these places. We played really well and were 2–1 up with just a minute to go, and then a massive mix-up gifted Bayern an equaliser. It was as if we had lost in the dressing room afterwards.

We were due to travel back tonight, but in a strange repeat of the past, our plane has broken down, so we are staying over.

GARY: We played so well against Munich that I can't believe we didn't win. With minutes to go it looked as if we were at last going to win a big away game in Europe, but then they grabbed a soft equaliser. We were absolutely gutted. We now have to beat Brondby twice to stand a chance of qualifying for the Quarter-Finals.

Champions' League / Olympiastadion / Att: 53,000

Bayern Munich 2
Kahn, Babel, Lizarazu, Strunz, Elber, Matthaus, Effenburg, Jeremies (Fink), Jancker (Dael), Salihamidzic (Goktan), Linke
Scorers: Elber 2
Manchester United
Schmeichel, G Neville, Irwin, Stam, Beckham, Sheringham, P Neville, Blomqvist (Cruyff), Keane, Scholes, Yorke
Scorers: Yorke, Scholes

Friday 2 October

GARY: Phil: and I were both named in the England squad to play Bulgaria. There is a lot of pressure on the team to win this one after the Sweden loss, but it's my first chance to get back in the side since then, so I'm looking forward to it.

Saturday 3 October   **Southampton 0 Manchester United 3**

GARY: At last, we've won at the Dell!

Southampton were without Mark Hughes, which helped. Sparky's been having yellow-card trouble this season and he was suspended. Referees always seem to single out players like Hughes who have an aggressive approach.

It's a great win for us. After all the early season talk of the Solskjaer-Yorke partnership, it looks like Cole and Yorke play together just as well. Andy set Dwight up for our first goal and produced an excellent finish himself to make it 3–0.

PHIL: I have had a run of games now which I think has restored my confidence. Southampton was my third in a row and it was a good game to play in, a bit of a stroll really. Coley and Yorkie, paired together for the first time since August, were brilliant, but I thought Jesper Blomqvist was our best player. It must have been really hard for him when he first arrived at the club because we were all away in Norway on our pre-season tour and he was on his own in Manchester training with the physios, instead of getting to know us and sharing in the banter. He's a lovely bloke, speaks excellent English and now he is showing what a great footballer he is.

GARY: I came on as substitute against Jesper four years ago in Gothenburg when he put us out of the Champions' League almost single-handedly. He looked a top-class player then and he's played at two big clubs in Milan and Parma after that. He's got so many tricks, he's quick and, like Ryan Giggs, he's incredibly strong on the ball for someone with such a slight frame.

Premiership / The Dell / Att: 15,251

Southampton 0
Jones, Palmer, Lundekvam (Gibbens), Monkou, Le Tissier, Ostenstad, Howells, Ripley (Beattie), Benali, Bridge, Warner
Manchester United 3
Van der Gouw, G Neville, Irwin (Brown), Stam, Beckham, Butt, P Neville, Blomqvist (Sheringham), Keane, Yorke (Cruyff), Cole
Scorers: Yorke, Cole, Cruyff

Sunday 4 October

GARY: There have been a few rumours in the press about what tablets and injections England players were given at France 98 and the medical staff at United have asked us about it. I had no qualms about telling them, because the England team medics would not have given us anything they thought was dangerous.

One of the things was creatine, and there have been a couple of cases of bodybuilders dying through creatine abuse. But they were taking massive doses whereas our intake was strictly monitored. If you swallowed a box of Paracetamol you'd struggle.

It is true I felt very sharp during the World Cup, but whether that was due to creatine or the injections I don't know. It could have just been adrenaline, because if you don't feel good about playing in the biggest competition in the world, when will you?

Saturday 10 October   England 0 Bulgaria 0

GARY: This was a poor performance when we really needed a win. We didn't create much in the way of chances and it must have been very uninspiring to watch. There's now a lot of pressure on us to play much better in Luxembourg.

Gazza has been admitted into a rehabilitation clinic. He's obviously got problems. All I know is that he's an absolutely brilliant lad, and I wish him all the best. At the moment it's easy to take Paul for granted, and I think people will only realise how badly we miss him when he's retired from the game. People like him don't come along every week.

European Championship qualifier / Wembley

England 0
Seaman, G Neville, Hinchcliffe (Le Saux), Lee, Campbell, Southgate, Anderton (Batty), Redknapp, Shearer, Owen, Scholes (Sheringham)
Bulgaria 0
Zdravkov, Yordanov, Zagorcic, Kirilov, Kishishev, Iliev (Gruev), Iankov, Petkov, Naidenov, Stoichkov (Bachev), Hristov (Ivanov)

Wednesday 14 October   Luxembourg 0 England 3

PHIL: I have to admit to being quite nervous for the game against Luxembourg. It was my first start for England since being left out of the World Cup squad in the summer. I thought I did all right, setting up our third goal for Gareth Southgate. The England fans there were on our back throughout the game. They were expecting us to score six or seven, so when we found it hard going they didn't get behind us.

Despite winning, we were all disappointed with the performance. Glenn Hoddle didn't say much to us afterwards.

GARY: I expected to play, so I was disappointed when Glenn Hoddle pulled me aside and told me I wasn't. Rio Ferdinand played instead and I have to say he was our best player on the night.

We got off to a nightmare start, conceding a penalty early on – luckily they missed. We passed it around well in the first half and being 2–0 up at half-time, the Boss told the lads to keep on attacking. Instead, our passing slowed down and we just killed the game.

European Championship qualifier / Luxembourg

Luxembourg 0
Koch, L Deville, Strasser, Funck, Ferron, Salbene, F Deville, Theis (Holtz), Posing, Cardoni, Christophe (Amodio)
England 3
Seaman, Ferdinand R, Neville P, Batty, Campbell, Southgate, Beckham, Anderton (Lee), Shearer, Owen, Scholes (Wright)
Scorers: Owen, Shearer (pen), Southgate

Thursday 15 October

GARY: Rumours have surfaced of a dressing-room argument between Alan Shearer and Glenn Hoddle last night. It's being implied that there was some kind of player revolt, but that simply didn't happen. As I recall, one or two things were said at half-time regarding our defending at free-kicks, but it was just normal dressing-room stuff. Nothing out of the ordinary.

| Saturday 17 October | Manchester United 5 Wimbledon 1 |

GARY: Like this time last season, when we thrashed Barnsley and Sheffield Wednesday, the goals are starting to flow. Yorke and Cole are flying.

Dwight has made a major impact. He moves off the ball, he makes quick turns, he can play deep or as a target man. Like Mark Hughes, he's brilliant at holding the ball up. As a defender, there's nothing better than knowing the ball will stick when you fire it forward to your strikers.

Dwight and Andy are best friends off the pitch and a lot of people think that helps their play on it. It obviously helps a bit, but it's easy to forget that Coley has also played well with Teddy and Ole. I think that generally, there is a good team spirit among the lads. Everyone is quite friendly with each other, but, from playing on the right with David Beckham, I know that being close mates probably is an advantage, especially when things aren't going so well.

PHIL: Coley and Yorkie destroyed Wimbledon today. Their partnership is beginning to be recognised as a potentially great one. Coley needed somebody like Dwight. Andy's loved by all the lads, but now he's got someone he's close with off the pitch, it's really helped him.

Dwight has fitted right in. The players and the fans all love him. From the first day he came into the dressing room, he's had a smile on his face and he never stops beaming. The lads joke with him that if someone told him he only had two weeks to live, he still wouldn't stop smiling.

Premiership / Old Trafford / Att: 55,265

Manchester United 5
Van der Gouw, G Neville (Curtis), Stam, Brown, P Neville, Beckham (Cruyff), Giggs (Scholes), Blomqvist, Keane, Yorke, Cole
Scorers: Cole 2, Giggs, Beckham, Yorke
Wimbledon 1
Sullivan, Cunningham, Kimble (Ardley), Perry, Blackwell, Thatcher, Earle, Roberts, Leaburn (Gayle), Hughes, Euell
Scorer: Euell

Wednesday 21 October   Brondby 2 Manchester United 6

GARY: A real pressure game, but it was one of those nights when everything seemed to go in. The Brondby players seemed nervous, in awe of us even.

Perhaps there was a carry-over from our pre-season friendly, because this was a team that beat Bayern Munich in their first Champions' League game.

Before the match, their goalkeeper Morgens Krogh was quoted as saying that he didn't rate Andy Cole and that Coley would never score past him. Andy responded by producing an excellent finish for his goal. Afterwards, Krogh was very anxious to tell our players that he'd been misquoted!

PHIL: Roy Keane scored his first goal of the season tonight. He has come back brilliantly from his injury. Everyone thought he'd play a couple of games then rest, but he hasn't missed a game or a training session. He's worked so hard. I think he's shown how much we missed him last year.

Champions' League / Parken Stadium / Att: 40,315

Brondby 2
Krogh, Bjur, Nielsen (M Jensen), Ravn, Daugaard, Rasmussen, Sand, Hansen (Bagger), Colding, B Jensen (Vragel), Lindrup
Scorers: Daugaard, Sand
Manchester United 6
Schmeichel, G Neville, Stam, P Neville, Brown, Blomqvist, Keane, Scholes, Giggs (Cruyff), Yorke (Wilson), Cole (Solskjaer)
Scorers: Giggs 2, Cole, Keane, Yorke, Solskjaer

Saturday 24 October   Derby County 1 Manchester United 1

PHIL: We gave a tired performance at Derby. Their tactics really nullified us. With three upfront, they didn't allow our defenders to get forward and so it turned into a bit of a stalemate.

I was pleased for my pal Jordi, who came on as a substitute and grabbed our important equaliser. He looked really sharp. He hasn't missed a single day's training, so at last people are beginning to see the real Jordi.

Premiership / Pride Park / Att: 30,867

Derby County 1
Hoult, Delap, Laursen (Dorigo), Stimac, Prior, Schnoor, Carsley, Powell, Burton, Sturridge, Wanchope
Scorer: Burton
Manchester United 1
Schmeichel, G Neville (Scholes), Stam, Beckham, Butt (Cruyff), Cole, Giggs (Blomqvist), P Neville, Keane, Yorke, Brown
Scorer: Cruyff

Wednesday 28 October   Manchester United 2 Bury 0 AET

GARY: About 8,000 Bury fans turned out for this Cup game, which is more than they get at home. The receipts from a total gate of 52,495 will help Bury keep their best players and survive in the First Division.

I thought they did quite well, but they never created a good chance and I felt their best chance would be to have a real go in the last half hour. They did take us to extra time though, but as soon as Ole Gunnar scored, I knew the game was over.

Of the young players in the team tonight, Jonathan Greening really stood out. He's a good dribbler and really aggressive for a forward. He doesn't mind doing his share of tackling either, and defenders like me appreciate that.

Worthington Cup / Old Trafford / Att: 52,495

Manchester United 2
Van der Gouw, May, P Neville, Curtis, Cruyff, Solskjaer, Berg, Clegg (Brown), Mulryne (Nevland), Wilson (Scholes), Greening
Scorers: Solskjaer, Nevland
Bury 0
Kiely, Woodward, Barrick, Daws, Lucketti, Redmond, Swailes, Patterson (Matthews), D'Jaffo (Preece), Johnrose, Ellis (James)

Thursday 29 October

GARY: Most of the England squad went to Buckingham Palace today to meet the Queen. It was a great opportunity, but unfortunately all of the United players, bar Teddy, had to give it a miss. Teddy is injured, so he won't be playing on Saturday. For the rest of us, being out all day two days before a game is not the best preparation. If we were to lose on Saturday, it wouldn't be acceptable.

for club and country

Saturday 31 October   Everton 1 Manchester United 4

GARY: We always seem to do well at Goodison Park and today, we put in an excellent performance. Jesper ran their full-back absolutely ragged and scored his first goal for the club.

Premiership / Goodison Park / Att: 40,079

Everton 1
Myhre, Ball, Dacourt, Watson, Unsworth, Collins, Ferguson, Short (Dunne), Materazzi, Bakayoko, Cadamarteri
Scorer: Ferguson
Manchester United 4
Schmeichel, G Neville, Stam, Beckham, Brown, P Neville (Irwin), Blomqvist, Keane, Scholes, Yorke, Cole
Scorers: Yorke, Cole, Blomqvist, Short (own goal)

Monday 2 November

GARY: After ten games we are in second place on 21 points, one behind Aston Villa. Villa have started brilliantly under John Gregory. They struggled last year when we thought they'd do quite well, but Gregory's added to the squad, bringing in some good solid professionals like Steve Watson, Alan Thompson and Paul Merson. When you sign those sort of players, you know exactly what you are getting. It's good to see a team full of English players at the top of the League.

John Gregory seems to have made the difference there. He has been quoted as saying that Villa are second only to United in this country and that he wants to get as close to what Alex Ferguson has achieved during his four-year contract.

He's confident, with a different approach to management and that's refreshing for the game. His players have certainly responded to him.

Wednesday 4 November   Manchester United 5 Brondby 0

PHIL: We were worried that the fans would expect another rout and it could prove difficult, but we just blitzed Brondby and were 4–0 up after half an hour. I scored my second goal for United as well and imitated Jesper Blomqvist with my celebration. Jesper always plays with his

266

sleeves pulled down over his hands, so I did the same and waved my empty sleeves about! I still got slaughtered for it by the lads afterwards.

Coley scored a brilliant goal, one of the best I've ever seen at Old Trafford. Everything went for us. Unfortunately, it couldn't last and I had to go off injured with a pulled hamstring.

GARY: Frank Leboeuf said recently that you need at least twenty good players in a squad to win the Premiership and a European trophy, and I agree. At United, the Gaffer has assembled a massive squad, and hopefully it will prove good enough to win one, two or even three trophies. Although this means there are a lot of good players on the side-lines at any one time. No footballer likes it when they are not selected, but I think it's easier for players to accept at a club like United, because when you do get in the team there's always something to play for.

Champions' League / Old Trafford / Att: 53,250

Manchester United 5
Schmeichel, G Neville, P Neville (Brown), Stam, Irwin, Beckham, Keane, Blomqvist (Cruyff), Scholes, Yorke, Cole (Solskjaer)
Scorers: Beckham, Cole, P Neville, Yorke, Scholes
Brondby 0
Andersen, Colding, Nielsen, Rasmussen, M Jensen, Bjur (Krogh), B Jensen, Daugaard, Bagger (Thygesen), Sand (Hensen), Skarbalijus

Thursday 5 November

GARY: John Gregory has struck again, buying Dion Dublin for £5.75 million. A few eyebrows were raised at the fee for a 29-year-old, but you know you are going to get four or five good years out of Dion. He's a solid character and a proven goalscorer in the Premiership – and he can play in defence. I think that's far better value for money than maybe bringing in a foreigner at the same price, who might just be coming for the money and will leave you at the first sign of trouble.

Friday 6 November

GARY: Roy Keane reckons that the 1994 United side have the edge on the present team, but that they didn't have enough quality in reserve, and I agree. The 1994 Double-winning first-choice eleven – Schmeichel, Parker, Bruce, Pallister, Irwin, Kanchelskis, Ince, Keane, Giggs, Cantona, Hughes – had power and class all over the park, but the squad wasn't big enough to deal with the Champions' League.

They also had the three-foreigners' rule to contend with then, and I think we are better equipped to do well in Europe now. The players around now were just getting close to the team back then and we can learn from their mistakes.

We won't get carried away though. After the Brondby game, John Jensen described us as "simply the best team in Europe". That's very kind, but we're not going to fall for that one again. After the last couple of years, we know how difficult it is to win the European Cup, so we're wary of any praise.

Saturday 7 November

GARY: Alex Ferguson said in an interview recently, "I am the last of a dying breed – I just can't see another manager lasting twelve years in a job."

It is becoming more like Italy in the Premiership with clubs swapping managers every one or two years, but you can't beat continuity and consistency, and that's what the Boss brings to the club.

Sunday 8 November   Manchester United 0 Newcastle United 0

GARY: The state-of-the-art pitch that was laid at Old Trafford in summer has turned out to be a bit of a nightmare. It was cutting up unbelievably today – if anyone slid into a tackle they'd bring up yard-long divots. But we can't just blame the pitch – it was yet another poor performance after a European game.

Newcastle's tactics worked quite well, but they never offered anything in attack. It was the sort of game we'd hope to win 1–0, but couldn't quite sneak a goal.

Premiership/Old Trafford/Att: 55,174

Manchester United 0
Schmeichel, Brown (Johnsen, Butt), Stam, G Neville, Irwin, Beckham, Keane, Scholes, Blomqvist (Solskjaer), Cole, Yorke
Newcastle United 0
Given, Charvet, Hughes, Dabizas, Griffin, Georgiadis, Hamann (Speed), Batty, Glass, Shearer, Dalglish

Wednesday 11 November   Manchester United 2 Nottingham Forest 1

GARY: Neither Phil or me played in this Worthington Cup match. Jordi had an excellent game, running the show in midfield. He supplied the passes for both of Ole Gunnar's goals. Ole is a natural finisher. It doesn't seem to make any difference to him that he hasn't played many full games recently.

Worthington Cup / Old Trafford / Att: 37,237

Manchester United 2
Van der Gouw, Clegg, Curtis, May (Wallwork), Berg, Butt, Wilson, Mulryne, Cruyff, Solskjaer, Greening
Scorer: Solskjaer 2
Nottingham Forest 1
Beasant, Louis-Jean, Rogers, Chettle, Stone, Gemmill, Bart-Williams, Freedman, Armstrong, Harewood (van Hooijdonk), Gray
Scorer: Stone

Thursday 12 November

GARY: Peter Schmeichel announced he will be leaving United at the end of the season. I found out on a TV bulletin. It's a big surprise and it will be a massive loss. Of all the players who have left the club in the last few years, I think he will be the hardest to replace. He was the best in his position in the world. It will be impossible to find someone with his character, presence and ability. He's won us so many games and it's going to be a frightening prospect for whoever comes in to replace him.

I don't think it will be a young keeper, because the pressure on him would be unbearable. I see it being an experienced pro who can handle everything that is going to be thrown at him, because comparisons with Peter will come with the job.

PHIL: I can honestly say, I had no idea about Peter's plans. It came as a shock. I heard there was a press conference at the ground and I assumed we were signing a player, so I was taken aback to find out on Teletext that Peter was leaving.

Tonight, Glenn Hoddle phoned to tell me he was leaving me out of the squad for next week's friendly against the Czech Republic but to keep going. He said he wanted to try out some younger players.

When I put down the phone I was absolutely gutted. It's hard to take. With the World Cup I knew it would be close, but I didn't see this coming.

Friday 13 November

PHIL: We were tip-toeing around Peter this morning, no one really wanted to ask him about his decision for some reason. No one really talked about it, life just goes on at this club. But later in the day I had a chat to him. He said he was finding it difficult to recover from games in time for the next one. Peter enjoys training, but with the number of games we play he doesn't have the time for it. His body can't take it.

The speculation has already started about who is going to replace him. I fancy the Dutch keeper, Edwin van der Sar.

GARY: The England squad for the Czech Republic game next Wednesday was made public today. I can't really understand Glenn Hoddle's explanation for leaving out Phil to try some younger players. The only youngsters he's brought in are Lee Hendrie, Emile Heskey and Richard Wright and none of them plays in Phil's position. Having played in the last England game, leaving Phil out of the squad can't do him any good. It rekindles bad memories from before the World Cup and puts him back to square one. But Glenn Hoddle picks the squad and you have to stand by that.

Saturday 14 November   Manchester United 3 Blackburn Rovers 2

GARY: We were killing them until Tim Sherwood was sent off. At 3–0 down with ten men, they suddenly started throwing men forward and by the last ten minutes we were hanging on.

The tackle by Tim Sherwood on David Beckham which led to his sending-off was horrendous. Every time we've played against him, there seems to be trouble. I didn't appreciate him spitting at me on his way off either.

Premiership / Old Trafford / Att 55, 198

Manchester United 3
Schmeichel, P Neville, Stam, G Neville, Curtis, Blomqvist (Solskjaer), Scholes (Cruyff, Keane), Butt, Beckham, Cole, Yorke
Scorers: Scholes 2, Yorke
Blackburn Rovers 2
Filan, Davidson (Croft), Peacock, Henchoz, Kenna, Duff (Marcolin), Johnson, Dailly, Sherwood, Davies (Gallacher), Blake
Scorers: Marcolin, Blake

Sunday 15 November

PHIL: Being left out of the squad to play the Czech Republic has affected me more than missing the World Cup. It has definitely hit me badly. The main thing Alex Ferguson has said to me since is that I play for Manchester United and that they ultimately pay my wages.

I have not played as many games as I would have liked this season, especially after missing out on the World Cup. I wanted to come back and have a good season with United, so it's not gone as well as I had hoped. I was actually getting a good run in the side, but then I got injured against Brondby and that set me back. There is a long way to go and with three competitions the manager is always going to give you a chance and everyone is going to get a fair amount of games, so hopefully my best is still to come.

I have been in and out all season and when I have been left out of a game the Gaffer has always taken me to one side and told me I'm doing well. He doesn't have to do that, but it's good management. He's told me to keep going and that my future is at the club.

That's all I need to hear.

Wednesday 18 November   England 2 Czech Republic 0

GARY: The whole team from the back three, through Nicky Butt and David Beckham in midfield up to Ian Wright, Dion Dublin and Paul

Merson – our 94-year-old strikeforce in attack, played really well. After the last couple of games, it was vital to put in an exciting performance to banish any doubts about the team.

Lee Hendrie came on as sub and made an impressive debut. All the team signed his shirt afterwards. He's a nice lad and he's fitted in well.

International Friendly / Wembley

England 2
Martyn, Keown, Campbell, Butt, R Ferdinand, Le Saux, Beckham, Anderton, Dublin, Wright (Fowler), Merson (Hendrie)
Scorers: Anderton, Merson
Czech Republic 0
Kouba, Latal (Lokvenc), Votava, Novotny (Baranek), Repka, Berger, Nemec (Kotulec), Poborsky, Kuka (Sloncik), Smicer (Vonasek), Bejbl

Saturday 21 November   Sheffield Wednesday 3 Manchester United 1

PHIL: The manager really laid into us after the game today. He was angry at how sloppy we were and thought we were behaving like big-game players. The players took it to heart and discussed it on the coach back to Manchester. The manager had a point, we let ourselves down, but then I'm sure we'll perform in Barcelona.

Coley had one chance today and put it away. That's the best way to answer Glenn Hoddle.

Premiership / Hillsborough / Att: 39,475

Sheffield Wednesday 3
Srnicek, Atherton, Walker, Hinchcliffe, Thome, Sonner, Jonk, Alexandersson, Rudi, Carbone, Booth
Scorers: Alexandersson 2, Jonk
Manchester United 1
Schmeichel, P Neville, Stam, G Neville, Irwin (Brown), Beckham, Scholes, Keane (Solskjaer), Blomqvist (Butt), Cole, Yorke
Scorer: Cole

Wednesday 25 November   Barcelona 3 Manchester United 3

Gary: Before tonight's game, Eric Cantona, who lives in Barcelona, surprised us by coming onto the team coach to wish us luck. Apparently, the Gaffer turned round during the game and saw Eric and his family urging us on, so he's obviously still behind us.

Although, Barcelona could still qualify, it looked as if their fans had given up on them. When we lost 4–0 in 1994, the Nou Camp was filled to its 120,000 capacity. This time, only about half that amount of people got to see a thriller.

We got off to an appalling start, and I was at fault for Sonny Anderson's goal in the first minute. The next twenty minutes or so we were wobbly, but once Dwight got us a goal, we settled down. After that, it was non-stop, end-to-end stuff. Even when we were attacking, Barcelona had five players up against our three. I've never seen anything like it. It's a brilliant way of playing, but in the end we capitalised on their lack of numbers at the back. Andy Cole and Dwight Yorke gave the finest attacking display I have ever seen. They ran them ragged.

At the end, I didn't know whether to be happy or not, because although I'd taken part in one of the best games you'll ever see, yet again we'd failed to win away against one of the best teams in Europe. It was there for us, but we didn't take it.

Champions' League / Nou Camp / Att: 67,650

Barcelona 3
Hesp, Okunowo, Sergi, Reiziger, Lopez, Xavi, Zenden, Figo, Rivaldo, Giovanni, Anderson
Scorers: Anderson, Rivaldo 2
Manchester United 3
Schmeichel, Brown, Irwin, G Neville, Stam, Beckham (Butt), Keane, Scholes, Blomqvist, Yorke, Cole
Scorers: Yorke 2, Cole

Sunday 29 November   Manchester United 3 Leeds United 2

GARY: The Old Trafford pitch was ripped up after the last home game and today we played on the new surface. It was still a little uneven in places because the turf hasn't bedded in yet.

It's rare for me to pay Leeds a compliment, but this was the best, most attacking Leeds team I've played against. Most Leeds sides I've encountered have played route-one football, using big forwards upfront like Lee Chapman or Brian Deane, but this team has pace and really tries to play football.

Since he took over, David O'Leary has thrown a lot of youngsters in there and they look the part. They are a good side now, but when the young players have had a couple more years they could well be challenging for the Premiership title.

Nicky Butt scored the winner for us. Nicky's had a tough spell recently. The two sendings-off saw him miss five games through suspensions. When you miss that many games, it's hard to get your rhythm back, but today he was back to his best.

Premiership / Old Trafford / Att: 55,172

Manchester United 3
Schmeichel, Brown, P Neville, G Neville, Stam (Berg), Butt, Keane, Scholes (Sheringham), Solskjaer, Cole (Giggs), Yorke
Scorers: Solskjaer, Keane, Butt
Leeds United 2
Martyn (Robinson), Halle, Hiden (Wetherall), Woodgate, Harte, Haaland, Hopkin, Ribeiro (Smith), McPhail, Kewell, Hasselbaink
Scorers: Hasselbaink, Kewell

Monday 30 November

GARY: ITV are screening a documentary about our efforts at France 98. I was pleased to take part in the programme as one of the interviewees, but it soon became apparent that the main reason they wanted me on it is because I'm close to David Beckham. The point I wanted to make was that all the condemnation of Becks came from the outside, no one in the team held the sending-off against him. Virtually every member of that squad has been sent off during his career. It happens.

PHIL: There is a growing anti-England feeling among United fans. They're just basically standing up for David Beckham after the World Cup. United fans have obviously seen England fans slaughtering their players in internationals and this is their response. Although I think chanting "Argentina" is going too far.

GARY: England fans at Wembley have never gone out of their way to help United players. It's only been during Euro 96 and World Cup matches that I've really felt they are behind all of us. It has escalated from shouts of, "You Manc bastard" and "You Red so-and-so" when you're warming up, to half the ground singing, "Stand Up If You Hate Man U" like when we played Saudi Arabia.

Since the World Cup, the hatred has been directed mainly at David Beckham and United fans have retaliated by singing "Argentina" to get back at them. Because of this, people are saying that United fans are the sickest in the country. But the "Argentina" chant just refers to a game of football which we happened to lose. For years, at every ground we visit, United fans have had to put up with opposition fans singing Munich songs and making aeroplane impressions. They are singing about a tragedy where people lost their lives. How sick is that?

I know supporters of southern teams are more into international football than people from the north. To be honest, my only ambition growing up was to play for United. Now, United comes first, because if I'm not playing well for United, the bonus of playing for my country doesn't come at all.

15

Farewell Kiddo

Tuesday 1 December

PHIL: Kiddo is being linked with the Blackburn job. I pray he doesn't go. It's been in all the papers for a few days now, but Kiddo has come in every day like nothing has happened, so I assume he's staying with us. A few players have mentioned it to him and he has just laughed it off, so I hope there's nothing to worry about.

Wednesday 2 December   Tottenham Hotspur 3 Manchester United 1

PHIL: Kiddo wasn't on the coach to Tottenham, so the rumour was he was having talks with Blackburn. We were told he was meeting us at White Hart Lane, but when we got there he was nowhere to be seen.

Just as we were about to go out for our warm-up, Kiddo turned up drenched in sweat. He said he'd been stuck in traffic so had got out of his car and run three miles through the streets of North London to make it to the game. He threw on his tracksuit and took us out for our warm-up. He didn't say anything about Blackburn, so we guessed he had turned them down. During the game in the dugout he was shouting instructions and as concentrated as ever.

GARY: I wasn't in the squad that travelled down to London for the Worthington Cup Quarter-Final, so I watched it on TV.

Although the Boss rested a few players, he still fielded a strong team. When Teddy scored to make it 2–1, we were in with a chance but a superb left-foot strike by David Ginola made the game safe for them.

Playing on the right flank against Ginola is a great test for any defender and he was handled very well. But you can't do anything about the goal he scored. I know because in a game against Newcastle three years ago, Ginola stole half a yard on me and smashed it in the top corner with his right foot. Ginola only needs half a yard on either side to whip in a cross or shot. Sometimes you can only applaud the quality of his play.

Worthington Cup / White Hart Lane / Att: 35,702

Tottenham Hotspur 3
Walker, Carr, Young, Campbell, Sinton, Nielsen, Calderwood (Fox), Anderton, Iversen, Ginola, Armstrong (Ferdinand)
Scorers: Armstrong 2, Ginola
Manchester United 1
Van der Gouw, Clegg, Johnsen, Berg, Curtis (Beckham), Greening (Blomqvist), Butt (Notman), P Neville, Giggs, Sheringham, Solskjaer
Scorer: Sheringham

Thursday 3 December

GARY: A sad day for all the players as Brian Kidd is confirmed as Blackburn manager. We've worked under Kiddo for so long and we all like him. He geared everything towards loving your football. He's been with myself, Phil, Scholesy, Becks and Nicky since the Under-14s and he had a big influence on us getting schoolboy, apprentice and pro contracts.

It is a bit of a shock to lose someone who has been such a big part of our lives, but I suppose it's been on the cards for the last year. Everton, Manchester City and others have all made offers and it was inevitable that he would eventually take up the challenge of being a manager.

To lose him in mid-season is a setback, but there would never have been a good time because his methods were tried and tested and they helped us win trophies. Obviously, the manager is the most important person at any club, but Ferguson and Kiddo were a great partnership.

Friday 4 December

PHIL: Kiddo came down to the Cliff to say his goodbyes. It was quite sad as everyone loved him. He had a smile on his face and was joking with all the players. He was the one who really trained us and he acted as the go-between for us and the manager. He was a real players' man. If you weren't in the team he would cheer you up. I remember many times when the manager named a team without me in it, Kiddo would come and sit next to me and make me laugh for ten minutes. He is a great bloke and a great coach, whom I will sorely miss.

I would like him to return to Manchester United one day, hopefully as successor to the manager when he finally retires. I have never known a better coach.

Saturday 5 December   Aston Villa 1 Manchester United 1

GARY: After Paul Scholes gave us the lead, we tried to keep it tight but Villa drove us back. Although Joachim's goal was one of the luckiest you'll ever see – his shot got an enormous deflection which left Peter stranded – a draw was a fair result.

Brian Kidd got off to a successful start at Blackburn with a 1–0 win over Charlton. He started off watching from the Directors' Box in the first half. But by the second half, he was in the dugout urging Blackburn on. That's where Kiddo is going to manage from. He's a down-in-the-trenches guy.

There seem to be a few unsettled players at Blackburn, but Kiddo will bring stability to the club. The players will respect him for what he's achieved at United and they will absolutely love his training methods, that's for sure. He will get the best out of them physically and mentally.

PHIL: It was strange to see Kiddo talking on Match Of The Day, as he rarely did interviews at United. But the funniest thing was seeing him in a big cashmere coat because he's really a tracksuit-and-trainers man. I suppose now he's a manager he's got to have a manager's coat!

Premiership / Villa Park / Att: 39,241

Aston Villa 1
Jones, Watson, Southgate, Ehiogu, Wright, Hendrie, Barry, Taylor, Thompson, Dublin, Joachim
Scorer: Joachim
Manchester United 1
Schmeichel, G Neville, Stam, Brown, Irwin, Blomqvist (Butt), Beckham, Keane, Scholes, Yorke, Cole (Butt)
Scorer: Scholes

Tuesday 8 December

GARY: John Giles of The Express has written that Peter Schmeichel is now too error prone and United should ditch him. Peter's been taking a lot of stick this season, but that is absolutely ridiculous. Where are you going to find a goalkeeper anywhere near Peter's class for a start? I can't believe people are actually saying this stuff.

Tonight, Liverpool were knocked out of the UEFA Cup. Chelsea and Manchester United are now the only English teams left in Europe and it's only December. It still seems English sides haven't quite grasped what it takes to succeed in Europe. We need to take a step further and get to the Final and win a European Cup to break the barrier.

Wednesday 9 December **Manchester United 1 Bayern Munich 1**

GARY: The pressure in the build-up to this game was immense, but we always felt that a draw would be enough. The mathematics meant results elsewhere would have to go horribly wrong for us not to qualify.

Bayern showed their experience during the game, but it was pretty even. They had five or six massive players in their line-up which caused us problems from set-pieces and that's where their goal came from. We probably lacked the height to deal with them.

Five minutes before full time, the message came from the bench that a draw would do, but I think Peter and I were the only people who realised. We just passed the ball between each other as Bayern Munich's players sat off us, but our fans were going absolutely mental. I could hear them shouting, "Come on", "What are you doing" (or words to that effect!) but I was happy to stay there all night. German or Italian fans would probably have cheered us, but it is the English mentality to go forward at all costs. In the end, Peter actually got a bit nervous and passed the ball out so I had to go forward.

The draw proved enough to complete the task of qualifying from a very tough group. We had also achieved what very few people believed possible – qualifying in second place.

PHIL: This was a strange game.

I was on the bench and at 1–1 deep into the second half, the Bayern Munich bench let us know that if the score remained the same we were both through to the Quarter-Finals.

The manager got word to the players not to bust a gut and just keep the game as it was. Andy Cole obviously didn't know, as he went sprinting after a defender and the manager was screaming, "Drop off, Coley, drop off!" Towards the end we just sat off each other and played out the game.

The only problem was that the crowd didn't have a clue what was going on and started to boo us when we didn't get it forward. The manager told all the substitutes to get down the touchlines and tell the crowd we were through. I was giving them the thumbs up, but they weren't getting the message. When I gave one bloke the good news, he just said, "Shut up, Neville!"

At the final whistle we were all jumping around, but some fans trooped home thinking we were out!

Champions' League / Old Trafford / Att: 54,434

Manchester United 1
Schmeichel, Brown, Stam, G Neville, Irwin (Johnsen), Beckham, Keane, Scholes, Giggs, Cole, Yorke (Butt)
Scorer: Keane
Bayern Munich 1
Kahn, Matthaus (Linker), Babbel, Kuffour, Strunz, Jeremies, Effenburg, Salihamidzic, Lizarazu, Elber (Jancker), Zickler (Basler)
Scorer: Salihamidzic

Thursday 10 December

PHIL: I'm being linked with a move to Blackburn. I suppose it's inevitable really. I have actually spoken to Kiddo since he left the club and nothing has been said about it. I will always be friends with Kiddo – he brought me to the club when I was just 11 years old. It's not something I have even thought about and it's nothing to worry about, I hope.

I don't believe Kiddo would come back to sign players from United. He would want to do it his own way, buying his own players. He's left United and probably wants to leave that part of his life behind him.

Friday 11 December

GARY: No matter who comes and goes at United within a week, we are getting on with it as normal. Brian Kidd's departure is one of the biggest of them all, but matches are coming thick and fast and you have to go back to work. Our reserve-team coach Jim Ryan has taken over and done a good job. Most of us have worked with Jimmy before – the players and the manager like and trust him. Naturally, some elements of the training sessions have changed, the Boss has been more involved on the pitch, but basically it's been a smooth transition.

Saturday 12 December   Tottenham Hotspur 2 Manchester United 2

GARY: We absolutely roasted them in the first forty minutes. It was as good a performance as we've had in a long time. Then I got sent off for a second bookable offence.

The first yellow card was for a studs-up tackle on Alan Nielsen. The second booking was for pulling back David Ginola. You could say it was a deserved sending-off, but some weeks I wouldn't have even got booked.

Ginola put his arm across me and I put my arm inside his arm and he fell down. If he'd stayed on his feet, I wouldn't have got sent off. Ginola is 6 foot tall, 13 stone of muscle and he's got amazing balance, so how does he fall over when someone my size puts an arm across him? I'm not saying he's wrong to dive though, because he won his team a point. Ginola is a brilliant player.

Putting aside my sending-off, because a few other referees would have come to the same decision, I wasn't happy with Uriah Rennie's refereeing performance. He likes to be the centre of attention. I've spoken to a lot of players about him and they all have the same view. Before a game, most referees will be waiting with his linesmen at the top of the tunnel for the teams. Not Rennie. He'll always wait for both teams to line up in the tunnel, then half a minute later, he'll march out from the referee's dressing room between the two lines of players.

Last December, early in a game against Everton, I went up for a header and won it cleanly. There was no question of a foul, but Rennie booked me. I didn't understand his decision but you can't speak to him, his word is law. Today, he booked Teddy just for saying, "I can't believe you gave a foul there."

PHIL: Gary: didn't deserve his first yellow card, but once he got another he had to go. Ginola's a big man, so he shouldn't go over so easily, but then again, if he played for us I wouldn't complain.

The Boss didn't have a go at Gary, but I had a joke with him, calling him a dirty player.

Premiership / White Hart Lane / Att: 36,079

Tottenham Hotspur 2
Walker, Young, Campbell, Carr, Sinton, Nielsen, Anderton, Fox (Allen), Ginola, Armstrong, Ferdinand
Scorer: Campbell 2
Manchester United 2
Schmeichel, Stam, Johnsen, P Neville, G Neville, Keane, Butt, Beckham, Giggs (Blomqvist,) Sheringham (Cole),
Solskjaer (Berg)
Scorer: Solskjaer 2

Wednesday 16 December   **Manchester United 1 Chelsea 1**

GARY: Today, the draw was made for the European Cup Quarter-Finals. On paper, Inter are the hardest possible draw, but I don't think it matters. Two years ago, we thrashed Porto and they'd already beaten AC Milan that year. Last season, Monaco were supposed to be the easiest and they knocked us out. It's just a great tie to look forward to and the ticket requests have started already!

PHIL: The draw with Inter is excellent. The bigger the opposition, the better we play. The manager alluded to that back in the autumn when he called us "big-time players". If we had drawn a smaller team our fans might have been blasé and expected us to go through, but this way, we're the underdogs so we should do well.

GARY: Chelsea have done well in the past few seasons. They put us under pressure throughout the second half tonight, and deserved at least a point. Afterwards, we were gutted. First, because we hadn't played well and second, because we had got ahead but couldn't hang on to our lead for the last few minutes.

Bernard Lambourde should have been sent off for a professional foul on Dwight Yorke. Tonight's referee Graham Barber was the same man who harshly sent off Nicky Butt at Highbury. It's very frustrating when referees are so inconsistent.

Premiership / Old Trafford / Att: 55,159

Manchester United 1
Schmeichel, Irwin, G Neville, Stam, Brown, Blomqvist (Giggs), Butt, Keane, Scholes (Sheringham), Cole, Yorke (Beckham)
Scorer: Cole
Chelsea 1
De Goey, Le Saux (Poyet), Lambourde, Duberry, Ferrer, Babayaro, Wise, Di Matteo, Petrescu, Zola, Flo
Scorer: Zola

Thursday 17 December

PHIL: It was no surprise that Kiddo appointed Brian McClair as his number two at Blackburn. Choccy used to help Kiddo with his coaching at United and a few times he took the youth team. They have always been very close, away from United as well. There were rumours that Choccy would come back to United to replace Kiddo, but I knew that would never be possible.

GARY: Kiddo has been active in the transfer market. He bought ex-United winger Keith Gillespie from Newcastle last week and now he's also bidding for Matt Jansen who's at Crystal Palace. He must have been impressed with Jansen when he came to United on trial. Jansen certainly impressed me and I thought we were going to sign him, but he chose Palace instead, where he was guaranteed first-team football and it's worked out well for him.

Saturday 19 December   Manchester United 2 Middlesbrough 3

PHIL: We arrived at Old Trafford to learn that the manager wasn't going to be at today's game because of a family bereavement. It was very strange not to have either the manager or Kiddo there, so we didn't want to let Jim Ryan down. Unfortunately, we did. We let Middlesbrough go three goals up and I was at fault for the third one when I tried to nip it around Brian Deane instead of booting it into the stand. We're all just tired at the end of a run of nine games in 24 days.

GARY: Quite rightly, our defenders have taken a lot of stick about the number of goals we've conceded recently, so going 3–0 down was depressing. I didn't play well at centre-half, their strikers Ricard and Deane were dominating us physically, and as a team we didn't play at all. We did better in the second half, getting it to 3–2 with twenty minutes to go, but we couldn't salvage a draw.

Premiership / Old Trafford / Att: 55,152

Manchester United 2
Schmeichel, P Neville (Solskjaer), Johnsen, G Neville, Irwin, Giggs, Keane, Butt, Beckham (Scholes), Cole, Sheringham
Middlesbrough 3
Schwarzer, Gordon, Vickers, Cooper, Pallister, Festa, Mustoe (Moore), Townsend, Maddison (Beck), Deane, Ricard
Scorers: Ricard, Gordon, Deane

Saturday 26 December   Manchester United 3 Nottingham Forest 0

GARY: After playing badly against Middlesbrough, I would have liked to play in this game, but the Spurs' sending-off meant I was suspended. I went along and watched. Forest were poor, lacking confidence and looking sure to be relegated.

Premiership / Old Trafford / Att: 55,216

Manchester United 3
Schmeichel, P Neville, Berg, Johnsen, Irwin, Beckham, Butt, Keane (Greening), Giggs (Blomqvist), Sheringham, Scholes (Solskjaer)
Scorers: Johnsen 2, Giggs
Nottingham Forest 0
Beasant, Louis-Jean, Chettle (Doig), Armstrong, Rogers, Bart-Williams (Bonalair), Stone (Hodges), Johnson, Quashie, Shipperley, Freedman

Wednesday 29 December   Chelsea 0 Manchester United 0

GARY: Chelsea carried on their Old Trafford form in the first half. They created at least six clear chances, most of which fell to Tore Andre Flo who just couldn't put it in the net.

It was only in the second half that we managed to put pressure on their defence. They tired markedly and we controlled the game and looked the most likely team to win in the end.

Frank Leboeuf should have been sent off for two bookable offences. I couldn't believe he stayed on the pitch. Decisions like that make my sending-off the other week even harder to take.

As their performances against us have shown, Chelsea are real Premiership title contenders, but I still feel Arsenal could prove to be the most dangerous team.

Premiership / Stamford Bridge / Att: 34,741

Chelsea 0
De Goey, Ferrer, Leboeuf, Duberry, Le Saux (Goldbaek), Petrescu, Morris (Desailly), Di Matteo, Babayaro, Flo, Zola
Manchester United 0
Schmeichel, G Neville, Johnsen, Stam, Irwin, Beckham, Keane, Butt, Giggs, Scholes (Sheringham), Cole

Epilogue

PHIL: Glenn Hoddle's reign as England manager came to end. Of course, I missed out on the World Cup, but I won most of my caps with him and I refuse to put the boot in.

What Hoddle said offended a lot of people, especially families with disabled children or relatives. He probably deeply regrets saying that. Maybe we'll find out exactly what he was trying to get across, but he realised he was never going to get away with it – the press were after him and even Tony Blair got in on the act.

On football matters, he deserved to keep his job. The FA contacted Alan Shearer, Paul Ince, Ian Wright and Dion Dublin and I'm sure they would have spoken well about him. I don't think he ever completely lost the respect of the players, of course he did the journalists, but not us. Most players were behind him for the way he got us to the World Cup.

My best experience with Glenn Hoddle was at Le Tournoi in the summer of 1997. He was good to me then. He looked after me and gave me confidence. He definitely improved the technical side of my game.

GARY: Glenn Hoddle's removal from the England manager's job didn't surprise me. In the few days after he made those comments about disabled people, I think we saw the amazing power of the media. Once public opinion was expressed through polls and phone-ins and the newspapers reacted to those opinions, it all snowballed out of control.

The decision was inevitable once the Prime Minister Tony Blair said he would have to go. I'm not sure it was the PM's place to speak on such matters, but after he had said that, I think the FA's hands were tied.

It is very harsh for a football manager to lose his job over a non-football issue, but I think there was more to it than that. Unfortunately, I don't think the Boss had enough credits in the bank with journalists to overcome it. If he had a clean slate in the eyes of the media, he may have survived.

Everyone was behind him when England qualified for the World Cup finals in Rome the October before last, but the media turned against him just before France with the Eileen Drewery issue. Then there were his comments that Michael Owen was not a natural goalscorer and Beckham was "unfocused". Not picking Gazza added fuel to the fire.

Journalists also didn't take kindly to Hoddle misleading them over team line-ups (even though that's hardly an unusual tactic among managers). After the World Cup, his book and the comments he made about Eileen Drewery – that she would have given us an extra 20 per cent – led to further cynicism.

It has also been said that he'd lost the respect of the players, but that's going too far. Footballers will play their hardest for England whoever the manager is and there are only a couple of things I might criticise him on.

First, I disagreed with him when he said that David Beckham was unfocused going into the World Cup. David is close to me and I know that wasn't the case. Even if the Boss did think it, I believe he was wrong to express that opinion publicly, especially during a World Cup, which is the biggest time in any player's career. Second, at United we are used to Alex Ferguson giving us a reason when he leaves you out or substitutes you, and that was not always the case with Glenn Hoddle.

But, both of the above criticisms are more about managerial style and certainly not sacking offences. Ultimately though, I think certain sections of the media have been after him and they were just waiting for one more slip. They got it with his interview with The Times.

It's Glenn Hoddle, his family and friends who have suffered most in all this. When you read that note his daughter sent to Ceefax and saw him making his final statement as England manager, you could only feel sorry for him.

A lot of positives came out of Glenn Hoddle's reign. He took over from Terry Venables, which was a very difficult job because Venables had done so well, and he kept the momentum going. He wanted us to play attractive football and, personally, I have a lot to thank him for because he picked me 17 times and selected me in every one of his squads.

People may ridicule him about Eileen Drewery, but that was just one aspect of the incredible detail he went into to prepare us to qualify for and play in the 1998 World Cup. The Boss said we couldn't have been any better prepared and I have to agree with him.

Glenn Hoddle won't struggle to find another top job in football.

His departure in the middle of a European Championship qualifying campaign is not ideal, but the players will just get on with it. I didn't want Terry Venables to leave two years ago, but England games are more important than any one person.

Managing England is a tough job and I'm sure Glenn Hoddle will wish whoever takes over better luck than he's had.

Other titles available from Manchester United Books

0 223 99178 6	Manchester United in the Sixties by Graham McColl	£12.99
0 233 99340 1	Manchester United: The Insider Guide	£7.99
0 233 99359 2	Sir Matt Busby: A Tribute by Rick Glanvill	£14.99
0 233 99359 2	Cantona on Cantona by Eric Cantona	£14.99
0 233 99047 X	Alex Ferguson: Ten Glorious Years by Jim Drewett and Alex Leith	£9.99
0 233 99368 1	A Will to Win: The Manager's Diary by Alex Ferguson with David Meek	£6.99
0 233 99362 2	Odd Man Out: A Player's Diary by Brian McClair with Joyce Woolridge	£6.99
0 233 99417 3	The Official Manchester United Quiz Book	£9.99
0 233 99148 4	David Beckham: My Story by David Beckham	£12.99
0 233 99153 0	Access All Areas by Adam Bostock and Roger Dixon	£14.99
0 233 99369 X	Red and Raw by Ivan Ponting	£14.99

All these books are available from your local bookshop or can be ordered direct from the publisher. Prices and availbility are subject to change without notice.

Send order to: Manchester United Cash Sales, 76 Dean Street, London W1V 5HA

Please send a cheque or postal order made payable to André Deutsch Ltd for the value of the book(s) and add the following for postage and packaging (remembering to give your name and address):

UK: £1.00 for the first book, 50p for the second and 30p for each additional book up to a maximum of £3.00.

OVERSEAS including Eire: £2.00 for the first book and £1.00 for the second and 50p for each additional book to a maximum of £5.00